American Society of Plumbing Engineers
Data Book
A Plumbing Engineer's Guide to System Design and Specifications

Volume 4

Plumbing Components and Equipment

American Society of Plumbing Engineers
8614 W. Catalpa Ave., Suite 1007
Chicago, IL 60656

The ASPE Data Book is designed to provide accurate and authoritative information for the design and specification of plumbing systems. The publisher makes no guarantees or warranties, expressed or implied, regarding the data and information contained in this publication. All data and information are provided with the understanding that the publisher is not engaged in rendering legal, consulting, engineering, or other professional services. If legal, consulting, or engineering advice or other expert assistance is required, the services of a competent professional should be engaged.

American Society of Plumbing Engineers
8614 W. Catalpa Ave., Suite 1007
Chicago, IL 60656
(773) 693–2773 • Fax: (773) 695–9007
E-mail: aspehq@aspe.org • Internet: www.aspe.org

Copyright © 2003 by American Society of Plumbing Engineers

ISBN 1–891255–19–3
Printed in the United States of America

10 9 8 7 6 5 4 3 2 1

Data Book
Volume 4
Plumbing Components and Equipment

Data Book Chairperson: Allan D. Otts. P.Ep., CIPE

ASPE Vice-President, Technical: J. Joe Scott II, CPD

Editorial Review: J. Joe Scott II, CPD

Technical and Research
Committee Chairperson: James N. Polando, P.E., CIPE

CONTRIBUTORS

Chapter 1: Plumbing Fixtures
Julius A. Ballanco, P.E., Chicago Chapter, JB
Engineering

Chapter 2: Piping Systems
William F. Hughes, Jr., CIPE, Boston Chapter,
Robinson Green Beretta
Joseph Barbera, P.E., CIPE, Boston Chapter,
Evergreen Engineering

Special Thanks to:
Brian Bowes, Plastic Pipe and Supply
Robert Carter, Jr., Zurn Industries
Dale Powell, Copper Development Association
Scott Frey, Victaulic Company
Michael Gillespie, Ridgid-Viega
Dewey Manus, Charlotte Pipe and Foundry
Company
Carl Parker, Blucher-Josam Company
Scott Planck, Duriron Manufacturing
William Rich, Omega Flex, Inc.

Chapter 3: Valves
Gary E. Mohr, CPD, Central Indiana Chapter,
Veazy, Parrott, Durkin & Shoulders

Chapter 4: Pumps
Roy Ahlgren, Chicago Chapter, ITT Fluid Handling

Chapter 5: Piping Insulation
Michael Frankel, CIPE, Miami Chapter

Chapter 6: Hangers and Supports
Stanley Wolfson, Chicago Chapter, American
Society of Plumbing Engineers

Chapter 7: Vibration Isolation
Ray W. Moore, P.E., CPD, Intermountain Chapter, Professional Engineering Services

Chapter 8: Grease Interceptors
L. Richard Ellis, CPD, Dallas/Ft. Worth Chapter,
Blum Consulting Engineers
William C. Whitehead, Boston Chapter, Plumbing
& Drainage Institute

Chapter 9: Cross–Connection Control
Norman Parks, CET, CPD, Raleigh Chapter, The
Wooten Company
Joel Goldmont, Smith and Stevenson, Charlotte, NC

Chapter 10: Water Treatment
Kevin M. Noble, P.E, Cleveland Chapter,
Scheeser, Buckley & Mayfield.

**Chapter 11: Thermal Expansion
and Contraction**
Patrick R. Powell, P.E., Houston Chapter, J.L.
Powell & Associates

**Chapter 12: Water Coolers: Potable Water
Coolers and Central Water Systems**
Gregory L. Mahoney, CPD, Nashville Chapter,
Quantum Engineering Group Inc

**Chapter 13: Bioremediation Pretreatment
Systems**
William M. Smith, Jay R. Smith Manufacturing
Company
Max Weiss, Jay R. Smith Manufacturing Company

About ASPE

The American Society of Plumbing Engineers (ASPE) is the international organization for professionals skilled in the design and specification of plumbing systems. ASPE is dedicated to the advancement of the science of plumbing engineering, to the professional growth and advancement of its members, and to the health, welfare, and safety of the public.

The Society disseminates technical data and information, sponsors activities that facilitate interaction with fellow professionals, and, through research and education programs, expands the base of knowledge of the plumbing engineering industry. ASPE members are leaders in innovative plumbing design, effective materials and energy use, and the application of advanced techniques from around the world.

Worldwide Membership — ASPE was founded in 1964 and currently has 7,500 members. Spanning the globe, members are located in the United States, Canada, Asia, Mexico, South America, the South Pacific, Australia, and Europe. They represent an extensive network of experienced engineers, designers, contractors, educators, code officials, and manufacturers interested in furthering their careers, their profession, and the industry. ASPE is at the forefront of technology. In addition, ASPE represents members and promotes the profession among all segments of the construction industry.

ASPE Membership Communication — All members belong to ASPE worldwide and have the opportunity to belong and participate in one of the 62 state, provincial or local chapters throughout the U.S. and Canada. ASPE chapters provide the major communication links and the first line of services and programs for the individual member. Communications with the membership is enhanced through the Society's bimonthly magazine, *Plumbing Systems and Design,* and the bimonthly newsletter *ASPE Report* which is incorporated as part of the magazine.

Technical Publications — The Society maintains a comprehensive publishing program, spearheaded by the profession's basic reference text, the *ASPE Data Book.* The *Data Book,* encompassing forty-six chapters in four volumes, provides comprehensive details of the accepted practices and design criteria used in the field of plumbing engineering. New additions that will shortly join ASPE's published library of professional technical manuals and handbooks include: *High-Technology Pharmaceutical Facilities Design Manual, High-Technology Electronic Facilities Design Manual, Health Care Facilities and Hospitals Design Manual,* and *Water Reuse Design Manual.*

Convention and Technical Symposium — The Society hosts biennial Conventions in even-numbered years and Technical Symposia in odd-numbered years to allow professional plumbing engineers and designers to improve their skills, learn original concepts, and make important networking contacts to help them stay abreast of current trends and technologies. In conjunction with each Convention there is an Engineered Plumbing Exposition, the greatest, largest gathering of plumbing engineering and design products, equipment, and services. Everything from pipes to pumps to fixtures, from compressors to computers to consulting services is on display, giving engineers and specifiers the opportunity to view the newest and most innovative materials and equipment available to them.

Certified in Plumbing Design — ASPE sponsors a national certification program for engineers and designers of plumbing systems, which carries the designation "Certified in Plumbing Design" or CPD. The certification program provides the profession, the plumbing industry, and the general public with a single, comprehensive qualification of professional competence for engineers and designers of plumbing systems. The CPD, designed exclusively by and for plumbing engineers, tests hundreds of engineers and designers at centers throughout the United States biennially. Created to provide a single, uniform national credential in the field of engineered plumbing systems, the CPD program is not in any way connected to state-regulated Professional Engineer (P.E.) registration.

ASPE Research Foundation — The ASPE Research Foundation, established in 1976, is the only independent, impartial organization involved in plumbing engineering and design research. The science of plumbing engineering affects everything . . . from the quality of our drinking water to the conservation of our water resources to the building codes for plumbing systems. Our lives are impacted daily by the advances made in plumbing engineering technology through the Foundation's research and development.

Table of Contents

CHAPTER 12 Water Coolers:

Potable Water Coolers and Central Water Systems **269**

CHAPTER 13 Bioremediation Pretreatment Systems **283**

ILLUSTRATIONS

ACRONYMS

ABS Acrylonitrile butadiene styrene
AC Alternating current
ACI American Concrete Institute
ADA Americans with Disabilities Act
AGA American Gas Association
AISI American Iron and Steel Institute
ANSI American National Standards Institute
API American Petroleum Institute
ARI Air-Conditioning and Refrigeration Institute
ASHRAE American Society of Heating, Refrigerating, and Air-Conditioning Engineers
ASJ All-service jacket
ASME American Society of Mechanical Engineers
ASSE American Society of Sanitary Engineers
ASTM American Standard for Testing and Material
AW Acid waste
AWWA American Water Works Association
BHP Brake horsepower
BOD Biological oxygen demand
BUNA-N Butadiene and acrylonitrile (nitrile rubber)
CAP College of American Pathologists
CE Coefficient of expansion
CISPI Cast Iron Soil Pipe Institute
CPM Cycles per minute
CPVC Chlorinated polyvinyl chloride
CRREL Cold Region Research and Engineering Laboratory (US Army)
CSA Canadian Standards Association
CSST Corrugated stainless steel tubing
CTS Copper tube size
CWP Cold working pressure
DC 1 Direct current; 2 Double containment
DI Deionizing
DWV Drain, waste, and vent
EPA Environmental Protection Agency
EPDM Ethylene-propylene diene monomer
FM Factory Mutual
FOG Fats, oils, and grease
FPS Feet per second
FR Flame retardant
FRP Fiberglass pipe
FRPP Flame-retardant pipe
FSK Fiberglass, skrim, kraft paper
GPD Gallons per day
GPG Grains per gallon (hardness)
GPH Gallons per hour
GPM Gallons per minute
GRD Grease/oil recovery device
HVAC Heating, ventilation, and air conditioning
IAPMO International Association of Plumbing and Mechanical Officials
IBBM Iron body, bronze mounted
ICC International Code Council
ID Inside diameter
IP Inch-pound
IPS Iron pipe size
IS Inside screw

kcal Kilocalorie
LP Liquefied petroleum
MEA Materials and Acceptance Division (New York City)
MIG Metallic inert gas
Mohm Megaohm
MSS Manufacturers Standardization Society
NBR Acrylonitrile-butadiene rubber
NC Noise criteria
NF Nanofiltration
NFPA National Fire Protection Association
NFPP Nonflame pipe
NM Nanometer
NPS Nominal pipe size
NPSH Net positive suction head
NRS Nonrising stem
NSF National Sanitation Foundation
OD Outside diameter
OS&Y Outside screw and yoke
PB Polybutylene
PDI Plumbing and Drainage Institute
PE Polyethylene
PEX Cross-linked polyethylene
PP Polypropylene
PPM Parts per million
PSI Pounds per square inch
PSIA Pounds per square inch absolute
PSIG Pounds per square inch gage
PTFE Polytetrafluoroethylene plastic
PVA Polyvinyl acetate
PVC Polyvinyl chloride
PVDF Polyvinylidene fluoride
RCP Reinforced concrete pipe
RO Reverse osmosis
RPM Revolutions per minute
RS Rising stem
RTRP Reinforced thermosetting resin pipe
S Siemens
SDI Service deionized water
SI International Standard
SWP Steam working pressure
TDS Total dissolved solids
TFE Tetrafluoroethylene
TIG Tungsten inert gas
TOC Total oxidizable carbon
TU Turbidity unit
UF Ultrafiltration
UL Underwriters' Laboratory
USC FCCC & HR University of Southern California Foundation for CrossConnection Control and Hydraulic Research
USEPA US Environmental Protection Agency
WC Water column
WCB Wrought carbon grade B
WOG Water, oil, gas
WWP Water working pressure

1 Plumbing Fixtures

It has been said that without plumbing fixtures there would be no indoor plumbing. A plumbing fixture is supplied with water, discharges water and/or waste, and performs a function for the user. Each fixture is designed for a specific activity to maintain public health and sanitation. As such, plumbing fixtures are often referred to as "sanitaryware."

The standard plumbing fixtures used in a plumbing system include

1. Water closets
2. Urinals
3. Lavatories
4. Kitchen sinks
5. Service sinks
6. Sinks
7. Laundry trays
8. Drinking fountains
9. Showers
10. Bathtubs
11. Bidets
12. Floor drains
13. Emergency fixtures.

In addition, there are fixture fittings used in connection with these plumbing fixtures, including

1. Faucets and fixture fittings
2. Shower valves
3. Tub fillers.

FIXTURE MATERIALS

The surface of any plumbing fixture must be smooth, impervious, and readily cleanable to maintain a high level of sanitation. Fixture materials are selected based on these requirements. Common plumbing fixture materials include the following:

- *Vitreous china* This is a unique material that is specially suited for plumbing fixtures. Unlike other ceramic materials, vitreous china will not absorb water on surfaces that are not glazed. It is not porous. While vitreous china plumbing fixture surfaces are glazed, the inside waterways are not. The exterior glazing provides a nice finish that is readily cleaned. Vitreous china is also an extremely strong material.

  Because vitreous china is nonporous, it has a very high shrinkage rate when fired in a kiln. This accounts for the slight difference between otherwise identical plumbing fixtures.

- *Nonvitreous china* Nonvitreous china is a porous ceramic that requires glazing to prevent any water absorption. Use of nonvitreous china for lavatories and similar fixtures has grown in popularity in recent years. The advantage of nonvitreous china is that there is not a high shrinkage rate. This allows the fixture to be more ornately designed.

- *Enameled cast iron* Enameled cast iron fixtures have a base that is a high-grade cast iron. The exposed surfaces have an enameled coating, which is fused to the cast iron, resulting in a hard, glossy, opaque, and acid-resistant surface. Enameled cast iron plumbing fixtures are strong, ductile, and long lasting.

- *Porcelain enameled steel* Porcelain enameled steel is a substantially vitreous or glossy inorganic coating that is bonded to sheet steel by fusion. The sheet steel must be designed for the application of the porcelain enamel to produce a high-quality product.

- *Stainless steel* A variety of stainless steels are used to produce plumbing fixtures. The different types include types 316, 304, 302, 301, 202, 201, and 430. One of the key ingredients in stainless steel is nickel. A higher nickel content tends to produce a superior finish in the stainless steel. Types 302 and 304 have 8% nickel and Type 316 has 10% nickel.

- *Plastic* Plastic is a generic category for a variety of synthetic materials used in plumbing fixtures. The various plastic materials used to produce plumbing fixtures include acrylonitrile butadiene styrene (ABS); polyvinyl chloride (PVC); gel-coated, fiberglass-reinforced plastic; acrylic; cultured marble; cast-filled fiberglass; polyester; cast-filled acrylic; gel-coated plastic; and cultured marble acrylic. Plastics used in plumbing fixtures are subject to numerous tests to determine their quality. Some of the testing includes an ignition (torch) test, a cigarette burn test, a stain-resistance test, and a chemical-resistance test.

- *Soapstone* This is an older material used predominantly in the manufacture of laundry trays and service sinks. Soapstone is steatite, which is extremely heavy and very durable.

ACCESSIBILITY

The Americans with Disabilities Act (ADA) and American National Standards Institute (ANSI) A117.1, *Accessible and Usable Buildings and Facilities*, require certain plumbing fixtures to be accessible. The requirements for accessibility are addressed in *ASPE Data Book*, Volume 1, Chapter 6.

APPLICABLE STANDARDS

Plumbing fixtures are regulated by nationally developed consensus standards. These standards specify the material, fixture design, and testing requirements.

While the standards for plumbing fixtures are considered voluntary, with reference to the standards in the plumbing code, the requirements become mandatory. Most fixture manufacturers have their products certified by a third-party testing laboratory as being in conformance with the applicable standard.

Table 1-1 identifies the most common consensus standards regulating plumbing fixtures. A complete list of standards is found in *Data Book*, Volume 1, Chapter 2.

Table 1-1 Plumbing Fixture Standards

Plumbing Fixture	Applicable Standard	Fixture Material
Water closet	ANSI/ASME A112.19.2	Vitreous china
	ANSI Z124.4	Plastic
Urinal	ANSI/ASME A112.19.2	Vitreous china
	ANSI Z124.9	Plastic
Lavatory	ANSI/ASME A112.19.1	Enameled cast iron
	ANSI/ASME A112.19.2	Vitreous china
	ANSI/ASME A112.19.3	Stainless steel
	ANSI/ASME A112.19.4	Porcelain enameled steel
	ANSI/ASME A112.19.9	Nonvitreous china
	ANSI Z124.3	Plastic
Sink	ANSI/ASME A112.19.1	Enameled cast iron
	ANSI/ASME A112.19.2	Vitreous china
	ANSI/ASME A112.19.3	Stainless steel
	ANSI/ASME A112.19.4	Porcelain enameled steel
	ANSI/ASME A112.19.9	Nonvitreous china
	ANSI Z124.6	Plastic
Drinking fountain	ANSI/ASME A112.19.1	Enameled cast iron
	ANSI/ASME A112.19.2	Vitreous china
	ANSI/ASME A112.19.9	Nonvitreous china
	ARI 1010	Water coolers
Shower	ANSI Z124.2	Plastic
Bathtub	ANSI/ASME A112.19.1	Enameled cast iron
	ANSI/ASME A112.19.4	Porcelain enameled steel
	ANSI/ASME A112.19.9	Nonvitreous china
	ANSI Z124.1	Plastic
Bidet	ANSI/ASME A112.19.2	Vitreous china
	ANSI/ASME A112.19.9	Nonvitreous china
Floor drain	ANSI/ASME A112.6.3	All materials
Emergency fixtures	ANSI Z358.1	All materials
Faucets and fixture fittings	ANSI/ASME A112.18.1	All materials
Waste fittings	ANSI/ASME A112.18.2	All materials

WATER CLOSETS

Passage of the Plumbing Product Efficiency Act of 1992 by the US government changed the design of a water closet. It imposed a maximum flushing rate of 1.6 gallons per flush (gpf) (6 L per flush). This was a significant drop in the quantity of water used, previously 3.5 gal per flush, and was considered to be a water savings. Prior to the first enactment of water conservation in the late 1970s, water closets typically flushed between 5 and 7 gal of water. The greatest water use, 7 gal per flush, was by blowout water closets.

With the modification in water flush volume, the style of each manufacturer's water closet changed. The former terminology for identifying water closets no longer fit. Water closets were previously categorized as blowout, siphon jet, washout, reverse trap, and wash down. (See Figure 1-1.) The new style of 1.6 gpf water closets fit between the cracks of these old categories. The standards have since changed, no longer identifying a water closet by these designations.

Water closets are currently placed into one of three categories:

- *A close-coupled water closet* is one with a two-piece tank and bowl fixture.
- *A one-piece water closet* is, as it suggests, one with the tank and bowl as one piece.
- *A flushometer style water closet* is a bowl with a spud connection that receives the connection from a flushometer valve. Flushometer type water closets are also referred to as "top spud" or "back spud bowls." The "spud" is the name for the connection for the flushometer valve and the top or rear identifies the location of the spud. (See Figure 1-2.)

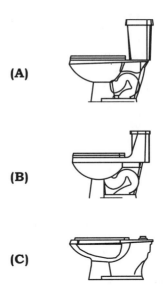

Figure 1-2 Water closets are identified as (A) close coupled, (B) one piece, and (C) flushometer types.

There are also three distinct means for identifying the flushing of a water closet:

- In *a gravity flush*, used with tank type water closets, the water is not under pressure and flushes by gravity.
- With *a flushometer tank*, also for tank type water closets, however, the water is stored in a pressurized vessel and flushed under a pressure ranging between 25 and 35 psi.
- A *flushometer valve* type of flush uses the water supply line pressure to flush the water closet. Because of the demand for a flush of a large volume of water in a short period of time, the water supply pipe must be larger in diameter than that for a gravity or flushometer tank type of flush.

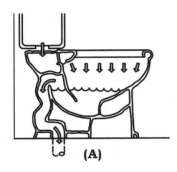 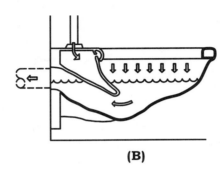 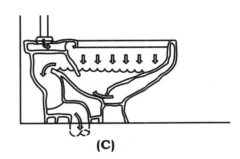

(A)   (B)   (C)

Figure 1-1 The older styles of water closets were identified as (A) reverse trap, (B) blowout, and (C) siphon jet, to name a few. Though still used in the industry, these terms are no longer used in the standards.

Another distinction used to identify a water closet is the manner of mounting and connection. The common designations for water closets are the following:

- A *floor-mounted water closet* is supported by the floor and connected directly to the piping through the floor. (See Figure 1-3.)

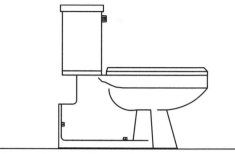

Figure 1-3 A floor-mounted, back outlet water closet is supported on the floor with the piping connection through the back wall.

- A *wall hung water closet* is supported by a wall hanger and never comes in contact with the floor. Wall hung water closets are considered superior for maintaining a clean floor in the toilet room since the water closet doesn't interfere with the cleaning of the floor. (See Figure 1-4.)

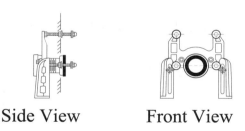

Side View   Front View

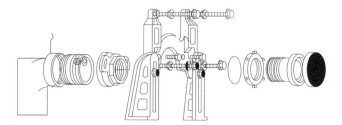

Figure 1-4 Carrier for a Water Closet

Source: Courtesy of Jay R. Smith Company.

- *Floor-mounted, back outlet water closets* are supported by the floor yet connect to the piping through the wall. The advantage of the floor-mounted, back outlet water closet is that the penetrations of the floor are reduced for the plumbing. It should be noted that with the change to 1.6 gal per flush it is more difficult for manufacturers to produce a floor-mounted, back outlet water closet that meets all of the flushing performance requirements in the standard. (See Figure 1-5.)

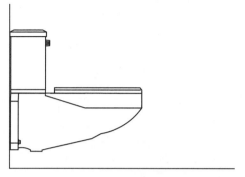

Figure 1-5 A wall hung water closet attaches to the back wall; the water closet does not contact the floor.

Shape and Size

A water closet bowl is classified as either a round front or elongated. An elongated bowl has an opening that extends 2 in. farther to the front of the bowl. Most plumbing codes require elongated bowls for public and employee use. The additional 2 in. provides a larger opening, often called a "target area." With the larger opening, there is a greater likelihood of maintaining a cleaner water closet for each user.

For floor-mounted water closets, the outlet is identified based on the rough-in dimension. The rough-in is the distance from the back wall to the center of the outlet when the water closet is installed. A standard rough-in bowl outlet is 12 in. Most manufacturers also make water closets with a 10-in. or 14-in. rough-in. (See Figure 1-6.)

The size of the bowl is also based on the height of the bowl rim measured from the floor:

- A *standard water closet* has a rim height of 14 to 15 in. This is the most common water closet to install.

- A *child's water closet* has a rim height of 10 in. above the floor. Many plumbing codes require child's water closets in day-care centers and kindergarten toilet rooms for use by small children.

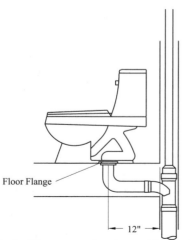

Figure 1-6 The standard rough-in dimension is 12 in. from the centerline of the water closet outlet to the back wall. The floor flange must be permanently secured to the building structure.

- A *water closet for juvenile use* has a rim height of 13 in.
- A *water closet for the physically challenged* has a rim height of 18 in. With the addition of the water closet seat, the fixture is designed to conform to the accessibility requirements.

Water Closet Seat

A water closet seat must be designed for the shape of the bowl to which it connects. There are two styles of water closet seat: solid and split rim. Plumbing codes typically require a split rim seat for public and employee use water closets. The split rim seat is designed to facilitate easy wiping by females, and to prevent contact between the seat and the penis with males. This is to maintain a high level of hygiene in public facilities.

A new style of water closet seat has a plastic wrap around the seat. The intent of this seat is to allow a clean surface for each use. The seat is intended to replace the split rim seat in public and employee locations.

Flushing Performance

The flushing performance requirements for a water closet are found in a separate standard, ANSI/American Society of Mechanical Engineers (ASME) A112.19.6. This standard identifies the test protocol that must be followed to certify a water closet. The tests include a ball removal test, granule test, ink test, dye test, water consumption test, trap seal restoration test, water rise test, back pressure test, rim top and seat fouling test, and a drain line carry test. At the time this chapter was written, an additional test was being considered for inclusion in the standard, a bulk media test.

The ball removal test utilizes 100 polypropylene balls that are ¾ in. in diameter. The water closet must flush at least an average of 75 balls on the initial flush of three different flushes. The polypropylene balls are intended to replicate the density of human feces.

The granule test utilizes approximately 2500 disc shaped granules of polyethylene. The initial flush of three different flushes must result in no more than 125 granules on average remaining in the bowl. The granule test is intended to simulate a flush of watery feces (diarrhea).

The ink test is performed on the inside wall of the water closet bowl. A felt tip marker is used to draw a line around the inside of the bowl. After flushing, no individual segment of line can exceed ½ in. The total length of the remaining ink line must not exceed 2 in. This test determines that the water flushes all interior surfaces of the bowl.

The dye test uses a color dye to add to the water closet trap seal. The concentration of the dye is determined both before and after flushing the water closet. The dilution ratio of 100:1 must be obtained for each flush. This test determines the evacuation of urine in the trap seal.

The water consumption test determines that the water closet meets the federal mandate of 1.6 gal per flush.

The trap seal restoration test determines that the water closet refills the trap of the bowl after each flush. The remaining trap seal must be a minimum of 2 in. in depth.

The water rise test evaluates the rise of water in the bowl when the water closet is flushed. The water cannot rise above a point 3 in. below the top of the bowl.

The back pressure test is used to determine that the water seal remains in place when exposed to a back pressure (from the outlet side of the bowl) of 2½ in. of water column (wc). This test determines that no sewer gas will escape through the fixture when high pressure occurs in the drainage system piping.

The rim top and seat fouling test determines if the water splashes onto the top of the rim or seat of the water closet. This test ensures that the user will not encounter a wet seat when using the water closet.

The drain line carry test determines the performance of the water closet flush. The water closet is connected to a 4-in. drain 60 ft in length pitched ¼ in./ft. The same 100 polypropylene balls used in the flush test are used in the drain line carry test. The average carry distance of all the polypropylene balls must be 40 ft in length. This test determines the ability of the water closet to flush the contents in such a manner that they properly flow down the drainage piping.

The new proposed bulk media test is a test of a large quantity of items placed in the bowl. The bowl cannot be stopped up by the bulk media during the flush, and a certain flushing performance of the bulk media will be required. The debate over this test is the repeatability of the test. It is expected that, after round robin testing is completed, the test will be added to the standard.

In Canada, water closets must conform to Canadian Standards Association (CSA) B45.1, CSA B45.4, or CSA B45.5. While Canada does not have a federal mandate requiring 1.6-gal-per-flush water closets, many areas require these water closets. It should also be noted that Canada requires a bulk media test for water closet flush performance.

Installation Requirements

The water closet must be properly connected to the drainage piping system. For floor-mounted water closets, a water closet flange is attached to the piping and permanently secured to the building. For wood framed buildings, the flange is screwed to the floor. For concrete floors, the flange sits on the floor.

Noncorrosive closet bolts connect the water closet to the floor flange. The seal between the floor flange and the water closet is made with either a wax ring or an elastomeric sealing connection. The connection formed between the water closet and the floor must be sealed with caulking or tile grout.

For wall hung water closets, the fixture must connect to a wall carrier. The carrier must transfer the loading of the water closet to the floor. A wall hung water closet must be capable of supporting a load of 500 lb at the end of the water closet. When the water closet is connected to the carrier, none of this load can be transferred to the piping system. Water closet carriers must conform to ANSI/ASME A112.6.1.

The minimum spacing required for a water closet is 15 in. from the centerline of the bowl to the side wall, and 21 in. from the front of the water closet to any obstruction in front of the water closet. The standard dimension for a water closet compartment is 30 in. wide by 60 in. in length. The water closet must be installed in the center of the standard compartment. The minimum distance required between water closets is 30 in. (See Figure 1-7.)

The change in the flushing performance of the 1.6-gal-per-flush water closet has affected the piping connection for back-to-back water closet installations. With a 3.5-gal-per-flush water closet, the common fitting used to connect back-to-back water closets was either a 3-in. double sanitary tee or a 3-in. double fixture fitting. With the superior flushing of the 1.6-gpf water closet, the plumbing codes have prohibited the installation of a double sanitary tee or double fixture fitting for back-to-back water closets. The only acceptable fitting is the double combination wye and eighth bend. The fitting, however, increases the spacing required between the floor and the ceiling.

The minimum spacing required to use a double sanitary tee fitting is 30 in. from the centerline of the water closet outlet to the entrance of the fitting. This spacing rules out a back-to-back water closet connection.

One of the problems associated with the short pattern fittings is the siphon action created in the initial flush of the water closets. This siphon action can draw the water out of the trap of the water closet connected to the other side of the fitting. Another potential problem is the interruption of flow when flushing a water closet. The flow from one water closet can propel water across the fitting, interfering with the other water closet. (See Figure 1-8.)

Flushing Systems

Gravity flush The most common means of flushing a water closet is a gravity flush. This is the flush with a tank type water closet, described

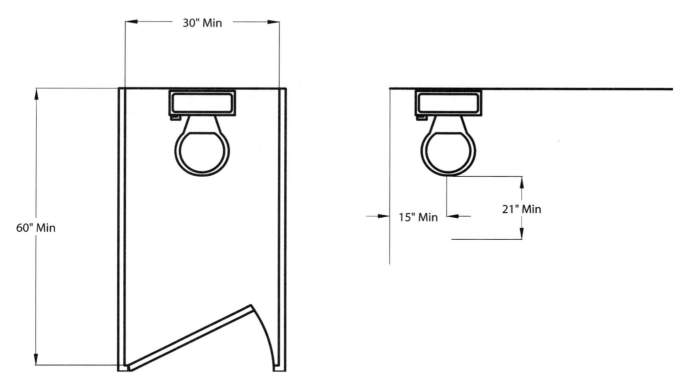

Figure 1-7 The minimum size water closet compartment is 30 in. × 60 in. Spacing is required from the centerline of the water closet to a side wall or obstruction and from the front lip of the water closet to any obstruction.

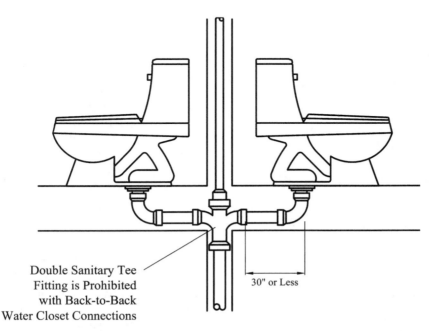

Double Sanitary Tee
Fitting is Prohibited
with Back-to-Back
Water Closet Connections

30" or Less

Figure 1-8 Both a double sanitary tee and a double fixture fitting are prohibited on a 3-in. connection to back-to-back water closets.

above, wherein the water is not pressurized in the tank. The tank stores a quantity of water to establish the initial flush of the bowl. A trip lever raises either a flapper or a ball, allowing the the flush is at the maximum siphon in the bowl, the flapper or ball reseals, closing off the tank from the bowl.

The ballcock, located inside the tank, controls the flow of water into the tank. A float mechanism opens and closes the ballcock. The ballcock directs the majority of the water into the tank and a smaller portion of water into the bowl to refill the trap seal. The ballcock must be

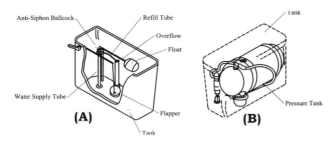

Figure 1-9 (A) A Gravity Tank and (B) a Flushometer Tank

an antisiphon ballcock conforming to American Society of Sanitary Engineers (ASSE) 1002. This prevents the contents of the tank from being siphoned back into the potable water supply. (See Figure 1-9.)

Flushometer tank   A flushometer tank has the same outside appearance as a gravity tank. However, inside the tank is a pressure vessel that stores the water for flushing. The water in the pressure vessel must be a minimum of 25 psi to operate properly. Thus, the line pressure on the connection to the flushometer tank must be a minimum of 25 psi. A pressure regulator prevents the pressure in the vessel from rising above 35 psi (typical of most manufacturers).

The higher pressure from the flushometer tank results in a flush similar to a flushometer valve. One of the differences between the flushometer tank and the flushometer valve is the sizing of the water distribution system. The water piping to a flushometer tank is sized the same way the water piping to a gravity flush tank is sized. Typically, the individual water connection is ½ in. in diameter. For a flushometer valve, there is a high flow rate demand, resulting in a large piping connection. A typical flushometer

valve for a water closet has a connection of 1 in. in diameter. (See Figure 1-9.)

Flushometer valve   A flushometer valve is also referred to as a "flush valve." The valve is designed with upper and lower chambers separated by a diaphragm. The water pressure in the upper chamber keeps the valve in the closed position. When the trip lever is activated, the water in the upper chamber escapes to the lower chamber, starting the flush. The flush of 1.6 gal passes through the flush valve. The valve is closed by line pressure as water reenters the upper chamber, closing off the valve.

For 1.6-gpf water closets, flushometer valves are set to flow 25 gpm at peak to flush the water closet. The flushing cycle is very short, lasting 4 to 5 s. The water distribution system must be properly designed to allow the peak flow during a heavy use period for the plumbing system.

Flushometer valves have either a manual or an automatic means of flushing. The most popular manual means of flushing is a handle mounted on the side of the flush valve. Automatic flushometer valves are available in a variety of styles. The automatic can be battery operated or directly connected to the power supply of the building.

URINALS

A urinal was developed as a fixture to expedite the use of a toilet room. It is designed for the removal of urine and the quick exchange of users. The Plumbing Product Efficiency Act of 1992 included requirements for the water consumption of urinals. A urinal is now restricted to a maximum water use of 1.0 gal per flush. This change in water consumption resulted in a modified design of the fixture.

One of the main concerns in the design of a urinal is the maintenance of a sanitary fixture. The fixture must contain the urine, flush it down the drain, and wash the exposed surfaces. Prior to the passage of the Plumbing Product Efficiency Act of 1992, urinals were developed using larger quantities of water to flush the contents. This included a blowout model that could readily remove any of the contents thrown into the urinal in addition to urine. Blowout urinals were popular in high-traffic areas such as assembly buildings. However, the older blowout urinals require more than 1 gal of water to flush. The newer urinals identified as blowout urinals do not have the same forceful flush.

Urinals have been considered a fixture for the male population. However, that has not always been the case. Various attempts have been made to introduce a female urinal. The concept of a female urinal has never been embraced by the female population. Problems that have been encountered include a lack of understanding of the use of the urinal. (The first female urinals required the woman to approach the urinal in the opposite way a man would. She would be facing away from the urinal slightly bent over.) Another continuing concern is privacy during use. Finally, there have been concerns regarding cleanliness with its use compared with that associated with the use of a water closet. Hence, very few female urinals remain in use in the United States and Canada.

Urinal Styles

Urinals are identified as blowout, siphon jet, washout, stall, and wash down. A stall urinal is a type of wash-down urinal. Blowout, siphon-jet, and washout urinals all have integral traps. Stall and wash-down urinals have an outlet to which an external trap is connected. Many plumbing codes continue to prohibit the use of stall and wash-down urinals in public and employee toilet rooms. One of the concerns with stall and wash-down urinals is the ability to maintain a high level of sanitation after each flush.

The style identifies the type of flushing action in the urinal. The blowout and siphon-jet types rely on a complete evacuation of the trap. Blowout urinals tend to force the water and waste from the trap to the drain. Siphon-jet urinals create a siphon action to evacuate the trap. Washout urinals rely on a water exchange to flush. There is no siphon action or complete evacuation of the trap way. Stall and wash-down urinals have an external trap. The flushing action is a water exchange; however, it is a less efficient water exchange than that of a washout urinal.

Urinals with an integral trap must be capable of passing a ¾-in. diameter ball. The outlet connection is typically 2 in. in diameter.

Stall and wash-down urinals can have a 1½-in. outlet with an external 1½-in. trap.

Flushing Performance

The flushing performance for a urinal is regulated by ANSI/ASME A112.19.6. There are three tests for urinals: the ink test, dye test, and water consumption test.

In the ink test a felt tip marker is utilized to draw a line on the inside wall of the urinal. The urinal is flushed and the remaining ink line is measured. The total length of ink line cannot exceed 1 in., and no segment can exceed ½ in. in length.

The dye test uses a colored dye to evaluate the water exchange rate in the trap. After one flush, the trap must have a dilution ratio of 100 to 1. The dye test is performed only on urinals with an integral trap. This includes blowout, siphon-jet, and washout urinals. It is not possible to test stall and wash-down urinals since they have external traps. This is one of the concerns that have resulted in the restricted use of these fixtures.

The water consumption test determines that the urinal flushes with 1 gal of water or less.

Installation Requirements

The minimum spacing required between urinals is 30 in. center to center. The minimum spacing between a urinal and the sidewall is 15 in. This spacing provides access to the urinal without

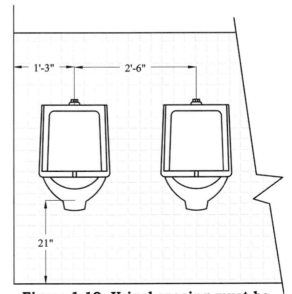

Figure 1-10 Urinal spacing must be adequate to allow adjacent users to access the urinals without interference.

the user coming in contact with the user of the adjacent fixture. The minimum spacing required in front of the urinal is 21 in. (See Figure 1-10.)

One of the debated issues regarding urinals is screening between urinals. A question of privacy is often raised during plumbing code discussions. At the time of this writing, screening is not required by any of the model plumbing codes. However, many local and some state plumbing codes require privacy barriers between urinals.

Urinals with an integral trap have the outlet located 21 in. above the floor for a standard height installation. Stall urinals are mounted on the floor. Wall hung urinals must be mounted on carriers that transfer the weight of the urinal to the floor.

Many plumbing codes require urinals for public and employee use to have a visible trap seal. This refers to blowout, siphon-jet, or washout urinals.

The building and/or plumbing codes require the walls and floor surrounding the urinal to be finished with waterproofed, smooth, readily cleanable, nonabsorbent material. This finished material must be applied to the wall for a distance of 2 ft to either side of the urinal and a height of 4 ft. It must also extend outward on the floor to a point 2 ft in front of the urinal. This protects the building material from damage that could result from splashing, which can occur with urinal use.

Flushing Requirements

With the federal requirements for water consumption, urinals must be flushed with a flushometer valve. The valve can be either manually or automatically actuated.

A urinal flushometer valve has a lower flush volume and flow rate than a water closet flushometer valve. The total volume is 1 gal per flush and the peak flow rate is 15 gpm. The water distribution system must be properly sized for the peak flow rate for the urinal.

Urinal flushometer valves operate the same as water closet flushometer valves. For additional information see the discussion of flushing systems under "Water Closets" earlier in this chapter.

There is also a new style of urinal available— the waterless urinal. Waterless urinals connect to the drainage system but do not have a water supply. Waterless urinals have a special solution that fills the trap seal. During the use of the fixture, the urine drops below the special trap solution entering the drainage system. The inside walls of the urinal are required to be washed with the special solution on a periodic basis.

LAVATORIES

A lavatory is a wash basin used for personal hygiene. In public locations, a lavatory is intended to be used for washing one's hands and face. Residential lavatories are intended for hand and face washing, shaving, applying makeup, cleaning contact lenses, and similar hygienic activities.

Lavatory faucet flow rates are regulated as a part of the Plumbing Product Efficiency Act of 1992. The original flow rate established by the government was 2.5 gpm at 80 psi for private use lavatories and 0.5 gpm, or a cycle discharging 0.25 gal, for public use lavatories. Since the initial regulations, there has been a change to 2.2 gpm at 60 psi for private (and residential) lavatories, and 0.5 gpm at 60 psi, or a cycle of 0.25 gal, for public lavatories.

Size and Shape

Manufacturers produce lavatories in every conceivable size and shape. The lavatories are square, round, oblong, rectangular, shaped for corners, with or without ledges, decorative bowls, and molded into countertops.

The standard outlet for a lavatory is 1¼ in. in diameter. The standard lavatory has three holes on the ledge for the faucet. A normal faucet hole pattern spaces the two outside holes 4 in. apart. The faucets installed in these lavatories are called 4-in. centersets. When spread faucets are to be installed, the spacing between the two outer holes is 8 in.

For many years, the fixture standards required lavatories to have an overflow. This requirement was based on the use of the fixture whereby the basin was filled prior to cleaning. If a user left the room while the lavatory was being filled, the water would not overflow onto the floor.

Studies have shown that lavatories are rarely used in this capacity. It is more common not to fill the basin with water during use. As a result, overflows became an optional item for lavatories. Some plumbing codes, however, still require overflows for lavatories.

To avoid a hygiene problem with the optional overflows, the fixture standard added a minimum size for the overflow. The minimum cross-sectional area must be 1⅛ in.[2]

Another style of lavatory is the circular or semicircular group washup. The plumbing codes consider every 20 in. of space along a group washup to be equivalent to one lavatory.

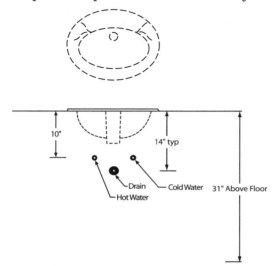

Figure 1-11 Recommended Installation Dimensions for a Lavatory

Installation

The standard height of a lavatory is 31 in. above the finished floor. A spacing of 21 in. is required in front of the lavatory to access the fixture. (See Figure 1-11.)

Lavatories can be counter mounted, under counter mounted, or wall hung. When lavatories are wall hung in public and employee facilities, they must be connected to a carrier that transfers the weight of the fixture to the floor.

KITCHEN SINKS

A kitchen sink is used for culinary purposes. There are two distinct classifications of kitchen sink—residential and commercial. It should be noted that residential kitchen sinks are installed in commercial buildings, typically in a kitchen used by employees. Commercial kitchen sinks are designed for restaurant and food handling establishments.

The Plumbing Product Efficiency Act of 1992 regulates the flow rate of faucets for residential kitchen sinks. The original flow rate established was 2.5 gpm at 80 psi. The fixture standards have since modified the flow rate to 2.2 gpm at 60 psi.

Residential Kitchen Sinks

Common residential kitchen sinks are single- or double-compartment (or bowl) sinks. There is no standard dimension for the size of the sink; however, most kitchen sinks are 22 in. measured from the front edge to the rear edge. For single-compartment sinks, the most common width of the sink is 25 in. For double-compartment kitchen sinks, the most common width is 33 in. The common depth of the compartments is 9 to 10 in.

Most plumbing codes require the outlet of a residential kitchen sink to be 3½ in. in diameter. This is to accommodate the installation of a food waste grinder.

There are specialty residential kitchen sinks that have three compartments. Typically, the third compartment is a smaller compartment that does not extend the full depth of the other compartments.

Kitchen sinks have one, three, or four holes for the installation of a faucet. Some single-lever faucets require only a single hole for installation. The three-hole arrangement is for a standard two-handle valve installation. The four holes are designed to allow the installation of a

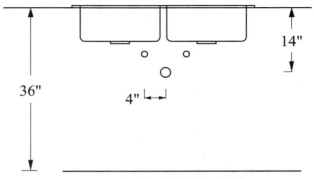

Figure 1-12 Standard dimensions for a kitchen sink include a counter height of 36 in. above the finished floor.

side spray or other kitchen appurtenance such as a soap dispenser.

The standard installation height for a residential kitchen sink is 36 in. above the finished floor. Most architects tend to follow the 6-ft triangle rule when locating a kitchen sink. The sink is placed no more than 6 ft to the range and 6 ft to the refrigerator. (See Figure 1-12.)

Residential kitchen sinks mount either above the counter or below the counter. Counter-mounting kitchen sinks are available with a self rimming ledge or a sink frame.

Commercial Kitchen Sinks

Commercial kitchen sinks are normally larger in size and have a deeper bowl than residential kitchen sinks. The depth of the bowl ranges from 16 to 20 in. for most commercial kitchen sinks. Commercial kitchen sinks are often free-standing sinks with legs to support the sink.

Because of health authority requirements, most commercial kitchen sinks are stainless steel. Another health authority requirement is for either a two- or three-compartment sink in every commercial kitchen. The more popular requirement is a three-compartment sink. The historical requirement for a three-compartment sink dates back to the use of the first compartment for washing of dishes, the second compartment for the rinsing of dishes, and the third compartment for sanitizing the dishes. With the increased use of dishwashers in commercial kitchens, some of the health codes have modified the requirements for a three-compartment sink.

Commercial kitchen sinks used for food preparation are required to connect to the drainage system through an indirect waste. This prevents the possibility of contaminating any of the food in the event of a drain-line backup resulting from a stoppage in the line.

Commercial kitchen sinks that could discharge grease-laden waste must connect to either a grease interceptor or a grease trap. Plumbing codes used to permit the grease trap to serve as the trap for the sink if it was located within 60 in. of the sink. Most plumbing codes have since modified this requirement by mandating a trap for each kitchen sink. The grease trap is no longer permitted to serve as a trap. A separate trap provides better protection from the escape of sewer gas. (See Figure 1-13.)

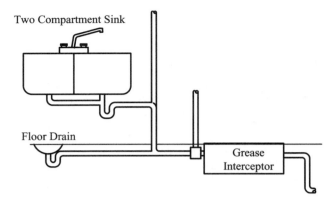

Figure 1-13 When grease-laden waste is possible, the sink must discharge to a grease interceptor.

SERVICE SINKS

A service sink is a general purpose sink intended to be used for facilitating the cleaning or decorating of a building. The sink is commonly used to fill mop buckets and dispose of their waste. It is also used for cleaning paint brushes, rollers, and paper hanging equipment.

There is no standard size, shape, or style of a service sink. They are available both wall mounted and floor mounted. Mop basins, installed on the floor, qualify as service sinks in the plumbing codes.

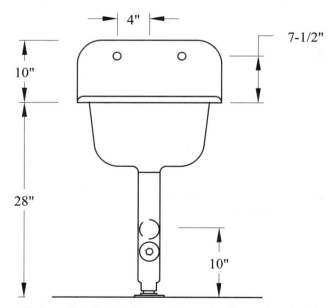

Figure 1-14 While not required, a standard 3-in. P trap service sink is still a popular fixture.

A service sink is typically located in a janitor's storage closet or a separate room for use by the custodial employees. There is no requirement specifying location in the plumbing codes. Neither is there a standard height for installing a service sink. Furthermore, there are no limitations on the flow rate from the service sink faucet.

Service sinks are selected based on the anticipated use of the fixture and the type of building in which it is installed. The plumbing codes require either a 1½- or a 2-in. trap for the service sink. (See Figure 1-14.)

SINKS

There is a general classification for sinks that are neither kitchen sinks nor service sinks; these are identified simply as "sinks." The general category of fixtures is typically those not required but installed for the convenience of the building users. Some typical installations include doctors' offices, hospitals, laboratories, photo-processing facilities, quick marts, and office buildings.

Sinks come in a variety of sizes and shapes. There are no height or spacing requirements. The flow rate from the faucet is not regulated. Most plumbing codes require a 1½-in. drain connection.

LAUNDRY TRAYS

A laundry tray, or laundry sink, is located in the laundry room and used in conjunction with washing clothes. The sink has either one or two compartments. The depth of the bowl is typically 14 in. There are no standard dimensions for the size of laundry trays; however, most single-compartment laundry trays measure 22 in. by 24 in. wide, and most double-compartment laundry trays measure 22 in. by 45 in.

Plumbing codes permit a domestic clothes washer to discharge into a laundry tray. The minimum size for a trap and outlet for a laundry tray is 1½ in.

At one time, laundry trays were made predominantly of soapstone. Today, the majority of laundry trays are plastic. However, there are also stainless steel, enameled cast iron, and porcelain enameled steel laundry trays.

FAUCETS

Every sink and lavatory needs a faucet to direct and control the flow of water into the fixture. A faucet performs the simple operations of opening, closing, and mixing hot and cold water. While the process is relatively simple, fixture manufacturers have developed extensive lines of faucets.

Faucet Categories

Faucets are categorized by application. The types of faucets include lavatory faucets, residential kitchen sink faucets, laundry faucets, sink faucets, and commercial faucets. The classification commercial faucets includes commercial kitchen faucets and commercial sink faucets. It does not include lavatory faucets. All lavatories are classified the same, whether they are installed in residential or commercial buildings. It should be noted, however, that there are styles of lavatory faucets used strictly in commercial applications. These include self-metering lavatory faucets that discharge a specified quantity of water and automatic lavatories that operate on sensors.

Flow Rates

The flow rates are regulated for lavatories and noncommercial kitchen sinks. Table 1-2 identifies the flow rate limitations of faucets.

Table 1-2
Faucet Flow Rate Restrictions

Type of Faucet	Maximum Flow Rate
Kitchen faucet	2.2 gpm @ 60 psi
Lavatory faucet	2.2 gpm @ 60 psi
Lavatory faucet (public use)	0.5 gpm @ 60 psi
Lavatory faucet (public use, metering)	0.25 gal per cycle

Backflow Protection

In addition to controlling the flow of water, a faucet must protect the potable water supply against backflow. This is often a forgotten requirement, since most faucets rely on an air gap to provide protection against backflow. When an air gap is provided between the outlet of the faucet and the flood level rim of the fixture (by manufacturer design), no additional protection is necessary.

Backflow protection becomes a concern whenever a faucet has a hose thread outlet, a flexible hose connection, or a pull-out spray connection. For these styles of faucet, additional backflow protection is necessary. The hose or hose connection eliminates the air gap by submerging the spout or outlet in a nonpotable water source.

The most common form of backflow protection for faucets not having an air gap is the use of a vacuum breaker. Many manufacturers include an atmospheric vacuum breaker in the design of faucets that require additional backflow protection. The standard atmospheric vacuum breaker must conform to ASSE 1001.

Faucets with pull-out sprays or goose-neck spouts can be protected by a vacuum breaker or a backflow system that conforms to ANSI/ASME A112.18.3. This standard specifies testing requirements for a faucet to be certified as protecting the water supply against backflow. Many of the newer pull-out spray kitchen faucets are listed in ANSI/ASME A112.18.3. These newer faucets have a spout attached to a flexible hose whereby the spout can detach from the faucet body and be used similarly to the way a side spray is.

Side-spray kitchen faucets must have a diverter that is listed in ASSE 1025. The diverter ensures that the faucet switches to an air gap whenever there is a lowering of the pressure in the supply line.

The most important installation requirement is the proper location of the backflow preventer (or the maintenance of the air gap). When atmospheric vacuum breakers are installed, they must be located a minimum distance above the flood level rim of the fixture, as specified by the manufacturer.

DRINKING FOUNTAINS

A drinking fountain is designed to provide drinking water to users. The two classifications of drinking fountains are water coolers and drinking fountains. A water cooler has a refrigerated component that chills the water. A drinking fountain is a nonrefrigerated water dispenser.

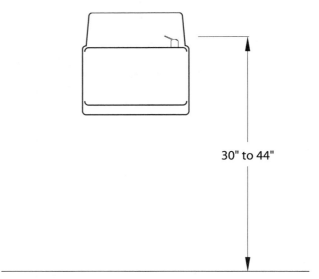

Figure 1-15 Drinking fountain height can vary depending on the application.

There are many styles of both drinking fountain and water cooler. The height of a drinking fountain is not regulated—other than accessible drinking fountains conforming to ANSI/International Code Council (ICC) A117.1. For grade school installations, drinking fountains are typically installed 30 in. above the finished floor to the rim of the fountain. Other locations typically have drinking fountains 36 to 44 in. above the finished floor. (See Figure 1-15.)

Space must be provided in front of the drinking fountain to allow proper access to the fixture. The plumbing code prohibits drinking fountains from being installed in toilets or bathrooms.

The water supply to a drinking fountain is ⅜ in. or ½ in. in diameter. The drainage connection is 1¼ in.

Many plumbing codes permit bottled water or the service of water in a restaurant to be substituted for the installation of a drinking fountain.

SHOWERS

A shower is designed to allow full body cleansing. The size and configuration of a shower must permit an individual to bend at the waist to clean the lower body extremities. The minimum size shower enclosure required in the plumbing codes is 30 in. by 30 in. The codes further stipulate that a shower have a 30-in. diameter circle within the shower to allow free movement by the bather.

The water flow rate for showers is regulated by the Plumbing Product Efficiency Act of 1992. The maximum permitted flow rate from a shower valve is 2.5 gpm at 80 psi.

There are three different types of shower available: the prefabricated shower enclosure, the prefabricated shower base, and the built-in-place shower. Prefabricated shower enclosures are available from plumbing fixture manufacturers in a variety of sizes and shapes. Prefabricated shower bases are the floors of the showers designed so that the walls can be either prefabricated assemblies or built-in-place ceramic walls. Built-in-place showers are typically ceramic installations for both the floor and walls.

Prefabricated shower enclosures and prefabricated shower bases have a drainage outlet designed for a connection to a 2-in. drain. Certain plumbing codes have lowered the shower drain size to 1½ in. The connection to a 1½-in. drain can also be made with prefabricated showers.

A built-in-place shower allows the installation of a shower of any shape and size. The important installation requirement for a built-

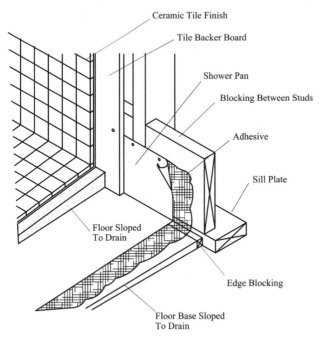

Figure 1-16 Built-in-place showers require a pan below the floor. The drain must have weep holes at the shower pan level.

in-place shower is the shower pan. The pan is placed on the floor prior to the installation of the ceramic base. The pan must turn up on the sides of the shower a minimum of 2 in. above the finished threshold of the shower (except the threshold entrance). The materials commonly used to make a shower pan include sheet lead, sheet copper, PVC sheet, and chlorinated polyethylene sheet. (See Figure 1-16.)

At the drainage connection to the shower pan, weep holes are required to be installed at the base of the shower pan. The weep holes and shower pan are intended to serve as a backup drain in the event that the ceramic floor leaks or cracks.

SHOWER VALVES

Shower valves must be thermostatic mixing, pressure balancing, or a combination of thermostatic mixing and pressure balancing and conform to ASSE 1016. The shower valves not only control the flow and temperature of the water, they also must control any variation in the temperature of the water. These valves provide protection against scalding as well as sudden changes in water temperature, which can cause slips and falls.

A pressure-balancing valve maintains a constant temperature of the shower water by constantly adjusting the pressure of the hot and cold water supply. If there is a change in pressure on the cold water supply, the hot water supply balances to the equivalent pressure setting. When tested, a pressure-balancing valve cannot have a fluctuation in temperature that exceeds 3°F. If the cold water shuts off completely, the hot water shuts off as well.

Thermostatic mixing valves adjust the temperature of the water by maintaining a constant temperature once the water temperature is set. This is accomplished by thermally sensing controls that modify the quantity of hot and cold water to keep the set temperature.

The difference between a thermostatic mixing valve and a pressure-balancing valve is that a thermostatic mixing valve will adjust the temperature when there is a fluctuation in the temperature of either the hot or cold water. With a pressure-balancing valve, when the temperature of either the hot or cold water changes, the temperature of the shower water will change accordingly.

The maximum flow rate permitted for each shower is 2.5 gpm at 80 psi. If body sprays are added to the shower, the total water flow rate is still 2.5 gpm at 80 psi for the total water flow.

The shower valve is typically located 48 to 50 in. above the floor. The installation height for

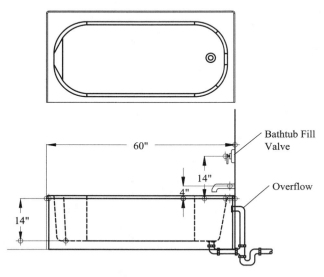

Figure 1-17 A standard bathtub is 5 ft in length.

a shower head ranges from 65 to 84 in. above the floor of the shower. The standard height is 78 in. for showers used by adult males.

BATHTUBS

The bathtub was the original fixture used to bathe or cleanse one's body. Eventually, the shower was added to the bathtub to expedite the bathing process. The standard installation was a combination tub/shower. With the introduction of the whirlpool bathtub, there has been a renaissance with a change to a separate whirlpool bathtub without an overhead shower and a separate shower. It is still common, however, to have a whirlpool bathtub with an overhead shower as the main bathing fixture.

The bathtub has been a traditional residential fixture. Bathtubs tend to be installed within residential units only. The standard bathtub size is 5 ft long by 30 in. wide with a depth of 14 to 16 in. The drain can be either a left-hand (drain hole on the left side as you face the bathtub) or right-hand outlet. (See Figure 1-17.)

All bathtubs must have an overflow drain. This is necessary since the bathtub is often filled while the bather is not present. Porcelain enameled steel and enameled cast iron bathtubs are required to have a slip-resistant base to prevent slips and falls. Plastic bathtubs are not required to have the slip-resistant surface since the plastic is considered to have an inherent slip resistance. However, slip resistance can be specified for plastic bathtub surfaces.

In addition to the standard 5-ft bathtub, there are a variety of sizes and shapes of bathtubs and whirlpool bathtubs. When whirlpool bathtubs are installed, the controls for the whirlpool must be accessible.

BATHTUB FILL VALVE

The two types of bathtub fill valve are the tub filler and the combination tub and shower valve. Tub and shower valves must be pressure-balancing, thermostatic mixing, or combination pressure-balancing and thermostatic mixing valves conforming to ASSE 1016. The tub filler is not required to meet these requirements, although there are pressure-balancing and thermostatic mixing tub filler valves available.

The spout of the tub filler must be properly installed to maintain a 2-in. air gap between the outlet and the flood level rim of the bathtub. If this air gap is not maintained, then the outlet must be protected from backflow by some other means. Certain decorative tub fillers have an atmospheric vacuum breaker installed to protect the opening that is located below the flood level rim.

The standard location of the bathtub fill valve is 14 in. above the top rim of the bathtub. The spout is typically located 4 in. above the top rim of the bathtub to the centerline of the pipe connection.

BIDET

The bidet is a fixture designed for cleaning the perineal area. The bidet is often mistaken to be a fixture designed for use by the female population only. However, the fixture is meant for both male and female cleaning. The bidet has a faucet that comes with or without a water spray connection. When a water spray is provided, the outlet must be protected against backflow since the opening is located below the flood level rim of the bidet. Manufacturers provide a decorative atmospheric vacuum breaker that is located on the deck of the bidet.

Bidets are vitreous china fixtures that are mounted on the floor. The fixture, being similar to a lavatory, has a 1¼-in. drainage connection. Access must be provided around the bidet to allow a bather to straddle the fixture and sit down on the rim. Most bidets have a flushing rim to cleanse the fixture after each use.

The bidet is used only for external cleansing. It is not designed for internal body cleansing. This is often misunderstood since the body spray may be referred to as a "douche" (the French word for shower).

FLOOR DRAINS

A floor drain is a plumbing fixture that is the exception to the definition of a plumbing fixture. There is no supply of cold and/or hot water to a floor drain. Every other plumbing fixture has a water supply. Floor drains are typically provided as an emergency fixture in the event of a leak or overflow of water. They are also used to assist in the cleaning of a toilet or bathroom.

Floor drains are available in a variety of shapes and sizes. The minimum size drainage outlet required by the plumbing code is 2 in. Most plumbing codes do not require floor drains; it is considered an optional fixture that the plumbing engineer may consider installing. Most public toilet rooms have a least one floor drain. Floor drains are also used on the lower level of commercial buildings and in storage areas, commercial kitchens, and areas subject to potential leaks.

Floor drains may also serve as indirect waste receptors for condensate lines, overflow lines, and similar indirect waste lines.

A trench drain is considered a type of floor drain. (See Figure 1-18.) Trench drains are continuous drains that can extend for a number of feet in length. Trench drains are popular in indoor parking structures and factory and industrial areas. Each section of trench drain must have a separate trap.

When floor drains are installed for emergency purposes, the lack of use can result in the evaporation of the trap seal and the escape of sewer

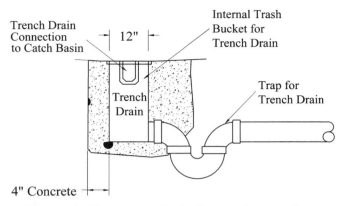

Figure 1-18 A trench drain can be used as a floor drain in a building. A separate trap is required for each section of trench drain.

gas. Floor drain traps subject to such evaporation are required to be protected with trap seal primer valves or devices. These valves or devices ensure that the trap seal remains intact and prevents the escape of sewer gas. (See Figure 1-19.)

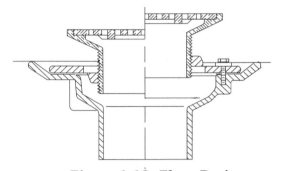

Figure 1-19 Floor Drain

Source: Courtesy of Jay R. Smith Company.

EMERGENCY FIXTURES

The two types of emergency fixture are the emergency shower and the eyewash station. These fixtures are designed to wash a victim with large volumes of water when there is a chemical spill or burn or another hazardous material is spilled on an individual.

Emergency fixtures are normally required by OSHA regulations. In industrial buildings and chemical laboratories, emergency fixtures are sometimes added at the owner's request in addition to the minimum number required by OSHA.

An emergency shower is also called a "drench shower" because of the large volume of water discharged through the emergency shower. (See

Figure 1-20 Emergency Shower

Source: Courtesy of Haws Corporation.

Figure 1-20.) A typical low-end flow rate through an emergency shower is 25 gpm. The flow rate can be as high as 100 gpm. The minimum size water connection is 1 in. The shower head is typically installed 7 ft above the finished floor.

Eyewash stations are for washing the eyes. Unlike in emergency showers, in eyewash stations the water flow rate is gentle so that the eyes can remain open during the washing process. The flow rates for an eyewash station range from 1.5 to 6 gpm.

There are also combination emergency shower and eyewash stations.

Most plumbing codes do not require a drain for emergency showers or eyewash stations. This is to allow greater flexibility in the location of the fixtures and the spot cleanup of any chemicals that may be washed off the victim.

The standard regulating emergency fixtures is ANSI Z358.1. This standard requires the water supply to emergency fixtures to be tepid. The temperature of tepid water is assumed to be in the range of 85°F. When controlling the water temperature, the thermostatic control valve must permit full flow of cold water in the event of a failure of the hot water supply. This can be accomplished with the use of a fail-safe thermostatic mixing valve or a bypass valve for the thermostatic mixing valve. Since the shower and eyewash stations are for extreme emergencies, there must always be an available supply of water to the fixtures.

MINIMUM FIXTURE REQUIREMENTS FOR BUILDINGS

The minimum number of required plumbing fixtures for buildings is specified in the plumbing codes. See Table 1-3, which reprints Table 403.1 of the ICC *International Plumbing Code*, and Table 1-4, which reprints Table 4-1 of the International Association of Plumbing and Mechanical Officials (IAPMO) *Uniform Plumbing Code*.

Both the *International Plumbing Code* and the *Uniform Plumbing Code* base the minimum number of plumbing fixtures on the occupant load of the building. This is the maximum loading permitted based on the exiting of the building. It should be recognized that the occupant load and occupancy of the building are sometimes significantly different. For example, in an office building, the occupancy is typically 25% of the occupant load. The minimum fixture tables have taken this into account in determining the minimum number of fixtures required.

Single-Occupant Toilet Rooms

The *International Plumbing Code* has added a requirement for a single-occupant toilet room for use by both sexes. This toilet room is also called a "unisex toilet room." The single-occupant toilet room must be designed to meet the accessible fixture requirements of ANSI/ICC A117.1. The purpose of the single-occupant toilet room is to allow a husband to help a wife or vice versa. It also allows a father to oversee a daughter or a mother to oversee a son. These rooms are especially important for those temporarily incapacitated and the severely incapacitated.

Table 1-3 Minimum Number Of Required Plumbing Fixtures

No.	Classification	Use Group	Description	Water Closets [a] Male	Water Closets [a] Female	Lavatories Male	Lavatories Female	Bathtubs/ Showers	Drinking Fountains [b]	Other
1	Assembly (see Sections 403.2, 403,5 and 403.6)	A-1	Theaters usually with fixed seats and other buildings for the performing arts and motion pictures	1 per 125	1 per 65	1 per 200		—	1 per 500	1 service sink
		A-2	Nightclubs, bars, taverns, dance halls and buildings for similar purposes	1 per 40	1 per 40	1 per 75		—	1 per 500	1 service sink
			Restaurants, banquet halls and food courts	1 per 75	1 per 75	1 per 200		—	1 per 500	1 service sink
		A-3	Auditoriums without permanent seating, art galleries, exhibition halls, museums, lecture halls, libraries, arcades and gymnasiums	1 per 125	1 per 65	1 per 200		—	1 per 500	1 service sink
			Passenger terminals and transportation facilities	1 per 500	1 per 500	1 per 750		—	1 per 1000	1 service sink
			Places of worship and other religious services. Churches without assembly halls	1 per 150`	1 per 75	1 per 200		—	1 per 1000	1 service sink
		A-4	Coliseums, arenas, skating rinks, pools and tennis courts for indoor sporting events and activities	1 per 75 for the first 1,500 and 1 per 120 for the remainder exceeding 1,500	1 per 40 for the first 1,500 and 1 per 60 for the remainder exceeding 1,500	1 per 200	1 per 150	—	1 per 1000	1 service sink
		A-5	Stadiums, amusement parks, bleachers and grandstands for outdoor sporting events and activities	1 per 75 for the first 1,500 and 1 per 120 for the remainder exceeding 1,500	1 per 40 for the first 1,500 and 1 per 60 for the remainder exceeding 1,500	1 per 200	1 per 150	—	1 per 1000	1 service sink
2	Business (see Sections 403.2, 403,4 and 403.6)	B	Buildings for the transaction of business, professional services, other services involving merchandise, office buildings, banks, light industrial and similar uses	1 per 25 for the first 50 and 1 per 50 for the remainder exceeding 50		1 per 40 for the first 50 and 1 per 80 for the remainder exceeding 50		—	1 per 1000	1 service sink
3	Educational	E	Educational facilities	1 per 50		1 per 50		—	1 per 100	1 service sink
4	Factory and Industrial	F-1 and F-2	Structures in which occupants are engaged in work fabricating, assembly or processing of products or materials	1 per 100		1 per 100		(See Section 411)	1 per 400	1 service sink

(continued)

Table 1-3 continued

Classification No.		Use Group	Description	Water Closets [a] Male	Water Closets [a] Female	Lavatories Male	Lavatories Female	Bathtubs/ Showers	Drinking Fountains [b]	Other
5	Institutional	I-1	Residential care	1 per 10	1 per 10	1 per 10		1 per 8	1 per 100	1 service sink
		I-2	Hospitals, ambulatory nursing home patients [c]	1 per room [d]		1 per room [d]		1 per 15	1 per 100	1 service sink per floor
			Employees, other than residential care [c]	1 per 25		1 per 35		—	1 per 100	—
			Visitors, other than residential care	1 per 75		1 per 100		—	1 per 500	—
		I-3	Prisons [c]	1 per cell		1 per cell		1 per 15	1 per 100	1 service sink
		I-3	Reformatories, detention centers, and correctional centers [c]	1 per 15		1 per 15		1 per 15	1 per 100	1 service sink
		I-4	Adult daycare and childcare [c]	1 per 15		1 per 15		1 per 15 [e]	1 per 100	1 service sink
6	Mercantile (see Sections 403.2, 403.5 and 403.6)	M	Retail stores, service stations, shops, salesrooms, markets and shopping centers	1 per 500		1 per 750		—	1 per 1,000	1 service sink
7	Residential	R-1	Hotels, motels, boarding houses (transient)	1 per guestroom		1 per guestroom		1 per guestroom	—	1 service sink
		R-2	Dormitories, fraternities, sororities and boarding houses (not transient)	1 per 10		1 per 10		1 per 8	1 per 100	1 service sink
		R-2	Apartment house	1 per dwelling unit		1 per dwelling unit		1 per dwelling unit	—	1 kitchen sink per dwelling unit; 1 automatic clothes washer connection per 20 dwelling units [f]
		R-3	One- and two-family dwellings	1 per dwelling unit		1 per dwelling unit		1 per dwelling unit	—	1 kitchen sink per dwelling unit; 1 automatic clothes washer connection per dwelling unit [f]
		R-4	Residential care/assisted living facilities	1 per 10		1 per 10		1 per 8	1 per 100	1 service sink
8	Storage (see Sections 403.2 and 403.4)	S-1 S-2	Structures for the storage of goods, warehouses, storehouses and freight depots. Low and Moderate Hazard.	1 per 100		1 per 100		1 per 1,000	See Section 411	1 service sink

Source: International Plumbing Code, Copyright 2003, International Code Council, Inc., Falls Church, Virginia. Reproduced with permission. All rights reserved.

Notes: 1. The fixtures shown are based on one fixture being the minimum required for the number of persons indicated or any fraction of the number of persons indicated. The number of occupants shall be determined by the International Building Code. 2. For further information, see International Plumbing Code, 2003, Sections 403.2 and 403.3. 3. All references to sections in this table refer to International Plumbing Code, 2003.
a. For urinals, see International Plumbing Code, 2003, Section 419.2.
b. See International Plumbing Code, 2003, Section 410.1.
c. Toilet facilities for employees shall be separate from facilities for inmates or patients.
d. A single-occupant toilet room with one water closet and one lavatory serving not more than two adjacent patient rooms shall be permitted where such room is provided with direct access from each patient room and with provisions for privacy.
e. For day nurseries, a maximum of one bathtub shall be required.
f. For attached one- and two-family dwellings, one automatic clothes washer connection shall be required per 20 dwelling units.

Table 1-4 Minimum Plumbing Facilities

Type of Building or Occupancy [a]	Water Closets [m] (Fixtures per Person)		Urinals [d,l] (Fixtures per Person)	Lavatories (Fixtures per Person)		Bathtubs or Showers (Fixtures per Person)	Drinking Fountains [b,l] (Fixtures per Person)
	Male	Female	Male	Male	Female		
Assembly Places– Theatres, Auditoriums, Convention Halls, etc. – for permanent employee use	1: 1-15 2: 16-35 3: 36-55 Over 55, add 1 fixture for each additional 40 persons.	1: 1-15 3: 16-35 4: 36-55	0: 1-9 1: 10-50 Add one fixture for each additional 50 males.	1 per 40	1 per 40		
Assembly Places – Theatres, Auditoriums, Convention Halls, etc. – for public use	1: 1-100 2: 101-200 3: 201-400 Over 400, add one fixture for each additional 500 males and 1 for each additional 125 females.	3: 1-50 4: 51-100 8: 101-200 11: 201-400	1: 1-100 2: 101-200 3: 201-400 4: 401-600 Over 600 add 1 fixture for each additional 300 males.	1: 1-200 2: 201-400 3: 401-750 Over 750, add one fixture for each additional 500 persons.	1: 1-200 2: 201-400 3: 401-750		1: 1-150 2: 151-400 3: 401-750 Over 750, add one fixture for each additional 500 persons
Dormitories [h] School or Labor	1 per 10 Add 1 fixture for each additional 25 males (over 10) and 1 for each additional 20 females (over 8).	1 per 8	1 per 25 Over 150, add 1 fixture for each additional 50 males.	1 per 12 Over 12 add one fixture for each additional 20 males and 1 for each 15 additional females.	1 per 12	1 per 8 For females, add 1 bathtub per 30. Over 150, add 1 per 20.	1 per 150 [x]
Dormitories – for staff use	1: 1-15 2: 16-35 3: 36-55 Over 55, add 1 fixture for each additional 40 persons.	1: 1-15 3: 16-35 4: 36-55	1 per 50	1 per 40	1 per 40	1 per 8	
Dwellings [c]							
Single Dwelling Multiple Dwelling or Apartment House	1 per dwelling 1 per dwelling or apartment unit			1 per dwelling 1 per dwelling or apartment unit		1 per dwelling 1 per dwelling or apartment unit	
Hospital waiting rooms	1 per room			1 per room			1 per 150 [k]
Hospitals – for employee use	1: 1-15 2: 16-35 3: 36-55 Over 55, add 1 fixture for each additional 40 persons.	1: 1-15 3: 16-35 4: 36-55	0: 1-9 1: 10-50 Add one fixture for each additional 50 males.	1 per 40	1 per 40		
Hospitals							
Individual Room Ward Room	1 per room 1 per 8 patients			1 per room 1 per 10 patients		1 per room 1 per 20 patients	1 per 150 [x]
Industrial [e] Warehouses Workshops, Foundries and similar establishments – for employee use	1: 1-10 2: 11-25 3: 26-50 4: 51-75 5: 76-100 Over 100, add 1 fixture for each additional 30 persons	1: 1-10 2: 11-25 3: 26-50 4: 51-75 5: 76-100		Up to 100, 1 per 10 persons Over 100, 1 per 15 persons [f,g]		1 shower for each 15 persons exposed to excessive heat or to skin contamination with poisonous, infectious, or irritating material	1 per 150 [k]
Institutional – Other than Hospitals or Penal Institutions (on each occupied floor	1 per 25	1 per 20	0: 1-9 1: 10-50 Add one fixture for each additional 50 males.	1 per 10	1 per 10	1 per 8	1 per 150 [12]
Institutional – Other than Hospitals or Penal Institutions (on each occupied floor) – for employee use	1: 1-15 2: 16-35 3: 36-55 Over 55, add 1 fixture for each additional 40 persons	1: 1-15 2: 16-35 3: 36-55	0: 1-9 1: 10-50 Add one fixture for each additional 50 males.	1 per 40	1 per 40	1 per 8	1 per 150 [12]
Office or Public Buildings	1: 1-100 2: 101-200 3: 201-400 Over 400, add one fixture for each additional 500 males and 1 for each additional 150 females.	3: 1-50 4: 51-100 8: 101-200 11: 201-400	1: 1-100 2: 101-200 3: 201-400 4: 401-600 Over 600 add 1 fixture for each additional 300 males.	1: 1-200 2: 201-400 3: 401-750 Over 750, add one fixture for each additional 500 persons.	1: 1-200 2: 201-400 3: 401-750		1 per 150 [k]

(continued)

Table 1-4 continued

Type of Building or Occupancy [a]	Water Closets [m] (Fixtures per Person) Male	Water Closets [m] (Fixtures per Person) Female	Urinals [d,l] (Fixtures per Person) Male	Lavatories (Fixtures per Person) Male	Lavatories (Fixtures per Person) Female	Bathtubs or Showers (Fixtures per Person)	Drinking Fountains [b,l] (Fixtures per Person)
Office or Public Buildings– for employee use	1: 1-15 2: 16-35 3: 36-55 Over 55, add 1 fixture for each additional 40 persons	1: 1-15 2: 16-35 3: 36-55	0: 1-9 1: 10-50 Add one fixture for each additional 50 males.	1 per 40	1 per 40		
Penal Institutions – for employee use	1: 1-15 2: 16-35 3: 36-55 Over 55, add 1 fixture for each additional 40 persons	1: 1-15 2: 16-35 3: 36-55	0: 1-9 1: 10-50 Add one fixture for each additional 50 males.	1 per 40	1 per 40		1 per 150 [k]
Penal Institutions –for prison use Cell Exercise Room	1 per cell 1 per exercise room		1 per exercise room	1 per cell 1 per exercise room			1 per cell block floor 1 per exercise room
Restaurants, Pubs and Lounges [j]	1: 1-50 2: 51-150 3: 151-300 Over 300, add 1 fixture for each additional 200 persons	1: 1-50 2: 51-150 4: 151-300	1: 1-150 Over 150, add 1 fixture for each additional 150 males	1: 1-150 2: 151-200 3: 201-400 Over 400, add 1 fixture for each additional 400 persons	1: 1-150 2: 151-200 3: 201-400		
Schools – for staff use All schools	1: 1-15 2: 16-35 3: 36-55 Over 55, add 1 fixture for each additional 40 persons	1: 1-15 2: 16-35 3: 36-55	1 per 50	1 per 40	1 per 40		
Schools – for student use Nursery	1: 1-20 2: 21-50 Over 50, add 1 fixture for each additional 50 persons	1: 1-20 2: 21-50		1: 1-25 2: 26-50 Over 50, add 1 fixture for each additional 50 persons	1: 1-25 2: 26-50		1 per 150 [k]
Elementary	1 per 30	1 per 25	1 per 75	1 per 35	1 per 35		1 per 150 [k]
Secondary	1 per 40	1 per 30	1 per 35	1 per 40	1 per 40		1 per 150 [k]
Others (Colleges, Universities, Adult Centers, etc.)	1 per 40	1 per 30	1 per 35	1 per 40	1 per 40		1 per 150 [k]
Worship Places Educational/Activities	1 per 150	1 per 75	1 per 150	1 per 2 water closets			1 per 150 [k]
Worship Places Principal Assembly Place	1 per 150	1 per 75	1 per 150	1 per 2 water closets			1 per 150 [k]

Source: Reproduced from the 2000 edition of the *Uniform Plumbing Code*™, Copyright 1999, with permission of the publishers, the International Association of Plumbing and Mechanical Officials. All rights reserved.

Notes: 1. The figures shown are based upon one fixture being the minimum required for the number of persons indicated or any fraction thereof. 2. Each building shall be provided with sanitary facilities, including provisions for the physically handicapped, as prescribed by the department having jurisdiction. For requirements for the handicapped, ANSI A117.1-1992, Accessible and Usable Buildings and Facilities, may be used. 3. The total occupant load shall be determined by minimum exiting requirements. The minimum number of fixtures shall be calculated at 50% male and 50% female based on the total occupant load.

[a] Building categories not shown on this table shall be considered separately by the administrative authority.

[b] Drinking fountains shall not be installed in toilet rooms.

[c] Laundry trays. One (1) laundry tray or one (1) automatic washer standpipe for each dwelling unit or one (1) laundry tray or one (1) automatic washer standpipe, or combination thereof, for each twelve (12) apartments. Kitchen sinks, one (1) for each dwelling or apartment unit.

[d] For each urinal added in excess of the minimum required, one water closet may be deducted. The number of water closets shall not be reduced to less than two-thirds (2/3) of the minimum requirement.

[e] As required by ANSI Z4.1-1968, Sanitation in Places of Employment.

[f] There where there is exposure to skin contamination with poisonous, infectious, or irritating materials, provide one (1) lavatory for each five (5) persons.

[g] Twenty-four (24) lineal inches (610 mm) of wash sink or eighteen (18) inches (457 mm) of a circular basin, when provided with water outlets for such space, shall be considered equivalent to one (1) lavatory.

[h] Laundry trays, one (1) for each fifty (50) persons. Service sinks, one (1) for each hundred (100) persons.

[i] General. In applying this schedule of facilities, consideration shall be given to the accessibility of the fixtures. Conformity purely on a numerical basis may not result in an installation suited to the need of the individual establishment. For example, schools should be provided with toilet facilities on each floor having classrooms.

   A. Surrounding materials, wall and floor space to a point two (2) feet (610 mm) in front of urinal lip and four (4) feet (1219 mm) above the floor, and at least two (2) feet (610 mm) to each side of the urinal shall be lined with nonabsorbent materials.

   B. Trough urinals shall be prohibited.

[j] A restaurant is defined as a business that sells food to be consumed on the premises.

   A. The number of occupants for a drive-in restaurant shall be considered as equal to the number of parking stalls.

   B. Employee toilet facilities shall not be included in the above restaurant requirements. Hand washing facilities shall be available in the kitchen for employees.

[k] Where food is consumed indoors, water stations may be substituted for drinking fountains. Offices, or public buildings for use by more than six (6) persons shall have one (1) drinking fountain for the first one hundred fifty (150) persons and one (1) additional fountain for each three hundred (300) persons thereafter.

[l] There shall be a minimum of one (1) drinking fountain per occupied floor in schools, theatres, auditoriums, dormitories, offices or public buildings.

[m] The total number of water closets for females shall be at least equal to the total number of water closets and urinals required for males.

The *International Plumbing Code* requires the single-occupant toilet room in mercantile and assembly buildings when the total number of water closets required (both men and women) is six or more. When installed in airports, the facilities must be located to allow use before an individual passes through the security checkpoint.

Another feature typically added to single-occupant toilet rooms is a diaper changing station. This allows either the mother or the father to change a baby's diaper in privacy. To allow all possible uses of the single-occupant toilet room, the rooms are often identified as family toilet rooms. This is to clearly indicate that the rooms are not reserved for the physically challenged.

Piping Systems

The selection of piping materials depends on pressure, velocity, temperature, the corrosiveness of the medium conveyed within, initial cost, installation costs, operating costs, and good engineering practice. This chapter is intended to provide information and guidance regarding common types of pipe materials. The information is offered to the plumbing engineer for general applications of various pipe materials and various applications of materials. It should be noted that plumbing codes and regulations differ from one state to another and should be referred to prior to the beginning of any design.

INSTALLATION

Pipes should be neatly arranged—straight, parallel or at right angles to walls—and cut accurately to established measurements. Pipes should be worked into place without springing or forcing. Sufficient headroom should be provided to enable the clearing of lighting fixtures, ductwork, sprinklers, aisles, passageways, windows, doors, and other openings. Pipes should not interfere with access to maintain equipment.

Pipes should be clean (free of cuttings and foreign matter inside) and exposed ends of piping should be covered during site storage and installation. Split, bent, flattened, or otherwise damaged pipe or tubing should not be used. Sufficient clearance should be provided from walls, ceilings, and floors to permit welding, soldering, or connecting joints and valves. A minimum of 6–10 in. (152.4–254 mm) clearance should be provided. Installation of pipe over electrical equipment, such as switchgear, panel boards, and elevator machine rooms, should be avoided. Piping systems should not interfere with safety or relief valves.

A means of draining the piping systems should be provided. A ½ or ¾-in. (12.7 or 19.1-mm) hose bib (provided with a threaded end and vacuum breaker) should be placed at the lowest point of the piping system for this purpose. Constant grades should be maintained for proper drainage, and piping systems should be free of pockets due to changes in elevation.

SPECIFICATION

Only new materials should be specified. A typical piping specification should include the following items:

1. Type of system,
2. Type of material,
3. Applicable standard(s),
4. Wall thickness,
5. Method of joining,
6. Methods of support,
7. Type of end connection,
8. Type of weld or solder,
9. Bolting,
10. Gasket materials, and
11. Testing.

Piping is usually tested at 1.5 times the working pressure of the system. It should not be buried, concealed, or insulated until it has been inspected, tested, and approved. All defective piping is to be replaced and retested.

Note: All domestic water piping and fittings are to conform to National Sanitation Foundation (NSF) Standard 61.

COMMON TYPES OF PIPE

Asbestos Cement

This type of pipe is made of asbestos fibers combined under pressure with Portland cement and silica flour to form a dense and homogeneous material. It is then autoclave cured for strength.

There are two types of pipe, pressure and nonpressure. Both types are available with or without an epoxy lining of 12, 20, or 40-mil thickness. The pressure type is used primarily unlined as water piping and secondarily as lined sewer force mains and industrial effluent and process piping. The nonpressure type is used for sanitary and storm drainage systems, casings for electric cables, and ductwork.

The size range is 4–36 in. (100–914 mm) in diameter for water piping and 4–42 in. (100–1067 mm) for nonpressure piping. The 4 and 6-in. (100 and 150-mm) diameter is available in either 10 or 13-ft (3 or 4-m) lengths and the 8–42-in. (200–1060-mm) diameter in 13-ft (4-m) lengths. Pressure pipe is available in 100, 150, and 200-psi (689.5, 1035.2, and 1379-kPa) working pressures. Sewer pipe is classified in grades of 1500, 2400, 3300, 4000, 5000, 6000, and 7000-lb/ft. (2234.3, 3574.8, 4468.5, 5958, 7447.5, 8937.2, and 10426.7-kg/m) crush strength. The selection of pipe is determined by such factors as working pressure, earth loading, and wheel or live loading.

The asbestos is not considered a health hazard because of the process by which it is bonded into the pipe. Very little asbestos cement piping is manufactured in the United States because of the hazard of breathing asbestos during the cutting and manufacturing of the pipe. Another reason it is seldom used is the high cost of disposal for unused and damaged piping.

Note: The use of asbestos cement piping has been banned in some states; the designer should check with the local code officials prior to use.

The applicable standard for asbestos cement water piping is American Standard for Testing and Material (ASTM) C-296 and for nonpressure drainage piping ASTM C-428.

Pipe joints are made with a machined spigot end on the pipe which pushes into a coupling. Fittings are belied. Both couplings and fittings bells are grooved, with a rubber gasket that fits between the groove and the spigot pipe end. This makes a watertight joint, permitting 2.5–5.0° deflection. Cast iron fittings are normally used for pressure pipe and miter cut and epoxy joint asbestos cement fittings for nonpressure pipe. Couplings for both pipes are asbestos cement. See Figure 2-1.

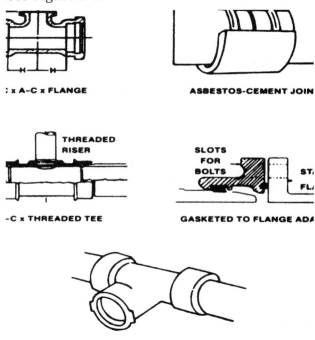

Figure 2-1 Asbestos-Cement Pressure Pipe Joints and Fittings

Applicable standards and specifications for asbestos cement piping include the following: for pressure pipe ASTM C-296, American Water Works Association (AWWA) C-400, and AWWA C-402, and for nonpressure pipe ASTM C-428.

Note: Environmental as well as health problems are asssociated with cutting asbestos cement pipe. The designer should check with local code officials, the local health authority, and pipe manufacturers' recommendations.

(Red) Brass (Copper Alloy) Pipe

(Red) brass pipe is an alloy of copper manufactured to the requirements of ASTM B-43, *Standard Specification for Seamless Red Brass Pipe, Standard Sizes*. It is manufactured from alloy C23000, which is composed of approximately 85% copper (Cu) with no greater than 0.05% lead (Pb) and 0.05% iron (Fe) and the remainder zinc (Zn).

Environmental Protection Agency (EPA) regulations have set a maximum concentration of 8% lead in brass piping. Lead was previously used in the manufacturing of pipe as a filler material. It was added to make the pipe softer, therefore making it easier to cut and shape.

Available sizes are ⅛–12-in. (3.18–304.8-mm) diameters in both standard weight (Schedule 40) and extra-strong weight (Schedule 80). Extra-strong pipe has the same outside diameter as standard weight piping; the difference is in the wall thickness, thus reducing the inside diameter. The standard length for (red) brass pipe is 12 ft (3.7 m). Brass piping dimensions are similar to those of steel piping.

Brass pipe is moderately resistant to many corrosive solutions and is often utilized for water supply and distribution.

Joints in (red) brass pipe can be threaded, flanged, or brazed to the fittings of the appropriate joint configuration. Fittings in the smaller sizes, normally those below 2-in. diameter are screwed cast copper alloy or brazed cup cast copper alloy. Fittings above 2-in. diameter are normally threaded, flanged, brazed, or—in some cases—grooved mechanical joint fittings.

Fittings used with (red) brass pipe include those meeting the applicable requirements of ANSI/ASME B16.15, *Cast Bronze Threaded Fittings*; ANSI/ASME B16.24, *Cast Copper Alloy Pipe Flanges and Flanged Fittings*, MIL F-1183, *Bronze Fittings for Brazed Joints* (threadless brass/bronze fittings).

Note: Many of the federal specification numbers have been replaced by the appropriate ASTM, ANSI/ASME numbers using the appropriate numbering format. See Figure 2-2.

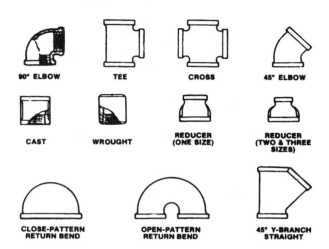

Figure 2-2 Cast-Bronze Threaded Fittings

Cast Iron Soil Pipe

Cast iron soil pipe used in the United States is classified into two major types: hub and spigot, and hubless (no hub).

Cast iron soil pipe is made of gray cast iron with a compact close grain. Three classifications arc used: XH (extra heavy), SV (service), and hubless. Cast iron soil pipe is primarily used for sanitary drain, waste, vent, and storm systems. The extra heavy class is often used for underground applications. Sizes include 2 to 15-in. diameters and 5 or 10-ft (1.5 or 3.1-m) lengths for extra heavy and service pipe. It is available in single and double hub. Traps can have removable cleanouts. Hubless class cast iron sizes include 1½ to 15-in. diameter, and it is manufactured in 5 to 10-ft (1.5 to 3.1-m) lengths. Piping is also available with beaded ends.

Hub and spigot pipe and fittings have hubs into which the spigot (plain end) of the pipe or fitting is inserted. The joint is sealed with a rubber (neoprene) compression gasket or molten lead and oakum. Hub and spigot pipe and fittings are available in two classes or thicknesses: service (SV) and extra heavy (XH). Because the additional wall thickness is added to the outside diameter, service and extra heavy classes have different outside diameters and are not readily interchangeable. These two different types of pipe and fittings can be connected with adapters available form the manufacturer. Hub and spigot pipe and fittings are available in 2 to 15-in. (50.8 to 381-mm) sizes. Compression gaskets, lubricants, and assembly tools are available from manufacturers.

Hubless cast iron soil pipe and fittings are simply pipe and fittings manufactured without a hub. The method of joining these pipes and fittings utilizes a hubless coupling, which slips over the plain ends of the pipe and fittings and is tightened to seal it. Hubless cast iron soil pipe and fittings are made in only one class, or thickness. There are many varied configurations of fittings, and both pipe and fittings range in size from 1½ to 10 in. (38.1 to 254 mm). Couplings

for use in joining hubless pipe and fittings are also available in these size ranges from various manufacturers.

Fittings vary in size and shape. See Figures 2-3, 2-4, and 2-5 and Tables 2-1, 2-2, and 2-3.

Applicable standards and specifications include: ASTM A-74, ASTM A-888, Cast Iron Soil Pipe Institute (CISPI) 301, and CISPI 310.

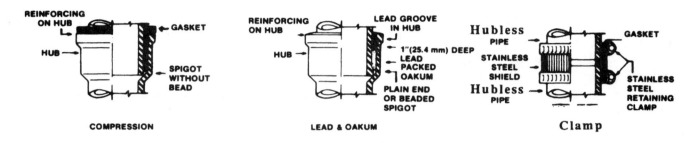

For Extra Heavy and Service Classes   **For Hubless Class**

Figure 2–3: Cast Iron Soil Pipe Joints

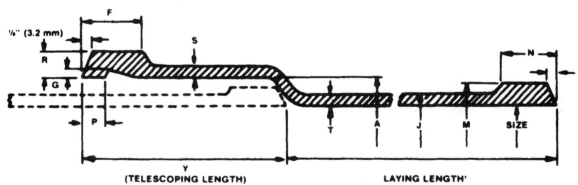

Figure 2-4 Cast-Iron Soil Pipe (Extra-Heavy and Service Classes)

Notes :1. Laying length, all sizes:single hub 5 ft; double hub 5 ft less Y, 5-ft lengths; single hub 10 ft; double hub 10 ft less Y, for 10 ft lengths. 2. If a bead is provided on the spigot end, M may be any diameter between J and M. 3. Hub ends and spigot ends can be made with or without draft, and spigot ends can be made with or without spigot bead.

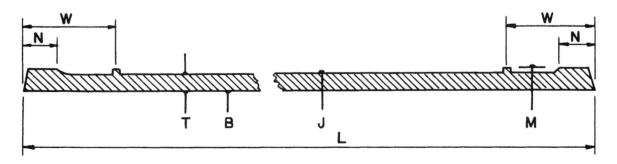

Figure 2-5 Hubless Cast-Iron Soil Pipe and Fittings

Table 2-1 Dimensions of Hubs, Spigots, and Barrels for Extra-Heavy Cast-Iron Soil Pipe and Fittings

Nominal Inside Diameter Size (in.)	Inside Diameter of Hub (in.)	Outside Diameter of Spigot [a] (in.)	Outside Diameter of Barrel (in.)	Telescoping Length (in.)	Thickness of Barrel (in.)	
	A	M	J	Y	T (nominal)	T (minimum)
2	3.06	2.75	2.38	2.50	0.19	0.12
3	4.19	3.88	3.50	2.75	0.25	0.18
4	5.19	4.88	4.50	3.00	0.25	0.18
5	6.19	5.88	5.50	3.00	0.25	0.18
6	7.19	6.88	6.50	3.00	0.25	0.18
8	9.50	9.00	8.62	3.50	0.31	0.25
10	11.62	11.13	10.75	3.50	0.37	0.31
12	13.75	13.13	12.75	4.25	0.37	0.31
15	17.00	16.25	15.88	4.25	0.44	0.37

Nominal Inside Diameter Size (in.)	Thickness of Hub (in.)		Width of Hub Bead [b] (in.)	Width of Spigot Bead [b] (in.)	Distance from Lead Groove to End, Pipe and Fittings (in.)	Depth of Lead Groove (in.)	
	Hub Body	Over Bead					
	S (minimum)	R (minimum)	F	N	P	G (minimum)	G (maximum)
2	0.18	0.37	0.75	0.69	0.28	0.10	0.13
3	0.25	0.43	0.81	0.75	0.28	0.10	0.13
4	0.25	0.43	0.88	0.81	0.28	0.10	0.13
5	0.25	0.43	0.88	0.81	0.28	0.10	0.13
6	0.25	0.43	0.88	0.81	0.28	0.10	0.13
8	0.34	0.59	1.19	1.12	0.38	0.15	0.19
10	0.40	0.65	1.19	1.12	0.38	0.15	0.19
12	0.40	0.65	1.44	1.38	0.47	0.15	0.19
15	0.46	0.71	1.44	1.38	0.47	0.15	0.19

Note: Laying length, all sizes:single hub 5 ft; double hub 5 ft less Y, 5-ft lengths; single hub 10 ft; double hub 10 ft less Y, for 10 ft lengths.

[a] If a bead is provided on the spigot end, M may be any diameter between J and M.

[b] Hub ends and spigot ends can be made with or without draft, and spigot ends can be made with or without spigot bead.

Table 2-1(M) Dimensions of Hubs, Spigots, and Barrels for Extra-Heavy Cast-Iron Soil Pipe and Fittings

Nominal Inside Diameter Size (in.)	Inside Diameter of Hub (mm)	Outside Diameter of Spigot [a] (mm)	Outside Diameter of Barrel (mm)	Telescoping Length (mm)	Thickness of Barrel (mm)	
	A	M	J	Y	T (nominal)	T (minimum)
2	77.72	69.85	60.45	63.50	4.83	3.05
3	106.43	98.55	88.90	69.85	6.35	4.57
4	131.83	123.95	114.30	76.20	6.35	4.57
5	157.23	149.35	139.70	76.20	6.35	4.57
6	182.63	174.75	165.10	76.20	6.35	4.57
8	241.30	228.60	218.95	88.90	7.87	6.35
10	295.15	282.70	273.05	88.90	9.40	7.87
12	349.25	333.50	323.85	107.95	9.40	7.87
15	431.80	412.75	403.35	107.95	11.18	9.40

(Continued)

(Table 2-1(M) continued)

Nominal Inside Diameter Size (in.)	Thickness of Hub (mm)		Width of Hub Bead [b] (mm)	Width of Spigot Bead [b] (mm)	Distance from Lead Groove to End, Pipe and Fittings (mm)	Depth of Lead Groove (mm)	
	Hub Body	Over Bead					
	S (minimum)	R (minimum)	F	N	P	G (minimum)	G (maximum)
2	4.57	9.40	19.05	17.53	7.11	2.54	3.30
3	6.35	10.92	20.57	19.05	7.11	2.54	3.30
4	6.35	10.92	22.35	20.57	7.11	2.54	3.30
5	6.35	10.92	22.35	20.57	7.11	2.54	3.30
6	6.35	10.92	22.35	20.57	7.11	2.54	3.30
8	8.64	14.99	30.23	28.45	9.65	3.81	4.83
10	10.16	16.51	30.23	28.45	9.65	3.81	4.83
12	10.16	16.51	36.58	35.05	11.94	3.81	4.83
15	11.68	18.03	36.58	35.05	11.94	3.81	4.83

Note: Laying length, all sizes: single hub 1.5 m; double hub 1.5 m less Y, 1.5 m lengths; single hub 3.1 m; double hub 3.1 m less Y, for 3.1 m lengths.
[a] If a bead is provided on the spigot end, M may be any diameter between J and M.
[b] Hub ends and spigot ends can be made with or without draft, and spigot ends can be made with or without spigot bead.

Table 2-2 Dimensions of Hubs, Spigots, and Barrels for Service Cast-Iron Soil Pipe and Fittings

Nominal Inside Diameter Size (in.)	Inside Diameter of Hub (in.)	Outside Diameter of Spigot [a] (in.)	Outside Diameter of Barrel (in.)	Telescoping Length (in.)	Thickness of Barrel (in.)	
	A	M	J	Y	T (nominal)	T (minimum)
2	2.94	2.62	2.30	2.50	0.17	0.12
3	3.94	3.62	3.30	2.75	0.17	0.13
4	4.94	4.62	4.30	3.00	0.18	0.14
5	5.94	5.62	5.30	3.00	0.19	0.15
6	6.94	6.62	6.30	3.00	0.20	0.16
8	9.25	8.75	8.38	3.50	0.22	0.17
10	11.38	10.88	10.50	3.50	0.26	0.21
12	13.50	12.88	12.50	4.25	0.28	0.22
15	16.75	16.00	15.62	4.25	0.30	0.25

Nominal Inside Diameter Size (in.)	Thickness of Hub (in.)		Width of Hub Bead [b] (in.)	Width of Spigot Bead [b] (in.)	Distance from Lead Groove to End, Pipe and Fittings (in.)	Depth of Lead Groove (in.)	
	Hub Body	Over Bead					
	S (minimum)	R (minimum)	F	N	P	G (minimum)	G (maximum)
2	0.13	0.34	0.75	0.69	0.28	0.10	0.13
3	0.16	0.37	0.81	0.75	0.28	0.10	0.13
4	0.16	0.37	0.88	0.81	0.28	0.10	0.13
5	0.16	0.37	0.88	0.81	0.28	0.10	0.13
6	0.18	0.37	0.88	0.81	0.28	0.10	0.13
8	0.19	0.44	1.19	1.12	0.38	0.15	0.19
10	0.27	0.53	1.19	1.12	0.38	0.15	0.19
12	0.27	0.53	1.44	1.38	0.47	0.15	0.19
15	0.30	0.58	1.44	1.38	0.47	0.15	0.19

Note: Laying length, all sizes: single hub 5 ft; double hub 5 ft less Y, 5-ft lengths; single hub 10 ft; double hub 10 ft less Y, for 10 ft lengths.
[a] If a bead is provided on the spigot end, M may be any diameter between J and M.
[b] Hub ends and spigot ends can be made with or without draft, and spigot ends can be made with or without spigot bead.

Table 2-2(M) Dimensions of Hubs, Spigots, and Barrels for Service Cast-Iron Soil Pipe and Fittings

Nominal Inside Diameter Size (in.)	Inside Diameter of Hub (mm)	Outside Diameter of Spigot [a] (mm)	Outside Diameter of Barrel (mm)	Telescoping Length (mm)	Thickness of Barrel (mm)	
	A	M	J	Y	T (nominal)	T (minimum)
2	74.68	66.55	58.42	63.50	4.32	3.05
3	100.08	91.95	83.82	69.85	4.32	3.30
4	125.48	117.35	109.22	76.20	4.57	3.56
5	150.88	142.75	134.62	76.20	4.83	3.81
6	176.28	168.15	160.02	76.20	5.08	4.06
8	234.95	222.25	212.85	88.90	5.59	4.32
10	289.05	276.35	266.70	88.90	6.60	5.33
12	342.90	327.15	317.50	107.95	7.11	5.59
15	425.45	406.40	396.75	107.95	7.62	6.35

Nominal Inside Diameter Size (in.)	Thickness of Hub (mm)		Width of Hub Bead [b] (mm)	Width of Spigot Bead [b] (mm)	Distance from Lead Groove to End, Pipe and Fittings (mm)	Depth of Lead Groove (mm)	
	Hub Body	Over Bead					
	S (minimum)	R (minimum)	F	N	P	G (minimum)	G (maximum)
2	3.30	8.64	19.05	17.53	7.11	2.54	3.30
3	4.06	9.40	20.57	19.05	7.11	2.54	3.30
4	4.06	9.40	22.35	20.57	7.11	2.54	3.30
5	4.06	9.40	22.35	20.57	7.11	2.54	3.30
6	4.57	9.40	22.35	20.57	7.11	2.54	3.30
8	4.83	11.18	30.23	28.45	9.65	3.81	4.83
10	6.86	13.46	30.23	28.45	9.65	3.81	4.83
12	6.86	13.46	36.58	35.05	11.94	3.81	4.83
15	7.62	14.73	36.58	35.05	11.94	3.81	4.83

Note: Laying length, all sizes: single hub 1.5 m; double hub 1.5 m less Y, 1.5 m lengths; single hub 3.1 m; double hub 3.1 m less Y, for 3.1 m lengths.
[a] If a bead is provided on the spigot end, M may be any diameter between J and M.
[b] Hub ends and spigot ends can be made with or without draft, and spigot ends can be made with or without spigot bead.

Table 2-3 Dimensions of Spigots and Barrels for Hubless Pipe and Fittings

Nom. Size (in.)	Inside Diam. Barrel (in.)	Inside Diam. Barrel (mm)	Outside Diam. Barrel (in.)	Outside Diam. Barrel (mm)	Outside Diam. Spigot (in.)	Outside Diam. Spigot (mm)	Width Spigot Bead (in.)	Width Spigot Bead (mm)	Thickness of Barrel (in.)	Thickness of Barrel (mm)	Thickness of Barrel (in.)	Thickness of Barrel (mm)	Gasket Positioning Lug (in.)	Gasket Positioning Lug (mm)	Laying Length, L [a, b] 5 Ft (in.)	Laying Length, L [a, b] 10 Ft (in.)
	B		J		M		N		T-Nom.		T-Min.		W		5 Ft	10 Ft
1½	1.50	3.81	1.90	4.83	1.96	4.98	0.25	0.64	0.16	0.38	0.13	0.33	1.13	2.87	60	120
2	2.00	5.08	2.35	5.97	2.41	6.12	0.25	0.64	0.16	0.38	0.13	0.33	1.13	2.87	60	120
3	3.00	7.62	3.35	8.51	3.41	8.66	0.25	0.64	0.16	0.38	0.13	0.33	1.13	2.87	60	120
4	4.00	10.16	4.38	11.13	4.44	11.28	0.31	0.79	0.19	0.48	0.15	0.38	1.13	2.87	60	120
5	4.94	12.70	5.30	13.46	5.36	13.61	0.31	0.79	0.19	0.48	0.15	0.38	1.50	3.81	60	120
6	5.94	15.24	6.30	16.00	6.36	16.15	0.31	0.79	0.19	0.48	0.15	0.38	1.50	3.81	60	120
8	7.94	20.32	8.38	21.29	8.44	21.44	0.31	0.79	0.23	0.58	0.17	0.43	2.00	5.08	60	120
10	10.00	25.40	10.56	26.82	10.62	26.97	0.31	0.79	0.28	0.71	0.22	0.56	2.00	5.08	60	120

[a] Laying lengths as listed are for pipe only.
[b] Laying lengths may be either 5 ft 0 in. or 10 ft 0 in. (1.5 or 3.1 m) long.

Ductile Iron Water and Sewer Pipe

Ductile iron pipe has replaced gray cast iron pressure pipe for water and sewer uses. Gray cast iron pressure pipe is no longer manufactured in the United States. Ductile iron pipe is a high-strength material and is available in seven classes (50–56) and in sizes from 3 to 64-in. (76 to 1626-mm) diameter. Ductile iron pipe is not as brittle as cast iron pipe. The pipe is manufactured with bell ends and has lengths of either 18 or 20 ft (5.49 or 6.1 m). Pressure ratings for the working pressure are available in all sizes to 350 psi (2414 kPa). The primary uses of this pipe are in water and sewer systems and industrial applications.

Standard joints for pipe and fittings are push-on, mechanical, and flanged. Other special joints are also available, such as restrained, ball and socket, and grooved and shouldered. Fittings are manufactured and available as either gray cast iron or ductile iron. See Figure 2-6.

Cement-lined piping is normally required for water distribution systems. The cement lining provides a protective barrier between the potable water supply and the ductile iron pipe to prevent impurities and contaminants form leaching into the water supply.

Applicable standards and specifications include the following:

- ANSI/AWWA C104/A21.4, *Cement Mortar Lining*
- ANSI/AWWA C105/A21.5, *Polyethylene Encasement*
- ANSI/AWWA CI10/A21.10, *Fitting*
- ANSI/AWWA C111/A21.11, *Rubber-Gasket Joints*
- ANSI/AWWA C115/A21.15, *Flanged Pipe*
- ANSI/AWWA C116/A21.16, *Fusion-Bonded Epoxy Coating*
- ANSI/AWWA C150/A21.50, *Thickness Design*
- ANSI/AWWA C151/A21.51, *Manufacturing*
- ANSI/AWWA C153/A21.53, *Compact Fittings*
- ANSI/AWWA C600, *Installation*
- AWWA C651, *Disinfecting*
- ASTM A716, *Culvert Pipe*
- ASTM A746, *Gravity Sewer Pipe.*

Concrete Pipe (Underground Use Only)

There are three commonly used processes for producing precast concrete pipe: packerhead, dry cast, and wet cast. Packerhead and dry cast are classified as immediate strip methods. Immediate strip is characterized by the use of no-slump concrete that is sufficiently compacted during the pipe-making cycle to allow removal of the inner core or outer form as soon as the pipe has been produced. Strip means the removal of the form from the pipe. Wet casting utilizes relatively wet concrete to fill the annular space between an inner core and outer form.

Nonreinforced concrete pipe is used for drainage and sewer lines, and for gravity-flow water supply lines if the joints are carefully made. This pipe is available in 4 to 36-in. (100 to 900-mm) diameters. Nonreinforced concrete pipe is not available in all markets.

Reinforced concrete pipe is (RCP) is made by the addition of steel wire or steel bars. Reinforced concrete pipe is used primarily for sewage and storm drainage and is available in 12 to 144-in. (300 to 3600-mm) diameters.

RCP is also the most commonly used drainage pipe for parking areas and roadways. RCP is installed by site contractors during site preparation more usually than it is installed by the plumbing trade. Joints are usually made with a cement plaster.

For use in sanitary sewers, the joints for both nonreinforced concrete pipe and RCP should be constructed utilizing rubber gaskets. More and more building codes are permitting only elastomeric gasket joints conforming to ASTM C-443 for use below buildings.

Applicable standards and specifications include ASTM C-14, *Standard Specification for Concrete Sewer, Storm Drain, and Culvert Pipe for Non-reinforced Concrete*; ASTM-C-76, *Standard Specification for Reinforced Concrete Culverts, Storm Drain, and Sewer Pipe*, and C-655, *Standard Specification for Reinforced Concrete D-Load Culvert Storm Drain and Sewer Pipe for Reinforced Concrete Pipe*; and ASTM C-443, *Standard Specification for Joints for Circular Concrete Sewer and Culver Pipe, Using Rubber Gaskets.*

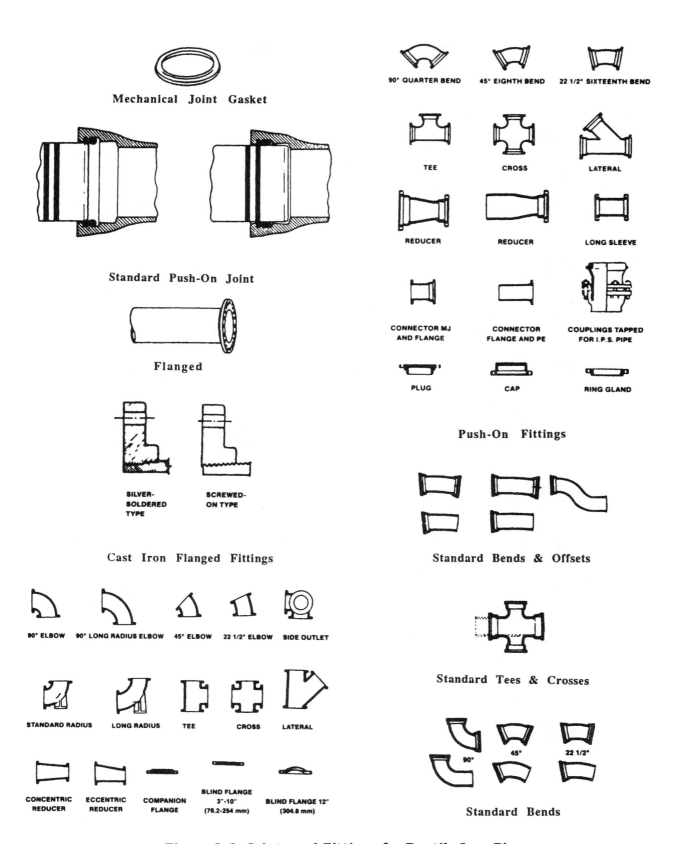

Figure 2-6 Joints and Fittings for Ductile-Iron Pipe

Copper Pipe

Copper pipe is almost pure copper manufactured to the requirements of ASTM B42, *Standard Specification for Seamless Copper Pipe, Standard Sizes*. It may be manufactured from any of five copper alloys (C10200, C10300, C10800, C12000, and C12200) that all conform to the chemical composition requirements of alloys containing a minimum of 99.9% Copper (Cu) and a maximum of 0.04% Phosphorous (P). Available sizes are ⅛ to 12-in. (3.18 to 304.8-mm) diameters in regular wall thickness and ⅛ to 10 in. (3.18 to 254 mm) in extra strong wall thickness. The standard length for copper pipe is 12 ft (3.7 m). Copper pipe dimensions are similar to those for brass and steel pipe.

Copper pipe is suitable for water supply; drain, waste, and vent (DWV); boiler feed lines; refrigeration; and similar purposes.

Joints in seamless copper pipe can be threaded, flanged, or brazed to fittings of the appropriate joint configuration. Fittings in the smaller sizes, normally those below 2-in. diameter, are screwed cast copper alloy or brazed cup cast copper alloy. Fittings above 2-in. diameter are normally threaded, flanged, or brazed; in some cases, grooved mechanical joint fittings are employed.

Fittings used with seamless copper pipe include those meeting the applicable requirements of ANSI/ASME B16.15, *Cast Bronze Threaded Fittings;* ANSI/ASME B16.24, *Cast Copper Alloy Pipe Flanges and Flanged Fittings;* and MIL F-1183, *Bronze Fittings for Brazed Joints* (threadless brass/bronze fittings).

Note: Many of the federal specification numbers have been replaced by the appropriate ASTM, ANSI/ASME numbers using the appropriate numbering format. See Table 2-4.

Copper Water Tube

Copper water tube is a seamless, almost pure copper material manufactured to the requirements of ASTM B88, *Standard Specification for Seamless Copper Water Tube*. It has three basic wall thickness dimensions, designated as types K, L, and M, type K being the thickest, type L being of intermediate thickness, and type M being the thinnest. All three types of tube are manufactured from copper alloy C12200, which has a chemical composition of a minimum of 99.9% copper (Cu) and silver (Ag) combined and

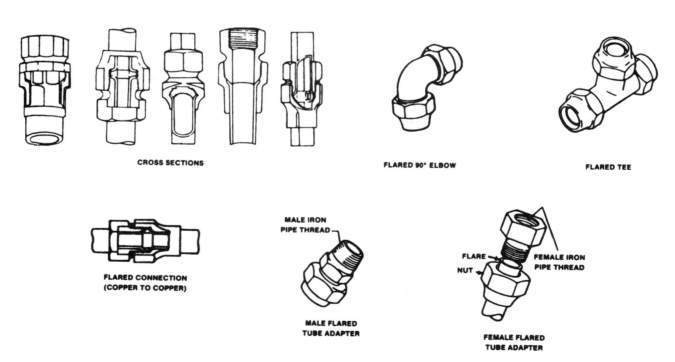

Figure 2-7 Copper Tube Flared Fittings

Table 2-4 Commercially Available Lengths of Copper Plumbing Tube

The first of the three principal classes of copper tubular products is commonly referred to as "commodity tube." It includes types K (heaviest), L (standard), and M (lightest) wall thickness schedules as classified by ASTM B88, *Specification for Seamless Copper Water Tube*; type DWV of ASTM B306, *Specification for Copper Drainage Tube (DWV)*; and medical gas tube of ASTM B819, *Specification for Seamless Copper Tube for Medical Gas Systems*. In each case, the actual outside diameter is ⅛ in. (0.32 cm) larger than the nominal or standard size.

Copper Tube—Types, Standards, Applications, Tempers, Lengths

Tube Type   **Color Code**
Type K   **Green ASTM B 88** [a]

	Commercially Available Lengths [b]			
	Straight Lengths		Coils	
Standard Applications [c]	Drawn	Annealed		
Domestic water service and distribution	¼ to 8 in. 20 ft	20 ft	¼ to 1 in.	60 ft
Fire protection	10 in. 18 ft	18 ft		100 ft
Solar	12 in. 12 ft	12 ft	1¼ and 1½ in.	60 ft
Fuel/fuel oil			2 in.	40 ft
HVAC				45 ft
Snow melting				

Tube Type   **Color Code**
Type L   **Blue ASTM B 88**

	Commercially Available Lengths [b]			
	Straight Lengths		Coils	
Standard Applications [c]	Drawn	Annealed		
Domestic water service and distribution	¼ to 8 in. 20 ft	20 ft	¼ to 1 in.	60 ft
Fire protection	12 in. 18 ft	18 ft		100 ft
Solar			1¼ and 1½ in.	60 ft
Fuel/fuel oil			2 in.	40 ft
Natural gas				45 ft
Liquefied petroleum (LP) gas				
HVAC				
Snow melting				

Tube Type   **Color Code**
Type M   **Red ASTM B 88**

	Commercially Available Lengths [b]		
	Straight Lengths		Coils
Standard Applications [c]	Drawn	Annealed	
Domestic water service and distribution	¼ to 12 in. 20 ft	N/A	
Fire protection			
Solar			
Fuel/fuel oil			
HVAC			
Snow melting			

(Table 2-4 continued)

Tube Type	Color Code					
DWV	**Yellow ASTM B 306**					

		Commercially Available Lengths [b]				
		Straight Lengths			Coils	
Standard Applications [c]		Drawn	Annealed			
Drain, waste, vent Solar HVAC		1¼ to 8 in.	20 ft	N/A		

Tube Type	Color Code					
ACR	**Blue ASTM B 280**					

		Commercially Available Lengths [b]				
		Straight Lengths			Coils	
Standard Applications [c]		Drawn	Annealed			
Air conditioning Refrigeration Natural gas Liquefied petroleum (LP) gas		⅜ to 4⅛ in.	20 ft	[d]	⅛ and 1⅝ in.	50 ft

Tube Type	Color Code					
OXY, MED **OXY/MED** **OXY/ACR** **ACR/MED**	**(K) Green** **(L) Blue ASTM B 819**					

		Commercially Available Lengths [b]				
		Straight Lengths			Coils	
Standard Applications [c]		Drawn	Annealed			
Medical gas		¼ to 8 in.	20 ft	N/A		

Tube Type	Color Code					
Type G	**Yellow ASTM B 837**					
Natural gas Liquid petroleum (LP) gas		⅜ to 1⅛ in.	12 ft 20 ft	12 ft 20 ft	⅜ to ⅞ in.	60 ft 100 ft

[a]   Tube made to other ASTM standards is also intended for plumbing applications, although ASTM B 88 is by far the most widely used. ASTM B 698, *Standard Classifications*, lists six plumbing tube standards, including ASTM B 88.

[b]   Individual manufacturers may have commercially available lengths in addition to those shown in this table.

[c]   There are many other copper and copper alloy tubes and pipes available for specialized applications. For information on these products, contact the Copper Development Association.

[d]   Available as special order only.

a maximum allowable range of phosphorous (P) of 0.015–0.040%.

Seamless copper water tube is manufactured in sizes ¼ to 12 in. (6.35 to 304.8 mm) nominal. Types K and L are manufactured in drawn temper (hard) ¼ to 12 in. (6.35 to 304.8 mm) and annealed temper (soft) coils ¼ to 2 in. (6.35 to 50.8 mm), while type M is manufactured only in drawn (hard) temper ¼ to 12 in. (6.35 to 304.8 mm).

Seamless copper water tube of drawn temper is required to be identified with a color stripe that contains the manufacturer's name or trademark, the type of tube, and the nation of origin. This color strip is green for type K, blue for type L, and red for type M. In addition to the color stripe, the tube is incised with the type of tube and the manufacturer's name or trademark at intervals not in excess of 1½ ft. Annealed (soft) coils or straight lengths are not required to be identified with a color stripe.

Fittings in copper water tube may be those conforming to ASME/ANSI B16.22, *Wrought Copper and Copper Alloy Solder-Joint Pressure Fittings*; ASME/ANSI B16.18, *Cast Copper Alloy Solder-Joint Pressure Fittings*; ASME/ANSI B16.26, *Cast Copper Alloy Fittings for Flared Copper Tube*; or ASME/ANSI B16.24, *Cast Copper Alloy Pipe Flanges and Flanged Fittings, Class 150, 300, 400, 600, 900, 1500, and 2500*. Various other fittings of the compression, grooved, and mechanical type may also be used.

Joints in copper water tube are normally soldered, flared, or brazed, although roll-grooved or mechanical joints are also permitted.

Soldered joints should be installed in accordance with the requirements and procedures detailed in ASTM B828, *Standard Practice for Making Capillary Joints by Soldering of Copper and Copper Alloy Tube and Fittings*; and the flux used should meet the requirements of ASTM B813, *Standard Specification for Liquid and Paste Fluxes for Soldering Applications of Copper and Copper Alloy Tube*.

The mechanical joining of copper tubing with a specially manufactured fitting and crimping tool with interchangeable jaws ½ to 4 in. (12.7 to 101.6 mm) is an alternate way of joining copper tubing.

Applicable standards and specifications include ASTM B-16.18 and ASME B-16.22. O-rings in fittings are to be ethylene-propylene diene monomer (EPDM). See Figures 2-7 and 2-8 and Tables 2-5, 2-6, and 2-7.

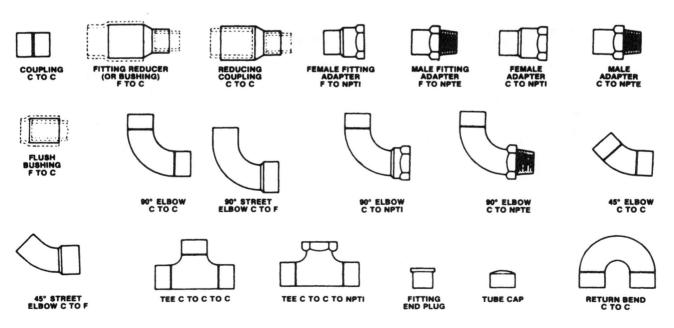

Figure 2-8 Copper and Bronze Joints and Fittings

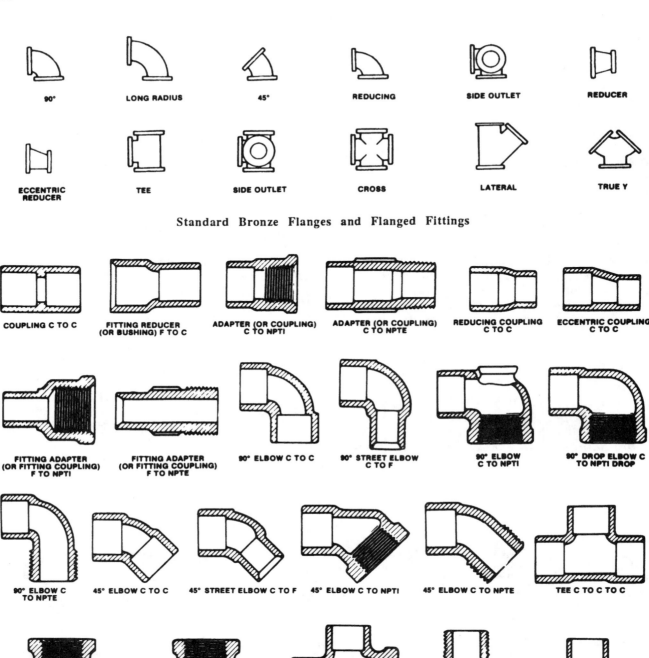

Standard Bronze Flanges and Flanged Fittings

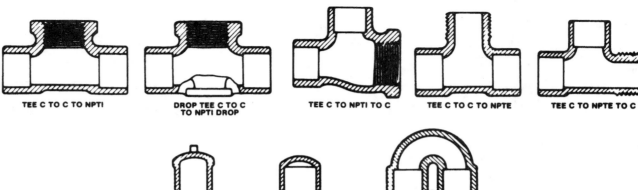

Cast Bronze Solder-Joint Pressure Fittings

(Figure 2-8 Continued)

Table 2-5 Dimensional and Capacity Data—Type K Copper Tube

Nominal (in.)	Actual inside	Actual outside	Wall thick-ness (in.)	Outside	Inside	Metal	of tube alone	of water in tube	of tube and water
¼	0.305	0.375	0.035	0.110	0.073	0.034	0.145	0.033	0.167
⅜	0.402	0.500	0.049	0.196	0.127	0.069	0.269	0.055	0.324
½	0.527	0.625	0.049	0.307	0.218	0.089	0.344	0.094	0.438
⅝	0.652	0.750	0.049	0.442	0.334	0.108	0.418	0.145	0.563
¾	0.745	0.875	0.065	0.601	0.436	0.165	0.641	0.189	0.830
1	0.995	1.125	0.065	0.993	0.778	0.216	0.839	0.338	1.177
1¼	1.245	1.375	0.065	1.484	1.217	0.267	1.04	0.53	1.57
1½	1.481	1.625	0.072	2.072	1.722	0.350	1.36	1.22	2.58
2	1.959	2.125	0.083	3.546	3.013	0.533	2.06	1.31	3.37
2½	2.435	2.625	0.095	5.409	4.654	0.755	2.93	2.02	4.95
3	2.907	3.125	0.109	7.669	6.634	1.035	4.00	2.88	6.88
3½	3.385	3.625	0.120	10.321	8.999	1.322	5.12	3.91	9.03
4	3.857	4.125	0.134	13.361	11.682	1.679	6.51	5.07	11.58
5	4.805	5.125	0.160	20.626	18.126	2.500	9.67	7.87	17.54
6	5.741	6.125	0.192	29.453	25.874	3.579	13.9	11.2	25.1
8	7.583	8.125	0.271	51.826	45.138	6.888	25.9	19.6	45.5
10	9.449	10.125	0.338	80.463	70.085	10.378	40.3	30.4	70.7
12	11.315	12.125	0.405	115.395	100.480	14.915	57.8	43.6	101.4

Nominal Diam. (in.)	Outside	Inside	Outside	Inside	Ft³	Gal	1 Ft³	1 Gal	1 Lb of Water
¼	1.178	0.977	0.098	0.081	.00052	.00389	1923	257	30.8
⅜	1.570	1.262	0.131	0.105	.00088	.00658	1136	152	18.2
½	1.963	1.655	0.164	0.138	.00151	.01129	662	88.6	10.6
⅝	2.355	2.047	0.196	0.171	.00232	.01735	431	57.6	6.90
¾	2.748	2.339	0.229	0.195	.00303	.02664	330	37.5	5.28
1	3.533	3.124	0.294	0.260	.00540	.04039	185	24.8	2.96
1¼	4.318	3.909	0.360	0.326	.00845	.06321	118	15.8	1.89
1½	5.103	4.650	0.425	0.388	.01958	.14646	51.1	6.83	0.817
2	6.673	6.151	0.556	0.513	.02092	.15648	47.8	6.39	0.765
2½	8.243	7.646	0.688	0.637	.03232	.24175	30.9	4.14	0.495
3	9.813	9.128	0.818	0.761	.04607	.34460	21.7	2.90	0.347
3 ½	11.388	10.634	0.949	0.886	.06249	.46745	15.8	2.14	0.257
4	12.953	12.111	1.080	1.009	.08113	.60682	12.3	1.65	0.197
5	16.093	15.088	1.341	1.257	.12587	.94151	7.94	1.06	0.127
6	19.233	18.027	1.603	1.502	.17968	1.3440	5.56	0.744	0.089
8	25.513	23.811	2.126	1.984	.31345	2.3446	3.19	0.426	0.051
10	31.793	29.670	2.649	2.473	.48670	3.4405	2.05	0.291	0.033
12	38.073	35.529	3.173	2.961	.69778	5.2194	1.43	0.192	0.023

Table 2-5(M) Dimensional and Capacity Data—Type K Copper Tube

	Diameter		Wall thick-ness (mm)	Cross-sectional area (10³ mm²)			Weight per Meter (kg)		
Nominal Diam. (in.)	Actual inside (mm)	Actual outside (mm)		Outside	Inside	Metal	of tube alone	of water in tube	of tube and water
¼	7.90	9.53	0.89	0.071	0.049	0.022	0.216	0.049	0.249
⅜	10.21	12.70	1.25	0.127	0.082	0.045	0.401	0.082	0.483
½	13.39	15.88	1.25	0.198	0.141	0.057	0.512	0.140	0.652
⅝	16.56	19.05	1.25	0.285	0.216	0.070	0.623	0.216	0.839
¾	18.92	22.23	1.65	0.388	0.281	0.107	0.955	0.282	1.236
1	25.27	28.58	1.65	0.641	0.501	0.139	1.250	0.504	1.753
1¼	31.62	34.93	1.65	0.957	0.785	0.172	1.549	0.789	2.339
1½	37.62	41.28	1.83	1.337	1.111	0.226	2.026	1.817	3.843
2	49.76	53.98	2.11	2.288	1.944	0.344	3.068	1.951	5.020
2½	61.85	66.68	2.41	3.490	3.003	0.487	4.364	3.009	7.373
3	73.84	79.38	2.77	4.948	4.280	0.668	5.958	4.290	10.248
3½	85.98	92.08	3.05	6.659	5.806	0.853	7.626	5.824	13.450
4	97.97	104.78	3.40	8.620	7.537	1.083	9.697	7.552	17.248
5	122.05	130.18	4.06	13.307	11.694	1.613	14.404	11.722	26.126
6	145.82	155.58	4.88	19.002	16.693	2.309	20.704	16.682	37.387
8	192.61	206.38	6.88	33.436	29.121	4.444	38.578	29.194	67.772
10	240.01	257.18	8.59	51.912	45.216	6.696	60.027	45.281	105.308
12	287.40	307.98	10.29	74.448	64.826	9.623	86.093	64.942	151.035

Nominal Diam. (in.)	Circumference (mm)		M² of surface per Meter		Contents of Tube per Lin. Meter		Lin. Meters to Contain		
	Outside	Inside	Outside	Inside	(L)	(L)	1 L	1 L	1 kg of Water
¼	29.92	24.82	0.030	0.025	0.048	0.048	20.699	20.696	20.678
⅜	39.88	32.06	0.040	0.032	0.077	0.082	12.228	12.240	12.219
½	49.86	42.04	0.050	0.042	0.140	0.140	7.126	7.135	7.117
⅝	59.82	51.99	0.060	0.052	0.216	0.216	4.639	4.638	4.632
¾	69.80	59.41	0.070	0.059	0.282	0.331	3.552	3.020	3.545
1	89.74	79.35	0.090	0.079	0.502	0.502	1.991	1.997	1.987
1¼	109.68	99.29	0.110	0.099	0.785	0.785	1.270	1.272	1.269
1½	129.62	118.11	0.130	0.118	1.819	1.819	0.550	0.550	0.549
2	169.49	156.24	0.170	0.156	1.944	1.943	0.515	0.515	0.514
2½	209.37	194.21	0.210	0.194	3.003	3.002	0.333	0.333	0.332
3	249.25	231.85	0.249	0.232	4.280	4.279	0.234	0.234	0.233
3½	289.26	270.10	0.289	0.270	5.806	5.805	0.170	0.172	0.173
4	329.01	307.62	0.329	0.308	7.537	7.536	0.133	0.133	0.132
5	408.76	383.24	0.409	0.383	11.694	11.692	0.086	0.085	0.085
6	488.52	457.89	0.489	0.458	16.693	16.690	0.060	0.060	0.060
8	648.03	604.80	0.648	0.605	29.121	29.115	0.034	0.034	0.034
10	807.54	753.62	0.807	0.754	45.216	42.724	0.022	0.023	0.022
12	967.05	902.44	0.967	0.903	64.826	64.814	0.015	0.016	0.015

Table 2-6 Dimensional and Capacity Data—Type L Copper Tube

Nominal	Diameter (in.) Actual inside	Actual outside	Wall thick-ness (in.)	Cross-sectional area (sq. in.) Outside	Inside	Metal	Weight per foot (lb) of tube alone	of water in tube	of tube and water
¼	0.315	0.375	0.030	0.110	0.078	0.032	0.126	0.034	0.160
⅜	0.430	0.500	0.035	0.196	0.145	0.051	0.198	0.063	0.261
½	0.545	0.625	0.040	0.307	0.233	0.074	0.285	0.101	0.386
⅝	0.666	0.750	0.042	0.442	0.348	0.094	0.362	0.151	0.513
¾	0.785	0.875	0.045	0.601	0.484	0.117	0.445	0.210	0.665
1	1.025	1.125	0.050	0.993	0.825	0.168	0.655	0.358	1.013
1¼	1.265	1.375	0.055	1.484	1.256	0.228	0.884	0.545	1.429
1½	1.505	1.625	0.060	2.072	1.778	0.294	1.14	0.77	1.91
2	1.985	2.125	0.070	3.546	3.093	0.453	1.75	1.34	3.09
2½	2.465	2.625	0.080	5.409	4.770	0.639	2.48	2.07	4.55
3	2.945	3.125	0.090	7.669	6.808	0.861	3.33	2.96	6.29
3½	3.425	3.625	0.100	10.321	9.214	1.107	4.29	4.00	8.29
4	3.905	4.125	0.110	13.361	11.971	1.390	5.38	5.20	10.58
5	4.875	5.125	0.125	20.626	18.659	1.967	7.61	8.10	15.71
6	5.845	6.125	0.140	29.453	26.817	2.636	10.2	11.6	21.8
8	7.725	8.125	0.200	51.826	46.849	4.977	19.3	20.3	39.6
10	9.625	10.125	0.250	80.463	72.722	7.741	30.1	31.6	61.7
12	11.565	12.125	0.280	115.395	104.994	10.401	40.4	45.6	86.0

Nominal Diam. (in.)	Circumference (in.) Outside	Inside	Ft² of Surface per Lineal Foot Outside	Inside	Contents of Tube per Lineal Foot Ft³	Gal	Lineal Feet to Contain 1 Ft³	1 Gal	1 Lb of Water
¼	1.178	0.989	0.098	0.082	.00054	.0040	1852	250	29.6
⅜	1.570	1.350	0.131	0.113	.00100	.0075	1000	133	16.0
½	1.963	1.711	0.164	0.143	.00162	.0121	617.3	82.6	9.87
⅝	2.355	2.091	0.196	0.174	.00242	.0181	413.2	55.2	6.61
¾	2.748	2.465	0.229	0.205	.00336	.0251	297.6	40.5	4.76
1	3.533	3.219	0.294	0.268	.00573	.0429	174.5	23.3	2.79
1¼	4.318	3.972	0.360	0.331	.00872	.0652	114.7	15.3	1.83
1½	5.103	4.726	0.425	0.394	.01237	.0925	80.84	10.8	1.29
2	6.673	6.233	0.556	0.519	.02147	.1606	46.58	6.23	0.745
2½	8.243	7.740	0.688	0.645	.03312	.2478	30.19	4.04	0.483
3	9.813	9.247	0.818	0.771	.04728	.3537	21.15	2.83	0.338
3½	11.388	10.760	0.949	0.897	.06398	.4786	15.63	2.09	0.251
4	12.953	12.262	1.080	1.022	.08313	.6218	12.03	1.61	0.192
5	16.093	15.308	1.341	1.276	.12958	.9693	7.220	1.03	0.123
6	19.233	18.353	1.603	1.529	.18622	1.393	5.371	0.718	0.0592
8	25.513	24.465	2.126	2.039	.32534	2.434	3.074	0.411	0.0492
10	31.793	30.223	2.649	2.519	.50501	3.777	1.980	0.265	0.0317
12	38.073	36.314	3.173	3.026	.72912	5.454	1.372	0.183	0.0219

Table 2-6(M) Dimensional and Capacity Data—Type L Copper Tube

Nominal (in.)	Actual inside (mm)	Actual outside (mm)	Wall thickness (mm)	Outside	Inside	Metal	of tube alone	of water in tube	of tube and water
	Diameter			Cross-sectional area (10³ mm²)			Weight per Meter (kg)		
¼	8.00	9.53	0.76	0.071	0.050	0.021	0.188	0.051	0.239
⅜	10.92	12.70	0.89	0.127	0.094	0.033	0.295	0.094	0.389
½	13.84	15.88	1.02	0.198	0.150	0.048	0.425	0.150	0.575
⅝	16.92	19.05	1.07	0.285	0.225	0.061	0.539	0.225	0.764
¾	19.94	22.23	1.14	0.388	0.312	0.076	0.678	0.313	0.991
1	26.04	28.58	1.27	0.641	0.532	0.108	0.976	0.533	1.509
1¼	32.13	34.93	1.40	0.957	0.810	0.147	1.317	0.812	2.129
1½	38.23	41.28	1.52	1.337	1.147	0.190	1.698	1.147	2.845
2	50.42	53.98	1.78	2.288	1.996	0.292	2.607	1.996	4.603
2½	62.61	66.68	2.03	3.490	3.077	0.412	3.694	3.083	6.777
3	74.80	79.38	2.29	4.948	4.392	0.556	4.960	4.409	9.369
3½	87.00	92.08	2.54	6.659	5.945	0.714	6.390	5.958	12.348
4	99.19	104.78	2.79	8.620	7.723	0.897	8.014	7.745	15.759
5	123.83	130.18	3.18	13.307	12.038	1.269	11.335	12.065	23.400
6	148.46	155.58	3.56	19.002	17.301	1.701	15.193	17.278	32.471
8	196.22	206.38	5.08	33.436	30.225	3.211	28.747	30.237	58.984
10	244.48	257.18	6.35	51.912	46.917	4.994	44.834	47.068	91.902
12	293.75	307.98	7.11	74.448	67.738	6.710	60.176	67.921	128.097

Nominal Diam. (in.)	Outside	Inside	Outside	Inside	(L)	(L)	1 L	1 L	1 kg of Water
	Circumference (mm)		M² of surface per Meter		Contents of Tube per Lin. Meter		Lin. Meters to Contain		
¼	29.92	25.12	0.030	0.025	0.050	0.050	19.935	20.132	19.872
⅜	39.88	34.29	0.040	0.034	0.093	0.093	10.764	10.710	10.742
½	49.86	43.46	0.050	0.044	0.151	0.150	6.645	6.652	6.626
⅝	59.82	53.11	0.060	0.053	0.225	0.225	4.448	4.445	4.438
¾	69.80	62.61	0.070	0.063	0.312	0.312	3.203	3.261	3.196
1	89.74	81.76	0.090	0.082	0.532	0.533	1.878	1.876	1.873
1¼	109.68	100.89	0.110	0.101	0.810	0.810	1.235	1.232	1.229
1½	129.62	120.04	0.130	0.120	1.149	1.149	0.870	0.870	0.866
2	169.49	158.32	0.170	0.158	1.995	1.994	0.501	0.502	0.500
2½	209.37	196.60	0.210	0.197	3.077	3.077	0.325	0.325	0.324
3	249.25	234.87	0.249	0.235	4.393	4.392	0.228	0.228	0.227
3½	289.26	273.30	0.289	0.273	5.944	5.943	0.168	0.168	0.169
4	329.01	311.46	0.329	0.312	7.723	7.722	0.130	0.130	0.129
5	408.76	388.82	0.409	0.389	12.038	12.037	0.078	0.083	0.083
6	488.52	466.17	0.489	0.466	17.301	17.298	0.058	0.058	0.040
8	648.03	621.41	0.648	0.621	30.225	30.225	0.033	0.033	0.033
10	807.54	767.66	0.807	0.768	46.917	46.903	0.021	0.021	0.021
12	967.05	922.38	0.967	0.922	67.738	67.728	0.015	0.015	0.015

Table 2-7 Dimensional and Capacity Data—Type M Copper Tube

Nominal	Diameter (in.) Actual inside	Actual outside	Wall thick-ness (in.)	Cross-sectional area (sq. in.) Outside	Inside	Metal	Weight per foot (lb) of tube alone	of water in tube	of tube and water
⅜	0.450	0.500	0.025	0.196	0.159	0.037	0.145	0.069	0.214
½	0.569	0.625	0.028	0.307	0.254	0.053	0.204	0.110	0.314
¾	0.811	0.875	0.032	0.601	0.516	0.085	0.328	0.224	0.552
1	1.055	1.125	0.035	0.993	0.874	0.119	0.465	0.379	0.844
1¼	1.291	1.375	0.042	1.48	1.31	0.17	0.682	0.569	1.251
1½	1.527	1.625	0.049	2.07	1.83	0.24	0.94	0.83	1.77
2	2.009	2.125	0.058	3.55	3.17	0.38	1.46	1.35	2.81
2½	2.495	2.625	0.065	5.41	4.89	0.52	2.03	2.12	4.15
3	2.981	3.125	0.072	7.67	6.98	0.69	2.68	3.03	5.71
3½	3.459	3.625	0.083	10.32	9.40	0.924	3.58	4.08	7.66
4	3.935	4.125	0.095	13.36	12.15	1.21	4.66	5.23	9.89
5	4.907	5.125	0.109	20.63	18.90	1.73	6.66	8.20	14.86
6	5.881	6.125	0.122	29.45	25.15	2.30	8.92	11.78	20.70
8	7.785	8.125	0.170	51.83	47.58	4.25	16.5	20.7	37.2
10	9.701	10.125	0.212	80.46	73.88	6.58	25.6	32.1	57.7
12	11.617	12.125	0.254	115.47	105.99	9.48	36.7	46.0	82.7

Nominal Diam. (in.)	Circumference (in.) Outside	Inside	Ft² of Surface per Lineal Foot Outside	Inside	Contents of Tube per Lineal Foot Ft³	Gal	Lineal Feet to Contain 1 Ft³	1 Gal	1 Lb of Water
⅜	1.570	1.413	0.131	0.118	0.00110	0.00823	909	122	14.5
½	1.963	1.787	0.164	0.149	0.00176	0.01316	568	76.0	9.09
¾	2.748	2.547	0.229	0.212	0.00358	0.02678	379	37.3	4.47
1	3.533	3.313	0.294	0.276	0.00607	0.04540	164.7	22.0	2.64
1¼	4.318	4.054	0.360	0.338	0.00910	0.06807	109.9	14.7	1.76
1½	5.103	4.795	0.425	0.400	0.01333	0.09971	75.02	10.0	1.20
2	6.673	6.308	0.556	0.526	0.02201	0.16463	45.43	6.08	0.727
2½	8.243	7.834	0.688	0.653	0.03396	0.25402	29.45	3.94	0.471
3	9.813	9.360	0.818	0.780	0.04847	0.36256	20.63	2.76	0.330
3½	11.388	10.867	0.949	0.906	0.06525	0.48813	15.33	2.05	0.246
4	12.953	12.356	1.080	1.030	0.08368	0.62593	11.95	1.60	0.191
5	16.093	15.408	1.341	1.284	0.13125	0.98175	7.62	1.02	0.122
6	19.233	18.466	1.603	1.539	0.18854	1.410	5.30	0.709	0.849
8	25.513	24.445	2.126	2.037	0.33044	2.472	3.03	0.405	0.484
10	31.793	30.461	2.649	2.538	0.51306	3.838	1.91	0.261	0.312
12	38.073	36.477	3.173	3.039	0.73569	5.503	1.36	0.182	0.217

Table 2-7(M) Dimensional and Capacity Data—Type M Copper Tube

Nominal (in.)	Diameter Actual inside (mm)	Diameter Actual outside (mm)	Wall thickness (mm)	Cross-sectional area (10^3 mm²) Outside	Cross-sectional area (10^3 mm²) Inside	Cross-sectional area (10^3 mm²) Metal	Weight per Meter (kg) of tube alone	Weight per Meter (kg) of water in tube	Weight per Meter (kg) of tube and water
⅜	11.43	12.70	0.64	0.127	0.103	0.024	0.216	0.103	0.319
½	14.45	15.88	0.71	0.198	0.164	0.034	0.304	0.164	0.468
¾	20.60	22.23	0.81	0.388	0.333	0.055	0.489	0.334	0.823
1	26.80	28.58	0.89	0.641	0.564	0.077	0.693	0.565	1.258
1¼	32.79	34.93	1.07	0.955	0.845	0.110	1.016	0.848	1.864
1½	38.79	41.28	1.25	1.336	1.181	0.155	1.400	1.236	2.636
2	51.03	53.98	1.47	2.290	2.045	0.245	2.175	2.011	4.186
2½	63.38	66.68	1.65	3.490	3.155	0.336	3.024	3.158	6.182
3	75.2	79.38	1.83	4.948	4.503	0.445	3.992	4.513	8.505
3½	87.86	92.08	2.11	6.658	6.065	0.596	5.332	6.077	11.409
4	99.95	104.78	2.41	8.619	7.839	0.781	6.941	7.790	14.731
5	124.64	130.18	2.77	13.310	12.194	1.116	9.920	12.214	22.134
6	149.38	155.58	3.10	19.000	16.226	1.484	13.286	17.546	30.832
8	197.74	206.38	4.32	33.439	30.697	2.742	24.577	30.833	55.410
10	246.41	257.18	5.39	51.910	47.664	4.245	38.131	47.813	85.944
12	295.07	307.98	6.45	74.497	68.381	6.116	54.665	68.517	123.182

Nominal Diam. (in.)	Circumference (mm) Outside	Circumference (mm) Inside	M² of surface per Meter Outside	M² of surface per Meter Inside	Contents of Tube per Lin. Meter (L)	Contents of Tube per Lin. Meter (L)	Lin. Meters to Contain 1 L	Lin. Meters to Contain 1 L	Lin. Meters to Contain 1 kg of Water
⅜	39.88	35.89	0.040	0.036	0.102	0.102	9.784	9.825	9.735
½	49.86	45.39	0.050	0.045	0.164	0.163	6.114	6.120	6.103
¾	69.80	64.69	0.070	0.065	0.033	0.333	4.080	3.004	3.001
1	89.74	84.15	0.090	0.084	0.564	0.564	1.773	1.772	1.772
1¼	109.68	102.97	0.110	0.103	0.845	0.845	1.183	1.184	1.182
1½	129.62	121.79	0.130	0.122	1.238	1.238	0.808	0.805	0.806
2	169.49	160.22	0.170	0.160	2.045	2.044	0.489	0.490	0.488
2½	209.37	198.98	0.210	0.199	3.155	3.154	0.317	0.317	0.316
3	249.25	237.74	0.249	0.238	4.503	4.502	0.222	0.222	0.222
3½	289.26	276.02	0.289	0.276	6.62	6.062	0.165	0.165	0.165
4	329.01	313.84	0.329	0.314	7.774	7.773	0.129	0.129	0.128
5	408.76	391.36	0.409	0.391	12.194	12.191	0.082	0.082	0.082
6	488.52	469.04	0.489	0.469	17.516	17.509	0.057	0.057	0.570
8	648.03	620.90	0.648	0.621	30.699	30.697	0.033	0.033	0.325
10	807.54	773.71	0.807	0.774	47.665	47.660	0.021	0.021	0.210
12	967.05	926.52	0.967	0.926	68.348	68.336	0.015	0.015	0.146

Copper Drainage Tube

Copper drainage tube for DWV applications is a seamless copper tube conforming to the requirements of ASTM B306, *Standard Specification for Copper Drainage Tube (DWV)*. Copper drainage tube is furnished in drawn (hard) temper only in sizes 1¼ to 8 in. (31.8 to 203.2 mm). It is required to be identified by a yellow stripe giving the manufacturer's name or trademark, the nation of origin, and the letters "DWV"; it is also required to be incised with the manufacturer's name or trademark and the letters "DWV" at intervals no greater than 1½ ft.

Fittings for use with drainage pipe are usually those conforming to either ASME/ANSI B16.23, *Cast Copper Alloy Solder-Joint Drainage Fittings,* or ASME/ANSI B16.29, *Wrought Copper and Wrought Copper Alloy Solder-Joint Drainage Fittings* and are required to carry the incised mark "DWV."

Joints for drainage applications can be soldered or brazed. See Figure 2-9 and Table 2-8.

Medical Gas Tube

Medical gas tube is a seamless copper tube manufactured to the requirements of ASTM B819, *Standard Specification for Seamless Copper Tube for Medical Gas Systems*. Medical gas tube is shipped cleaned and capped and is furnished in type K or L wall thickness in drawn (hard) temper only.

Medical gas tube is identified with an incised mark containing the manufacturer's name or trademark at intervals not in excess of 1½ ft; it is color coded green for type K and blue for type L.

Fittings in copper water tube may be those conforming to ASME/ANSI B16.22, *Wrought Copper and Copper Alloy Solder-Joint Pressure Fittings;* ASME/ANSI B16.18, *Cast Copper Alloy Solder-Joint Pressure Fittings* (where wrought copper fittings are not available); or ASTM B16.50, *Wrought Copper Braze Fittings*, or they may be fittings meeting the requirements of Manufacturers Standardization Society (MSS) SP-73, *Brazing Joints for Copper and Copper Alloy Pressure Fittings.*

Joints in medical gas systems are of the socket/lap type and are normally brazed with copper-phosphorous or copper-phosphorous-silver (BCuP) brazing alloys while being purged with oil-free nitrogen.

Applicable standards and specifications dealing with the installation of medical gas systems may be but are not limited to the following: National Fire Protection Association (NFPA) 99, *Standard for Health Care Facilities*; NFPA 99C, *Gas and Vacuum Systems*; and ASSE 6000, *Professional Qualifications Standard for Medical Gas Systems Installers, Inspectors, Verifiers, Maintenance Personnel and Instructors.*

Glass Pipe

Glass pipe is used in the mechanical industry in two ways: as pressure ½ to 8 in. (13 to 203 mm) pipe and as drainage 1½ to 6 in. (38 to 153 mm) pipe. It is available in standard 5 and 10-ft (1.5 and 3.1-m) lengths. Glass is unique for several reasons: First, it is clear, you can see through it; and second, it is the piping system that is least susceptible to fire. Glass will not burn; with enough heat, it can melt. This is why in build-

Table 2-8 Dimensional Data—Type DWV Copper Tube

Nominal Size (in.)	Outside Diameter (in.)	(mm)	Inside Diameter (in.)	(mm)	Wall Thickness (in.)	(mm)	Cross-Sectional Area of Bore (in.²)	(cm²)	External Surface (ft² / lin ft)	(m²/m)	Internal Surface (ft² /lin ft)	(m²/m)	Weight kg (/lf)	(/m)
1¼	1.375	34.93	1.295	32.89	.040	1.02	1.32	8.52	0.360	0.03	0.339	0.03	0.65	0.29
1½	1.625	41.28	1.541	39.14	.042	1.07	1.87	12.06	0.425	0.04	0.403	0.04	0.81	0.37
2	2.125	53.98	2.041	51.84	.042	1.07	3.27	21.10	0.556	0.05	0.534	0.05	1.07	0.49
3	3.125	79.38	3.030	76.96	.045	1.14	7.21	46.52	0.818	0.08	0.793	0.07	1.69	0.77
4	4.125	104.78	4.009	101.83	.058	1.47	12.6	81.29	1.08	0.10	1.05	0.10	2.87	1.30
5	5.125	130.18	4.981	126.52	.072	1.83	19.5	125.81	1.34	0.12	1.30	0.12	4.43	2.01
6	6.125	155.58	5.959	151.36	.083	2.11	27.9	180.00	1.60	0.15	1.56	0.15	6.10	2.77
8	8.125	206.38	7.907	200.84	.109	2.77	49.1	316.77	2.13	0.20	2.07	0.19	10.6	4.81

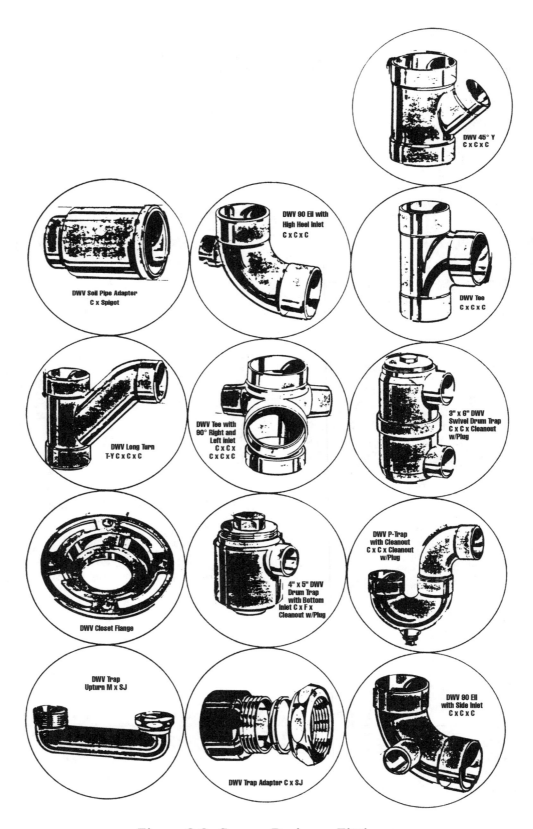

Figure 2-9 Copper Drainage Fittings

ings with a return air plenum for heating, ventilation, and air-conditioning (HVAC), most plastics are not acceptable by fire codes and glass is a solution for meeting this building code requirement.

Glass pipe (see Figure 2-10) is made of low-expansion borosilicate glass with a low alkali content. It is most commonly used for chemical waste drain lines, vent piping, and purified water piping. Nonstandard lengths are available or it can be field cut or fabricated to special lengths. Glass can be installed aboveground (padded or with coated hangers) or buried (with styrofoam blocking around the pipe). Glass is fragile, so care must be taken to prevent scratches or impact by sharp objects. Glass is used for chemical waste-DWV systems in high schools, colleges, labs, industrial plants, and hospitals when hot fluids are put down the systems constantly. (Hot fluids are those at 200°F with no dilution.)

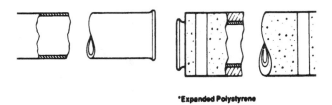

*Expanded Polystyrene

Figure 2-10 Standard Glass Pipe

Glass is installed by cutting the pipe to the exact fixed length. It is held together with either of two types of coupling, depending on whether it is a "bead to bead" or "bead to cut glass end" application. See Figures 2-11 and 2-12(A).

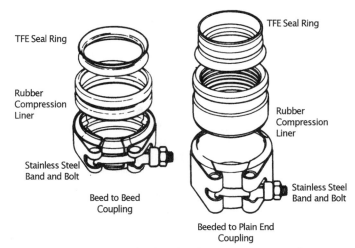

Figure 2-11 Standard Glass Pipe Couplings

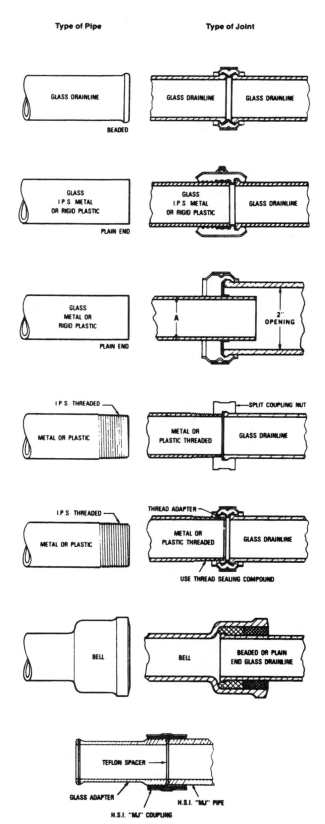

Figure 2-12 (A) Typical Glass Pipe Joint Reference Chart

**Figure 2-12 (B) Typical Threaded Fittings
for Galvanized or Steel Pipe**

Joints are made by using compression type couplings consisting of 300 series stainless steel outer bands, electrometric compression liners, and sealing members of chemically inert tetrafluoroethylene (TFE). The coefficient of glass expansion is 0.2 in./100 ft/100°F (5 mm/30.4 m/37.8°C), and glass is very stable and can operate up to 300°F (148.9°C).

Fittings are made of borosilicate glass and include a full range of sanitary and plumbing fittings (see Figure 2-13).

The applicable standards and specifications include ASTM C-599-77.

Steel Pipe

Steel pipe may be either seamless (extruded) or welded. The welding of steel piping is accomplished by two methods: continuous or electric-resistance welding (ERW). Continuous welded pipe is heated and formed. Electric-resistance welding is cold rolled and then welded. Steel pipe also may be black iron or galvanized (zinc coated). Galvanized steel pipe is dipped and zinc coated to produce a galvanized protective coating both inside and out.

Steel pipe is produced in three basic weight classifications: standard weight, extra strong and double extra strong. Steel pipe in standard weight and various weights or "schedules"—ranging from Schedule 10, also known as "light wall pipe," to Schedule 160—is normally supplied in random lengths of 6 to 22 ft (1.8 to 6.7 m) and is available in ⅛ to 24-in. (3.2 to 660-mm) diameters. Exceptions to this are butt-welded standard weight and extra strong, which are not available in diameters larger than 4 in., and butt-welded double extra-strong steel pipe, which is not made in diameters larger than 2½ in. Steel pipe specified for heating, air-conditioning, plumbing, gas, and air lines conforms to ASTM A-53. Steel pipe conforming to ASTM A-53 is intended for coiling, bending, forming, or other special purposes. Steel pipe that meets the requirements of ASTM A-106 is used for high-temperature service and is suited for coiling, bending, and forming. Steel pipe conforming to ASTM A-135 is made in sizes through 12 in. by the electric-resistance welding method only. Grade A is suitable for flanging or binding. Pipe meeting ASTM A-135 is used extensively for light wall pipe in fire sprinkler systems. See Tables 2-9, 2-10, and 2-11.

Joints and fittings for welded pipe may be butt welded, electric-resistance welded, or grooved. Pipe is supplied with threaded ends and couplings or plain or beveled ends.

Closer mill tolerances for pipe and fittings permit a close dimensional control. The fittings used are elbows, 45° elbows, tees, crosses, couplings, and reducers. See Figure 2-12(B).

Applicable specifications and standards include the following: ANSI B36.1, ASTM A-53, ASTM A-106, and ASTM A-135. Applicable specifications and standards for fittings include the following: ASME B-16.9, ASME B-16.11, and ASME B16.28.

Lead Pipe

Lead pipe was made of 99.7 pig lead and various alloys for special applications. It was used primarily in chemical waste and venting lines, for handling corrosive materials, in laboratory drainage, for processing systems, and for radioactive wastes. Lead piping was also used as water piping and can still be found in some of the older homes in the northeast.

Internal diameter (ID) ranged from ¼ to 12 in. The wall thickness varied according to the intended use. Lead pipe in smaller sizes was sold in coils. Larger diameters were available in standard lengths, generally 10 ft (3.1 m). Check with all codes, including local and federal, before using this type of piping for any application.

Joints and fittings were molten lead with wiped joints or mechanical flange. The applicable standard and specification is ASTM B-29.

Note: Lead piping is no longer manufactured but is listed here in the event repairs or modifications are made to existing systems.

Vitrified Clay Pipe

Vitrified clay pipe is extruded from a suitable grade of shale or clay and fired in kilns at approximately 2000°F (1100°C). Vitrification takes place at this temperature, producing an ex-

tremely hard and dense, corrosion-resistant material. Because of its outstanding corrosion and abrasion resistance, clay pipe is used for industrial wastes in addition to its wide use in domestic sewer and drainage systems. It is used in a building sewer starting outside of the building and connecting to the main sewer. Clay pipe is suitable for most gravity-flow systems and is not intended for pressure service. Available sizes include 3 to 48-in. (75 to 1220-mm) diameters and lengths up to 10 ft (3.05 m) in standard or extra strength grades as well as perforated. See Tables 2-12 and 2-13. Pipe and fittings are joined with prefabricated compression seals.

The applicable standards and specifications are ASTM C-4, ASTM C-12, ASTM C-301, ASTM C-425, ASTM C-700, ASTM C-828 and ASTM C-896.

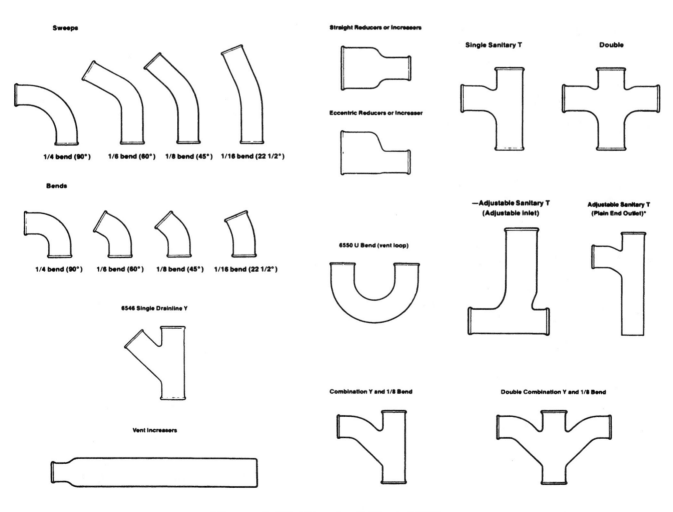

Figure 2-13 Standard Glass Fittings

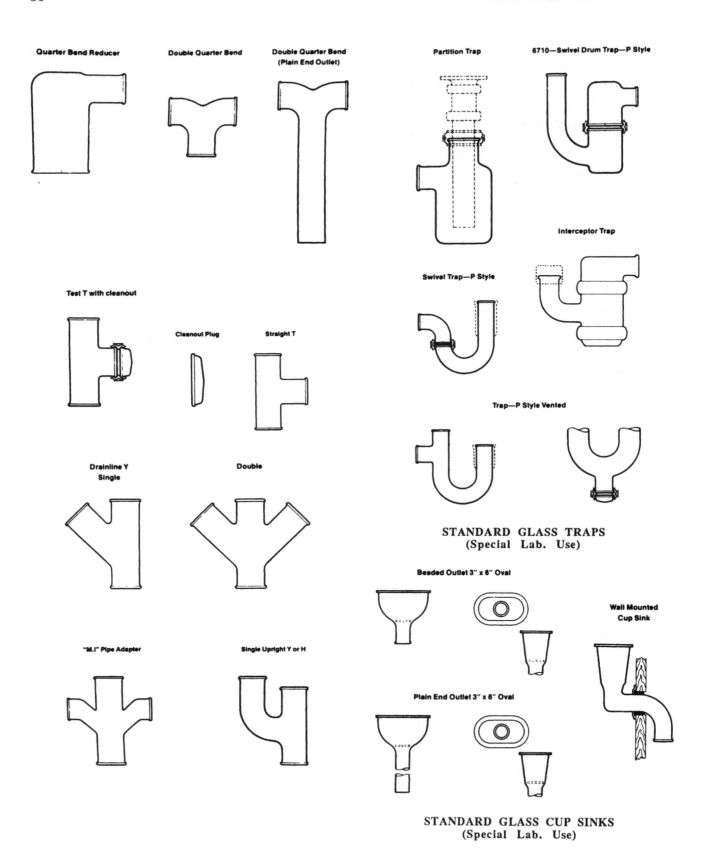

Quarter Bend Reducer

Double Quarter Bend

Double Quarter Bend (Plain End Outlet)

Partition Trap

6710—Swivel Drum Trap—P Style

Interceptor Trap

Swivel Trap—P Style

Test T with cleanout

Cleanout Plug

Straight T

Trap—P Style Vented

STANDARD GLASS TRAPS
(Special Lab. Use)

Drainline Y Single

Double

Beaded Outlet 3" x 6" Oval

Wall Mounted Cup Sink

Plain End Outlet 3" x 6" Oval

"M.I" Pipe Adapter

Single Upright Y or H

STANDARD GLASS CUP SINKS
(Special Lab. Use)

(Figure 2-13 Continued)

Table 2-9 Dimensional and Capacity Data—Schedule 40 Steel Pipe

Nominal	Actual inside	Actual outside	Wall thickness (in.)	Outside	Inside	Metal	of tube alone	of water in tube	of tube and water
⅛	0.269	0.405	0.068	0.129	0.057	0.072	0.25	0.028	0.278
¼	0.364	0.540	0.088	0.229	0.104	0.125	0.43	0.045	0.475
⅜	0.493	0.675	0.091	0.358	0.191	0.167	0.57	0.083	0.653
½	0.622	0.840	0.109	0.554	0.304	0.250	0.86	0.132	0.992
¾	0.824	1.050	0.113	0.866	0.533	0.333	1.14	0.232	1.372
1	1.049	1.315	0.133	1.358	0.864	0.494	1.68	0.375	2.055
1¼	1.380	1.660	0.140	2.164	1.495	0.669	2.28	0.649	2.929
1½	1.610	1.900	0.145	2.835	2.036	0.799	2.72	0.882	3.602
2	2.067	2.375	0.154	4.431	3.356	1.075	3.66	1.454	5.114
2½	2.469	2.875	0.203	6.492	4.788	1.704	5.80	2.073	7.873
3	3.068	3.500	0.216	9.621	7.393	2.228	7.58	3.201	0.781
3½	3.548	4.000	0.226	12.568	9.888	2.680	9.11	4.287	3.397
4	4.026	4.500	0.237	15.903	12.730	3.173	10.80	5.516	6.316
5	5.047	5.563	0.258	24.308	20.004	4.304	14.70	8.674	3.374
6	6.065	6.625	0.280	34.474	28.890	5.584	19.00	12.52	31.52
8	7.981	8.625	0.322	58.426	50.030	8.396	28.60	21.68	50.28
10	10.020	10.750	0.365	90.79	78.85	11.90	40.50	34.16	74.66
12	11.938	12.750	0.406	127.67	113.09	15.77	53.60	48.50	02.10
14	13.126	14.000	0.437	153.94	135.33	18.61	63.30	58.64	21.94
16	15.000	16.000	0.500	201.06	176.71	24.35	82.80	76.58	59.38
18	16.876	18.000	0.562	254.47	223.68	30.79	105.00	96.93	201.93
20	18.814	20.000	0.593	314.16	278.01	36.15	123.00	120.46	243.46

Nominal Diam. (in.)	Outside	Inside	Outside	Inside	Ft³	Gal	1 Ft³	1 Gal	1 Lb of Water
⅛	1.27	0.84	0.106	0.070	0.0004	0.003	2533.775	338.74	35.714
¼	1.69	1.14	0.141	0.095	0.0007	0.005	1383.789	185.00	22.222
⅜	2.12	1.55	0.177	0.129	0.0013	0.010	754.360	100.85	12.048
½	2.65	1.95	0.221	0.167	0.0021	0.016	473.906	63.36	7.576
¾	3.29	2.58	0.275	0.215	0.0037	0.028	270.034	36.10	4.310
1	4.13	3.29	0.344	0.274	0.0062	0.045	166.618	22.38	2.667
1¼	5.21	4.33	0.435	0.361	0.0104	0.077	96.275	12.87	1.541
1½	5.96	5.06	0.497	0.422	0.0141	0.106	70.733	9.46	1.134
2	7.46	6.49	0.622	0.540	0.0233	0.174	42.913	5.74	0.688
2½	9.03	7.75	0.753	0.654	0.0332	0.248	30.077	4.02	0.482
3	10.96	9.63	0.916	0.803	0.0514	0.383	19.479	2.60	0.312
3½	12.56	11.14	1.047	0.928	0.0682	0.513	14.565	1.95	0.233
4	14.13	12.64	1.178	1.052	0.0884	0.660	11.312	1.51	0.181
5	17.47	15.84	1.456	1.319	0.1390	1.040	7.198	0.96	0.115
6	20.81	19.05	1.734	1.585	0.2010	1.500	4.984	0.67	0.080
8	27.90	25.07	2.258	2.090	0.3480	2.600	2.878	0.38	0.046
10	33.77	31.47	2.814	2.622	0.5470	4.100	1.826	0.24	0.029
12	40.05	37.70	3.370	3.140	0.7850	5.870	1.273	0.17	0.021
14	47.12	44.76	3.930	3.722	1.0690	7.030	1.067	0.14	0.017
16	53.41	51.52	4.440	4.310	1.3920	9.180	0.814	0.11	0.013
18	56.55	53.00	4.712	4.420	1.5530	11.120	0.644	0.09	0.010
20	62.83	59.09	5.236	4.920	1.9250	14.400	0.517	0.07	0.008

Table 2-9(M) Dimensional and Capacity Data—Schedule 40 Steel Pipe

	Diameter		Wall thick-ness (mm)	Cross-sectional area (10³ mm²)			Weight per Meter (kg)		
Nominal (in.)	Actual inside (mm)	Actual outside (mm)		Outside	Inside	Metal	of tube alone	of water in tube	of tube and water
⅛	6.8	10.3	1.7	0.083	0.037	0.047	0.37	0.04	0.41
¼	9.3	13.7	2.2	0.148	0.067	0.081	0.64	0.07	0.71
⅜	12.5	17.2	2.3	0.231	0.123	0.108	0.85	0.12	0.97
½	15.8	21.3	2.8	0.357	0.196	0.161	1.28	0.20	1.48
¾	20.9	26.7	2.9	0.559	0.344	0.215	1.7	0.35	2.05
1	26.7	33.4	3.4	0.876	0.557	0.319	2.5	0.56	3.06
1¼	35.1	42.2	3.6	1.396	0.965	0.432	3.4	0.97	4.37
1½	40.9	48.3	3.7	1.829	1.314	0.516	4.05	1. 31	5.36
2	52.5	60.3	3.9	2.859	2.165	0.694	5.45	2.17	7.62
2½	62.7	73.0	5.2	4.188	3.089	1.099	8.64	3.09	11.73
3	77.9	88.9	5.5	6.207	4.77	1.437	11.29	4.77	16.06
3½	90.1	101.6	5.7	8.108	6.379	1.729	13.57	6.39	19.96
4	102.3	114.3	6.0	10.26	8.213	2.047	16.09	8.22	24.31
5	128.2	141.3	6.6	15.68	12.91	2.777	21.9	12.92	34.82
6	154.1	168.3	7.1	22.24	18.64	3.603	28.3	18.65	46.95
8	202.7	219.1	8.2	37.69	32.28	5.417	42.6	32.29	74.89
10	254.5	273.1	9.3	58.57	50.87	7.677	60.33	50.88	111.21
12	303.2	323.9	10.3	82.37	72.96	10.17	79.84	72.24	152.08
14	333.4	355.6	11.1	99.32	87.31	12.01	94.29	87.34	181.63
16	381.0	406.4	12.7	129.72	114.01	15.71	123.33	114.07	237.4
18	428.7	457.2	14.3	164.17	144.31	19.87	156.4	144.38	300.78
20	477.9	508.0	15.1	202.68	179.36	23.32	183.21	179.43	362.64

Nominal Diam. (in.)	Circumference (mm)		M² of surface per Meter		Contents of Tube per Lin. Meter		Lin. Meters to Contain		
	Outside	Inside	Outside	Inside	(L)	(L)	1 L	1 L	1 kg of Water
⅛	32.26	21.34	0.032	0.021	0.037	0.037	27.27	27.28	23.98
¼	42.93	28.96	0.043	0.029	0.065	0.062	14.9	14.9	14.92
⅜	53.85	39.37	0.054	0.039	0.121	0.124	8.12	8.12	8.09
½	67.31	49.53	0.067	0.051	0.195	1.199	5.1	5.1	5.09
¾	83.57	65.53	0.084	0.066	0.344	0.348	2.91	2.91	2.89
1	104.9	83.57	0.105	0.084	0.576	0.559	1.79	1.79	1.79
1¼	132.33	109.98	0.133	0.11	0.966	0.956	1.04	1.04	1.03
1½	151.38	128.52	0.152	0.129	1.31	1.316	0.76	0.76	0.76
2	189.48	164.85	0.19	0.165	2.165	2.161	0.46	0.46	0.46
2½	229.36	196.85	0.23	0.199	3.084	3.08	0.32	0.32	0.32
3	278.38	244.6	0.279	0.245	4.775	4.756	0.21	0.21	0.21
3½	319.02	282.96	0.319	0.283	6.336	6.37	0.16	0.16	0.16
4	358.9	321.06	0.359	0.321	8.213	8.196	0.12	0.12	0.12
5	443.74	402.34	0.444	0.402	12.91	12.92	0.08	0.08	0.08
6	528.57	483.87	0.529	0.483	18.67	18.63	0.05	0.05	0.05
8	688.09	636.78	0.688	0.637	32.33	32.29	0.03	0.03	0.03
10	857.76	799.34	0.858	0.799	50.82	50.91	0.02	0.02	0.02
12	1017.27	957.58	1.027	0.957	72.93	72.89	0.013	0.014	0.014
14	1196. 85	1136.9	1.198	1.135	99.31	87.3	0.011	0.011	0.011
16	1356.61	1308.61	1.353	1.314	129.32	114.0	0.009	0.009	0.009
18	1436.37	1346.2	1.436	1.347	144.28	138.09	0.007	0.007	0.007
20	1595.88	1500.89	1.596	1.5	178.84	178.82	0.006	0.006	0.006

Table 2-10 Dimensional and Capacity Data—Schedule 80 Steel Pipe

	Diameter (in.)		Wall thick-ness (in.)	Cross-sectional area (sq. in.)			Weight per foot (lb)		
Nominal	Actual inside	Actual outside		Outside	Inside	Metal	of tube alone	of water in tube	of tube and water
⅛	0.215	0.405	0.091	0.129	0.036	0.093	0.314	0.016	0.330
¼	0.302	0.540	0.119	0.229	0.072	0.157	0.535	0.031	0.566
⅜	0.423	0.675	0.126	0.358	0.141	0.217	0.738	0.061	0.799
½	0.546	0.840	0.147	0.554	0.234	0.320	1.087	0.102	1.189
¾	0.742	1.050	0.154	0.866	0.433	0.433	1.473	0.213	1.686
1	0.957	1.315	0.179	1.358	0.719	0.639	2.171	0.312	2.483
1¼	1.278	1.660	0.191	2.164	1.283	0.881	2.996	0.555	3.551
1½	1.500	1.900	0.200	2.835	1.767	1.068	3.631	0.765	4.396
2	1.939	2.375	0.218	4.431	2.954	1.477	5.022	1.280	6.302
2½	2.323	2.875	0.276	6.492	4.238	2.254	7.661	1.830	9.491
3	2.900	3.500	0.300	9.621	6.605	3.016	10.252	2.870	13.122
3½	3.364	4.000	0.318	12.568	8.890	3.678	12.505	3.720	16.225
4	3.826	4.500	0.337	15.903	11.496	4.407	14.983	4.970	19.953
5	4.813	5.563	0.375	24.308	18.196	6.112	20.778	7.940	28.718
6	5.761	6.625	0.432	34.474	26.069	8.405	28.573	11.300	39.873
8	7.625	8.625	0.500	58.426	45.666	12.750	43.388	19.800	63.188
10	9.564	10.750	0.593	90.79	71.87	18.92	64.400	31.130	95.530
12	11.376	12.750	0.687	127.67	101.64	26.03	88.600	44.040	132.640
14	12.500	14.000	0.750	153.94	122.72	31.22	107.000	53.180	160.180
16	14.314	16.000	0.843	201.06	160.92	40.14	137.000	69.730	206.730
18	16.126	18.000	0.937	254.47	204.24	50.23	171.000	88.500	259.500
20	17.938	20.000	1.031	314.16	252.72	61.44	209.000	109.510	318.510

Nominal Diam. (in.)	Circumference (in.)		Ft² of Surface per Lineal Foot		Contents of Tube per Lineal Foot		Lineal Feet to Contain		
	Outside	Inside	Outside	Inside	Ft³	Gal	1 Ft³	1 Gal	1 Lb of Water
⅛	1.27	0.675	0.106	0.056	0.00033	0.0019	3070	527	101.01
¼	1.69	0.943	0.141	0.079	0.00052	0.0037	1920	271	32.26
⅜	2.12	1.328	0.177	0.111	0.00098	0.0073	1370	137	16.39
½	2.65	1.715	0.221	0.143	0.00162	0.0122	616	82	9.80
¾	3.29	2.330	0.275	0.194	0.00300	0.0255	334	39.2	4.69
1	4.13	3.010	0.344	0.251	0.00500	0.0374	200	26.8	3.21
1¼	5.21	4.010	0.435	0.334	0.00880	0.0666	114	15.0	1.80
1½	5.96	4.720	0.497	0.393	0.01230	0.0918	81.50	10.90	1.31
2	7.46	6.090	0.622	0.507	0.02060	0.1535	49.80	6.52	0.78
2½	9.03	7.320	0.753	0.610	0.02940	0.220	34.00	4.55	0.55
3	10.96	9.120	0.916	0.760	0.0460	0.344	21.70	2.91	0.35
3½	12.56	10.580	1.047	0.882	0.0617	0.458	16.25	2.18	0.27
4	14.13	12.020	1.178	1.002	0.0800	0.597	12.50	1.675	0.20
5	17.47	15.150	1.456	1.262	0.1260	0.947	7.95	1.055	0.13
6	20.81	18.100	1.734	1.510	0.1820	1.355	5.50	0.738	0.09
8	27.09	24.000	2.258	2.000	0.3180	2.380	3.14	0.420	0.05
10	33.77	30.050	2.814	2.503	0.5560	4.165	1.80	0.241	0.03
12	40.05	35.720	3.370	2.975	0.7060	5.280	1.42	0.189	0.02
14	47.12	39.270	3.930	3.271	0.8520	6.380	1.18	0.157	0.019
16	53.41	44.970	4.440	3.746	1.1170	8.360	0.895	0.119	0.014
18	56.55	50.660	4.712	4.220	1.4180	10.610	0.705	0.094	0.011
20	62.83	56.350	5.236	4.694	1.7550	13.130	0.570	0.076	0.009

Table 2-10(M) Dimensional and Capacity Data—Schedule 80 Steel Pipe

Diameter			Wall thickness (mm)	Cross-sectional area (10³ mm²)			Weight per Meter (kg)		
Nominal (in.)	Actual inside (mm)	Actual outside (mm)		Outside	Inside	Metal	of tube alone	of water in tube	of tube and water
⅛	5.46	10.29	2.41	0.083	0.023	0.06	0.468	0.024	0.492
¼	7.67	13.72	3.02	0.148	0.047	0.101	0.797	0.046	0.843
⅜	10.74	17.15	3.2	0.231	0.091	0.14	1.099	0.091	1.19
½	13.87	21.34	3.73	0.357	0.151	0.207	1.619	0.152	1.771
¾	18.85	26.67	3.91	0.559	0.279	0.279	2.194	0.317	2.511
1	24.31	33.4	4.55	0.876	0.464	0.412	3.234	0.465	3.698
1¼	32.46	42.16	4.85	1.396	0.828	0.569	4.463	0.827	5.289
1½	38.1	48.26	5.08	1.829	1.14	0.689	5.408	1.14	6.548
2	49.25	60.33	5.54	2.859	1.906	0.953	7.48	1.907	9.386
2½	59	73.03	7.01	4.188	2.734	1.454	11.411	2.726	14.137
3	73.66	88.9	7.62	6.207	4.261	1.946	15.27	4.275	19.545
3½	85.45	101.6	8.08	8.108	5.736	2.373	18.626	5.541	24.167
4	97.18	114.3	8.56	10.26	7.417	2.843	22.317	7.403	29.72
5	122.25	141.3	9.53	15.683	11.739	3.943	30.949	11.827	42.776
6	146.33	168.28	10.97	22.241	16.819	5.423	42.56	16.831	59.391
8	193.68	219.08	12.7	37.694	29.462	8.232	64.627	29.492	94.119
10	242.93	273.05	15.06	58.574	46.368	12.206	95.924	46.368	142.292
12	288.95	323.85	17.45	82.368	65.574	16.794	131.97	65.598	197.568
14	317.5	355.6	19.05	99.316	79.174	20.142	159.377	79.212	238.588
16	363.58	406.4	21.41	129.716	103.819	25.897	204.062	103.863	307.925
18	409.6	457.2	23.8	164.174	131.768	32.406	254.705	131.821	386.526
20	455.63	508	26.19	202.684	163.045	39.639	311.306	163.115	474.421

Nominal Diam. (in.)	Circumference (mm)		M² of surface per Meter		Contents of Tube per Lin. Meter		Lin. Meters to Contain		
	Outside	Inside	Outside	Inside	(L)	(L)	1 L	1 L	1 kg of Water
⅛	32.26	17.15	0.032	0.017	0.031	0.024	33.05	42.44	67.82
¼	42.93	23.95	0.043	0.024	0.048	0.046	20.67	21.82	21.66
⅜	53.85	33.73	0.054	0.034	0.091	0.091	14.75	11.03	11
½	67.31	43.56	0.067	0.044	0.151	0.152	6.63	6.6	6.58
¾	83.57	59.18	0.084	0.059	0.279	0.317	3.6	3.16	3.15
1	104.9	76.45	0.105	0.077	0.465	0.464	2.15	2.16	2.16
1¼	132.33	101.85	0.133	0.102	0.818	0.827	1.23	1.21	1.21
1½	151.38	119.89	0.152	0.12	1.143	1.14	0.88	0.88	0.88
2	189.48	154.69	0.19	0.155	1.914	1.906	0.54	0.53	0.52
2½	229.36	185.93	0.23	0.186	2.731	2.732	0.37	0.37	0.37
3	278.38	231.65	0.279	0.232	4.274	4.272	0.23	0.23	0.24
3½	319.02	268.73	0.319	0.269	5.732	5.687	0.18	0.18	0.18
4	358.9	305.31	0.359	0.305	7.432	7.414	0.14	0.14	0.13
5	443.74	384.81	0.444	0.385	11.706	11.76	0.09	0.09	0.09
6	528.57	459.74	0.529	0.46	16.909	16.826	0.06	0.06	0.06
8	688.09	609.6	0.688	0.61	29.543	29.555	0.03	0.03	0.03
10	857.76	763.27	0.858	0.763	51.654	51.721	0.02	0.02	0.02
12	1017.27	907.29	1.027	0.907	65.59	65.567	0.015	0.015	0.014
14	1196.85	997.46	1.198	0.997	79.154	79.227	0.013	0.013	0.013
16	1356.61	1142.24	1.353	1.142	103.773	103.814	0.01	0.01	0.009
18	1436.37	1286.76	1.436	1.286	131.737	131.755	0.008	0.008	0.007
20	1595.88	1431.29	1.596	1.431	163.046	163.048	0.006	0.006	0.006

Table 2-11 Dimensions and Weights for Plain End Steel Pipe

Pipe Size, Nom. Outside Diam. in. (mm)	STD Wall in.	STD Wt./Ft. lb	X.S. Wall in.	X.S. Wt./Ft. lb	X.X.S. Wall in.	X.X.S. Wt./Ft. lb	10 Wall in.	10 Wt./Ft. lb	20 Wall in.	20 Wt./Ft. lb	30 Wall in.	30 Wt./Ft. lb	40 Wall in.	40 Wt./Ft. lb	60 Wall in.	60 Wt./Ft. lb	80 Wall in.	80 Wt./Ft. lb	100 Wall in.	100 Wt./Ft. lb	120 Wall in.	120 Wt./Ft. lb	140 Wall in.	140 Wt./Ft. lb	160 Wall in.	160 Wt./Ft. lb
⅛ (0.405)	.068	.24	.095	.31	-	-	-	-	-	-	-	-	.068	.24	-	-	.095	.31	-	-	-	-	-	-	-	-
¼ (0.540)	.088	.42	.119	.54	-	-	-	-	-	-	-	-	.088	.42	-	-	.119	.54	-	-	-	-	-	-	-	-
⅜ (0.675)	.091	.57	.126	.74	-	-	-	-	-	-	-	-	.091	.57	-	-	.126	.74	-	-	-	-	-	-	-	-
½ (0.840)	.109	.85	.147	1.09	.294	1.71	-	-	-	-	-	-	.109	.85	-	-	.147	1.09	-	-	-	-	-	-	.188	1.31
¾ (1.050)	.113	1.13	.154	1.47	.308	2.44	-	-	-	-	-	-	.113	1.13	-	-	.154	1.47	-	-	-	-	-	-	.219	1.94
1 (1.315)	.133	1.68	.179	2.17	.358	3.66	-	-	-	-	-	-	.133	1.68	-	-	.179	2.17	-	-	-	-	-	-	.250	2.84
1¼ (1.660)	.140	2.27	.191	3.00	.382	5.21	-	-	-	-	-	-	.140	2.27	-	-	.191	3.00	-	-	-	-	-	-	.250	3.76
1½ (1.900)	.145	2.72	.200	3.63	.400	6.41	-	-	-	-	-	-	.145	2.72	-	-	.200	3.63	-	-	-	-	-	-	.281	4.86
2 (2.375)	.154	3.65	.218	5.02	.436	9.03	-	-	-	-	-	-	.154	3.65	-	-	.218	5.02	-	-	-	-	-	-	.344	7.46
2½ (2.875)	.203	5.79	.276	7.66	.552	13.69	-	-	-	-	-	-	.203	5.79	-	-	.276	7.66	-	-	-	-	-	-	.375	10.01
3 (3.500)	.216	7.58	.300	10.25	.600	18.58	-	-	-	-	-	-	.216	7.58	-	-	.300	10.25	-	-	-	-	-	-	.438	14.32
3½ (4.000)	.226	9.11	.318	12.50	-	-	-	-	-	-	-	-	.226	9.11	-	-	.318	12.50	-	-	-	-	-	-	-	-
4 (4.500)	.237	10.79	.337	14.98	.674	27.54	-	-	-	-	-	-	.237	10.79	-	-	.337	14.98	-	-	.438	19.00	-	-	.531	22.51
5 (5.563)	.258	14.62	.375	20.78	.750	38.55	-	-	-	-	-	-	.258	14.62	-	-	.375	20.78	-	-	.500	27.04	-	-	.625	32.96
6 (6.625)	.280	18.97	.432	28.57	.864	53.16	-	-	-	-	-	-	.280	18.97	-	-	.432	28.57	-	-	.562	36.39	-	-	.719	45.35
8 (8.625)	.322	28.55	.500	43.39	.875	72.42	-	-	.250	22.36	.277	24.70	.322	28.55	.406	35.64	.500	43.39	.594	50.95	.719	60.71	.812	67.76	.906	74.69
10 (10.750)	.365	40.48	.500	54.74	1.000	104.13	-	-	.250	28.04	.307	34.24	.365	40.48	.500	54.74	.594	64.43	.719	77.03	.844	89.29	1.000	104.13	1.125	115.64
12 (12.750)	.375	49.56	.500	65.42	1.000	125.49	-	-	.250	33.38	.330	43.77	.406	53.52	.562	73.15	.688	88.63	.844	107.32	1.000	125.49	1.125	139.67	1.312	160.27
14 (14.000)	.375	54.57	.500	72.09	-	-	.250	36.71	.312	45.61	.375	54.57	.438	63.44	.594	85.05	.750	106.13	.938	130.85	1.094	150.79	1.250	170.21	1.406	189.11
16 (16.000)	.375	62.58	.500	82.77	-	-	.250	42.05	.312	52.27	.375	62.58	.500	82.77	.656	107.50	.844	136.61	1.031	164.82	1.219	192.43	1.438	223.64	1.594	245.25
18 (18.000)	.375	70.59	.500	93.45	-	-	.250	47.39	.312	58.94	.438	82.15	.562	104.67	.750	138.17	.938	170.92	1.156	207.96	1.375	244.14	1.562	274.22	1.781	308.50
20 (20.000)	.375	78.60	.500	104.13	-	-	.250	52.73	.375	78.60	.500	104.13	.594	123.11	.812	166.40	1.031	208.87	1.281	256.10	1.500	296.37	1.750	341.09	1.969	379.17
22 (22.000)	.375	86.61	.500	114.81	-	-	.250	53.07	.375	86.61	.500	114.81	-	-	.875	197.41	1.125	250.81	1.375	302.88	1.625	353.61	1.875	403.00	2.125	451.06
24 (24.000)	.375	94.62	.500	125.49	-	-	.250	63.41	.375	94.62	.562	140.68	.688	171.29	.969	238.35	1.219	296.58	1.531	367.39	1.812	429.39	2.062	483.12	2.344	542.13

Note: mm = in. × 25.4

kg = lb × 2.2

Table 2-12 Dimensions of Class 1 Standard Strength Perforated Clay Pipe

Size (in.)	Laying length Min.	Limit of minus variation (in. per ft. of length)	Maximum difference in length of two opposite sides (in.)	Outside diameter of barrel (in.) Min.	Outside diameter of barrel (in.) Max.	Inside diameter of socket at ½ in. above base, (in.) Min.	Rows of perforations	Perforations per row 2 ft.	3 ft.	4 ft.	5 ft.	Depth of socket (in.) Nominal	Min.	Thickness of barrel (in.) Nominal	Min.	Thickness of socket at ½ in. from outer end (in.) Nominal	Min.
4	2	¼	5⁄16	4 ⅞	5⅛	5 ¾	4	7	9	11	13	1 ¾	1 ½	½	7⁄16	7⁄16	⅜
6	2	¼	⅜	7 1⁄16	7 7⁄16	8 3⁄16	4	7	9	11	13	2 ¼	2	⅝	9⁄16	½	7⁄16
8	2	¼	7⁄16	9 ¼	9 ¾	10 ½	4	7	9	11	13	2 ½	2 ¼	¾	11⁄16	9⁄16	½
10	2	¼	7⁄16	11 ½	12	12 ¾	6	7	9	11	13	2 ⅝	2 ⅜	⅞	13⁄16	⅝	9⁄16
12	2	¼	7⁄16	13 ¾	14 5⁄16	15 ⅛	6	—	—	—	—	2 ¾	2 ½	1	15⁄16	¾	11⁄16
15	3	¼	½	17 3⁄16	17 13⁄16	18 ⅝	6	—	10	14	17	2 ⅞	2 ⅝	1 ¼	1 ⅛	15⁄16	⅞
18	3	¼	½	20 ⅝	21 7⁄16	22 ¼	8	—	10	14	17	3	2 ¾	1 ½	1 ⅜	1 ⅛	1 1⁄16
21	3	¼	9⁄16	24 ⅛	25	25 ⅞	8	—	10	14	17	3 ¼	3	1 ¾	1 ⅝	1 5⁄16	1 3⁄16
24	3	⅜	9⁄16	27 ½	28 ½	29 ⅜	8	—	10	14	17	3 ⅜	3 ⅛	2	1 ⅞	1 ½	1 ⅜

Source: Table from ASTM Specification C700.

Table 2-12(M) Dimensions of Class 1 Standard Strength Perforated Clay Pipe

Size (in.)	Laying Length Minimum (m)	Limit of Minus Variation (mm/m)	Maximum Difference in Length of 2 Opposite Sides (mm)	Outside Diameter of Barrel (mm) Minimum	Maximum	Inside Diameter of Socket at 12.7 mm Above Base (mm)
4	0.61	20.8	7.94	123.83	130.18	146.05
6	0.61	20.8	9.53	179.39	188.91	207.96
8	0.61	20.8	11.11	234.95	247.65	266.70
10	0.61	20.8	11.11	292.10	304.80	323.85
12	0.61	20.8	11.11	349.25	363.54	348.18
15	0.94	20.8	12.70	436.56	452.44	473.08
18	0.94	20.8	12.70	523.88	544.51	565.15
21	0.94	20.8	14.29	612.78	635.00	657.23
24	0.94	31.3	14.29	698.50	723.90	746.13

Size (in.)	Rows of Perforations	Perforations per Row 0.61 m	0.91 m	1.22 m	1.52 m	Depth of Socket (mm) Nominal	Minimum	Thickness of Barrel (mm) Nominal	Minimum	Thickness of Socket at 12.7 mm from Outer End (mm) Nominal	Minimum
4	4	7	9	11	13	44.45	38.10	12.70	11.11	11.11	9.53
6	4	7	9	11	13	57.15	50.80	15.88	14.29	12.70	11.11
8	4	7	9	11	13	63.50	57.15	19.05	17.46	14.29	12.70
10	6	7	9	11	13	66.68	60.33	22.23	20.64	15.88	14.29
12	6	—	—	—	—	69.85	63.50	25.40	23.81	19.05	17.46
15	6	—	10	14	17	73.03	66.68	31.75	28.58	23.81	22.23
18	8	—	10	14	17	76.20	69.85	38.10	34.93	28.58	26.99
21	8	—	10	14	17	82.55	76.20	44.45	41.28	33.34	30.16
24	8	—	10	14	17	85.73	79.38	50.80	48.63	38.10	34.93

Source: Table from ASTM Specification C700.

Table 2-13 Dimensions of Class 1 Extra Strength Clay Pipe

Size (in.)	Laying length Min.	Limit of minus variation (in. per ft. of length)	Maximum difference in length of two opposite sides (in.)	Outside diameter of barrel (in.) Min.	Outside diameter of barrel (in.) Max.	Inside diameter of socket at ½ in. above base (in.) Min.	Depth of socket (in.) Nominal	Depth of socket (in.) Min.	Thickness of barrel (in.) Nominal	Thickness of barrel (in.) Min.	Thickness of socket at ½ in. from outer end (in.) Nominal	Thickness of socket at ½ in. from outer end (in.) Min.
4	2	¼	5⁄16	4 ⅞	5 ⅛	5 ¾	1¾	1 ½	⅝	9⁄16	7⁄16	⅜
6	2	¼	⅜	7 1⁄16	7 7⁄16	8 3⁄16	2 ¼	2	11⁄16	9⁄16	½	7⁄16
8	2	¼	7⁄16	9 ¼	9 ¾	10 ½	2 ½	2 ¼	⅞	¾	9⁄16	½
10	2	¼	7⁄16	11 ½	12	12 ¾	2 ⅝	2 ⅜	1	⅞	⅝	9⁄16
12	2	¼	7⁄16	13 ¾	14 5⁄16	15 ⅛	2 ¾	2 ½	1 3⁄16	1 1⁄16	¾	11⁄16
15	3	¼	½	17 3⁄16	17 13⁄16	18 ⅝	2 ⅞	2 ⅝	1 ½	1 ⅜	15⁄16	⅞
18	3	¼	½	20 ⅝	21 7⁄16	22 ¼	3	2 ¾	1 ⅞	1 ¾	1 ⅛	1 1⁄16
21	3	¼	9⁄16	24 ⅛	25	25 ⅞	3 ¼	3	2 ¼	2	1 5⁄16	1 3⁄16
24	3	⅜	9⁄16	27 ½	28 ½	29 ⅜	3 ⅜	3 ⅛	2 ½	2 ¼	1 ½	1 ⅜
27	3	⅜	⅝	31	32 ½	33	3 ½	3 ¼	2 ¾	2 ½	1 11⁄16	1 9⁄16
30	3	⅜	⅝	34 ⅜	35 ⅝	36 ½	3 ⅝	3 ⅜	3	2 ¾	1 ⅞	1 ¾
33	3	⅜	⅝	37 ⅝	38 15⁄16	39 ⅞	3 ¾	3 ¼	3 ¼	3	2	1 ¾
36	3	⅜	11⁄16	40 ¾	42 ¼	43 ¼	4	3 ¾	3 ½	3 ¼	2 1⁄16	1 ⅞

Source: Table from ASTM Specification C700.

Table 2-13(M) Dimensions of Class 1 Extra Strength Clay Pipe

Size (in.)	Laying Length Minimum (m)	Limit of Minus Variation (mm/m)	Maximum Difference in Length of 2 Opposite Sides (mm)	Outside Diameter of Barrel (mm) Minimum	Outside Diameter of Barrel (mm) Maximum	Socket Inside Diam. 12.7 mm Above Base (mm) Min.
4	0.61	20.8	7.94	123.83	130.18	146.05
6	0.61	20.8	9.53	179.39	188.91	207.96
8	0.61	20.8	11.11	234.95	247.65	266.70
10	0.61	20.8	11.11	292.10	304.80	323.85
12	0.61	20.8	11.11	349.25	363.54	384.18
15	0.91	20.8	12.70	436.56	452.44	473.08
18	0.91	20.8	12.70	523.88	544.51	565.15
21	0.91	20.8	14.29	612.78	635.00	657.23
24	0.91	31.3	14.29	698.50	723.90	746.13
27	0.91	31.3	15.88	787.40	815.98	838.20
30	0.91	31.3	15.88	873.13	904.88	927.10
33	0.91	31.3	15.88	955.68	989.01	1012.83
36	0.91	31.3	17.46	1035.05	1073.15	1098.55

Size (in.)	Depth of Socket (mm) Nominal	Depth of Socket (mm) Minimum	Thickness of Barrel (mm) Nominal	Thickness of Barrel (mm) Minimum	Thickness of Socket at 12.7 mm from Outer End (mm) Nominal	Thickness of Socket at 12.7 mm from Outer End (mm) Minimum
4	44.45	38.10	15.88	14.29	11.11	9.53
6	57.15	50.80	17.46	14.29	12.70	11.11
8	63.50	57.15	22.23	19.05	14.29	12.70
10	66.68	60.33	25.40	22.23	15.88	14.29
12	69.85	63.50	30.16	26.99	19.05	17.46
15	73.03	66.68	38.10	34.93	23.81	22.23
18	76.20	69.85	47.63	44.45	28.58	26.99
21	82.55	76.20	57.15	50.80	33.34	30.16
24	85.73	79.38	63.50	57.15	38.10	34.93
27	88.90	82.55	69.85	63.50	42.86	39.69
30	92.08	85.73	76.20	69.85	47.63	44.45
33	95.25	88.90	82.55	76.20	50.80	44.45
36	101.60	95.25	88.90	82.55	52.39	47.63

Source: Table from ASTM Specification C700.

Note: There is no limit for plus variation.

Plastic Pipe

Plastic pipe is available in compositions designed for various applications, including DWV, water supply, gas service and transmission lines, and laboratory and other chemical drainage and piping systems. Fuel double-containment systems; high-purity pharmaceutical or electronic grade water; and R-13, R-13A fire protection sprinkler systems are additional uses.

There are two basic types of plastic pipe: thermoset and thermoplastic. A *thermoset* plastic has the property of being permanently rigid. Epoxy and phenolics are examples of thermosets. A *thermoplastic* is a material having the property of softening when heated and hardening when cooled. ABS, PVC, PB, PE, polypropylene (PP), cross-linked polyethylene (PEX), and CPVC are thermoplastics. With thermoplastics, consideration must be given to the temperature-pressure relationship when selecting the support spacing and method of installation. Some common plastic pipe materials are discussed below. See Figure 2-14 and Tables 2-14 and 2-15.

Note: Some codes require hangers 4 ft 0 in. apart.

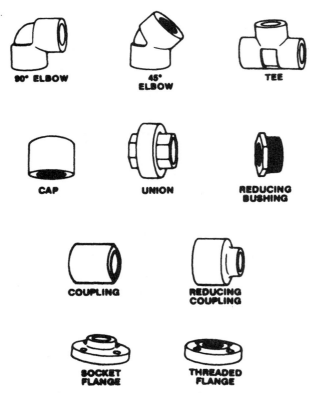

Figure 2-14 Plastic Pipe Fittings

Polybutylene (PB) Polybutylene is a flexible thermoplastic that was manufactured to pipe and tubing specifications. Polybutylene tubing is no longer manufactured; as a result, pipe material will no longer be available once existing supplies run out. The tubing is listed here in the event that repairs or modifications are made to existing systems.

Polybutylene is an inert polyolefin material, meaning that it is chemically resistant. That is why polybutylene pipe cannot be solvent cemented like other plastic piping systems. Polybutylene pipe was one of the most flexible piping materials acceptable for potable water. It was typically blue or gray in color.

Its applications included hydronic slab heating systems, fire sprinklers systems, hot and cold water distribution and plumbing and water supply.

Joints were made by mechanical, flared, heat fusion methods.

Applicable standards and specifications include ASTM D-2662 (pipe), ASTM D-2666 (tubing), ASTM D-3309 (water distribution), and CSA CAN3-B137.8.

Polyethylene (PE) Polyethylene is an inert polyolefin material, meaning that it is chemically resistant.

Polyethylene is available in basically two resins: 2406 MDPE (medium density) or 3408 HDPE (high density). These two types of resin have been used extensively for 50 years in the low-pressure street main distribution network for natural and propane gas. MDPE is presently used only in the buried gas transmission industry, in sizes ranging from ½ to 16 in. (12.7 to 406.4 mm), and is joined by butt and socket fusion.

HDPE is 90% of the polyethylene piping industry. It has a wide variety of below and aboveground applications, including domestic water supply, well water systems, lawn sprinkler systems, irrigation systems, skating rinks, buried chilled water pipe, underground Factory Mutual (FM) approved fire mains, chemical lines, snow making lines at ski slopes, pressurized chilled water piping underground between buildings and a central heating or cooling plant, methane gas collection piping, leachate collection lines at landfills, relining water and sewer mains to save redigging streets, water transmis-

Table 2-14 Plastic Pipe Data

Material	Schedule Numbers	Pipe Sizes (in.)	Fitting Sizes (in.)	Temperature Limit (°F)	Joining Methods
PVC I	40, 80, 120 SDR	¼–20	¼–8	150	Solvent weld, thread, flange, thermal weld
PVC II [a]	40, 80, 120 SDR	¼–20	¼–8	130	Solvent weld, thread, flange, thermal weld
Polypropylene	40–80	½–8	½–8	150	Thermal fusion, flange, thread, compression
CPVC	40–80	½–8	½–8	210	Solvent weld, thread, flange
Poyethylene	40, 80 SDR	½–6	½–6	120–140	Thermal fusion, compression
ABS	40, 80 SDR	⅛–12	½–6	160	Solvent weld, thread, flange
Polybutylene	SDR	¼–6	¼–6	210	Thermal fusion, flare, compression, insert

[a] The usage of PVC II is limited to electrical conduit.

Table 2-14(M) Plastic Pipe Data

Material	Schedule Numbers	Pipe Sizes (in.)	Fitting Sizes (mm)	Temperature Limit (°C)	Joining Methods
PVC I	40, 80, 120 SDR	¼–20	6.4 to 203.2	65.6	Solvent weld, thread, flange, thermal weld
PVC II [a]	40, 80, 120 SDR	¼–16	6.4 to 203.2	54.4	Solvent weld, thread, flange, thermal weld
Polypropylene	40–80	½–8	12.7 to 203.2	65.6	Thermal fusion, flange, thread, compression
CPVC	40–80	½–8	12.7 to 203.2	98.9	Solvent weld, thread, flange
Poyethylene	40, 80 SDR	½–6	12.7 to 152.4	48.9 to 60	Thermal fusion, compression
ABS	40, 80 SDR	⅛–12	3.2 to 152.4	71.1	Solvent weld, thread, flange
Polybutylene	SDR	¼–6	6.4 to 152.4	98.9	Thermal fusion, flare, compression, insert

[a] The usage of PVC II is limited to electrical conduit.

sion mains over highway bridges (it absorbs vibration), brine at skating rinks, and residential swimming pools.

Sizes range from ½ to 63 in. (12.7 to 1600.2 mm) diameter both iron pipe size (IPS) and copper tube size (CTS); pressures range from 50 psi to 250 psi depending on wall thickness, etc.

Polyethylene pipe cannot be solvent cemented like other plastic piping systems. This type of piping is normally supplied in blue or black for water applications. Orange-colored polyethylene piping is typically used for gas pipe installations.

Note: The joints are made with an inserts and clamps and by heat fusion. (PE cannot be threaded or solvent welded).

Typically, HDPE is installed with mechanical barbed joints or compression fittings through 2 in. (50.8 mm), and the pipe comes in coils. It is also available heat socket fused from ½ to 40 in. (12.7 to 1016 mm), butt fused from 2 to 63 in. (50.8 to 1600.2 mm), electro fused from 1½ to 30 in. (38.1 to 762 mm) diameter.

Table 2-15 Physical Properties of Plastic Piping Materials

Material		Specific Gravity	Tensile Strength (psi at 73°F)	Modulus of Elasticity in Tension (psi at 73°F × 10⁵)	Compress-ive Strength (psi)	Flexural Strength (psi)	Resistance to Heat (continu-ous) (°F)	Coefficient of Expansion (in./in./°F × 10⁻⁶)	Thermal Conduct-ivity (Btuh ft² /°F/in.)	Burning Rate	Heat Distortion Temp (°F at 264 psi)	Water Absorp-tion (%/24 hr at 73°F)	Izod Impact (73°F ft lb /in. notch)
PVC	Type I	1.38	7,940	4.15	9,600	14,500	140	3.0	1.2	Self Extinguishing	160	.05	.65
	Type II ª	1.35	6,000	3.5	8,800	11,500	140	5.55	1.35	Self Extinguishing	155	.07	2-15
CPVC	Type IV	1.55	8,400	4.2		15,600	210	3.8	.95	Self Extinguishing	221	.05	—
Polyethylene													
	Type I	.92	1,750	1.9–.35		1,700	120	10.0	2.3	Slow	NA	.01	16
	Type III	.95	2,800	1.5		2,000	120	7.3	3.5	Slow	NA	0.0	3.0
Polypropylene		.91	4,900	1.5	8,500		160–212	3.8	1.3	Slow	150	0.03	2.1
ABS													
	Type I	1.03	5,300	3.0	7,000	8,000	160	6.0	1.9	Slow	197	.20	5-9
	Type II	1.08	8,000		10,000	12,000	170	3.8	2.5	Slow	225	.20	4
Polyvinylidene Floride (PDVF)		1.76	7,000	1.2	10,000		200–250	8.5	1.05	Self Extinguishing	195	.04	3.0
Polybutylene		.93	4,800	.38	—	—	—	7.1	1.5	Slow	NA	‹ .01	no break

Notes: 1. Above data compiled in accordance with ASTM test requirements.
2. NA = Not Applicable.
ª The usage of PVC II is limited to electrical conduit.

Table 2-15(M) Physical Properties of Plastic Piping Materials

Material		Specific Gravity	Tensile Strength (MPa at 22.8°C)	Modulus of Elasticity in Tension (10⁵ kPa at 22.8°C)	Compress-ive Strength (MPa)	Flexural Strength (MPa)	Resistance to Heat (continu-ous) (°C)	Coefficient of Expansion (10⁻⁵ mm /mm/°C)	Thermal Conduct-ivity (W/m²°K)	Burning Rate	Heat Distortion Temp (°C at 1.82 MPa)	Water Absorp-tion (%/24h at 22.8°C)	Impact (J/mm notch at 22.8°C)
PVC	Type I	1.38	48.26	28.61	66.19	99.98	65.6	127.0	5.96	Self Extinguishing	73.9	0.07	0.04
	Type II ª	1.25	41.37	24.13	60.67	79.29	60.0	251.73	7.56	Self Extinguishing	68.3	0.07	0.53–0.80
CPVC	NA	NA	NA	NA	NA	NA	NA	NA	NA	NA	NA	NA	NA
Polyethylene													
	Type I	0.92	12.07	131.0–2.41	—	11.72	48.9	453.57	13.06	Slow	—	–0.01	0.85
	Type III	0.95	13.79	10.34	—	13.79	48.9	331.11	19.87	Slow	—	0	0.16
Polypropylene		0.91	33.79	10.34	58.61	—	71.1–100	172.36	7.38	Slow	65.6	0.03	0.11
ABS													
	Type I	1.03	36.54	20.68	48.26	55.16	71.1	272.14	10.79	Slow	91.7	0.20	0.27–0.48
	Type II	1.08	55.16	—	68.95	82.74	76.7	172.36	14.20	Slow	107.2	0.20	0.21
Polyvinylidene Floride (PDVF)		1.76	48.26	8.27	68.95	—	93.3–121.1	385.54	5.96	Self Extinguishing	90.6	0.04	0.16
Polybutylene		0.93	33.10	2.62	—	—	—	180.34	8.51	Slow	NA	‹ .01	no break

Notes: 1. Above data compiled in accordance with ASTM test requirements.
2. NA = Not applicable.
ª The usage of PVC II is limited to electrical conduit.

HDPE comes in a wide variety of fittings and pipe. Depending on diameter, ½ to 2 in. (12.7 to 50.8 mm) comes in rolled coils, which can be 100 to 5000 ft (30.5 to 1542 mm) on special reels, and 2 to 63 in. (50.8 to 1600.2 mm) diameter generally comes as 40 ft (12.2 m) pipe lengths.

The designer should not consider HDPE a fixed, rigid, perfectly straight pipe—it bends. When designing systems with HDPE, expansion must be preplanned and best efforts should be made to determine what direction it will take; i.e., bury the pipe in an "S" or snake pattern to let it try to expand or contract.

Both pipe and tubing (IPS and CTS) are manufactured using a standard dimension ratio (SDR) series, not Schedule 40, Schedule 80!

The upper operating maximum temperature limit is 160°F, but as always, the manufacturer of the product should be consulted on temperature versus pressure.

The color is typically black for HDPE, which according to ASTM means 2% carbon black has been blended with the resin to give the minimum 50-year life span at full pressure in direct sunlight. Two unique properties of HDPE pipe are that (1) should it freeze; it would swell and not break, and (2) since its specific gravity is 0.95, it will float in water. This is why HDPE pipe can be preassembled and thousands of feet can be floated to a certain position and then sunk with concrete collars.

The applicable specifications and standards are HDPE ASTM F-876, ASTM D-1148, ASTM D-2239, ASTM D-2609 (fitting), ASTM D-2737 (tubing), and CSA CAN/CSA-B137.1.

Crossed-linked polyethylene (PEX) Crossed-linked polyethylene tubing has been extensively used in Europe for many years for hot and cold potable water distribution systems.

A specially controlled chemical reaction takes place during the manufacturing of the polyethylene pipe to form crossed-linked polyethylene. Cross-linked molecular structuring gives the pipe greater resistance to rupture over a wider range of temperatures and pressures than other polyolefin piping (PB, PE, and PP).

Because of PEX pipe's unique molecular structure and heat resistance, heat fusion is not permitted as a joining method. Being a member of the polyolefin plastic family, PEX is resistant to solvents and cannot be joined by solvent cementing. Mechanical connectors and fittings for PEX piping systems are proprietary in nature and must be used only with the pipe for which they have been designed. A number of mechanical fastening techniques have been developed for joining PEX pipe; manufacturer's installation instructions are to be consulted for properly identifying the authorized fittings for the intended system use.

PEX pipe is flexible, allowing it to be bent. It is bent by two methods: hot and cold bending. See manufacturer's instructions for the exact requirements of bending methods. The tubing can be bent to a minimum radius of six times the outside diameter for cold bending and a minimum of two and one-half times the outside diameter for hot bending.

The material is available in sizes nominal pipe size (NPS) ¼ through 2 in. (6.4 through 51 mm).

The applicable specifications and standards are ASTM F-876, ASTM F-877, and CSA CAN/CSA-B137.5

Crossed-linked polyethylene/aluminum/crossed-linked polyethylene (PEX-AL-PEX)
PEX-AL-PEX is a composite of pipe made of an aluminum tube laminated to interior and exterior layers of cross-linked polyethylene. The layers are bonded with an adhesive.

The cross-linked molecular structuring described above and the addition of the aluminum core makes the pipe more resistant to rupture. Therefore, along with other system usages, the pipe is suitable for hot and cold water distribution. The pipe is rated for 125 psi at 180°F (862 kPa at 82°C).

Mechanical joints are the only methods currently available to join PEX-AL-PEX pipe. A number of mechanical compression type connectors have been developed for joining this type of pipe material to permit transition to other types of pipe and fittings. The installation of any fitting is to be in accordance with the manufacturer's installation instructions.

Although it is partially plastic, PEX-AL-PEX pipe resembles metal tubing in that it can be bent by hand or with a suitable bending device while maintaining its shape without fittings or supports. The minimum radius is five times the outside diameter.

The material is available in sizes NPS ¼ through 1 in.

The applicable specifications and standards are ASTM F-1281 and CSA CAN/CSA-B137.10.

Polyethylene/aluminum/polyethylene (PE-AL-PE) PE–AL-PE is identical to the PEX-AL-PEX composite pipe except for the physical properties of the polyethylene.

Polyethylene does not display the same resistance to temperature and pressure as the cross-linked polyethylene. Therefore, this type of pipe is limited to cold water applications or applications with other suitable fluids up to 110°F at 150 psi (43°C at 1034 kPa) of pressure.

The applicable specifications and standards are ASTM F-1282 and CSA CAN/CSA-B137.9.

Polyvinyl chloride (PVC) Polyvinyl chloride is rigid, pressure or drainage type pipe that resists chemicals and corrosion. There are two types available: Schedule 40 and Schedule 80. PVC water service piping is a different material than PVC drainage pipe, although both pipe materials are white in color. For pressure SDR 21 (200 psi) or SDR 26 (160 psi) is used. PVC is used for water distribution, irrigation, storm drainage, sewage, laboratory and hospital wastes, chemical lines, chilled water lines, heat pumps, underground FM approved fire mains, animal rearing facilities, hatcheries, and gray water piping.

The working pressure varies with the temperature: As the temperature increases, tensile strength decreases. The maximum working pressure is to be continuously marked on the pipe along with the manufacturer's name, ASTM or CSA standard, and the grade of PVC material. Temperature should be limited to 140 to 150°F (60 to 65.6°C). The joints are solvent welded or threaded. Schedule 40 PVC cannot be threaded and it can be used only with socket fittings. Schedule 80 can be threaded through the 4-in. (101.6-mm) size and used with either socket or threaded fittings. However, it can also be installed with mechanical grooved couplings or bell and gasket (underground only and thrust blocked).

The applicable standards and specifications for water service are ASTM D-1784, ASTM D-1785, ASTM D-2241, ASTM D-2665, ASTM D-2672 and CSA CAN/CSA-B137.3 (pipe). The standards for fittings are ASTM D-2464, ASTM D-2466, ASTM D-2467, ASTM D-3139, ASTM F-477, and CSA CAN/CSA-B137.2.

PVC is available in sizes:

- DWV: 1¼–24 in. (31.75–609.6 mm)
- Schedule 40: ½–30 in. (12.7–762 mm)
- Schedule 80: ⅛–30 in. (3.17–762 mm)
- SDR21: 1½–24 in. (38.1–609.6 mm)
- SDR26: 1½–24 in. (38.1–609.6 mm)

The maximum temperature rating for PVC is 140°F (60°C). The coefficient of linear expansion is 2.9 × 2–5°F. The specific gravity of PVC is 1.35.

Chlorinated polyvinyl chloride (CPVC) CPVC finds application in hot and cold water distribution and chemical process piping.

The higher-temperature version of PVC is CPVC pipe. This piping network comes in a variety of pressure applications of CTS or IPS (iron pipe sizes of Schedule 40 or Schedule 80). CPVC has an upper maximum temperature limit of 200°F. It is commonly used and is code accepted where residential water would quickly deteriorate copper pipe. Because of its size ranges—CTS: ½ to 2 in. (12.7 to 50.8 mm), Schedule 80: ¼–16 in. (6.3–406.4 mm)—it can be used in a wide variety of hot or cold water systems. CPVC has also been used extensively in wet fire protection systems in hotels, motels, residences, office buildings, dormitories, etc. (all applications that fall in the categories of 13 and 13R of NFPA). Pipe sizes for fire protection systems are ¾ to 3 in. (19 to 76.2 mm) and are ideally suited for the retrofit market.

Joining methods are solvent welding, threads, flanges, compression fittings, O-rings, transition fittings, bell-rings, and rubber gaskets.

The applicable standards and specifications are ASTM F-437, ASTM F-438, ASTM F-439(fittings), ASTM F-440 (tubing), ASTM F-441 (pipe), ASTM F-442 (SDR-PR pipe), ASTM F-937 (fittings), ASTM D-2846 (hot water distribution), and CSA CAN/CSA-B137.6.

Note: PVC and CPVC piping systems are not recommended for compressed air lines. Compensation for *both* thermal expansion and contraction must be taken into account!

Acrylonitrile-butadiene-styrene (ABS) ABS is

manufactured in Schedules 40 and 80 and in special dimensions for main sewers and utility conduits. It is commonly used for DWV plumbing (in the color black), main sanitary and storm sewers, underground electrical conduits, and applications in the chemical and petroleum industries. The joints are solvent welded for Schedule 40 and welded or threaded for Schedule 80.

The piping sizes are 1½, 2, 3, 4, and 6 in. (38.1, 50.8, 76.2, 101.6, and 152.4 mm) with the appropriate fittings. The system is joined together only with solvent cement.

For industrial applications, ABS piping is "gray" for low temperature [−40 to 176°F (−72 to 80°C)] and pressure up to 230 psi in sizes ½ to 8 in. (12.7 to 203.2 mm). It is joined only by solvent cementing per ASTM 648. The coefficient of linear expansion is 5.6 × 2–5 in./in.°F. Fittings are available for pressure only. The outside diameter of the pipe is nominal IPS, and a second product in the industrial area is "Airline" which is designed to be used in delivering compressed air for machine tools from ⅝ to 4 in. (16 to 101 mm).

The applicable standards and specifications are ASTM F-628, ASTM D-1527 (pipe Schedules 40 and 80), ASTM D-1788 (material), fittings are molded to ASTM D-2661 (DWV), ASTM D-2751 (sewer pipe), ASTM D-2680 (composite sewer pipe), ASTM D2468, and ASTM D-2282 (SDR-PR pipe).

Polypropylene (PP) PP is manufactured in a wide variety of systems.

The DWV systems are for chemical, special waste, or acid waste systems, both buried and aboveground applications. Pipe is available in Schedule 40 or Schedule 80 black (underground) or flame retardant (FR) for aboveground installation. Polypropylene acid waste (AW) pipe systems come either with mechanical joints—sizes 1½, 2, 3, 4, and 6 in. (38.1, 50.8, 76.2, 101.6, and 152.4 mm)—or with an internal wire heat fused—sizes 1½, 2, 3, 4, 6, 8, 10, 12, 14, 16, and 18 in. (38.1, 50.8, 76.2, 101.6, 152.4, 203.2, 254, 304, 355.6, 406.4, and 457.2 mm)—molded—sizes 1½ to 6 in. (38.1 to 152.4 mm)—and fabricated—sizes 8 to 18 in. (203.2 to 457.2 mm).

Fittings are made in both pressure type and DWV configurations. PP is used for a wide range of industrial liquids, salt water disposal, and corrosive waste systems. It is available in sizes of ½ to 24 in. (12.7 to 609.6 mm). Pipe is available in 10 and 20 ft (3.05 and 6.1 m) lengths. The joints cannot be solvent welded. Joints are made mechanically or by heat fusion (electric coil or socket fusion). (See Figure 2-15.) The applicable standards are ASTM F-1412, *Standard Specification for Polyolefin Pipe and Fittings for Corrosive Waste Drainage Systems*, and ASTM D-4101, *Standard Specification for Polypropylene Injection and Extrusion Materials*.

Figure 2-15 Fusion Lock Process in Operation

A wide selection of fittings is available to meet specific needs.

The following specification and standard applies: ASTMD-635, *Polypropylene Heat Fused.*

Polypropylene systems for acid waste installed aboveground must utilize FR pipe and fittings.

Polypropylene comes in a variety of pressure systems. It can be natural in color for high-purity systems or it may be black or beige with the added color pigment. Polypropylene pipe is available in both metric and IPS sizes.

Typically, polypropylene is joined by heat fusion, whether small diameter—½ to 4 in. (12.7 to 101.6 mm)—by socket fusion, or larger diameter—2 to 24 in. (50.8 to 609.6 mm)—by butt fusion.

Smaller diameter—½ to 2 in. (12.7 to 50.8 mm)—polypropylene may be joined by threading with a greatly reduced pressure rating, or certain manufacturers have molded fittings with stainless steel rings to restrain or help strengthen the threads for full pressure ratings.

Note: No glue can be used to join any polypropylene, polyethylene pipe, or polyvinylidene fluoride!

Double containment of polypropylene systems is a greatly expanded area of the DWV acid waste market. Double containment polypropylene systems are typically nonflame pipe (NFPP) for underground and flame-retardant pipe (FRPP) for aboveground applications. Double containment polypropylene can be installed with or without leak-detection systems. See discussion in Double Containment section below.

Note: It is critical what the temperature conditions of the ambient environment are and how the double containment system was tested, which depend on the manufacturer of the polypropylene double containment system.

Polyvinylidene fluoride (PVDF) is manufactured in Schedules 40 and 80. Polyvinylidene fluoride is a strong, tough, abrasion-resistant fluorocarbon material. It has widely used in high-purity electronic or medical grade water or chemical piping systems that need to remain pure but function at higher temperature. Other uses include a wide range of industrial liquids, salt water disposal, and corrosive waste systems, again where high-temperature performance is required. It is also often used for corrosive waste applications in return air plenum spaces. PVDF offers excellent flame and smoke-resistant characteristics.

The coefficient of thermal expansion is 7.9 in./in.°F × 2–5 per ASTM D696. It is available in metric and IPS sizes ranging from ⅜ to 12 in. (9.5 to 304.8 mm). Pipe is available in 10 ft (3.04 m) lengths.

The color is normally natural and the resin is not affected by UV light; however, if the media it is transporting is affected, a red coloring is added to the resin resulting in a red colored piping system. Normally, PVDF is available in a pressure system pattern of fittings. What makes PVDF a piping system of choice is its ability to withstand higher temperature for elevated-temperature cleaning.

Fittings are made in both pressure and DWV configurations. The joints cannot be solvent welded. Joints are made mechanically or by heat fusion (electric coil or socket fusion). The applicable standards are ASTM D-638; ASTM F-1673, *Standard Specification for Polyvinylidene Fluoride Corrosive Waste Drainage Systems*; and ASTM D-3222, *Specification for Unmodified Polyvinylidene Fluoride (PVDF) Molding, Extrusion and Coating Materials.*

Teflon (PTFE) Teflon, or polytetrafluoroethylene (PTFE), has outstanding resistance to chemical attack by most chemicals and solvents. It has a temperature range of –200 to 500°F (–128.9 to 260°C). Typically, we think of Teflon as tubing; however, it can be joined by threading in pipe sizes ⅛ to 4 in. (3.2 to 101.6 mm). Teflon piping is well suited for low-pressure—not to exceed (NTE) 15 psi—laboratory or process industry applications. If higher pressure or hotter temperatures are needed, Teflon lined steel pipe is generally used. Lined steel pipe is 1 to 12 in. (25.4 to 304.8 mm) and can take corrosive chemicals as well as high-pressure applications.

Low extractable PVC Rather recent to the expensive high-purity piping market is the less expensive low extractable PVC resin that is used in pressure piping loops for the conveyance of ultrapure water (UPW). Pipe and fittings with valves are joined by solvent cementing; fluids being conveyed cannot exceed 140°F (60°C). Pipe is in Schedule 80 wall thickness and sizes of ½ to 4 in. (12.7 to 101.6 mm). Fittings are made conforming to ASTM D2467, and pipe conforms to ASTM D1785.

This piping network is for economical engineering in UPW water loops such as in kidney dialysis and pharmaceutical and electronic industrial applications when an economical solution is imperative to solve problems in cold water loops in lieu of stainless steel or PVDF. Tests have been done to ASTM D5127 to prove resistivity is maintained at greater than 18 megaohms (Mohm) and on-line total oxidizable carbon (TOC) averaging less than 5 ppb.

Fiberglass Pipe (FRP), Reinforced Thermosetting Resin Pipe (RTRP) Fiberglass pipe is joined by using epoxy to join pipe and fittings. It normally is used in a pressure pattern mode and has not only good chemical resistance but also excellent stability in its upper temperature limit of 275°F (135°C). Many systems are joined with epoxy resins and heating blankets; however, dependent on the manufacturer, it can also be joined mechanically with bell and spigot, plain, or butt and wrap methods. It is manufactured in sizes of 1 to 48 in. (25.4 to 1219 mm) and can be custom made in much larger diameters. It is especially helpful in resisting attacks from the various oils used in the petroleum industry.

Different products require different approvals. Some must meet American Petroleum Institute (API), Underwriters' Laboratories (UL), or military (MIL) specifications MIL-P-29206A, or for potable water NSF Standard no. 14 per ASTM D2996, RTRP-11AF1, or ANSI/NSF Standard no. 61 for drinking water.

The coefficient of linear thermal expansion is 1.57 × 2–5 in./in./°F per ASTM D696.

As with all plastics, certain considerations must be reviewed before installation. These include code compliance, chemical compatibility, correct maximum temperature, and allowance for proper expansion and contraction movement. Certain plastics are installed with solvent cements, others require heating to join piping networks along with mechanical joints. The designer should consult the manufacturer's recommendations for the proper connection of all piping systems.

Duriron Pipe

Duriron is a 14.5% silicon iron that possess nearly universal corrosion resistance. For nearly 90 years, duriron pipe and fittings have provided a durable and reliable means of transporting corrosive waste safely. Anywhere there are acids, bases, solvents, or other aggressive fluids, duriron can be used.

Duriron bell-and-spigot pipe and fittings are available in sizes from 2 to 15 in. and are installed using traditional plumbing techniques. (See Figure 2-16.) Duriron mechanical joint pipe and fittings are available from 1½ to 4 in. and offer ease of installation through the use of couplings.

The duriron bell-and-spigot joint is made using conventional plumbing tools, virgin lead, and a special acid-resistant caulking yarn. The caulking yarn is packed into the bell of the duriron joint and a small amount of lead is poured over the yarn to fill the hub. It is the caulking yarn not the lead that seals the joint.

Duriron mechanical joints are designed for fast and easy assembly through the use of the two-bolt mechanical coupling. A calibrated ratchet

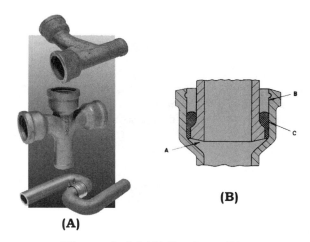

Figure 2-16 (A) Duriron Pipe, (B) Duriron Joint

Source: Courtesy of Duriron.

is necessary to complete the joint. The nuts are tightened to 10 ft-lb 24 h prior to testing.

Duriron conforms to ASTM specifications A518, A861, and A518.

SPECIAL-PURPOSE PIPING MATERIALS

Stainless steel and aluminum are the most common special-purpose piping materials used for a wide range of applications where performance requirements outweigh costs. Stainless steel and aluminum require specialized skills in design and fabrication. Many alloys are available for specific applications.

Aluminum

Aluminum is extruded or drawn in a variety of alloys. Its uses include cryogenic systems with temperatures as low as –423°F (–252.8°C), process systems, heat transfer, and pressure lines. The joints can be brazed or welded. It should be noted that special techniques are often required, depending on the type of alloy. Aluminum is available in 8 through 48-in. diameters, depending on the type.

Stainless Steel

Stainless steel is manufactured in three basic types: martensitic (hardenable, straight chromium alloy), ferritic (straight chromium, for corrosive service where nickel steel is undesirable), and austenitic (18% chromium and 8% nickel, for general corrosive service). Stainless steel is used where sanitation and product contamination resistance are critical (dairies, food processing, etc.). In processing systems, stainless steel is used to resist corrosion. The joints can be butt welded, socket welded, screwed, or flanged. Pipe and fittings are available in ⅛ through 48-in. diameters.

Stainless steel is a clean, durable, corrosion-resistant and long-lasting material. All stainless steels have inherent corrosion resistance, but the austenitic group of stainless steels has greater resistance.

Products are chemically descaled (acid pickled) to enhance the natural corrosion resistance and provide a uniform, aesthetically pleasing matt silver finish.

The designation "stainless steel" applies to a number of alloys with different properties. Common to all stainless steels, is the fact they contain at least 12% chromium.

The austenitic chromium-nickel steel is the best of the stainless steels. This steel is resistant to many different chemical products and most detergents.

Stainless steel uses include applications in the food industry, shipbuilding, pharmaceutical industry, breweries and dairies, industrial kitchens and institutions. When increased acid resistance is required, and spot and crevice corrosion may occur, molybdenum-alloyed chromium-nickel steels may be used. These acid-resistant steels resist a number of organic and inorganic acids.

However, acid-proof steels are only partially resistant to solutions containing chlorides.

The steel's ability to resist impacts and shocks is, in austenitic steel, excellent at all temperatures. This also applies at very low temperatures. Hard blows to the material may in certain cases cause dents, but it is very difficult to actually damage the steel.

Stainless steel cannot burn and is consequently classified as nonflammable. This means that pipes and drains made of stainless steel may penetrate floor partitions without the need for special fire insulation. Likewise, no harmful fumes or substances are released from the steel in case of fire.

Due to their very low heat expansion coefficient, drain products in stainless steel are not in any way influenced by temperatures occurring in drain installations. Furthermore, drain products need not be stored or installed at specific temperatures. Neither heat nor cold affects the stainless steel.

Stainless steel press fit piping system Stainless steel piping is manufactured in two different grades: 304, which is suitable for most environments, and 316, which is suitable for corrosive environments. Piping is available in single hub. Pipes are available in eight lengths: 0.5, 0.8, 1.6, 3.3, 4.9, 6.6, 9.8, 16.4 ft (150, 250, 500, 1000, 1500, 2000, 3000, and 5000 mm) and 2 to 6 in. (50.8 to 152.4 mm). It is necessary to determine the lengths required between fitting location points and to select the pipe lengths that will best minimize waste and eliminate field cuts when possible. A stainless steel piping system is lightweight and easy to install. A pipe joint can be made in a few seconds.

Corrugated stainless steel tubing Corrugated stainless steel tubing (CSST) is a flexible gas piping system made from 300 series stainless steel. The tubing is suitable for natural gas and propane. It can be used for both above- and underground installations. See specific manufacturer's recommendations for underground use and installation. The tubing is protected with a fire-retardant polyethylene jacket. It is manufactured in ⅜ to 2-in. (9.52 to 50.8-mm) sizes and in coils of up to 1000 ft (304.8 m) based on pipe sizes.

Mechanical joints are the only methods currently available to join CSST tubing. A number of mechanical compression type connectors have been developed for joining this type of pipe material to permit transition to other types of pipe and fittings. The installation of any fitting is to be in accordance with the manufacturer's installation instructions.

Manufacturers have specific protective devices and termination fittings for their products. The designer should consult with the manufacturer for all required accessories.

Applicable standards and specifications include ASTM A-240 for tubing, ANSI/ASME B-1.20.1 for fittings, and ASTM E-84 for jacket material.

DOUBLE CONTAINMENT

Double containment (DC) has proven to be needed both under- and aboveground for a multitude of purposes. Typically, to avoid a failed single-walled chemical pipe, a second, walled enclosure pipe is added. DC is marketed for preventing corrosive chemicals from getting into soils or spilling from a single-walled overhead pipe to people or objects below. Now DC is available in both drainage and pressure systems. Double containment is available in PVC DWV × PVC DWV, PVC Schedule 40/80 × PVC DWV; PVC 40/80 × PVC 40/80 CPVC 80 × PVC 80; DWV-PP × DWV PP; FRP × FRP. It can be ordered with or without a leak detection cable. DC has at the present time no ASTM standards to meet, but an attempt is being made to eliminate as many fabricated inner fittings as possible, especially for drainage. When planning for DC, the designer should leave plenty of space; labor costs are five to seven times those for installing single-walled pipe. When testing DC, the designer should doublecheck manufacturer's requirements for procedures to test inner and outer pipe. A simple DC size variation is 6 in. inner and 10 in. outer diameter, so there is a great difference in size; a typical 6-in. trap may take up 15 to 18 in. now and a 6 × 10-in. trap may take up 48 in of space. So to maintain pitch requires a very different site plan and pitch elevation plan.

JOINING PRACTICES

Mechanical Joints

Mechanical joints include transition, compression, and threaded joints. Mechanical joints shall incorporate a positive mechanical system for axial restraint in addition to any restraint provided by friction. All internal grab rings shall be manufactured from corrosion-resistant steel. Polyethylene sealing rings shall be Type 1 (LDPE) compound.

Compression Joints

Compression type gaskets have been used in pressure pipe joints for years. The compression joint uses hub-and-spigot pipe and fittings (as does the lead and oakum joint). The major difference is the one-piece neoprene rubber gasket. When the spigot end of the pipe or fitting is pulled or drawn into the gasketed hub, the joint is sealed by displacement and compression of the neoprene gasket. The resulting joint is leak free, and it absorbs vibration and can be deflected up to 5° without leaking or failing. Gaskets are precision molded of durable neoprene. Note that service gaskets must be used with service weight pipe and fittings. Extra-heavy gaskets must be used with extra-heavy pipe and fittings. The standard specification for rubber gaskets for joining cast-iron soil pipe and fittings is ASTM C564. Neoprene will not support combustion and gasket materials can be safely used up to 212°F. Maximum deflection should not exceed ½ in. per foot of pipe. This would allow 5 in. of deflection for a 10-ft piece of pipe and 2½ in. for 5 ft of pipe. For more than 5° of deflection, fittings should be used.

Lead and Oakum Joints (Caulked Joints)

Hub-and-spigot cast-iron soil pipe and fitting joints can be made with oakum fiber and molten lead, which provides a leak-free, strong, flexible, and root-proof joint. The waterproofing characteristics of oakum fiber have long been recognized by the plumbing trades, and when molten lead is poured over the oakum in a cast-iron soil pipe joint, it completely seals and locks the joint. This is because the hot lead fills a groove in the bell end of the pipe or fitting, firmly anchoring the lead in place after cooling. To make a caulked joint, the spigot end of a pipe or fitting is placed inside the hub of another pipe or fitting. Oakum is placed around the spigot in the hub using a yarning tool and then the oakum is packed to the proper depth using a packing tool. Molten lead is then poured into the joint making sure the lead is brought up near the top of the hub. After the lead has cooled sufficiently, it is caulked with a caulking tool to form a solid lead insert. The result is a locktight soil pipe joint with excellent flexural characteristics. If horizontal joints are to be made, a joint runner must be used to retain the molten lead. Customary safety precautions should be taken when handling molten lead.

Shielded Hubless Coupling

The shielded coupling for hubless cast-iron soil pipe and fittings is a plumbing concept that provides a more compact arrangement without sacrificing the quality and performance of cast iron. The hubless coupling system typically uses a one-piece neoprene gasket, a shield of stainless steel retaining clamps. The hubless coupling is manufactured in accordance with CISPI 310 and ASTM C1277. The great advantage of the system is that it permits joints to be made in limited-access areas. The 300 series stainless steel, which is always used with hubless couplings, was selected because of its superior corrosion resistance. It is resistant to oxidation, warping and deformation, offers rigidity under tension with substantial tension strength, and yet provides sufficient flexibility. The shield is corrugated in order to grip the gasket sleeve and give maximum compression distribution to the joint. The stainless steel worm gear clamps compress the neoprene gasket to seal the joint. The neoprene gasket absorbs shock and vibration and completely eliminates galvanic action between the cast iron and the stainless steel shield. Neoprene will not support combustion and can be safely used up to 212°F. The neoprene sleeve is completely protected by a nonflammable stainless steel shield, and as a result a fire rating is not required. Joint deflection using a shielded hubless coupling has a maximum limit of up to 5°. Maximum deflection should not exceed ½ in. per foot of pipe. This would allow 5 in. of deflection for a 10-ft piece of pipe. For more than 5° of deflection, fittings should be used.

Mechanically Formed Tee Fittings for Copper Tube

Mechanically formed tee fittings shall be formed in a continuous operation consisting of drilling a pilot hole and drawing out the tube surface to form a tee having a height of not less than three times the thickness of the branch tube wall so as to comply with the American Welding Society's lap joint weld. The device shall be fully adjustable to ensure proper tolerance and complete uniformity of the joint. (See Figure 2-17.)

The branch tube shall be notched to conform to the inner curve of the run tube and have two dimple/depth stops pressed into the branch tube, one ¼ in. (6.4 mm) atop the other so as to serve as a visual point of inspection. The bottom dimple is to ensure that penetration of the branch tube into the tee is of sufficient depth for brazing and that the branch tube does not obstruct the flow in the main line tube. Dimple/

Figure 2-17 Copper Pipe Mechanical T-Joint

Source: Courtesy of T-Drill.

depth stops shall be in line with the run of the tube.

Mechanically formed tee fittings shall be brazed in accordance with the Copper Development Association's *Copper Tube Handbook* using BCuP series filler metal.

Note: Soft soldered joints will not be permitted. Mechanically formed tee fittings shall conform to ASTM F 2014-00, ANSI B 31.9, *Building Services Piping*, and ASME *Code for Pressure Piping*, ANSI B 31.5c.

Mechanical Joining of Copper Pipe

The tubing should be severed with a tube cutter or fine-toothed steel saw and all burrs are to be removed both inside and out. The seal located inside the fitting should be checked; the seal is made of EPDM material. While being turned slightly, the fitting should be slid and pressed onto the pipe until properly seated. The insertion depth should be marked. The appropriate clamping jaw should be set into the pressing tool and pushed in until the jaw locks in place. The clamping jaw should be opened and placed at a right angle on the fitting; and the insertion depth should be verified. The pressing procedure should be started upon completion of the pressing cycle. The clamping jaw should be opened; the joint is completed.

Brazing

"Brazing" is defined as a process where the filler metals (alloys) melt at a temperature greater than 840°F and the base metals (tube and fittings) are not melted. Most commonly used brazing filler metals melt at temperatures around 1150 to 1550°F.

Soldering

"Soldering" is defined as a process wherein the filler metal (solder) melts at a temperature of less than 840°F and the base metals (tube and fittings) are not melted. Most commonly used leak-free solders melt at ranges around 350 to 600°F. Lead-free solders must contain less than 0.2% lead (Pb) in order to be classified as no lead.

Making up soldered joints Soldered joints should be installed in accordance with the requirements, steps, and procedures outlined in ASTM B828, *Standard Practice for Making Capillary Joints by Soldering of Copper and Copper Alloy Tube and Fittings* and the procedures found in the *Copper Tube Handbook* of the Copper Development Association.

Fluxes used for the soldering of copper and copper alloys should be those meeting the requirements of ASTM B813, *Standard Specification for Liquid and Paste Fluxes for Soldering Applications of Copper and Copper Alloy Tube.*

The tubing should be severed with a tube cutter and all burrs should be removed. The outside of the tubing and the inside fitting should be cleaned to bright metal with a medium-grade emery cloth or sandpaper. The flux must be evenly applied with a brush to the outside tubing and inside fitting. The fitting should be slipped on the tubing and twisted to distribute the flux. The joint should be soldered immediately, before moisture collects in the flux. (This could cause corrosion later on.) It should be heated evenly with the specified solder then filled with solder, and the excess should be wiped off.

Joining Plastic Pipe

Schedule 80 plastic pipe can be threaded. Schedule 40 must be solvent welded. The pipe and socket must be cleaned, burrs must be removed, and solvent should be applied to both. The pipe must be assembled quickly and twisted one-quarter turn to spread the solvent. The joint usually sets within two minutes.

Assembling Flanged Joints

The face of the flange should be cleaned with a solvent-soaked rag to remove any rust-preventive grease. Any dirt should be cleaned from the gasket. The pipe and the flanges should be aligned to eliminate any strain on the coupling. The gasket should be coated with graphite and oil or some other recommended lubricant, inserted, and then bolted. Thread lubricant should be applied to the bolts. The bolts should be evenly tightened with a wrench. The nuts should be hand tightened. When tightening the bolts, care should be exercised that they are diametrically opposed; adjacent bolts should never be tightened.

Making Up Threaded Pipe

Male and female threads should be cleaned with a wire brush. Pipe dope should be applied only to the male thread. (If dope is applied to female thread, it will enter the system). The pipe and coupling should be aligned and hand tightened and then finished by turning with a wrench. A few imperfect threads should be left exposed. Sections of the assembled piping should be blown out with compressed air before being placed in the system.

Thread Cutting

The pipe should be cut with a pipe cutter. It should be clamped in a vise and the pipe stock and die engaged with short jerks; when the cutter catches, it should then be pulled slowly with a steady movement using both hands. Enough cutting oil should be used during the cutting process to keep the die cool and the edges clean. The die should be backed off frequently to free the cutters, and the follower should be watched when reversing the dies against the jumping threads, cross-threading, or the stripping of threads. Leaky threaded joints are usually caused by faulty or improper lubricants.

Welding

Basic welding processes include electric arc, oxyacetylene, and gas shielded. Commercial welding fittings are available with ends designed for butt welding or for socket-joint welding. The type of joint used depends on the type of liquid, the pressure in the system, the pipe size and material, and the applicable codes. The butt joint is frequently used with a liner (backing ring). See Figures 2-18 and 2-19.

Electric arc welding Electric arc welding is used for standard, extra-heavy, or double extra-heavy commercial steel pipe. ASTM A-53 grades of low-carbon steel butt-welded pipe are the most weldable.

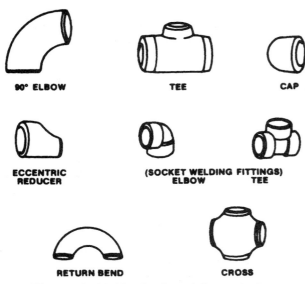

Figure 2-18 Typical Welding Fittings

Oxyacetylene welding In this welding process, the flame develops a temperature to 6300°F (3482.2°C), completely melting commercial metals to form a bond. The use of rod increases strength and adds extra metal to the seam. This process is used with many metals (iron, steel, stainless steel, cast iron, copper, brass, aluminum, bronze and other alloys) and can be used to join dissimilar metals. When cut on site, the pipe ends must be beveled for welding; this can be accomplished with an oxyacetylene torch.

Gas-shielded arcs This process keeps the atmosphere from the molten puddle and is good for nonferrous metals since flux is not required, producing an extremely clean joint. There are two types of gas-shielded arc: tungsten inert gas (TIG) and metallic inert gas (MIG). Gas-shielded arcs are used for aluminum, magnesium, low-alloy steel, carbon steel, stainless steel, copper nickel, titanium, and others.

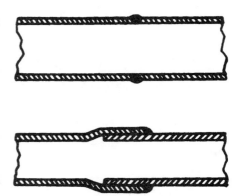

Figure 2-19 Types of Welded Joints

Joining Glass Pipe

The joints are either bead to bead or bead to plain end. The bead-to-bead coupling is used for joining factory-beaded or field-beaded end pipe and fittings. The bead-to-plain-end coupling is used to join a pipe section or fitting that has a beaded end to a pipe section that has been field cut to length and is not beaded.

Bending Pipe and Tubing

Pipe bending (cold or hot method) is usually done with a hydraulic pipe bender. The radius of the bend should be large enough to free the surface of cracks or buckles (see ANSI B31.1). Some bends are specifically designed to be creased or corrugated. Corrugated bends are more flexible than conventional types and may have smaller radii. Straight sections of pipe are sometimes corrugated to provide flexibility. Copper tube is usually bent with a spring tube bender, grooved wheel and bar, bending press, or machine. Sharp bends are usually made by filling the pipe with sand or other material to prevent flattening or collapsing. Bending pipe or tubing is easier and more economical than installing fittings. Bends reduce the number of joints (which could leak) and also minimize friction loss through the pipe.

Electrofusion Joining

Electrofusion is a heat fusion joining process wherein a heat source is an integral part of the fitting. Where electric current is applied, heat is produced, melting and joining its components. Fusion occurs when the joint cools below the melting temperature of the material. The applicable standard is ASTM F-1290-98 9, *Electrofusion Joining Polyolefin Pipe and Fittings.*

Both PP and PVDF are not generally suitable for threaded joints, these materials simply do not take a satisfactory thread. It is noted that thermal fusion is generally considered the best joining method.

ACCESSORIES AND JOINTS

Anchors

Anchors are installed to secure piping systems against expansion or contraction and to eliminate pipe variation. During the installation of anchors, damage to building wall or steel must be prevented. Common anchor materials are strap steel, cast iron, angles, steel plate, channels, and steel clamps. See Figure 2-20.

Dielectric Unions or Flanges

Dielectric unions or flanges are installed between ferrous and nonferrous piping to resist corrosion. Dielectric fittings prevent electric current from flowing from one part of the pipe to another. The spacer should be suitable for the system pressure and temperature. See Figure 2-21.

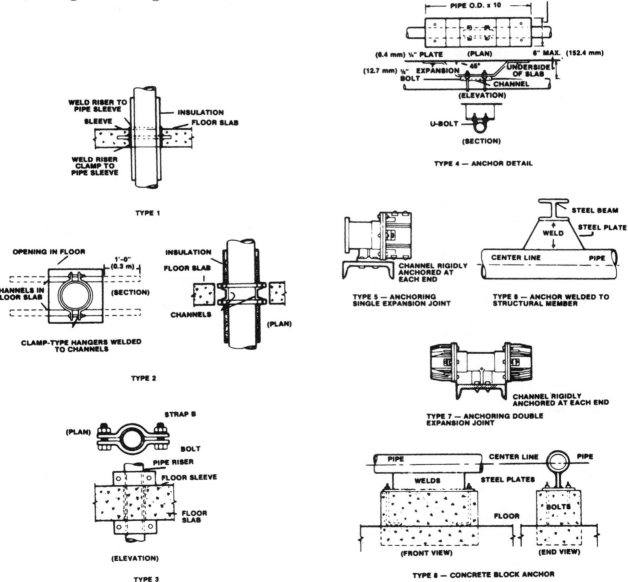

Figure 2-20 Anchors and Inserts

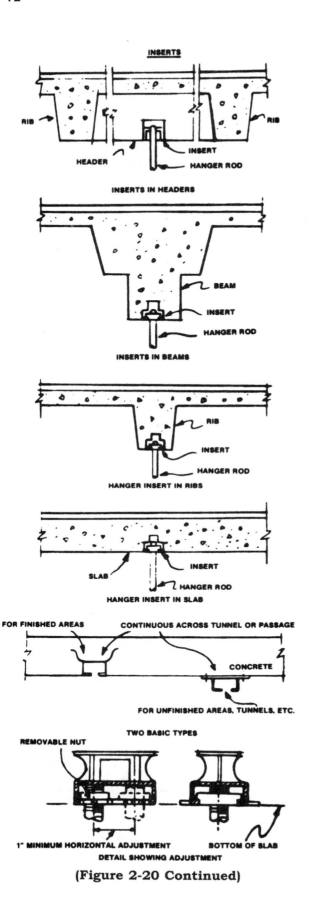

(Figure 2-20 Continued)

Expansion Joints and Guides

Expansion joints and guides are designed to permit free expansion and contraction and to prevent excessive bending at joints, hangers, and connections to the equipment caused by heat expansion or vibration. Expansion guides should be used where the direction of the expansion is critical. See Figure 2-22.

Ball Joints

Ball joints are used in hydronic systems, where pipe flexibility is desired, for positioning pipe, and where rotary or reciprocal movement is required. Ball joints are available with threaded, flanged, or welded ends of stainless steel, carbon steel, bronze, or malleable iron.

Flexible Couplings (Compression or Slip Type)

Flexible couplings do not require the same degree of piping alignment as flanges and threaded

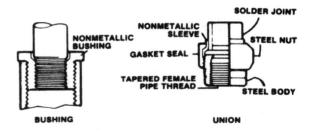

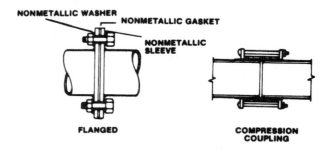

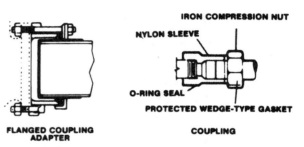

Figure 2-21 Dielectric Fittings

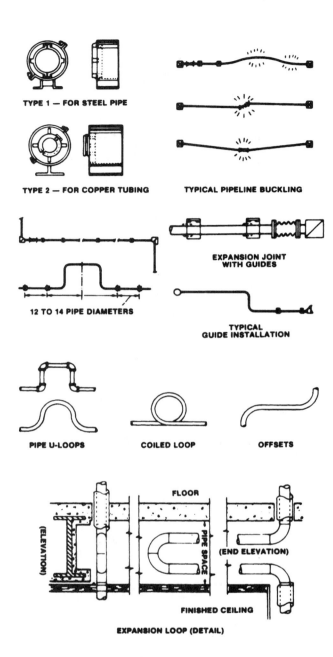

TYPE 1 — FOR STEEL PIPE

TYPE 2 — FOR COPPER TUBING

TYPICAL PIPELINE BUCKLING

12 TO 14 PIPE DIAMETERS

EXPANSION JOINT WITH GUIDES

TYPICAL GUIDE INSTALLATION

PIPE U-LOOPS

COILED LOOP

OFFSETS

FLOOR

(ELEVATION)

PIPE SPACE

(END ELEVATION)

FINISHED CEILING

EXPANSION LOOP (DETAIL)

Figure 2-22 Expansion Joints and Guides

couplings. They provide ¼ to ⅜ in. (6 to 9.5 mm) of axial movement because of the elasticity in the gaskets. These couplings should not be used as slip type expansion joints or as replacements for flexible expansion joints. See Figure 2-23.

Gaskets (Flanged Pipe)

Gaskets must withstand pressure, temperature, and attack from the fluid in the pipe. Gaskets normally should be as thin as possible. ANSI B 16.21 designates the dimensions for nonmetallic gaskets.

Mechanical Couplings

Mechanical couplings are self-centering, lock-in-place grooves or shouldered pipe and pipe fitting ends. The fittings provide some angular pipe deflection, contraction, and expansion. Mechanical couplings are often used instead of unions, welded flanges, screwed pipe connections, or soldered tubing connections. Mechanical couplings are available for a variety of piping materials, including steel and (galvanized steel), cast iron, copper tubing, and plastics. Bolting methods are standard bolts or vandal-resistant bolts are available. The gasketing material will vary, based on the fluid in the piping system. See Figure 2-24.

Hangers and Supports

Pipe should be securely supported with an ample safety factor. Horizontal suspended pipe should be hung using adjustable pipe hangers with bolted, hinged loops or turnbuckles. Chains, perforated strap irons, or flat steel strap hangers are not acceptable. Pipes 2 in. in diameter and smaller (supported from the side wall) should have an expansion hook plate. Pipes 2½ in. in diameter and larger (supported from the side wall) should have brackets and clevis hangers. Rollers should be provided wherever necessary. Trapeze hangers, holding several pipes, may be preferred over individual pipeline hangers. For individual hangers of pipes 2 in. in diameter and smaller, clevis type hangers should be used. Where hangers are attached to concrete slabs, slabs should have more concrete reinforcing rods at the point of support. The risers can be supported vertically using approved methods such as: (1) resting on the floor slab with an elbow support, (2) resting on the floor sleeve with a clamp, and (3) anchoring to the wall.

Consideration must also be given to seismic conditions in pipe hanging. The designer should consult with local, state, and all other governing agencies for specific requirements.

Pipe supports should be spaced according to the following:

- Less than ¾ in. pipe: On 5-ft (1.5-m) centers
- 1 and 1¼-in. pipe: On 6-ft (1.8-m) centers

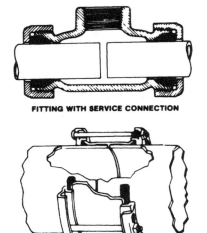

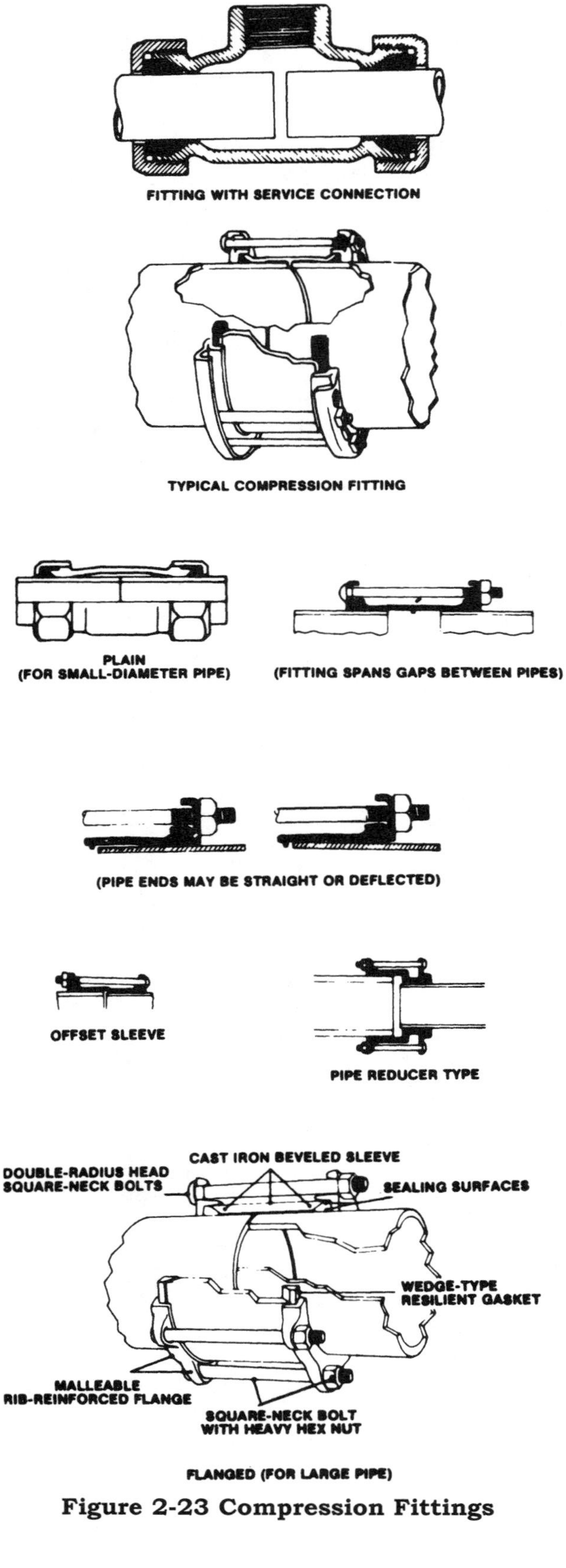

FITTING WITH SERVICE CONNECTION

TYPICAL COMPRESSION FITTING

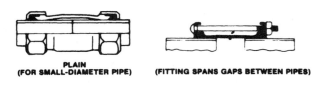

PLAIN
(FOR SMALL-DIAMETER PIPE)

(FITTING SPANS GAPS BETWEEN PIPES)

(PIPE ENDS MAY BE STRAIGHT OR DEFLECTED)

OFFSET SLEEVE

PIPE REDUCER TYPE

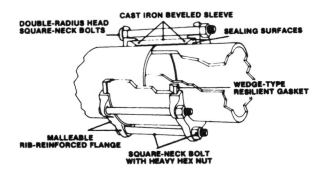

DOUBLE-RADIUS HEAD
SQUARE-NECK BOLTS

CAST IRON BEVELED SLEEVE

SEALING SURFACES

WEDGE-TYPE
RESILIENT GASKET

MALLEABLE
RIB-REINFORCED FLANGE

SQUARE-NECK BOLT
WITH HEAVY HEX NUT

FLANGED (FOR LARGE PIPE)

Figure 2-23 Compression Fittings

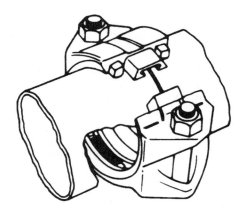

Figure 2-24 Mechanical Joint

- 1½ to 2½-in. pipe: On 10-ft (3.1-m) centers
- 3 and 4-in. pipe: On 12-ft (3.7-m) centers
- 6 in. and larger pipe: On 15-ft (4.6-m) centers

Pipes installed in finished trenches or tunnels should rest on a suitable sidewall or floor supports. See Figure 2-25.

Hanger and support installation for copper piping The hanger spacing and rod size requirements given are from MSS-SP-69. Designers should consult the local plumbing, mechanical, or building code for required hanger spacing requirements.

A. Install hangers for horizontal piping with the following maximum spacing and minimum rod sizes:

Nominal Tube Size (in.)	Copper Tube Max. Span (ft)	Min. Rod Diameter (in.)
Up to ¾	5	⅜
1	6	⅜
1 ¼	7	⅜
1 ½	8	⅜
2	8	⅜
2 ½	9	½
3	10	½
3 ½	11	½
4	12	½
5	13	½
6	14	⅝
8	16	¾
10	18	¾
12	19	¾

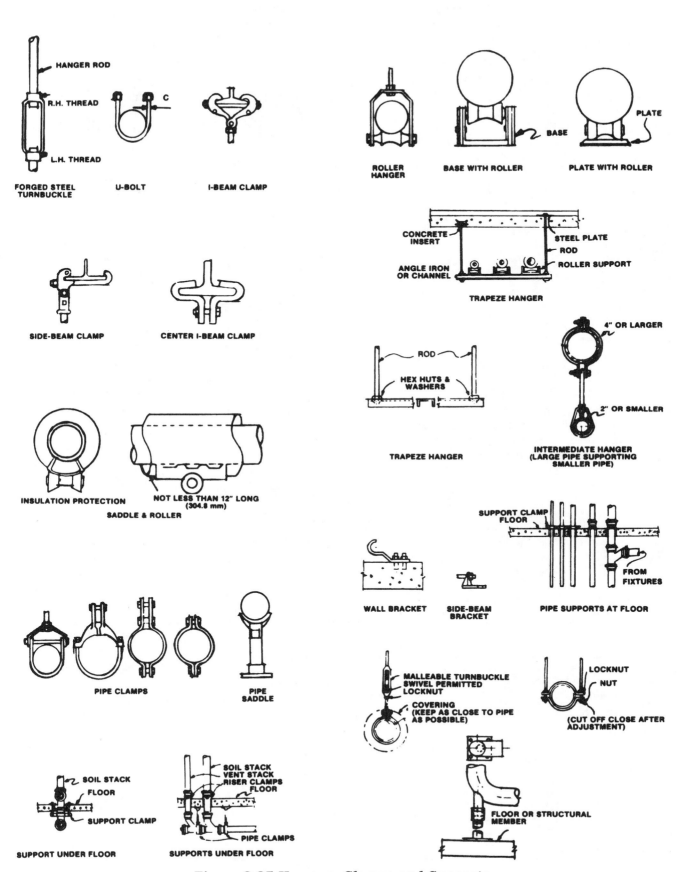

Figure 2-25 Hangers, Clamps and Supports

B. Support vertical copper tube, copper pipe, or brass pipe at each floor.

C. In areas where excessive moisture is anticipated, either the piping or the support shall be wrapped with an approved tape or otherwise isolated to prevent contact between dissimilar metals and inhibit galvanic corrosion of the supporting member.

Pipe Unions (Flanged Connections)

Pipe unions are installed at several locations to facilitate dismantling. They are usually installed close to the control valves, regulators, water heaters, meters, check valves, pumps, compressors, and boilers so that equipment can be readily disconnected for repair or replacement. See Figure 2-26 and Table 2-16.

Pipe Sleeves

For pipes passing through walls, sleeves should extend completely through the construction, flush with each surface. The sleeves should be caulked with graphite packing and a suitable plastic waterproof caulking compound. Pipe sleeves in rated walls are to be installed to suit the specific manufacturer's hourly fire rating. Packing and sealing compounds are to be the required thickness to meet the specific hourly ratings assembly. Sleeves in bearing walls should be of steel pipe, cast-iron pipe, or terra-cotta pipe. Sleeves in other masonry structures may be of sheet metal, fiber, or other suitable material. Sleeves for 4-in. pipe and smaller should be at least two pipe sizes larger than the pipe passing

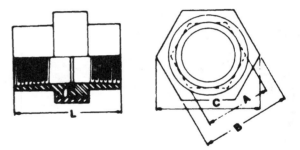

Figure 2-26 Pipe Union

through. For larger pipes, sleeves should be at least one pipe size larger than the enclosed pipe. The ID of pipe sleeves should be at least ½ in. (12.7 mm) larger than the outside diameter (OD) of the pipe or covering. See Figure 2-27.

Service Connections (Water Piping)

Hand drilled, self-tapping saddle, or cut-in sleeves should be used. Two types of cut-in sleeves are available: for pressures to 50 psi (344.7 kPa) and for pressures to 250 psi (1727.7 kPa). Tapping valves are for working pressures of 175 psi (1206.6 kPa) for 2 to 12-in. (50.8 to 304.8-mm) pipe and 150 psi (1034.2 kPa) for 16-in. pipe.

PIPING EXPANSION AND CONTRACTION

Piping, subject to changes in temperature, expands (increases in length) and contracts (decreases in length), and each material has its own characteristics. Piping expands as the temperature increases and contracts as the

Table 2-16 Pipe Union Dimensions

Pipe Size (in.)	Standard A (250 lb)(113.5 kg) (in.)	(mm)	B (250 lb)(113.5 kg) (in.)	(mm)	C (250 lb)(113.5 kg) (in.)	(mm)	L (250 lb)(113.5 kg) (in.)	(mm)	Normal Thread Engagement (in.)	(mm)
⅛	0.505	12.8	0.935	23.8	1.080	27.4	1.484	37.7	¼	6.4
¼	0.638	16.2	1.113	28.3	1.285	32.6	1.641	41.7	⅜	9.5
⅜	0.787	20.0	1.264	32.1	1.460	37.1	1.766	44.9	⅜	9.5
½	0.950	24.1	1.456	37.0	1.681	42.7	2.000	50.8	½	12.7
¾	1.173	29.8	1.718	43.6	1.985	50.4	2.141	54.4	⁹⁄₁₆	14.3
1	1.440	36.6	2.078	52.8	2.400	61.0	2.500	63.5	¹¹⁄₁₆	17.5
1¼	1.811	46.0	2.578	65.5	2.978	75.6	2.703	68.7	¹¹⁄₁₆	17.5
1½	2.049	52.1	2.890	73.4	3.338	84.8	2.875	73.0	¹¹⁄₁₆	17.5
2	2.563	65.1	3.484	88.5	4.025	102.2	3.234	82.1	¾	19.1
2½	3.109	79.0	4.156	105.6	4.810	122.2	3.578	90.9	¹⁵⁄₁₆	23.8
3	3.781	96.0	4.969	126.2	5.740	145.8	3.938	100.0	1	25.4

temperature decreases. The coefficient of expansion (CE) of a material is the material's characteristic unit increase in length per 1°F (0.56°C) temperature increase. Values for CE of various materials are given in Marks and Baumeister's *Standard Handbook for Mechanical Engineers* and manufacturer's literature.

Provisions must be made for the expansion and contraction of piping. If the piping is restrained, it will be subject to compressive (as the temperature increases) and tensile (as the temperature decreases) stresses. The piping usually withstands the stresses; however, failures may occur at the joints and fittings.

Two common methods to absorb piping expansion and contraction are the use of expansion joints, expansion loops, and offsets.

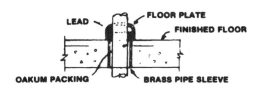

SLEEVE THROUGH FLOOR

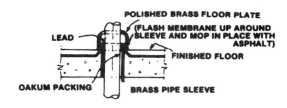

HIGH PIPE SLEEVE THROUGH MEMBRANED FLOOR

TYPICAL SLEEVE THROUGH FLOOR SLAB WITH MEMBRANE

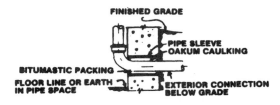

PIPE THROUGH EXTERIOR WALL

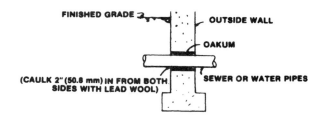

SLEEVE THROUGH FOUNDATION WALLS

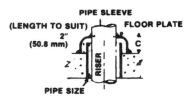

CONCRETE FLOOR SLEEVE

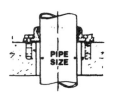

WATER-TIGHT RISER SLEEVE

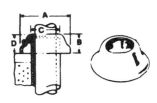

TYPICAL CEILING & FLOOR PLATE FOR SLEEVE

Figure 2-27 Sleeves

REFERENCES

1. American Iron and Steel Institute. *Handbook of steel pipe*. Washington, DC.

2. Cast Iron Soil Pipe Institute (CISPI). *Cast iron soil pipe and fittings handbook*. Vol. 2. McLean, VA.

3. Copper Development Association. *Copper tube handbook*. New York.

4. King, Reno C. *Piping handbook*. New York: McGraw-Hill.

5. Lead Industries Association. *Standard handbook*. New York.

6. Marks, L. S., and T. Baumeister. *Standard handbook for mechanical engineers*. New York: McGraw-Hill.

3

Valves

Valves serve the purpose of controlling the fluids in building service piping. They come in many shapes, sizes, design types, and materials to accommodate different fluids, piping, pressure ranges, and types of service. Proper selection is important to ensure the most efficient, cost-effective, and long-lasting systems. No single valve is best for all services. This chapter is limited to manually operated valves that start, stop, and regulate flow, and prevent its reversal.

FUNCTIONS

Valves are designed to perform four principal functions:

1. Starting and stopping flow
2. Regulating (throttling) flow
3. Preventing the reversal of flow
4. Regulating or relieving the flow pressure.

SERVICE CONSIDERATIONS

1. Pressure
2. Temperature
3. Type of fluid
   A. Liquid
   B. Gas, i.e., steam or air
   C. Dirty or abrasive (erosive)
   D. Corrosive

4. Flow
   A. On-off
   B. Throttling
   C. Need to prevent flow reversal
   D. Concern for pressure drop
   E. Velocity
5. Operating conditions
   A. Frequency of operation
   B. Accessibility
   C. Overall space/size available
   D. Manual or automated control
   E. Need for bubble-tight shut-off
   F. Concerns about body joint leaks
   G. Fire safe design
   H. Speed of closure.

APPROVALS

1. Manufacturers Standardization Society (MSS)
2. Fire protection: UL and Factory Mutual (FM)
3. State and local codes
4. American Petroleum Industries (API).

TYPES OF VALVE

Gate Valve

With starting and stopping flow its prime function, the gate valve is intended to operate either fully open

Table 3-1 Representative Equivalent Length, in Pipe Diameters, of Various Valves and Fittings

Description of Product				Equivalent Length in Pipe Diameters, L/D
Globe Valves	Conventional	With no obstruction in flat, bevel, or plug type seat	Fully open	340
		With wing or pin-guided disc	Fully open	450
	Y-pattern	(No obstruction in flat, bevel, or plug type seat)		
		With stem 60° from run of pipeline	Fully open	175
		With stem 45° from run of pipeline	Fully open	145
Angle Valves	Conventional	With no obstruction in flat, bevel, or plug type seat	Fully open	145
		With wing or pin-guided disc	Fully open	200
Gate Valves	Conventional wedge disc, double disc, or plug disc		Fully open	13
			Three-quarters open	35
			One-half open	160
			One-quarter open	900
	Pulp stock		Fully open	17
			Three-quarters open	50
			One-half open	260
			One-quarter open	1200
	Conduit pipeline		Fully open	3[a]
Check Valves	Conventional swing	0.5 (3.5)[b] . . .Fully open		135
	Clearway swing	0.5 (3.5)[b] . . .Fully open		50
	Globe lift or stop	2.0 (13.8)[b] . . . Fully open		Same as globe
	Angle lift or stop	2.0 (13.8)[b] . . . Fully open		Same as angle
	In-line ball	2.5 (17.3) vertical and 0.25 (1.7) horizontal[b] . . . Fully open		150
Foot Valves with Strainer		With poppet lift type disc	0.3 (2.1)[b] . . . Fully open	420
		With leather-hinged disc	0.4 (2.8)[b] . . . Fully open	75
Butterfly Valves (6 in. and larger) (152.4 mm and larger)			Fully open	20
Cocks	Straight-through	Rectangular plug port area equal to 100% of pipe area	Fully open	18
	Three-way	Rectangular plug port area equal to 80% of pipe area (fully open)	Flow straight through	44
			Flow through branch	140

Source: Extracted from a table published by Crane Co.

a Exact equivalent length is equal to the length between flange faces or welding ends.

b Minimum calculated pressure drop [psi) (kPa)] across valve to provide sufficient flow to lift disc fully.

Problem

Solution

Based on the use of Schedule 40 pipe, find the equivalent length in pipe diameters (L/D), resistance factor (K) and equivalent length in feet (m) of pipe (L) for 1, 5 and 12-inch, fully opened, conventional type gate valves.

To Find	Procedure (note dashed lines in charts)	1-in.	5-in.	12-in.
L/D	See Table 3-1. Read L/D value for conventional type gate valve, fully opened.	13.00	13.00	13.00
K	See Figure 3-1. From Schedule 40 pipe sizes (1, 5, 12 in.) draw lines upward from L/D value (13). Draw horizontal line. Intersecting points are K values.	0.30	0.20	0.17
L	Connect L/D value of 13 to Schedule 40 pipe sizes (1, 5, 12 in.) on d scale. At intersecting points on center scale read L values.	1.10 (0.34 m)	5.50 (1.68 m)	13.00 (3.96 m)

or fully closed. When fully open, it has the least resistance to flow of all the valve types, as illustrated in Table 3-1 and Figure 3-1.

From an examination of Figure 3-2, it becomes readily apparent how the gate valve got its name. A gate-like disc, actuated by a stem screw and hand wheel, moves up and down at right angles to the path of flow and seats against two faces to shut off flow. As the disc of the gate valve presents a flat surface to the oncoming flow, this valve is not suited for regulating or throttling flow. Flow through a partially open gate valve creates vibration and chattering and subjects the disc and seat to inordinate wear.

There is a wide variety of seats and discs to suit the conditions under which the valve is to operate. For relatively low pressures and temperatures and for ordinary fluids, seating materials are not a particularly difficult problem. Bronze and iron valves usually have bronze or bronze-faced seating surfaces; iron valves may be all iron. Nonmetallic "composition" discs are available for tight seating or hard-to-hold fluids, such as air and gasoline.

Gate discs can be classified as solid-wedge discs, double discs or split-wedge discs. In the solid-wedge design, a single tapered disc, thin at the bottom and thicker at the top, is forced into a similarly shaped seat.

In the double and split-wedge disc designs, two discs are employed back to back, with a spreading device between them. As the valve wheel is turned, the gate drops into its seat (as with any other gate valve), but on the final turns of the wheel, the spreader forces the discs outward against the seats, effecting tighter closure.

Bypass valves should be provided where the differential pressure exceeds 200 psi (1378 kPa) on valves sized 4 to 6 in. (101.6 to 152.4 mm),

and 100 psi (689 kPa) on valves 8 in. (203.2 mm) or larger. Bypass valves should be ½ in. (12.7 mm) for 4-in. (101.6-mm) valves, and ¾ in. (19.1 mm) for 5-in. (127-mm) valves or larger.

Globe Valve

The globe valve (which is named for the shape of its body) is much more resistant to flow than the gate valve, as can be seen by examining the path of flow through it (Figure 3-3) and the data in Table 3-1 and Figure 3-1. Its main advantages over the gate valve are its use as a throttling valve to regulate flow and its ease of repair.

Because all contact between seat and disc ends when flow begins, the effects of wire drawing (seat erosion) are minimized. The valve can operate just barely open or fully open with little change in wear. Also, because the disc of the globe valve travels a relatively short distance between fully open and fully closed, with fewer turns of the wheel required, an operator can gauge the rate of flow by the number of turns of the wheel.

As with the gate valve, there are a number of disc and seat arrangements. These are classified as conventional disc, plug type, and composition disc.

The conventional disc is relatively flat, with beveled edges. On closure it is pushed down into a beveled, circular seat.

Plug type discs differ only in that they are far more tapered, thereby increasing the contact surface between disc and seat. This characteristic has the effect of increasing their resistance to the cutting effects of dirt, scale, and other foreign matter.

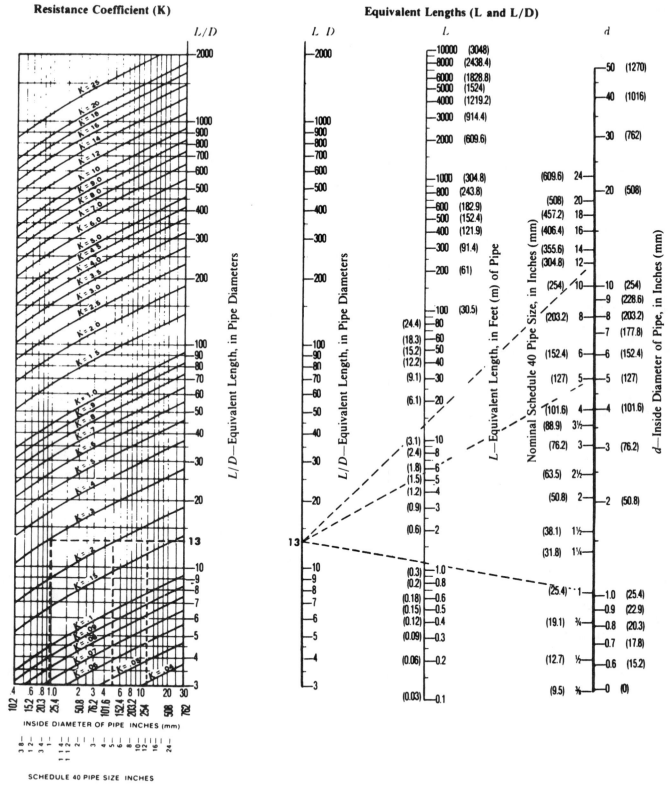

Figure 3-1 Valve Data for Use with Table 3-1

Source: Extracted from a table published by Crane Co.

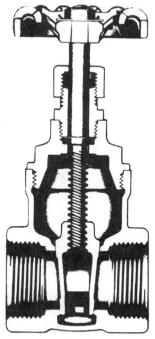

Figure 3-2 Gate Valve

The composition disc differs from the others in that it does not fit into the seat opening but over it, much as a bottle cap fits over the bottle opening. This seat adapts the valve to many services, including use with hard-to-hold substances such as compressed air, and makes it easy to repair.

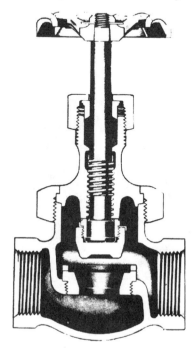

Figure 3-3 Globe Valve

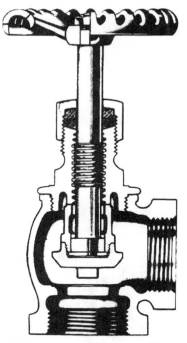

Figure 3-4 Angle Valve

Angle Valve

Very much akin to the globe valve, the angle valve (Figure 3-4) can cut down on piping installation time, labor, and materials by serving as both valve and 90° elbow. It is less resistant to flow than the globe valve, as flow must change direction twice instead of three times. It is also available with conventional, plug type, or composition discs.

Ball Valve

The ball valve derives its name from the drilled ball that swivels on its vertical axis and is operated by a handle, as shown in Figure 3-5. Its advantages are its straight-through flow, minimum turbulence, low torque, tight closure, and compactness. Also, a quarter turn of the handle

Figure 3-5 Ball Valve

makes it a quick-closing or -opening valve. Reliability, ease of maintenance, and durability have made the ball valve popular in industrial, chemical, and gas transmission applications.

Butterfly Valve

Figure 3-6 illustrates a butterfly valve, the valve most commonly used in place of a gate valve in cases where absolute, bubble-free shut-off is required. It is manufactured in nominal diameters from 1 to 72 in. (25.4 to 1828.8 mm).

In addition to its tight closing, one of the valve's advantages is that it can be placed into a very small

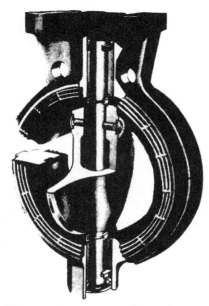

Figure 3-6 Butterfly Valve

space between pipe flanges. It is available with several types of operator, motorized and manual, and a variety of component material combinations.

Screwed-lug type valves should be provided so that equipment may be removed without draining down the system.

Check Valve

Swing checks and lift checks are the most common forms of check valve. Both are designed to prevent reversal of flow in a pipe. The swing check, Figure 3-7, permits straight-through flow when open and is, therefore, less resistant to flow than the lift check.

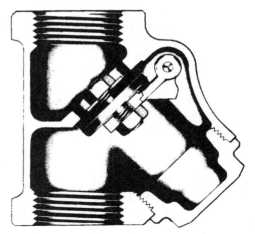

Figure 3-7 Swing Check

Note: A word of caution regarding the swing check: There have been instances when a swing check stayed open a few seconds after the reversal of flow began, allowing the velocity of backflow to rise to such a point that, when closure finally did occur, it was instantaneous and the resulting shock to the valve and system caused serious damage. Good insurance against such a possibility is a lever and weight or a spring to ensure immediate closure upon reversal of flow.

The lift check, Figure 3-8, is primarily for use with gases or compressed air or in fluid systems where pressure drop is not critical.

Figure 3-8 Lift Check

VALVE MATERIALS

A single valve may be constructed of several materials. It may have a bronze body, a monel seat, and an aluminum wheel. Material specifications depend on the operating conditions.

Brass and Bronze

Brass usually consists of 85% copper, 5% lead, 5% tin, and 5% zinc. Bronze has a higher copper content, ranging from 86 to 90%, with the remaining percentage divided among lead, tin, and zinc.

Of particular importance is the zinc content. Industry maximum is set at 15%, but certain military and government specifications allow no more than 6%.

Under certain circumstances, a phenomenon known as "dezincification" will occur in valves or pipes containing zinc. The action is a result of electrolysis; in effect, the zinc is actually drawn out and removed from the brass or bronze, leaving a porous, brittle, and weakened material. The higher the zinc content, the greater the susceptibility to dezincification. To slow or prevent the process, tin, phosphorus antimony, and other inhibitors are added. Brass valves should not be used for operating temperatures above 450°F (232.2°C). The maximum for bronze in 550°F (287.8°C).

Iron

Iron used in valves usually conforms to ASTM Standard A26. Although iron-bodied valves are manufactured in sizes as small as ¼-in. (6.4-mm) nominal diameter, they are most commonly stocked in sizes of 2 in. (50.8 mm) and above. In these larger sizes, they are considerably less expensive than bronze.

The higher weight of iron valves, as compared to bronze valves, should be considered when figuring hanger spacing and loads. A typical 2-in. (50.8-mm) screwed, bronze, globe valve rated at 125 psi (861.3 kPa) weighs about 13 lb (5.9 kg). The same valve in iron weighs 15 lb (6.8 kg) and, if specified with a yoke bonnet, about 22 lb (10 kg).

Malleable Iron

Malleable iron valves are stronger, stiffer, and tougher than iron-bodied valves and hold tighter pressures. Toughness is most valuable for piping subjected to stresses and shocks.

Stainless Steel

For highly corrosive fluids, stainless steel valves provide the maximum corrosion resistance, high strength, and good wearing properties. Seating surfaces, stems, and discs of stainless steel are suitable where foreign materials in the fluids handled could have adverse effects.

VALVE RATINGS

Most valve manufacturers rate their products in terms of saturated steam pressure; or pressure of nonshock cold water, oil, or gas (WOG); or both. These ratings usually appear on the body of the valve. For instance, a valve with the markings "125" with "200 WOG" will operate safely at 125 psi (861.3 kPa) of saturated steam or 200 psi (1378 kPa) cold water, oil, or gas.

The engineer should be familiar with the markings on the valves specified and should keep them in mind during construction inspection. A ruptured valve can do much damage.

VALVE COMPONENTS

Stems

Stem designs fall into four basic categories: rising stem with outside screw, rising stem with inside screw, nonrising stem with inside screw, and sliding stem.

Rising stem with outside screw This design is ideal where the valve is infrequently used and the possibility of sticking would constitute a hazard, such as in a fire-protection system. In this arrangement, the screws are not subject to corrosion or elements in the line fluid that might cause damage because they are outside the valve body. Also, being outside, they can easily be lubricated.

As with any other rising stem valve, sufficient clearance must be allowed to enable a full opening.

Rising stem with inside screw This design is the simplest and most common stem design for gate, globe, and angle valves. The position of the hand wheel indicates the position of the disc, opened or closed.

Nonrising stem These are ideal where headroom is limited. They are generally limited to use with gate valves. In this type, the screw does not raise the stem but rather raises and lowers the disc. As the stem only rotates and does not rise, wear on packings is slightly lessened.

Sliding stem These are applied where quick opening and closing are required. A lever replaces the hand wheel, and stem threads are eliminated.

Bonnets

In choosing valves, the service characteristics of the bonnet joint should not be overlooked. Bonnets and bonnet joints must provide a leakproof closure for the body. There are many modifications, but the three most common types are screwed-in bonnet, screwed union-ring bonnet, and bolted bonnet.

Screwed-in bonnet This is the simplest and least expensive construction, frequently used on bronze gate, globe, and angle valves and recommended where frequent dismantling is not needed. When properly designed with running threads and carefully assembled, the screwed-in bonnet makes a durable, pressure-tight seal that is suited for many services.

Screwed union-ring bonnet This construction is convenient where valves need frequent inspection or cleaning—also for quick renewal or changeover of the disc in composition disc valves. A separate union ring applies a direct load on the bonnet to hold the pressure-tight joint with the body. The turning motion used to tighten the ring is split between the shoulders of the ring and bonnet. Hence, the point of seal contact between the bonnet and the body is less subject to wear from frequent opening of the joint.

Contact faces are less likely to be damaged in handling. The union ring gives the body added strength and rigidity against internal pressure and distortion.

While ideal on smaller valves, the screwed, union-ring bonnet is impractical on large sizes.

Bolted bonnet joint A practical and commonly used joint for larger size valves or for higher-pressure applications, the bolted bonnet joint has multiple boltings with smaller diameter bolts that permit equalized sealing pressure without the excessive torque needed to make large threaded joints. Only small wrenches are needed.

END CONNECTIONS

Valves are available with screwed, welded, brazed, soldered, flared, flanged, and hub ends.

Screwed End

This is by far the most widely used type of end connection. It is found in brass, iron, steel, and alloy piping materials. It is suited for all pressures but is usually confined to smaller pipe sizes. The larger the pipe size, the more difficult it is to make up the screwed joint.

Welded End

This type of end is available only in steel valves and fittings and is mainly for higher-pressure and -temperature services. It is recommended for lines not requiring frequent dismantling. There are two types of welded end materials: butt end socket welding. Butt-welding valves and fittings come in all sizes; socket-welding ends are usually limited to smaller sizes.

Brazed End

This is available on brass materials. The ends of such materials are specially designed for the use of brazing alloys to make the joint. When the equipment and brazing material are heated with a welding torch to the temperature required by the alloy, a tight seal is formed between the pipe and valve or fitting. While made in a manner similar to a solder joint, a brazed joint can withstand higher temperatures due to the brazing materials used.

Soldered Joint

This is used with copper tubing for plumbing and heating lines and for many low-pressure industrial services. The joint is soldered by applying heat. Because of close clearance between the tubing and the socket of the fitting or valve, the solder flows into the joint by capillary action. The use of soldered joints under high temperatures is limited because of the low melting point of the solder. Silver solder or silfos are used for higher pressures and temperatures.

Flared End

This is commonly used on valves and fittings for metal and plastic tubing up to 2 in. (50.8 mm) diameter. The end of the tubing is skirted or flared and a ring nut is used to make a union type joint.

Flanged End

This is generally used when screwed ends become impractical because of cost, size, strength of joint, etc. Flanged ends are generally used for larger-diameter lines due to ease of assembly and dismantling. Flanged facings are available in various designs depending on service requirements. One important rule is to match facings. When bolting iron valves to forged steel flanges, the facing should be of the flat face design on both surfaces.

Hub End

This is generally limited to valves for water-supply and sewage piping. The joint is assembled on the socket principle, with the pipe inserted in the hub end of the valve or fitting then caulked with oakum and sealed with molten lead.

WATER-PRESSURE REGULATORS

A pressure regulator is an automatic valve controlled by an inner valve connected to a diaphragm or piston, or both. The diaphragm, held in the extreme travel, or open, position by a preloaded spring, is positioned in the downstream portion of the valve and closes the valve when the desired pressure has been reached.

The effectiveness of the diaphragm and the amount of preloading must be related to allow the diaphragm to move the inner valve to the extreme opposite travel, or closed, position immediately after the pressure on the diaphragm passes the desired operating pressure.

To change the operating pressure, tension on the diaphragm is increased or decreased by turning the adjusting screw.

Normally, a regulator does not go from closed to fully open or from open to fully closed immediately but moves between these extreme positions in response to system requirements. The regulator adjusts to a fully open position instantaneously only if maximum system demand is imposed quickly, which is not a common occurrence, unless the regulator is undersized. The degree of valve opening, therefore, depends entirely on the regulator's ability to sense and respond to pressure changes.

A reducing pressure change that causes a valve to open is known as a "reduced pressure fall-off," or "droop," and is an inherent characteristic of all self-operated or pilot-operated regulators. Technically, fall-off is expressed as the deviation in pressure from the set value that occurs when a regulator strokes from the minimum flow position to a desired flow position. The amount of fall-off necessary to open a valve to its rated capacity varies with different types of valve.

It is important to realize that the installation of a regulator sets up a closed system, and, therefore, it is necessary to install a relief valve to eliminate excessive pressure caused by the thermal expansion of water in the hot water tank.

Every manufacturer makes regulators with an integral bypass to eliminate relief valve dripping caused by thermal expansion. During normal operation, the bypass is held closed by high initial pressure. However, when thermal expansion pressure becomes equal to initial pressure, the bypass opens, passing the expanded water back into the supply line. The effectiveness of this feature is limited to systems where initial pressure is less than the pressure setting of the relief valve.

The integral bypass is not a replacement for the relief valve; it is used only to eliminate excessive drip from the relief valve.

Regulator Selection and Sizing

Selection of the correct type of regulator depends entirely on the accuracy of regulation required. The valve plug in oversized valves tends to remain close to the seat, causing rapid wire drawing and excessive wear.

Unfortunately, there is no set standard for rating a pressure-regulating valve, or for capacity sizing it to the system. The many methods proposed for selecting the proper valve are often a cause of confusion to the engineer.

The capacity rating of a pressure-regulating valve is usually expressed in terms of some single value. This value, to be useful, must specify all the conditions under which the rating was established, otherwise it is impossible to adapt it to different system conditions.

Manufacturers attempt to recognize the inherent characteristics of their own design and to stipulate those factors that, in their opinion, must be considered in sizing the valve to the system. Some firms stress the importance of the difference between initial and reduced pressure-differential pressure. Set pressure and allowable reduced pressure fall-off are very important factors in sizing a valve. A fall-off of 15 to 17 psi (103.4 to 117.1 kPa) is considered reasonable for the average residential installation and, in well-designed valves, will produce a good rating.

Another procedure for establishing valve performance is on the basis of rate of flow, with a reduced pressure fall-off of 15 to 17 psi (103.4 to 117.1 kPa) below reduced lockup or no-flow pressure. For general use, this approach provides an adequate means of valve selection. However, it is not specific enough to enable the selection of the valve best suited to specific conditions.

Other manufacturers rate their valves on the basis of a stipulated flow rate at a specific pressure differential, with the valve open to the atmosphere, without regard to change in pressure drop when the system demand is zero. This method does not provide ample information for proper judgment of valve behavior and capability, and could result in the selection of a valve that would, under no-demand conditions, permit a reduction in pressure great enough to damage equipment in the system.

The maximum pressure permitted on a system under no-flow conditions is a most important factor, for both physical and economic reasons, and should be stipulated in the specification.

The rule-of-thumb method frequently employed is a size-to-size selection, that is, using a valve having the same connection sizes as the pipeline in which it is to be installed. This is a gamble, inasmuch as the actual capacities of many valves are inadequate to satisfy the service load specified for a pipeline of corresponding size. Consequently, the system may be starved and

the equipment operate in a most inconsistent manner.

The only sound valve selection procedure to follow is to capacity size a valve on the basis of known performance data related to system requirements.

Common Regulating Valves

Direct-acting, diaphragm-actuated valve This valve is simple in construction and operation, requiring minimum attention after installation. The spring-loaded type pressure regulator does not regulate the delivery pressure with extreme accuracy.

Pilot-operated valve The pilot-controlled valve operates efficiently because the pilot magnifies the control valve travel for a given change in control pressure.

The pilot type regulator consists of a small, direct-acting, spring-loaded valve and a main valve. The pilot valve opens just enough to supply the necessary pressure for operating the main valve. Extreme accuracy is effected as there is practically a constant load on the adjusting spring and variations in initial pressure have little effect.

Direct-acting, balanced-piston valve This valve is a combination piston and diaphragm and requires little attention after installation. With the dependability of the diaphragm and the simplicity of direct acting, this valve is only slightly affected by variations in initial pressure.

Common Types of Regulator Installation

Single regulator in supply line This type of installation is most common in domestic service and is self-explanatory.

Two regulators in series in supply line This type of installation gives extra protection when the main pressure is so excessive that it must be reduced to two stages to prevent a high-velocity noise in the system.

Multiple regulators used as a battery in supply line In many instances, a battery installation is preferable to the use of a single valve, as it provides closer regulation over a wide demand variation.

This type of installation consists of a group of parallel regulators, all receiving water from a common manifold. After flowing through the battery of valves, water enters a common manifold of sufficient size to service the system at the reduced pressure. The battery installation is advantageous because it allows maintenance work to be performed without the necessity of turning off the entire system. It also gives better performance where demands vary from one extreme to the other.

For example, at a school with a 3-in. (76.2-mm) service, demand on drinking fountains during classes may be approximately 6 to 7 gpm (22.7 to 26.5 L). However, between classes, when all services are in use, the demand may be at a maximum. With a single 3-in. (76.2-mm) regulator in the system, when the faucet is turned on, the regulator must open to allow a small draw. Each time this is done, it cuts down on the service life of the large regulator.

In comparison, with a battery installation of two or three regulators set at a graduated pressure, with the smallest valve set 2 to 3 psi (13.8 to 20.7 kPa) higher than the larger ones, the system is more efficient. For a small demand, only the smallest valve will open. As the demand increases, the larger valves will also open, providing the system with the capacity of all valves in the battery.

ABBREVIATIONS

AGA American Gas Association

AISI American Iron and Steel Institute

ANSI American National Standards Institute

API American Petroleum Institute

ASME American Society of Mechanical Engineers

ASTM American Standard for Testing and Material

AWWA American Water Works Association

BUNA-N Butadiene and acrylonitrile (nitrile rubber)

CSA Canadian Standards Association (*also* CSA International) (approval agency for AGA)

CWP Cold working pressure

EPDM Ethylene-propylene diene monomer

IBBM Iron body, bronze mounted (trim)

IS Inside screw

MSS Manufacturers Standardization Society of the Valve and Fittings Industry

NBR Acrylonitrile-butadiene rubber

NFPA National Fire Protection Association

NRS Nonrising stem

OS&Y Outside screw and yoke

PSI Pounds per square inch

PTFE Polytetrafluoroethylene plastic

RS Rising stem

SWP Steam working pressure

TFE Tetrafluoroethylene plastic

WCB Wrought carbon, grade B

WOG Water, oil, gas (cold working pressure)

WWP Water working pressure

GLOSSARY

Ball A valve consisting of a single drilled ball that is operated by a handle attached to the vertical axis of the ball, which permits fluid flow in a straight-through direction. The ball within the valve body may be rotated fully opened or fully closed by one quarter turn of the handle.

Body That part of the valve that attaches to the pipeline or equipment—with screwed ends, flanged ends, or soldered/welded joint ends—and encloses the working parts of the valve.

Bonnet The part of the valve housing through which the stem extends. It provides support and protection to the stem and houses the stem packing. It may be screwed or bolted to the body.

Butterfly A type of valve consisting of a single disc that is operated by a handle attached to the disc, which permits fluid flow in a straight-through direction. The valve is bidirectional. The disc within the valve body may be rotated fully open or fully closed by one quarter turn of the handle.

Cap The top part of the housing of a check valve (equivalent to the bonnet of a gate or globe valve), which may be either screwed or bolted onto the main body.

Check valve An automatic, self-closing valve that permits flow in only one direction. It automatically closes by gravity when liquid ceases to flow in that direction.

Clapper A common term that is used to describe the disc of a swing type, check valve.

Disc The disc-shaped device that is attached to the bottom of the stem and that is brought into contact with or lifted off the seating surfaces to close or open a globe valve or butterfly valve.

Flanged bonnet A type of bonnet so constructed that it attaches to the body by means of a flanged, bolted connection. The whole bonnet assembly, including the hand wheel, stem, and disc, may be quickly removed by unscrewing the nuts from the bonnet stud bolts.

Gate valve A valve that is used to open or close off the flow of fluid through a pipe. It is so named because of the wedge (gate) that is either raised out of or lowered into a double-seated sluice to permit full flow or completely shut off flow. The passageway through a gate valve is straight through, uninterrupted, and is the full size of the pipeline into which the valve is installed.

Gland bushing A metal bushing installed between the packing nut and the packing to transmit the force exerted by the packing nut against the packing.

Globe valve A valve that is used for throttling or regulating the flow through a pipe. It is so named because of the globular shape of the body. The disc is raised off a horizontal seating surface to permit flow or lowered against the horizontal seating surface to shut off flow. The disc may be lifted completely to permit full flow or lifted only slightly to throttle or regulate flow. The flow through a globe valve has to make two 90° turns.

Hand wheel The wheel-shaped turning device by which the stem is rotated, thus lifting or lowering the disc or wedge.

Hinge pin The valve part that the disc or clapper of a check valve swings.

Outside screw and yoke A type of bonnet so constructed that the operating threads of the stem are outside the valve housing, where they may be easily lubricated and do not come into contact with the fluid flowing through the valve.

Packing A general term describing any yielding material used to affect a tight joint. Valve packing is generally "jam packing"; it is pushed into a stuffing box and adjusted from time to time by tightening down a packing gland or packing nut.

Packing gland A device that holds and compresses the packing and provides for additional compression by manual adjustment of the gland as wear of the packing occurs. A packing gland may be screwed or bolted in place.

Packing nut A nut that is screwed into place and presses down upon a gland bushing, which transmits the force exerted by the packing nut to the packing. It serves the same purpose as the packing gland.

Rising stem A threaded component that is unscrewed or screwed through the bonnet to open or close the valve. The hand wheel may rise with the stem, or the stem may rise through the hand wheel.

Screwed bonnet A type of bonnet so constructed that it attaches to the body by means of a screwed joint. A bonnet may be attached to the body by screwing over the body or inside the body, or by means of a union type, screwed connection.

Solid wedge A wedge consisting of one solid piece into which the valve stem is attached, so it seals against the valve seating surfaces to ensure a tight seal when the valve is closed.

Split wedge A wedge consisting of two pieces into which the valve stem is screwed, so it expands the two pieces against the valve seating surfaces to ensure a tight seal when the valve is closed.

Standard port The area through the valve is less than the area of standard pipe.

Stem The usually threaded shaft to which is attached the hand wheel at the top and the disc or wedge at the lower end. The stem may also be called the "spindle."

Stop plug An adjusting screw that extends through the body of a check valve. It adjusts and controls the extent of movement of the disc or clapper.

Swing check valve A check valve that uses a

hinged disc or clapper to limit the direction of flow. The pressure exerted by the fluid flowing through the valve forces the disc away from the seating surface. When the flow ceases, the clapper falls to its original position, preventing flow in the opposite direction.

Union A coupling fitting consisting of three parts (a shoulder piece, a thread piece, and a ring) that is used for coupling the ends of pipe sections. Adjoining faces of shoulder and thread pieces are lapped together to form a tight joint. Unions permit easy disconnection for repair and replacement of piping and fittings.

Union bonnet A type of bonnet that is so constructed that the whole bonnet assembly, including the hand wheel, stem, and disc assembly, may be quickly removed by unscrewing the bonnet union ring from the valve body.

Union ring A large nut-like component that secures the union thread and the union shoulder together. It slips over and against the shoulder piece and screws onto the union thread piece.

Union shoulder piece A part of the union fastened to the pipe that retains the union ring.

Union threaded piece That part of the union that is fastened to the pipe and has external threads over which the union ring is screwed to effect a coupling.

Wedge (See also *disc.*) The wedge-shaped device that fits into the seating surfaces of a gate valve and that is drawn out of contact with the seating surfaces to permit flow or is pushed down into contact with the seating surfaces to close off flow with the valve.

100% area (full port) The area through the valve is equal to or greater than the area of standard pipe.

MSS STANDARD PRACTICES

Number

SP-25 *Standard Marking System for Valves, Fittings, Flanges and Unions*

SP-42 *150 lb. Corrosion Resistant Cast Flanged Valves*

SP-67 *Butterfly Valves*

SP-70 *Cast Iron Gate Valves, Flanged and*

Threaded Ends

SP-71 *Cast Iron Swing Check Valves, Flanged and Threaded Ends*

SP-72 *Ball Valves with Flanged or Butt-Welding Ends for General Service*

SP-78 *Cast Iron Plug Valves*

SP-80 *Bronze Gate, Globe, Angle and Check Valves*

SP-81 *Stainless Steel, Bonnetless, Flanged, Wafer, Knife Gate Valves*

SP-82 *Valve Pressure Testing Methods*

SP-85 *Cast Iron Valves*

SP-110 *Ball Valves*

Notes: 1. Use of the last approved revision of all standards shall be used. 2. A large number of former MSS Standard Practices have been approved by the American National Standards Institute (ANSI) as ANSI Standards. To maintain a single source of authoritative information, MSS withdraws its Standard Practices when they are approved as ANSI Standards.

VALVE DESIGN CHOICES

1. Multiturn type
    A. Gate
    B. Globe/angle-globe
    C. End connection
2. Check type (backflow prevention)
    A. Swing
    B. Lift
    C. Silent or nonslam
    D. End connection
3. Quarter-turn type
    A. Ball
    B. Butterfly-resilient seated
    C. Plug
    D. End connection.

DESIGN DETAIL: GATE VALVES

Advantages and Recommendations

1. Good choice for on-off service
2. Full flow, low pressure drop

3. Bidirectional

4. Bypass valves should be provided where the differential pressure exceeds 200 psi on valves 4½ to 6 in. and 100 psi on valves 8 in. and larger. Bypass valves should be ½ in. for 4-in. valves and ¾ in. for 5-in. valves or larger.

Disadvantages

1. Not for throttling: Use fully open or fully closed. Flow through a partially open gate valve causes vibration and chattering and subjects the disc and seat to inordinate wear.

2. Metal-to-metal seating means not best choice for frequent operation. Bubble-tight seating should not be expected with metal-to-metal design.

3. Difficult to automate.

Disc and Seat Designs

1. Bronze or bronze-faced seating surfaces are used with bronze and iron valves. Iron valves may use all-iron seating surfaces. These are preferred for low pressures and temperatures and for ordinary fluids. Stainless steel is used for high-pressure steam and erosive media.

2. Nonmetallic, "composition" discs are available for tight seating or hard-to-hold fluids, such as air and gasoline.

3. Solid-wedge disc design is thinner at the bottom, thicker at the top, and forced into the seat of a similar shape.

4. Double-disc or split-wedge disc design are two discs employed back to back with a spreading device between them. As the valve wheel is turned, the gate drops into its seat (as with any other gate valve), but on the final turns of the wheel, the spreader forces the discs outward against the seats, effecting tighter closure.

5. Resilient wedge is a rubber encapsulated metal wedge that seals against an epoxy-coated body. Resilient wedge is limited to cold-water applications.

DESIGN DETAIL: GLOBE/ANGLE-GLOBE VALVE

Advantages and Recommendations

1. Recommended for throttling applications.

2. Positive bubble-tight shut-off when equipped with resilient seating.

3. Good for frequent operation.

4. Easy to repair.

Disadvantages

1. Flow path causes a significant pressure drop.

2. Globe valves are more costly than alternative valves.

Disc and Seat Designs

1. Resilient (soft) seat discs are preferred over metal-to-metal except where temperatures, very close throttling or abrasive flow make all-metal seating a better choice. Stainless steel trim is available for medium- to high-pressure steam and abrasive applications. Tetrafluoroethylene (TFE) is the best resilient disc material for most services, although rubber's softness gives good performance in cold water. TFE is good up to 400°F. Butadiene and acrylonitrile (Buna-N) is good up to 200°F.

2. Automatic, steam, stop-check, angle-globe valves are best on medium-pressure steam service.

3. Where the sliding action of the semiplug disc assembly permits the valve to serve as a shut-off valve, throttling valve, and or a check valve.

DESIGN DETAIL: CHECK VALVES (BACKFLOW PREVENTION)

1. Swing type check valves offer the least pressure drop and offer simple automatic closure; when fluid flow stops, gravity and flow reversal close the valve. Many bronze valves offer a Y-pattern body with an angle seat for improved performance. Resilient Teflon seating is preferred for tighter shut-off.

2. Lift checks come in an in-line or globe-style body pattern. Both cause greater pressure drop than the swing type, with the horizontal pattern similar in restriction to globe valves.

3. Some styles are spring actuated and center guided for immediate closure when flow stops. The in-line, spring-actuated lift check is also referred to as the "silent check" because the spring closes the valve before gravity and fluid reversal can slam the valve closed. Resilient seating is recommended.

4. Double-disc check valves have twin discs on a spring-loaded center shaft. These valves have better flow characteristics than lift checks and most often use a wafer body for low cost and easy installation. Resilient seating is recommended.

DESIGN DETAIL: QUARTER-TURN BALL VALVES

Advantages and Recommendations

1. Bubble-tight shut-off from resilient (TFE) seats

2. Quick, 90° open/close, not torque dependent for seating

3. Straight-through, unobstructed flow, bidirectional

4. Easier to automate than multiturn valves

5. More compact than multiturn valves

6. Offer long cycle life.

Disadvantages

1. Temperature and pressure range limited by seat material.

2. Cavity around ball traps media and does not drain entrapped media. Susceptible to freezing, expansion, and increased pressure due to increased temperature.

Body Styles

1. One-piece valves have no potential body leak path but have a double reduced port, thus, significant pressure drop occurs. Not repairable, they are used primarily by chemical and refining plants.

2. Two-piece end entries are used most commonly in building services. They are the best value valves and are available in full- or standard-port balls. They are recommended for on-off or throttling service and not recommended to be repaired.

3. Three-piece type valves are more costly but are easier to disassemble and offer the possibility of in-line repair. They are available in full- or standard-port balls.

Port Size

1. Full-port ball valves provide a pressure drop equal to the equivalent length of the pipe, slightly better than gate valves.

2. Standard- (conventional-) port balls are up to one pipe size smaller than the nominal pipe size but still have significantly better flow characteristics than globe valves.

3. Reduced-port ball valves have greater than one pipe size flow restriction and are not recommended in building services piping but rather are used for process piping for hazardous material transfer.

End Connections

1. Threaded ball valves with ANSI female taper threads are most commonly used with pipe up to 2 in.

2. Soldered-end valves permit the direct connection of bronze ball valves to 2-in. copper tubing. Care must be taken not to overheat and damage the valves during the soldering process.

Handle Extensions

1. Insulated handle extensions or extended handles should be used to keep insulated piping systems intact.

DESIGN DETAIL: QUARTER-TURN BUTTERFLY VALVES

Advantages and Recommendations

1. Bubble-tight shut-off from resilient seats

2. Quick, 90° open/close; easier to automate than multiturn valves

3. Very cost-effective compared to alternative valve choices

4. Broad selection of trim materials to match different fluid conditions

5. More compact than multiturn valves

6. Offer long cycle life

7. Dead-end service.

Disadvantages

1. Not to be used with steam.

2. Gear operators are needed for 8 in. and larger valves to aid in operation and protect against operating too quickly and causing destructive line shock.

Body Styles

1. *Wafer style valves* are held in place between two pipe flanges. They are easy to install but cannot be used as isolation valves.

2. *Lug-style valves* have wafer bodies but tapped lugs matching up to bolt circles of class 125/150-lb flanges. They are easily installed with cap screws from either side. Lug style designs from some manufacturers permit dropping the pipe from one side while the valve holds full pressure if needed.

3. *Groove butterfly valves* directly connect to pipe using iron-pipe-size, grooved couplings. While more costly than wafer valves, grooved valves are the easiest to install.

DESIGN DETAIL: QUARTER-TURN VALVES, LUBRICATED PLUG COCKS

Advantages and Recommendations

1. Bubble-tight shut-off from stem seal of re-inforced Teflon. Leakproof, spring-loaded ball and lubricated, sealed check valve and combination lubricant screw and button head fitting prevent foreign matter from being forced into the lubrication system.

2. Quick, 90° open/close, not dependent on torque for seating.

3. Straight-through, unobstructed flow, bidirectional flow, three-way flow, or four-way flow.

4. Offers long cycle life.

5. Adjustable stop for balancing or throttling service.

6. Can be supplied with round, diamond, or rectangular (standard) plug.

7. Mechanism for power operation or remote control of any size and type to operate with air, oil, or water.

Disadvantages

1. Temperature and pressure range limited by type of lubricant sealant and ANSI Standard rating, i.e. 150 psi steam working pressure (SWP) and 200 psi nonshock, cold working pressure (CWP), and water, oil, gas (WOG).

GENERAL VALVE SPECIFICATION BY SERVICE

Hot and Cold Domestic Water Service

Gate valve

2 in. and smaller Valves 2 in. and smaller shall be class 125, rated 125 psi SWP, 200 psi nonshock CWP, rising stem. Body, union bonnet, and solid wedge shall be of ASTM B-62 cast bronze with threaded ends. Stems shall be of dezincification-resistant silicon bronze, ASTM B-371, or low-zinc alloy, ASTM B-99. Packing glands shall be of bronze, ASTM B-62, with aramid fiber, nonasbestos packing, complete with malleable hand wheel. Valves shall comply with MSS SP-80.

2½ in. and larger Valves 2½ in. and larger shall be class 125, rated 100 psi SWP, 150 psi nonshock CWP; and have an iron body, bronze-mounted outside screw and yoke (OS&Y), with body and bolted bonnet conforming to ASTM A-126 class B cast-iron, flanged ends, with aramid fiber, nonasbestos packing and two-piece packing gland assembly. Valves shall comply with MSS SP-70.

All domestic water valves 4 in. and larger that are buried in the ground shall be iron body, bronze-fitted, with O-ring stem seal; and have epoxy coating inside and outside and a resilient-seated gate valve with nonrising stem and mechanical joint or flanged ends as required. All valves furnished shall open left. All internal parts shall be accessible without removing the valve body from the line. Valves shall conform to AWWA C509-89, *Standard for Resilient-Seated Gate Valves.* Epoxy coating shall conform to AWWA C550-90, *Standard for Protective Epoxy Interior Coating for Valves.*

Ball valves

2 in. and smaller Valves 2 in. and smaller shall be rated 150 psi SWP, 600 psi nonshock CWP; and have two-piece, cast brass bodies, replaceable reinforced Teflon seats, full-port ¼–1 in., conventional-port 1¼–2 in., blowout-proof stems, chrome-plated brass ball, and threaded or soldered ends. Valves shall comply with MSS SP-110

Globe valves

2 in. and smaller Valves 2 in. and smaller shall be of class 125, rated 125 psi SWP, 200 psi nonshock CWP; body and bonnet shall be of ASTM B-62 cast-bronze composition with threaded or soldered ends. Stems shall be of dezincification-resistant silicon bronze, ASTM B-371, or low-zinc alloy, ASTM B-99. Packing glands shall be of bronze, ASTM B-62, with aramid fiber, nonasbestos packing, complete with malleable hand wheel. Valves shall comply with MSS SP-80.

2½ in. and larger Valves 2½ in. and larger shall be class 125, rated 125 psi SWP, 200 psi nonshock CWP; and have an iron body, bronze-mounted OS&Y, with body and bolted bonnet conforming to ASTM A-126 class B cast-iron, flanged ends, with aramid fiber, nonasbestos packing, and two-piece packing gland assembly. Valves shall comply with MSS SP-85.

Butterfly valves

2½ in. and larger Valves 2 ½ in. and larger shall be rated 200 psi nonshock CWP; and have a lug or IPS grooved type body with 2-in. extended neck for insulating. They shall be ductile iron, ASTM A 536; with stainless steel disc; 416 stainless steel stem; ethylene-propylene diene monomer (EPDM) O-ring stem seals; and resilient, EPDM rubber molded to seat. Sizes 2½ to 6 in. shall be lever operated with a ten-position throttling plate; sizes 8 to 12 in. shall have gear operators; sizes 14 in. and larger shall have worm gear operators only. They are suitable for use as bidirectional isolation valves and, as recommended by the manufacturer, on dead-end service at full pressure without the need for downstream flanges.

Valves shall comply with MSS SP-67.

Note: Butterfly valves in dead-end service require both upstream and downstream flanges for proper shut-off and retention or must be certified by the manufacturer for dead-end service without downstream flanges.

Check valves

2 in. and smaller Valves 2 in. and smaller shall be class 125, rated 125 psi SWP, 200 psi nonshock CWP; and have threaded or soldered ends, with body and cap conforming to ASTM B-62 cast bronze composition, y-pattern swing type disc. Valves shall comply with MSS SP-80

Note: Class 150 valves meeting the above specifications may be used where system pressure requires. For class 125 seat disc, specify Buna-N for WOG service and TFE for steam service. For class 150 seat disc, specify TFE for steam service.

2½ in. and larger Valves 2½ in. and larger shall be class 125, rated 125 psi SWP, 200 psi nonshock CWP; iron body, bronze mounted, with body and bolted bonnet conforming to ASTM A-126 class B cast-iron, flanged ends, swing type disc, and nonasbestos gasket. Valves shall comply with MSS SP-71.

Alternative check valves (2½ in. and larger) shall be class 125/250 iron body, bronze mounted, wafer check valve, with ends designed for flanged type connection, aluminum bronze disc, EPDM seats, 316 stainless steel torsion spring, and hinge pin.

A spring-actuated check valve is to be used on pump discharge. Swing check with outside lever and spring (not center guided) is to be used on sewage ejectors or storm-water sump pumps.

Compressed-Air Service

Ball valves

2 in. and smaller

Mainline Valves 2 in. and smaller shall be rated 150 psi SWP, 600 psi nonshock CWP; and have two-piece, cast-bronze bodies; reinforced Teflon seats; full port; blowout-proof stems; chrome-plated brass ball, and threaded or soldered ends. Valves shall comply with MSS SP-110.

Branch line Valves 2 in. and smaller shall be rated 150 psi SWP, 600 psi nonshock CWP; and have two-piece, cast-bronze, ASTM B-584, bodies with reinforced Teflon seats. Full-port ¼–1-in. valves and conventional-port 1¼–2-in. valves require blowout-proof stems, chrome-plated brass ball with a safety vent hole on the downstream side with threaded or soldered ends and lock-out-tag-out handles. Lock-out-tag-out handles must meet the requirements of OSHA-1910.147. Valves shall comply with MSS SP-110.

Butterfly valves

2½ in. and larger Valves 2½ in. and larger shall be rated 200 psi nonshock CWP. Valves shall be lug or IPS, grooved type body with a 2-in. extended neck for insulating and shall be ductile iron, ASTM A-536, with a Buna-N seat; ductile iron, nickel-plated disc, ASTM A-582; Type 416 stainless steel stem; and Buna-N O-ring stem seals. Sizes 2½–6 in. shall be lever operated with a ten-position throttling plate; sizes 8–12-in. valves shall have gear operators. Lever-operated valves shall be designed to be locked in the open or closed position. Butterfly valves on dead-end service or valves needing additional body strength shall be lug type conforming to ASTM A-536, ductile iron, drilled and tapped, other materials and features as specified above. Valves shall comply with MSS SP-67.

Notes: 1. Dead-end service requires lug pattern or grooved type bodies. 2. For dead-end service, flanges are required upstream and downstream for proper shut-off and retention or valves must be certified by manufacturer for dead-end service without downstream flanges. 3. Ductile iron bodies are preferred.

Check valves

2 in. and smaller Valves 2 in. and smaller shall be of class 125, rated 125 psi SWP, 200 psi nonshock CWP, and have threaded ends, with body and cap conforming to ASTM B-62, cast-bronze composition, y-pattern, swing type with TFE seat disc, or spring-loaded lift type with resilient seating. Valves shall comply with MSS SP-80.

2½ in. and larger Valves 2½ in. and larger shall be class 125, rated 200 psi nonshock CWP, and have maximum temperature to 200°F; ASTM A 126 class B cast-iron body; wafer check valve,

with ends designed for flanged type connections; Buna-N resilient seats, molded to body, ASTM A 584; bronze disc; 316 stainless steel torsion spring; and hinge pin. Valves shall conform to ANSI B 16.1.

Note: If compressor is reciprocating type, check valves shall be downstream of receiver tank.

Vacuum Service

Ball valves

2 in. and smaller Valves 2 in. and smaller shall be rated 150 psi SWP, 600 psi nonshock CWP; and have two-piece, cast-brass bodies, reinforced Teflon seats, a full port, blowout-proof stems, a chrome-plated brass ball, and threaded or soldered ends. Valves shall comply with MSS SP-110.

Butterfly valves

2½ in. and larger Valves 2½ in. and larger shall be rated 200 psi nonshock CWP. Valves shall be lug or IPS grooved type body with a 2-in. extended neck for insulating; and shall be ductile iron, ASTM A 536, with a Buna-N seat; ductile iron, nickel-plated disc, ASTM A 582 type 416 stainless steel stem, and Buna-N O-ring stem seals. Sizes 2½–6 in. shall be lever operated with a ten-position throttling plate; sizes 8–12 in. shall have gear operators. Lever-operated valves shall be designed to be locked in the open or closed position.

For butterfly valves on dead-end service or requiring additional body strength, valves shall be lug type, conforming to ASTM A-536, ductile iron, drilled and tapped; other materials and features as specified above. Valves shall comply with MSS SP-67.

Notes: 1. Dead-end service requires lug pattern or grooved type bodies. 2. For dead-end service, flanges are required upstream and downstream for proper shutoff and retention or valves must be certified by manufacturer for dead-end service without downstream flanges. 3. Ductile iron bodies are preferred.

Medical Gas Service

Ball valves

2 in. and smaller Valves 2 in. and smaller shall be rated 600 psi nonshock CWP, 200 psi for medical gas; and have three-piece, cast-bronze, ASTM

B 584, bodies, replaceable reinforced TFE seats, a full port, blowout-proof stems, a chrome-plated brass/bronze ball, and brazed ends. Valves shall be provided by the manufacturer cleaned and bagged for oxygen service. Valves shall comply with MSS SP-110.

2½ in. and larger Valves 2½ in. and larger shall be rated 600 psi nonshock CWP, 200 psi for medical gas; and have three-piece, cast-bronze, ASTM B 584, bodies, replaceable reinforced TFE seats, a full port, blowout-proof stems, a chrome-plated brass/bronze ball, and brazed ends. Valves shall be provided by the manufacturer cleaned and bagged for oxygen service. Valves shall comply with MSS SP-110.

Note: Where piping is insulated, ball valves shall be equipped with 2-in. extended handles of nonthermal, conductive material. Also a protective sleeve that allows operation of the valve without breaking the vapor seal or disturbing the insulation should be provided.

Low-Pressure Steam and General Service

This includes service up to 125 psi saturated steam to 353° F (178° C).

Butterfly valves Butterfly valves are not allowed in steam service unless stated as acceptable for the application by the manufacturer.

Gate valves

2 in. and smaller Valves 2 in. and smaller shall be class 125, rated 125 psi SWP, 200 psi nonshock CWP, and have a rising stem. Body, union bonnet, and solid wedge shall be of ASTM B-62, cast bronze with threaded ends. Stems shall be of dezincification-resistant silicon bronze, ASTM B-371, or low-zinc alloy, ASTM B-99. Packing glands shall be of bronze, ASTM B-62, with aramid fiber, nonasbestos packing, complete with malleable hand wheel. Class150 valves meeting the above specifications may be used where pressures approach 100 psi. Valves shall comply with MSS SP-80.

2½ in. and larger Valves 2½ in. and larger shall be class 125, rated 100 psi SWP, 150 psi nonshock CWP; and have an iron body, bronze-mounted OS&Y, with body and bolted bonnet conforming to ASTM A-126 class B cast-iron, flanged ends, with aramid fiber, nonasbestos packing and two-piece packing gland assembly. Class 250 valves meeting the above specifications

may be used where pressures approach 100 psi. Valves shall comply with MSS SP-70.

Ball valves

2 in. and smaller Valves 2 in. and smaller shall be 150 psi SWP and 600 psi nonshock CWP, WOG, and have two-piece, cast bronze bodies; reinforced Teflon seats; a full port, blowout-proof stems, an adjustable packing gland, a stainless steel ball and stem, and threaded ends. Valves shall comply with MSS SP-110.

Notes: 1. A standard port may be used where pressure drop is not a concern. 2. For on-off service use ball valves with stainless steel balls; for throttling use globe valves.

Globe valves

2 in. and smaller Valves 2 in. and smaller shall be class 125, rated 125 psi SWP, 200 psi nonshock CWP, and have a body and bonnet of ASTM B-62 cast-bronze composition, with threaded ends. Stems shall be of dezincification-resistant silicon bronze, ASTM B-371, or low-zinc alloy, ASTM B-99. Packing glands shall be of bronze, ASTM B-62, with aramid fiber, nonasbestos packing, complete with malleable hand wheel. Valves shall comply with MSS SP-80.

2½ in. and larger Valves 2½ in. and larger shall be class 125, rated 125 psi SWP, 200 psi nonshock CWP, and have an iron body, bronze-mounted OS&Y, with body and bolted bonnet conforming to ASTM A-126 class B cast-iron, flanged ends with aramid fiber, nonasbestos packing and two-piece packing gland assembly. Class 250 valves meeting the above specifications may be used where pressures approach 100 psi. Valves shall comply with MSS SP-85.

Check valves

2 in. and smaller Valves 2 in. and smaller shall be class 125, rated 125 psi SWP, 200 psi nonshock CWP, threaded ends with body and cap conforming to ASTM B-62 and cast-bronze composition, y-pattern swing type with TFE seat disc or spring-loaded lift type with resilient seating. Valves shall comply with MSS SP-80.

Note: Class 150 valves meeting the above specifications may be used where system pressure requires them. For class 150 seat discs TFE for steam service should be specified.

2½ in. and larger Valves 2½ in. and larger shall be class 125, rated 125 psi SWP, 200 psi nonshock CWP, iron body, bronze mounted, with body and bolted bonnet conforming to ASTM A-126, class B cast-iron, flanged ends, a swing type disc, and nonasbestos gasket. Valves shall comply with MSS SP-71.

Medium-Pressure Steam Service

This includes up to 200 psi saturated steam to 391°F (201°C).

Butterfly valves Butterfly valves are not allowed in steam service unless stated as acceptable for the application by the manufacturer.

Gate valves

2 in. and smaller Valves 2 in. and smaller shall be class 200, rated 200 psi SWP, 400 psi nonshock CWP, and have a rising stem; body and union bonnet of ASTM-B-61 cast bronze; threaded ends; ASTM B 584 solid wedge; silicon bronze ASTM B 371 stem; bronze ASTM B 62 or ASTM B 584 packing gland; aramid fiber nonasbestos packing; and malleable hand wheel. Valves shall comply with MSS SP-80.

2½ in. and larger Valves 2 ½ in. and larger shall be class 250, rated 250 psi SWP, 500 psi nonshock CWP, and have an iron body; bronze-mounted OS&Y with body and bolted bonnet conforming to ASTM-A-126; class B cast-iron, flanged ends; with aramid fiber nonasbestos packing; and two-piece packing gland assembly. Valves shall comply with MSS SP-70.

Globe valves

2 in. and smaller Valves 2 in. and smaller shall be class 200, rated 200 psi SWP, 400 psi nonshock CWP, and have a rising stem, body and union bonnet of ASTM-B-61 cast bronze, threaded ends, ASTM-A-276 type 420 stainless steel plug type disc and seat ring, silicon bronze ASTM B 371 alloy stem, bronze ASTM B 62 or ASTM B 584 packing gland, aramid fiber nonasbestos packing, and malleable iron hand wheel. Valves shall comply with MSS SP-80.

2½ in. and larger Valves 2½ in. and larger shall be class 250, rated 250 psi SWP, 500 psi nonshock CWP, and have an iron body; bronze-mounted OS&Y with body and bolted bonnet conforming to ASTM-A-126; class B cast-iron, flanged ends; with aramid fiber nonasbestos pack-

ing and two-piece packing gland assembly. Where steam pressure approaches 150 psi/366°F then gray iron or ductile iron shall be used. Valves shall comply with MSS SP-85.

Check valves

2 in. and smaller Valves 2 in. and smaller shall be class 200, rated 200 psi SWP, 400 psi nonshock CWP, and have threaded ends with body and cap conforming to ASTM-B-61, cast-bronze composition, and a y-pattern swing type disc. Valves shall comply with MSS SP-80.

2½ in. and larger Valves 2½ in. and larger shall be class 250, rated 250 psi SWP, 500 psi nonshock CWP, and have an iron body, bronze mounted, with body and bolted bonnet conforming to ASTM-A-126, class B cast-iron, flanged ends; and a swing type disc assembly. Where steam pressure approaches 150 psi/366°F then gray iron or ductile iron shall be used. Valves shall comply with MSS SP-71.

High-Pressure Steam Service

This includes up to 300 psi saturated steam to 421°F (216°C).

Gate valves

2 in. and smaller Valves 2 in. and smaller shall be class 300, rated 300 psi SWP, nonrising stem (NRS); body and union bonnet shall be of ASTM-B-61 cast-bronze composition, with threaded ends, bronze ASTM B 61 disc, bronze ASTM B 371 stem, stainless steel ASTM A 276 type 410 seat rings, bronze packing gland, aramid fiber nonasbestos packing, and malleable hand wheel. Valves shall comply with MSS SP-80.

2½ in. and larger Valves 2½ in. and larger shall be class 300, rated 300 psi SWP, and have a cast-carbon steel ASTM A 216 wrought-carbon grade B (WCB) body and bolted bonnet. Disc and stem shall be ASTM-A-217 grade CA 15, cast 12–14% chromium stainless steel, with stellite faced seat rings, flanged ends, and two-piece packing gland assembly. Valves shall comply with MSS SP-70.

Globe valves

2 in. and smaller Valves 2 in. and smaller shall be class 300, rated 300 psi SWP, and have a body and union bonnet of ASTM-B-61 cast-bronze composition, threaded ends, stainless steel ASTM A 276 hardened plug type disc and seat ring, silicon bronze ASTM B 371 stem, bronze ASTM B 62 or ASTM B 584 packing gland, aramid fiber nonasbestos packing, and malleable hand wheel. Valves shall comply with MSS SP-80.

2½ in. and larger Valves 2½ in. and larger shall be class 300, rated 300 psi SWP, and have a cast-carbon steel ASTM A 216 grade WCB body and bolted bonnet. Disc, stem, and seat rings shall be ASTM-A-217 grade CA 15, cast 12–14% chromium stainless steel, flanged or welded ends, with two-piece packing gland assembly. Valves shall comply with MSS SP-85.

Check valves

2 in. and smaller Valves 2 in. and smaller shall be class 300, rated 300 psi SWP, and have threaded ends with body and cap conforming to ASTM-B-61, cast-bronze composition, and y-pattern swing type disc. Valves shall comply with MSS SP-80.

2½ in. and larger Valves 2½ in. and larger shall be class 300, rated 300 psi SWP, and have a cast-carbon steel ASTM A 216 grade WCB body and bolted bonnet. Disc and seat ring shall be ASTM-A-217 grade CA 15, cast 12–14% chromium stainless steel, with flanged or welded ends. Valves shall comply with MSS SP-71.

High-Temperature Hot-Water Service

This includes service to 450°F.

Nonlubricated plug valves Valves shall be ANSI class 300, with 70% port nonlubricated, wedge plug, and bolted bonnet. Body, bonnet, and packing gland flange shall be cast-carbon steel ASTM-A-216, grade WCB.

Plug shall be cast from high-tensile, heat-treated alloy iron. The plug shall have two Teflon O-rings inserted into dovetail-shaped grooves machined into the plug faces. O-rings shall provide double seating and ensure vapor-tight shut-off on both upstream and downstream seats. Valves are to be seated in both open and closed positions to protect body seats.

Stem shall be high-strength alloy steel conforming to AISI 4150 sulphurized, face-to-face dimensions to meet ANSI B-16.10.

Each valve shall be provided with a position indicator for visual indication of the 90° rotation of the plug. Valves are to be equipped with a provision for bypass connections.

Types of operator

1. Valves 3 in. and smaller: hand wheel or wrench.
2. Valves 4 in. and larger: enclosed gear with hand wheel.

Each valve shall be certified to have passed the following minimum test requirements:

- *Shell test*

  1100 psi hydrostatic

- *Seat test*

  750 psi hydrostatic (both sides to be tested)

  100 psi air underwater (both sides to be tested)

Gasoline and LPG Service

Plug valves Valves shall be ANSI class 150, 70% port, nonlubricated tapered plug, bolted bonnet type. Valve body shall be ASTM-A-216, grade WCB steel with drain plug, suitable for double block and bleed service.

The plug seals shall be two Teflon O-rings inserted into dovetail-shaped, grooves machined into the plug faces. Operation is to be such that the plug is lifted clear of the seats before rotating 90°.

End connections shall be ANSI class 150 raised face, and flanged. Face-to-face dimensions are to meet ANSI B 16.10.

Fire-Protection System

Gate valves

2 in. and smaller Valves 2 in. and smaller shall be of class 175 psi water working pressure (WWP) or greater, with body and bonnet conforming to ASTM-B-62, cast-bronze composition, threaded ends, OS&Y, solid disc *and listed by UL, FM approved, and in compliance with MSS SP-80.*

2½ in. and larger Valves 2½ in. and larger shall be rated 175 psi WWP or greater, and have an iron body, bronze mounted or with resilient rubber encapsulated wedge, with body and bonnet conforming to ASTM A-126, class B cast-iron,

OS&Y, class 125 flanged or grooved ends. If of resilient wedge design, interior of valve is to be epoxy coated. Valves shall meet or exceed AWWA C509-89, *Standard for Protective Epoxy Interior Coating for Valves. Valves are to be UL listed, FM approved, and in compliance with MSS SP-70.*

Valves 4 in. and larger for underground bury shall be rated 200 psi WWP or greater, with body and bonnet conforming to ASTM A-126, class B cast iron, bronze mounted, resilient-seated gate valve with nonrising stem, with O-ring stem seal, epoxy coating inside and outside, flanged or mechanical joint ends as required. All valves furnished shall open left. All internal parts shall be accessible without removing the valve body from the line. Valves shall conform to AWWA C509-89, *Standard for Resilient-Seated Gate Valves.* Epoxy coating shall conform to AWWA C550-90, *Standard for Protective Epoxy Interior Coating for Valves. Valves shall come complete with mounting plate for indicator post and be UL listed, FM approved, and in compliance with MSS SP-70.*

When required, a vertical indicator post may be used on underground valves. Posts must provide a means of knowing if the valve is open or shut. *Indicator posts must be UL listed and FM approved.*

High-Rise Service

Gate valves

2½- to 12-in. Gate valves 2½ to 10 in. shall be rated 300 psi WWP or greater, 12 in. shall be rated 250 psi WWP, and have an iron body, bronze mounted, with body and bonnet conforming to ASTM A-126, class B, cast iron, OS & Y, with flanged ends for use with class 250/300 flanges. *They shall be UL listed, FM approved, and in compliance with MSS SP-70.*

Check valves

2½- to 12-in. Check valves 2½ to 10 in. shall be rated 300 psi WWP or greater, 12 in. shall be rated 250 psi WWP, and have an iron body, bronze mounted, with a horizontal swing check design, with body and bonnet conforming to ASTM A 126 Class B, cast iron, with flanged ends for use with class 250/300 flanges. *They shall be UL listed, FM approved, and in compliance with MSS SP-71.*

Note: In New York City, valves are to be approved by the New York City Materials and Equipment Acceptance Division (MEA), in addition to the above specifications.

Ball valves

2 in. and smaller Valves 2 in. and smaller shall be constructed of commercial bronze, ASTM B 584, rated 175 psi WWP or higher, with reinforced TFE seats. Valves shall have a gear operator with a raised position indicator and two internal supervisory switches. Valves shall have threaded or IPS grooved ends and shall have blowout-proof stems and chrome-plated balls. *They shall be UL listed, FM approved, and in compliance with MSS SP-110 for fire-protection service.*

Butterfly valves

4 to 12 in. Butterfly valves may be substituted for gate valves, where appropriate. Valves shall be rated for 250 psi WWP, 175 psig working pressure, *UL listed, FM approved and in compliance with MSS SP-67.*

Valves furnished shall have ductile-iron ASTM A-536 body, and may have ductile-iron ASTM A-395 (nickel-plated) discs or aluminum bronze discs, depending upon the local water conditions. In addition, wafer style for installation between class 125/150 flanges or lug style or grooved body may be specified, depending upon the system needs.

Valves shall be equipped with weatherproof gear operator rated for indoor/outdoor use, with hand wheel and raised position indicator with two internal supervisory switches.

Check valves Valves 2½ in. and larger shall be 500 psi WWP, bolted bonnet, with body and bonnet conforming to ASTM A-126, class B cast iron, flanged end with composition y-pattern, horizontal, swing type disc. *They shall be UL listed, FM approved, and in compliance with MSS SP-71 type 1 for fire-protection service.*

4

Pumps

Centrifugal pumps, which impart energy, or head, to a flowing liquid by centrifugal action, are the most commonly used pumps in plumbing systems. In a conventional, volute type pump, the liquid enters near the axis of a high-speed impeller and is thrown radially outward into the pump casing. Impeller vanes are shaped to ensure a smooth flow of the liquid. Velocity head, imparted to the liquid by the impeller vanes, is converted into pressure head. Conversion, or pump efficiency, depends on the design of the impeller and casing as well as the physical properties of the liquid.

Centrifugal pumps used in plumbing systems are classified, on the basis of internal casing design, as volute or regenerative (turbine). On the basis of the main direction of discharge of liquid, the impellers are classified as radial, axial, or mixed flow. Other means of classification are casing design (vertical, horizontal, or split case); axis of shaft rotation (vertical, horizontal, or inclined); direction of pump suction, or discharge (side, top, or bottom); number of impellers, or stages (single- or multistage); type of coupling of motor to pump (close-coupled or flexible-coupled, base-mounted); position of the pump in relation to the liquid supply (wet- or dry-pit, mounted or in-line); and pump service (water, sewage, corrosive chemicals, slurries, etc.).

TYPES OF PUMP

Horizontal, Volute, Centrifugal Pumps

The volute, centrifugal pump is probably the pump most frequently specified by plumbing de-signers. Liquid entering at the eye of the impeller is thrown to the periphery in a progressively widening spiral casing, creating a lower pressure in the eye and causing more liquid to flow.

As the pumped liquid flows within the casing (gradually reducing in velocity), conversion of the velocity into pressure head results. Both turbulence and recirculation are reduced as the number of impeller vanes is increased. The effect of reduced internal recirculation is to increase the developed head. However, the angle of the tip of the blades has a profound effect on the centrifugal pump's characteristics. Enclosed impellers generate head between the two shrouds of the rotating impeller. Semiopen impellers generate head between one wall of the rotating impeller and one stationary wall of the casing. Open impellers generate head between the two stationary walls of the casing.

An enclosed impeller, as seen in Figure 4-1, has several surfaces, and original efficiencies can be maintained over most of its useful life. Conversely, an open or semiopen impeller, as illustrated in Figure 4-2, requires close clearances between the rotating vanes and the adjacent wall of the casing. Under these conditions, wear results in increased clearances, greater leakage losses, and lower efficiencies. Open impellers are used in pumps discharging liquid containing suspended solids.

Figure 4-3 illustrates a typical, double-suction, volute pump. It is normally selected for operation at pressures and volumes that are higher than those of the single-suction volute, since the liquid is supplied from identical suction chambers located at each impeller side,

**Figure 4-1 An Enclosed
Impeller**

substantially reducing hydraulic unbalance.
Double-suction pumps, by virtue of lower liquid
velocities at the eye of the pump, may have lower
net positive suction head requirements, which
can be used to advantage.

Most applications of double-suction pumps
involve horizontally split casings, although vertical, split-case, double-suction pumps are
available too. Single-suction pumps generally
have vertically split casings (see Figure 4-4). One
obvious advantage of horizontally split casings
is that they can be disassembled for service without previously removing the lower half from the
piping. However, most of the vertically split-case,
end-suction pumps are made available with a
back pullout design to enable removal of the
pumps for service without disturbing the piping
or the pump body.

One of the ways that internal recirculation
is reduced (or efficiency increased) is through
the use of casing seal (or wearing) rings, either
renewable or permanent. Worn renewable wearing rings can be readily replaced. Restoring rings
cannot be replaced; and original clearances can

be restored only by machining the worn surfaces
and installing replaceable rings; renewing worn
surfaces by building them up by welding and
remachining; or replacing the impeller or the casing or both. It should be pointed out that
replacement is the usual practice with the
smaller, less costly pumps. Also, wearing rings
are not used with open impellers; close clearances between exposed vanes and the casing wall
provide the required seal. Thus, open impellers
are replaced when they become worn.

**Figure 4-3 Typical Double-Suction,
Volute Pump**

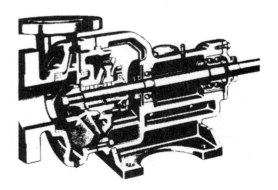

**Figure 4-4 Typical End-Suction,
Single-Stage, and Single-Suction,
Volute Pump**

Table 4-1 shows the operating ranges of some
common single-stage, volute, centrifugal pumps.
For heads in excess of 500 ft (152.4 m), when
operating at 3500 revolutions per minute (rpm),
multistage, volute, centrifugal pumps with horizontally split-case and enclosed impellers are
used. Figure 4-5 illustrates a single-suction, vertically split-case, multistage pump. Its
mechanical seal is under suction pressure, which
allows the pump to operate at a higher discharge
pressure using a standard mechanical seal.

Figure 4-2 An Open Impeller

Both horizontal and vertical, multistage pumps were developed for high-pressure service, i.e., fire or booster service. In such pumps, the output of each prior stage becomes the input to the next stage, so that the heads generated by each impeller are cumulative. Multistage, centrifugal pumps may use single- or double-suction impellers. Single-suction impellers are hydraulically unbalanced and, when used in multistage pumps, have equal numbers of nozzles discharging in opposite directions. Since double-suction impellers are not subject to hydraulic unbalance, they are not so limited.

Volute, centrifugal pumps may be frame- or cradle-mounted or close-coupled. In frame-mounted pumps, the motor driver is connected to the pump shaft through a flexible coupling, as illustrated in Figure 4-6. In close-coupled pumps, illustrated in Figure 4-7, the impeller is mounted directly on the motor shaft. However, cradle-mounted units with oil-lubricated bearings must be used horizontally. Although use of close-coupled pumps virtually eliminates alignment problems, their service is limited by temperature. The motor on frame-mounted pumps can be changed and repaired without breaking into the piping.

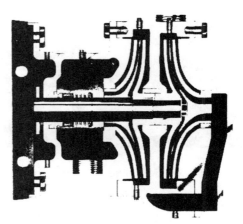

Fire 4-5 Typical Multistage Pump with Vertically Split Case

In-Line Pumps

In-line centrifugal pumps, as illustrated in Figure 4-8, have found widespread application in plumbing services. They are available in capacities up to 1000 gpm (63.1 L/s) at 450 ft (137.2 m) of head and in a wide range of construction materials. Initial and installation costs are approximately 30–40% lower than those of comparable conventional, volute pumps since they require less space, need no permanent foundation, and are easily maintained.

Table 4-1 Operating Ranges for Common Centrifugal Pumps

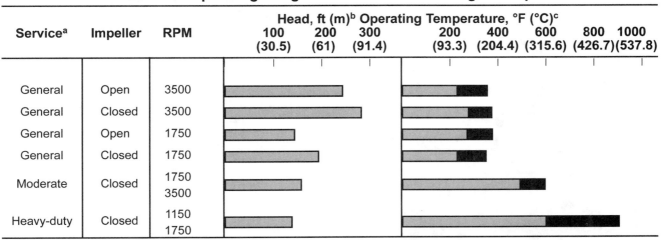

Service[a]	Impeller	RPM	Head, ft (m)[b]			Operating Temperature, °F (°C)[c]				
			100 (30.5)	200 (61)	300 (91.4)	200 (93.3)	400 (204.4)	600 (315.6)	800 (426.7)	1000 (537.8)
General	Open	3500								
General	Closed	3500								
General	Open	1750								
General	Closed	1750								
Moderate	Closed	1750 3500								
Heavy-duty	Closed	1150 1750								

a   All pumps are single-stage, single-suction designs. Medium-duty and heavy-duty service pumps are both end-suction and top-suction pumps. All pumps have packed stuffing boxes.

b   Heads taken at the best efficiency point.

c   Key [gray] Operating ranges for cast-iron, bronze, and ductile-iron pumps.

[black] Operating range extensions with alloy pumps.

Figure 4-6 Typical Frame-Mounted Pump with Horizontally Split Case

The in-line pump consists of a flanged head mounted directly in the piping, usually with a close-coupled drive positioned above the pump casing. Although smaller in-line pumps, similar to the one illustrated in Figure 4-9, are often mounted directly in horizontal or vertical piping, larger pumps usually require a rest plate to prevent undue strain on the piping (see Figure 4-8). For this reason, larger pumps are usually mounted in the vertical position.

The simplicity of the connection between the drive and pump (four to eight studs) permits rapid disassembly. To repair the pump, the studs are merely loosened and the entire motor-impeller unit is lifted clear of the pump casing. As piping remains intact and realignment is unnecessary on reassembly, downtime is minimal.

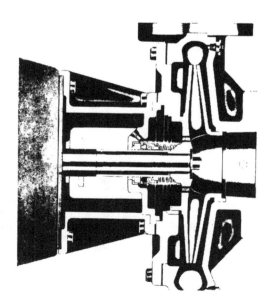

Figure 4-7 Typical Close-Coupled Pump

Sewage Pumps

Sewage pumps are designed to transport liquid-solid mixtures without clogging and are usually equipped with large suction and discharge ports free of obstructions, as illustrated in Figure 4-10. Nonclogging pumps usually are equipped with single- or two-port impellers designed to pass materials that would build up and clog other types of pumps. The impellers have rounded edges and large vane clearances. Narrow repelling vanes on the outer shroud operate to dislodge solids caught between the shroud and the casing wall. The shaft is usually kept clear of the suction port and chamber to avoid clogging prior to the impeller eye. End-clearance impeller and casing wearing rings are usually provided to maintain optimum clearance for efficient operation.

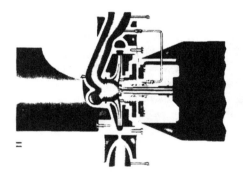

Figure 4-8 Typical In-Line Pump (Larger Unit)

Grinder Pumps

A grinder pump is a special class of sewage pump with an outstanding solids-handling capability. This capability is achieved by the incorporation of an integral in-line grinder as a part of the pumping machinery. The grinder pump has the ability to handle both normal sewage solids and a wide variety of foreign objects, which are often found in sewage.

Because the solids are reduced to tiny particles, the pump's passages and discharge piping can be much smaller than conventional sizes. This results in a higher efficiency and makes possible a high-head, low-flow pump for residential applications using a 1-hp (745.7-W) motor. Since the piping is smaller, scouring velocities are achieved at much lower flow rates.

Grinder pumps find application in completely pressurized sewage collection systems as well as in lifting sewage from a residence into a nearby gravity sewer located at a higher elevation. Grinder pumps are available as both centrifugals and positive displacement pumps. Centrifugal grinder pumps are made with steep characteristic curves. Since the parallel operation of centrifugal pumps into a common pressure header may drive some of them to heads above the shut-off point, pumps with a nearly vertical curve should be specified for such system applications. The positive displacement pump discharges at a nearly constant rate, even over extremely wide fluctuations in head. This means that a single-model pump can work well anywhere in a complex system. Its performance is predictable and consistent, whether it operates alone at a particular moment or shares the pipeline with several other pumps.

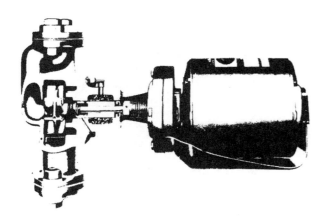

**Figure 4-9 Typical In-Line Pump
(Smaller Unit)**

The key factor in pipe sizing for pressure sewer systems is the design flow. This is based on a maximum number of pumps operating simultaneously. Based on mathematical analysis and empirical relations, the recommended design flows for a pressure sewer system using positive displacement pumps have been developed. These recommended flows are shown in Table 4-2 for various numbers of pumps connected.

Vertical, Pit-Mounted Pumps

Vertical, volute-pump impellers discharge radially and horizontally against that section of the casing known as the "bowl." The resulting pressure forces liquid up the vertical discharge column. The pumping chamber of the wet-pit-mounted pump is located below the liquid supply

Figure 4-10 Typical Sewage Pump

level with the discharge line usually elevated to floor or grade level in duplex configuration, as illustrated in Figure 4-11. Bottom-suction units are more common, but side-suction units are also available.

By contrast, the pumping chamber of dry-pit-mounted, vertical, volute pumps is located above the liquid supply level, as illustrated in Figure 4-12.

Some vertical pumps have cantilevered impeller shafts to avoid support problems with bearings, busings, and sleeves. Shafts are supported at two points at the top of the shaft, with the remainder of the shaft running completely

Table 4-2 Maximum Number of Grinder Pump Cores Operating Daily

Number Grinder Cores	Maximum Daily Number Of Grinder Pump Cores Operating Simultaneously
1	1
2 - 3	2
4 - 9	3
10 - 18	4
19 - 30	5
31 - 50	6
51 - 80	7
81 - 113	8
114 - 146	9
147 - 179	10
180 - 212	11
213 - 245	12
246 - 278	13
279 - 311	14
312 - 344	15

Note: Design flow = Maximum number of pumps running simultaneously × 11 gpm (0.69 L/s).

free. The shaft must be large in diameter and short to prevent excessive vibration, rarely extending more than 6 or 7 ft (1.8 or 2.1 m) below the bottom outboard steady bearing. For greater lengths, center support bearings are placed at approximately 4 ft (1.2 m).

In some wet-pit installations, long shafts can be avoided by using a close-coupled, totally submersible motor located beneath the pump chamber, as illustrated in Figure 4-13. The motors are filled with either oil or water. Oil-filled units have hermetically sealed windings and a pressure-equalizing diaphragm to compensate for expansion and contraction under varying temperatures. A mechanical seal prevents solid particles from entering the motor area. Oil-filled

Figure 4-11 Typical Wet-Pit-Mounted, Vertical Pump

motors are completely isolated from the pumped liquid. A double-mechanical-seal assembly prevents oil from leaking out or foreign material from entering the motor and a moisture-sensor probe indicates seal failure. Submersible-motor, volute pumps require less space at ground level and use less power than comparable long-shaft units.

Regenerative Pumps

In a regenerative pump (commonly called a "turbine type pump"), the liquid does not discharge freely from the tip (see Figure 4-14). Instead, it circulates back to a lower point on the impeller diameter and recirculates several times before leaving the impeller. This recirculation enables these pumps to develop heads several times those of volute pumps of the same impeller diameter and speed. Because of the close clearances be-

Figure 4-12 Typical Dry-Pit-Mounted, Vertical Pump

tween the impeller and casing, only clear liquids can be pumped. Regenerative turbine pumps are also available in multistage units, in capacities from 1 to 200 gpm (0.06 to 12.6 L/s). Single-stage units generate heads up to 500 ft (152.4 m); multistage units (e.g., five-stage units) can generate heads up to 2500 ft (762 m).

Vertical turbine pumps may be water or oil lubricated. The drive shaft of water-lubricated units is located directly in the path of the discharged process liquid, which lubricates the shaft bushings, packing, and stabilizers. This

Figure 4-13 Typical Submersible Pump

Figure 4-14 Typical Regenerative (Turbine Type) Pump

type of pump is used for raising water to the surface from deep wells and is often called a "deep-well pump." See Figure 4-15.

Water-lubricated pumps are prone to wear at the shaft packing and bushings. When used with abrasive or corrosive liquids, the pump will be subject to excessive maintenance problems. Oil-lubricated pumps are used for the latter service; however, they tend to contaminate the fluid being pumped. In oil-lubricated pumps, a tube enclosing the drive shaft is filled with oil for the bushings and sleeves. Thus, the internal parts do not come into contact with the liquid pumped.

Oil- and water-lubricated, vertical, deep-well pumps often use a screen or stainer in the suction line to prevent clogging. To permit satisfactory solids disengagement, the screen

Figure 4-15 Typical Vertical Turbine

area should be about four times the eye area of the impeller.

A short version of the vertical turbine pump, sometimes called the "short coupled" or "pot pump," is often mounted in a sump with the motor above the ground. (See Figure 4-16.) This is used widely in fire-protection systems, industrial-waste handling, and pipeline booster service for pumping water from lakes or slumps.

PUMP PERFORMANCE

Conventional volute pumps have a relatively long life, require little maintenance, and can undergo a significant amount of corrosion or erosion before the performance is significantly affected. Turbine type pumps have approximately one-third the life of conventional volute pumps in

Figure 4-16 Typical Pot Type Turbine

comparable service with clean, noncorrosive liquids. Nevertheless, turbine type pumps are ideally suited for relatively high-head, low-capacity service in which conventional volute pumps would be required to operate near their shut-off points.

All centrifugal pumps have one major disadvantage: performance is highly sensitive to changes in liquid viscosity, capacity varying inversely with viscosity. Volute pumps are normally not self-priming: turbine type pumps are, provided there is sufficient liquid to seal the close clearances.

PUMP HEADS

The concept of head applies to open systems. In a closed system, the static height (or the difference in elevation between the suction and discharge levels) is of no physical significance when determining the energy head pressure drop. This follows from the fact that, independent of path, the static heights of the supply and return piping legs are in balance. In a closed system, the energy required to raise the liquid to the highest point in the piping loop (from the pump centerline) is balanced by the energy head regain in the piping loop, as liquid flows down to this level.

In closed systems, the designer is concerned only with the friction head necessary to overcome the resistance to flow in pipe, appliances, and fittings. Open systems are more complex. Net pump head requirements depend on the statics of the system as well as the friction head losses. Open systems may be characterized as follows:

1. Applications in which the vertical distance from the centerline of the pump to the free level of the liquid source is greater or lesser than the vertical elevation from the centerline of the pump to the point of free discharge.

2. Applications in which the centerline of the pump is at an intermediate elevation between the free level of the liquid source and the point of free discharge.

All conditions of pump suction and discharge must be included in an accurate determination of the pump head.

With an increase in the liquid flow rate, the frictional head losses increase and the suction and available net positive suction head for a system decrease. "Net positive suction head" (NPSH) is a term that combines all the factors that limit the pump suction: static suction lift, suction friction losses, vapor pressure, and prevailing atmospheric conditions. In addition, the designer must differentiate between required and available NPSH. Required NPSH is a function of each pump, varying with the pump capacity and speed change and is always listed by the pump manufacturer, as shown in Figure 4-17. Available NPSH is a system characteristic and is defined as the net positive suction head above the vapor pressure available at the suction flange of the pump to maintain a liquid state.

CENTRIFUGAL PUMP RELATIONS

At any rotational speed, a centrifugal pump can operate at any capacity ranging from zero to some maximum value depending on the size and the design of the pump. A typical total head/capacity characteristic curve is also illustrated in Figure 4-17. Most pump manufacturers provide such curves for operation with water only. However, the corresponding curves for other liquid viscosities can be determined by using Figure 4-18, and the manufacturer's rating for pumps in water service can be adjusted by the factors indicated. Total head in feet (meters) (of liquid flowing) developed by a centrifugal pump at a given impeller speed and capacity is independent of the liquid's density.

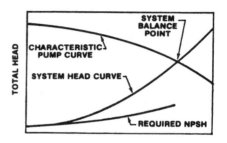

Figure 4-17 Pump Curves for a Typical System and Pump

A centrifugal pump can operate at only one particular capacity along its total head/capacity characteristic curve. That point, where the pump total head curve crosses the system total curve, is identified as the system balance point (see Figure 4-17). Implied in the construction of Figure 4-18 is that the available NPSH in the system is adequate to support the liquid flow rate into the pump suction. If available NPSH is lower than that required by the pump, cavitation will occur and normal curves will not be applicable.

Two centrifugal pumps are considered geometrically similar when the ratio of the corresponding internal dimensions of one pump is equal to that of the other pump. Geometrical similarity exists between two pumps of different size when the wetted surfaces in each pump have the same shape. Such pumps are also referred to as "homologous pumps."

Two concepts provide a convenient means of characterizing pumps: specific speed and suction-specific speed. The specific speed of a centrifugal pump is defined as the rotational speed (in rpm) at which a theoretical homologous pump (of smaller size) would operate while delivering 1 gpm (0.06 L/s) against a total head of 1 ft (0.3 m) at the most efficient point of the pump. The suction-specific speed is defined as the speed (in rpm) at which a theoretical homologous pump (of smaller size) would operate to give 1 gpm (0.06 L/s) at 1 ft (0.3 m) of required NPSH. Although there is considerable disagreement among pump manufacturers concerning the practical significance of these definitions, they lead to the derivations that formulate the basis

of the very useful Pump Affinity laws. These laws can be used to calculate the effect of changes in the impeller speed and diameter on the performance of a given centrifugal pump. Simply stated, they are

1. Pump capacity (Q) varies directly with speed (in revolutions per minute) or impeller diameter ratio change.

2. Pump head (Δh) varies directly as the square of the speed (rpm) or impeller ratio change.

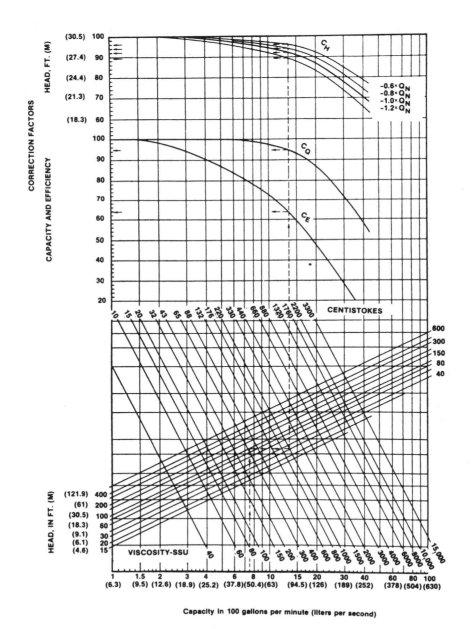

Figure 4-18 Viscosity Correction Curves for Centrifugal Pump Performance

3. Pump work, in brake horsepower (bhp), varies directly as the cube of the speed (rpm) or impeller diameter ratio.

Pump Affinity laws can be used for resizing impellers on pumps and applied to pump selections for speeds other than those given in the available manufacturer's data. It should be pointed out, however, that these relations hold only for small changes in impeller diameter.

CHARACTERISTIC CURVES

Although Pump Affinity laws provide useful relationships, system curve analyses provide more practical procedures. For example, consider the total head/capacity characteristic curve for the conventional volute centrifugal pump, as given in Figure 4-19. The maximum head for a pump with this characteristic is developed at zero capacity and decreases as the flow rate is increased. Other pumps have very steep total head/capacity curves, as illustrated in Figure 4-20, or very flat curves, as illustrated in Figure 4-21. Figure 4-22 is typical of a less common characteristic curve often referred to as a "drooping curve."

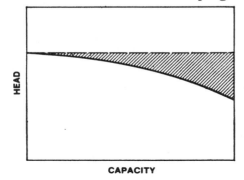

Figure 4-19 Normal Characteristic of Volute, Centrifugal Pumps

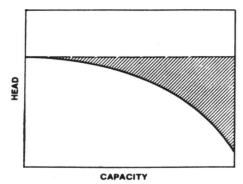

Figure 4-20 Steep Characteristic of Volute, Centrifugal Pumps

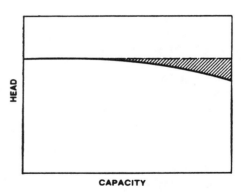

Figure 4-21 Flat Characteristic of Volute, Centrifugal Pumps

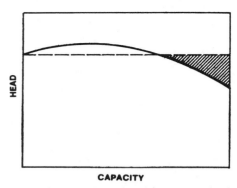

Figure 4-22 Drooping Characteristic of Volute, Centrifugal Pumps

When dealing with the latter characteristic, the same head can be developed for two different capacities. Although a small amount of droop may present no problem, care must be taken to avoid a selection in which the flow rate tends to go back and forth between two capacities, thereby setting up dangerous vibrations, particularly with two similar pumps operating in parallel.

Power/capacity characteristic curves are also useful in determining pump selections. In Fig-

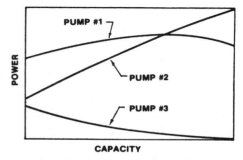

Figure 4-23 Power Capacity Characteristic for Three Typical, Volute, Centrifugal Pumps

ure 4-23, the power requirement for pump no. 1 has a maximum value at some predetermined flow rate. This is typical of nonoverloading centrifugal pumps. Pump no. 2 typifies an overloading curve. Power requirements continue to rise with an increase in the flow rate. Conversely, pump no. 3 is indicative of an overloading curve showing that the power requirement continues to rise with a decrease in flow rate (as in a turbine type pump).

The shape of the characteristic curve is a function of the geometries of the impeller and pump casing. Pumps are often designed to exhibit a combination of the characteristics illustrated in Figures 4-19 through 4-23. For example, it is quite common to find a total head/capacity characteristic curve that is quite flat over a specified range of flow and very steep beyond a certain flow rate. Nonclogging pumps are normally low-head pumps and have steep total head/capacity characteristic curves.

In summary, the capacity obtained from a given centrifugal pump at a specified total head, speed, and liquid viscosity can be determined from an analysis of its characteristic curve.

MULTIPLE PUMP SYSTEMS

It is often necessary in plumbing design work to consider the use of two or more centrifugal pumps in series or parallel. In parallel, the total head for each pump must equal the total system head. Thus, the sum of the individual pump capacities equals the system flow rate at the system total head. Similarly, in a series pump arrangement, the capacity of each pump must equal the system flow rate and the sum of individual pump heads must equal the system total head at the system flow rate.

With simple graphic procedures, the designer can easily determine the characteristics of multiple pumping systems. To select a minimum of two pumps, for example, to be installed in a closed piping system of known resistance to deliver 440 gpm (27.8 L/s) at 30 ft (9.1 m) total head, the designer can evaluate both parallel and series pump arrangements to determine the most favorable selection in terms of (1) overall performance between anticipated maximum and minimum variations of flow rate and total head in actual operation, (2) net horsepower requirements, and (3) effect on delivered flow rate if any one pump should fail. The utilization of horizontal, split-case, centrifugal pumps equipped with 9-in. (228.6-mm) impellers is assumed. (See Figure 4-24.)

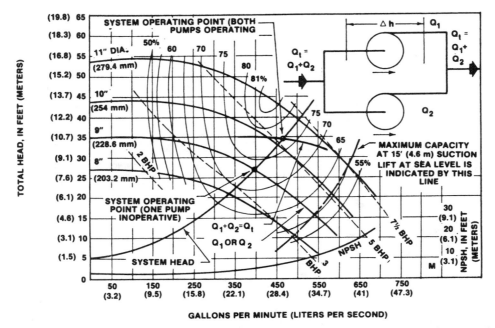

Figure 4-24 Pumps in Parallel—Chart for Estimating Total Head Capacity

The total head capacity characteristic curve for the two pumps, in parallel, can be plotted directly by adding the capacities of the individual pumps ($Q_1 + Q_2$) with a 9-in. (228.6-mm) impeller for various total heads (Δh) selected at random. The system head curve is then plotted on the pump characteristic curve. The point of intersection of the two curves represents the operating capacity (Q_1) and total head (Δh) for stable pump operation. Each pump is operating at half the total system flow and at full system head. Also, each pump should be provided with a 5-hp (3.7-kW) motor to prevent overloading.

If a pump of the type illustrated in Figure 4-24 is selected to operate in series, then a pump equipped with an 8-in. (203.2-mm) impeller for an identical piping system should be chosen.

Again, the total head/capacity characteristic curve for the two pumps in series can be plotted directly, as in Figure 4-25, by adding the total heads of the individual pumps ($\Delta h_1 + \Delta h_2$) with an 8-in. (203.2-mm) impeller for various capacities (Q). The system head curve and the point of intersection of the two curves represent the operating capacity (Q) and the total head (Δh) for stable operation.

Comparing the parallel and series selections using the same system (resistance), the resulting flow rates are within 7% of each other—470 vs. 435 gpm (29.7 vs. 27.4 L/s). The pump heads respectively developed are within 10% of each other—34 vs. 31 ft (10.4 vs. 9.5 m)—and the pump efficiencies are identical, 77%.

Both solutions result in approximately the same capacities; however, there are two basic differences worth noting. First, the resulting series pump system characteristic is steep (compared with that developed in Figure 4-24) and slight changes in system head will have a negligible effect upon the system flow rate. Second, the pumps in series require only 3-hp (2.2-kW) motors for nonoverloading operation, as compared with 5 hp (3.7 kW) per pump for parallel operation.

Before a final determination is made, consideration should be given to a pump suddenly becoming inoperative. Flow rate for the parallel pump arrangement would drop to 400 gpm (25.2 L/s), a reduction of only 15%, and the flow rate for the series pump arrangement would drop to 335 gpm (21.1 L/s), a reduction of 25%. Therefore, although a higher installed horsepower (wattage) is required in the parallel pump arrangement, the brake horsepower (wattage) requirements are approximately the same and, further, a failure in one of the two operating pumps will result in a considerably smaller reduction in system flow rate. This configuration, therefore, appears to be a better selection.

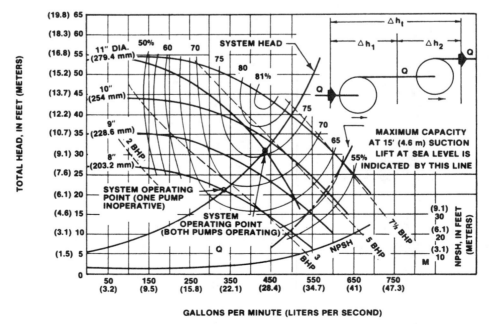

Figure 4-25 Pumps in Series—Chart for Estimating Total Head and Capacity

INSTALLATION AND OPERATING PROBLEMS

The designer should keep the following in mind when laying out the pumping system:

1. Suction and discharge piping should be as short and straight as possible to avoid excessive friction losses. Reducers in the piping should be eccentric.

2. Pumps should not support piping.

3. Line sizes should not be smaller than the pump nozzles.

4. The suction line should be of greater diameter than the suction nozzle of the pump.

5. High points in suction piping, which can promote the formation of air pockets, should be avoided.

6. Pumps should be located below the suction-side liquid level, where possible.

7. A nonslam check valve should be installed in the discharge piping to protect against sudden surges and reverse rotation of the impeller.

8. Where a discharge line of greater diameter than the discharge nozzle is employed, an eccentric increaser, check valve, and gate valve (in that order) should be used.

9. A line strainer in the pump suction piping should be provided, unless the pump is equipped with a nonclog impeller.

10. Pumps should be checked for correct alignment at the time of installation.

11. Pump suction lines should be checked for tightness to avoid drawing air into the pump. Entrained air tends to accumulate in the center of the impeller and causes a reduction in developed head and air lock.

12. When pump suction is directly connected to an open, shallow tank, baffles should be placed at the entrance of the suction pipe to break up any vortexes and to cause the incidence of the entrained air entering the pump to air lock.

13. When cavitation is diagnosed as the source of pump noise (characteristically, a crackling sound), installation of a throttling valve in the discharge piping used to reduce pump capacity should materially reduce the problem.

14. Noise may arise from any of the following conditions:

    A. Excessive velocities in the interconnecting piping or from improperly supported piping.

    B. Motor and/or bearing noise in high-speed pumps.

    C. Poor selection, with operating point substantially higher or lower than manufacturer's recommended "best efficiency point."

    D. Excessive vibration of pump or driver caused by misalignment, bent shaft, loose mounts or unbalanced hydraulic forces acting on impeller.

    E. Improper installation and sizing of the piping, which may cause noise transmission to the building.

    F. Improper vibration mounting of pumps.

15. Reverse rotation of impeller or impeller installed in reverse direction (though direction of rotation is correct), results in substantially reduced developed head and capacity with a higher power demand than the manufacturer indicates for measured flow rate.

16. Lack of liquid delivery can be due to lack of prime, insufficient available NPSH, clogged strainer, or system total head at zero capacity.

17. Loss of pump prime while operating can be due to loss of suction-line liquid vaporizing in suction line.

18. Excessive pump power can be due to excessive impeller speed, tight shaft packing, lack of sufficient clearance between impeller and casing, or higher than specified liquid density or viscosity, in addition to other contributing causes mentioned above.

5

Piping Insulation

Insulation and its ancillary components are a major consideration in the design and installation of the plumbing and piping systems of modern buildings. The insulation and methods discussed are used on a regular basis primarily for plumbing and drainage work. Insulation is used for the following purposes:

1. The retardation of heat or cooling temperature loss through pipe.

2. The elimination of condensation on piping

3. Personnel protection by keeping the surface temperature low enough to touch.

4. The appearance of the pipe, where aesthetics are important.

5. The protection of pipe from abrasion or damage from external forces.

6. The reduction of noise from a piping system.

To make certain that the reader understands the mechanism of heat, the following glossary of terms has been provided.

GLOSSARY

British thermal unit (Btu) The heat required to raise the temperature of 1 lb of water 1° Fahrenheit.

Conductance Also known as "conductivity," this measures the flow of heat through an arbitrary thickness of material, rather than the 1-in. thickness used in thermal conductivity. (See also "thermal conductivity.")

Convection The large-scale movement of heat through a fluid (liquid or gas). It cannot occur through a solid. The difference in density between hot and cold fluids will produce a natural movement of heat.

Degree Celsius This is the measurement used in international standard (SI) units and is found by dividing the ice point and steam point of water into 100 divisions.

Degree Fahrenheit This is the measurement used in inch-pound (IP) units and is found by dividing the ice point and steam point of water into 180 divisions.

Heat A type of energy that is produced by the movement of molecules. The more movement of molecules, the more heat. All heat (and movement) stops at absolute zero. It flows from a warmer body to a cooler body. It is calculated in such units such as Btu, calories, or watt-hours.

Kilocalorie (kcal) The heat required to raise 1 kilogram of water 1° Celsius.

Thermal conductivity The ability of a specific solid to conduct heat. This is measured in Btu/h and is referred to as the "k" factor. The standard used in the measurement is the heat that will flow in 1 hour through a material 1 in. thick, with a temperature difference of 1° Fahrenheit over an area of 1 ft.^{2} The metric equivalent is watts per square meter per degree kelvin (W/m^2/K). As the "k" factor increases, so does the flow of heat.

Thermal resistance Abbreviated "R," this is the reciprocal of the conductance value. (See "conductance.")

Thermal transmittance Known as the "U" factor, this is the rate of flow, measured in thermal resistance, through several different layers of materials taken together as a whole. It is measured in Btu per hour per square foot per degree Fahrenheit ($Btu/h/ft^2/°F$).

WATER VAPOR

Water vapor is present in the air at all times. A water vapor barrier does not stop the flow of water vapor, rather it serves as a means of controlling and reducing the rate of flow and is the only practical solution to the passage of water vapor. Its effectiveness depends on its location within the insulation system, which is usually as close to the outer surface of the insulation as practical. Water vapor has a vapor pressure that is a function of both temperature and relative humidity. The effectiveness of an insulation system is best when it is completely dry.

The water vapor transmission rate is a measure of water vapor diffusion into or through the total insulation system and is measured in perms. A perm is the weight of water, in grains, that is transmitted through 1 ft^2 of insulation 1 in. thick in 1 h. A generally accepted value of 0.30 perms is considered the maximum rate for an effective vapor barrier. A formula for the transmission of water vapor diffusing through insulation systems is given in Equation 5-1.

Equation 5-1

$$W = \mu A T \Delta \frac{P}{L}$$

where

W = Total weight of vapor transmitted (grains) (7000 grains = 1 lb water)

μ = Permeability of insulation (grains/ ft^2/ h/in. Hg ΔP/in.)

A = Area of cross-section of the flow path (ft^2)

T = Time during which the transmission occurred (h)

ΔP = Difference of vapor pressure between ends of the flow path (in. Hg)

L = Length of flow path (in.)

SMOKE AND FIRE REQUIREMENTS

When a fire starts within a building, many of its contents will contribute to the fire by either generating smoke (if the product is incombustible) or supporting combustion. Code limits for these factors have been established. These ratings are for complete insulation systems tested as a whole and not for individual components. The maximum code values for smoke developed is 50 or less, and a flame spread value of 25 or less. These values have been established for noncombustible construction. Combustible construction may be different.

The tunnel test is used to find the requirements for the different combinations of materials that are used. They are tested for smoke developed and flame spread. The ratings are compared to red oak flooring (rated at 100) and asbestos-cement board (rated at 0). Each test is given a different name by the agency that conducts it. The American Standard for Testing Materials calls it ASTM E-84, the National Fire Protection Association calls it NFPA 255 and Underwriters' Laboratories calls it UL 723.

A test conducted by the Underwriters' Laboratories has determined, however, that a smoke developed rating of 200 or less did not appreciably reduce visibility for periods of up to 6 min. From this report it seems likely that smoke ratings of up to 200 could provide good visibility.

CLEANING AND STERILIZATION

Insulation used for the chemical, pharmaceutical, and food processing industries (for example) must have the ability to withstand repeated cleaning by various methods. This is provided by the application of the proper jacketing material. Important properties of this jacket shall be resistance to growth of any organism, smooth finish, resistance to repeated cleaning by the method of choice by the owner, and nontoxicity.

TYPES OF INSULATION

All the various named types of insulation have different trade names given by manufacturers. The discussions that follow use the generic names for the most often used material in the plumbing and drainage industry. The various properties are based on the following conditions:

1. All materials have been tested to ASTM, NFPA and UL standards for a flame spread rating of 25 and a smoke developed rating of 50.
2. The temperature at which the k and R ratings were calculated was 75°F (24°C).

Fiberglass

Fiberglass insulation shall conform to ASTM C 547. It is manufactured from glass fiber bonded with a phenolic resin. It is the chemical composition of this resin that determines the highest temperature rating of this insulation. Consult the manufacturers for exact figures. This insulation is tested to fall below the rating of 50 for smoke developed and 25 for flame spread. It has a low water absorption and no to very limited combustibility. It has poor abrasion resistance.

This is the most commonly used insulation for the retardation of heat loss from plumbing lines and equipment. The recommended temperature range is from 35 to 800°F (1.8 to 422°C), with ratings dependent upon the binder. It is available as premolded pipe insulation, boards, and blankets. Typical k values range from 0.22 to 0.26 and R values range from 3.8 to 4.5. Its density is about 3–5 lb/ft^3 (48–80 kg/m^3).

Fiberglass by itself is not strong enough to stay on a pipe or piece of equipment, prevent the passage of water vapor, or present a finished appearance. Because of this a covering or jacket must be used.

Elastomeric

Elastomeric insulation, commonly called "rubber," shall conform to ASTM C 534. This is a flexible, expanded foam, closed cell material manufactured from nitrile rubber and polyvinyl chloride resin. This insulation is dependent on its thickness to fall below a specific smoke developed rating. All thickness has a flame spread rating of 50. This prevents it by code from being used in all types of construction. It will absorb 5% of its weight in water and has a perm rating of 0.17. Its density is in a range of between 3 and 8 lb/ft^3.

The recommended temperature range is from –35 to 220°F (–37 to 103°C). A typical k value is 0.27 and a typical R value is 3.6. Recommended use for this insulation includes preformed insulation for pipe sizes up to 5 in. (DN 125) in both ½ and ¾ in. thickness. It is also available in wide rolls up to 48 in. (1200 mm) long and in sheet sizes up to 36 × 48 in. (900 × 1200 mm) in size. An adhesive must be used to adhere it to pipes and equipment. It is generally the adhesive that determines the ultimate temperature for application. The manufacturer should be consulted for the exact figures.

Rubber insulation can be painted without treatment. It finds wide use in mechanical equipment rooms and pipe spaces where code requirements may be relaxed and the ease of application would make it less costly. The recommended temperature range is from 35 to 800°F (1.8 to 422°C)

Cellular Glass

Cellular glass shall conform to ASTM C 552. This insulation is pure glass foam manufactured with hydrogen sulfide and has closed cell air spaces. The smoke developed rating is 0 and the flame spread is 5. The recommended application temperature is between –450 and 450°F (–265 and 230°C) with the adhesive used to secure the insulation to the pipe or equipment the limiting factor. It has no water retention and poor surface abrasion resistance.

It is rigid and strong and commonly used for high-temperature installations. It is generally manufactured in blocks and must be fabricated by the contractor to make insulation for pipes or equipment. A saw is used for cutting. It has a typical k value of 0.37 and an R rating of 2.6. Its density is 8 lb/ft^3.

It is resistant to common acids and corrosive environments. It shall be provided with a jacket of some type.

Foamed Plastic

Foamed plastic insulation is a rigid, closed cell product, which shall conform to the following standards, depending on the material. Polyurethane shall conform to ASTM C 591, polystyrene shall conform to ASTM C 578, and polyethylene shall conform to ASTM C 578. It is made by the expansion of plastic beads or granules in a closed mold or using an extrusion process. The fire rating developed varies among manufacturers, but the combustibility is high. Additives can be used to increase the fire retardancy. It is available molded into boards or premolded into pipe insulation.

This is most commonly used in 3 or 4-in. thickness for insulation of cryogenic piping. The recommended temperature range for installation is from cryogenic to 220°F (103°C). The density varies between 0.7 and 3 lb/ft^3. The k value varies between 0.32 and 0.20, depending on the density and age of the material. The average water absorption is 2%.

Calcium Silicate

Calcium silicate shall conform to ASTM C 533. It is a rigid granular insulation composed of calcium silicate, asbestos-free reinforcing fibers and lime. This material has a k value of 0.38 and an R rating of 2.0.

A mineral fiber commonly referred to as "calsil," it is used for high-temperature work and does not find much use in the plumbing industry except as a rigid insert for installation at a hanger to protect the regular insulation from being crushed by the weight of the pipe.

Insulating Cement

This insulation is manufactured from fibrous and/or granular material and cement mixed with water to form a plastic substance. Sometimes referred to as "mastic," it has typical "k" values ranging between 0.65 and 0.95, depending on the composition.

This material is well suited for irregular surfaces.

TYPES OF JACKET

A jacket is any material, except cement or paint, that is used to protect or cover insulation installed on a pipe or over equipment. It allows the insulation to function for a long period of time by protecting the underlying material and extending its service life. The jacket is used for the following purposes:

1. As a vapor barrier to limit the entry of water into the insulation system.

2. As a weather barrier to protect the underlying insulation from the outside.

3. To prevent mechanical abuse due to accidental conditions or personnel.

4. Corrosion and additional fire resistance.

5. Appearance.

6. Cleanliness and disinfection.

All-Service Jacket

Known as "ASJ," the all-service jacket is a lamination of brown (kraft) paper, fiberglass cloth (skrim), and a metallic film. A vapor barrier is also included. This jacket is also called an "FSK" jacket because of the fiberglass cloth, skrim and kraft paper. It is most often used to cover fiberglass insulation.

The fiberglass cloth is used as a reinforcement for the kraft paper. The paper is generally a bleached 30-lb (13.5-kg) material, which actually weighs 30 lb per 30,000 ft^2 (2790 m^2). The metallic foil is aluminum. It is this complete jacket that gives the fire rating for the insulation system.

The jacket is adhered to the pipe with either self-sealing adhesive or staples. The butt joint ends are first sealed with adhesive, placed together, and then covered with lap strips during installation. Staples are used when the surrounding conditions are too dirty or corrosive to use self-sealing material. The staple holes shall be sealed with adhesive.

Aluminum Jacket

Aluminum jackets shall conform to ASTM B 209. They are manufactured in corrugated or smooth shape and available in various thicknesses ranging from 0.010 to 0.024, with 0.016 in. being the most common. The corrugated material is used where expansion and contraction of the piping may be a problem. These jackets are also made in various tempers and alloys. Vapor barrier material can also be applied. This vapor barrier may be necessary to protect the aluminum from any corrosive ingredient in the insulation. Fittings are fabricated in the shop.

Aluminum jackets may be secured by either of three methods: banded by straps on 9-in. (180-mm) centers, by a proprietary S or Z shape, or by sheet metal screws.

Stainless Steel Jacket

Stainless steel jackets shall conform to ASTM A 240. They are manufactured in corrugated or smooth shape and available in various thicknesses ranging from 0.010 to 0.019, with 0.016 in. being the most common. They are also available in various alloy types, among them are ASTM A 304 and A 316, with A 304 being the most common. They can be obtained in different finishes. Vapor barrier material can also be applied, although it is not required for corrosive ingredients except where chlorine or fluorides are present.

Stainless steel jackets are used for hygienic purposes and are adhered in a manner similar to that used for aluminum.

Plastic Jacket

Plastic jackets are manufactured from PVC, PVDF, ABS, polyvinyl acetate (PVA), and acrylics. Thicknesses range from 3 to 35 mils. The local code authorities shall be consulted prior to use.

They are adhered by the use of an appropriate adhesive.

Wire Mesh

Wire mesh is available in various wire diameters and various widths. Materials for manufacture are Monel, stainless steel, and Inconel. Wire mesh is used where a strong flexible covering that can be easily removed is needed.

It is secured with lacing hooks or stainless steel wire that must be additionally wrapped with tie wire or metal straps.

Lagging

Lagging is the covering of a previously insulated pipe or piece of equipment with a cloth or fiberglass jacket. It is used where appearance is the primary consideration, since this type of jacket offers little or no additional insulation protection. This material is also used as a combination system that will serve as a protective coat and adhesive.

This jacket is usually secured to the insulation with the use of lagging adhesive and/or sizing. It is available in a variety of colors and may eliminate the need for painting.

INSTALLING INSULATION FOR VALVES AND FITTINGS FOR PIPING

The fittings and valves on a piping system require specially formed or made-up sections of insulation to complete the installation.

One type of insulation is the preformed type that is manufactured by specific size and shape to fit over any particular fitting or valve. Such insulation is available in two sections that are secured with staples, adhesive or pressure sensitive tape depending on the use of a vapor barrier. This is the quickest method of installation but the most costly.

Another system uses a preformed plastic jacket the exact size and shape of the fitting or valve. A fiberglass blanket or sheet is cut to size and wrapped around the bare pipe, then the jacket is placed over the insulation. The exposed edges are tucked in and the jacket is secured with special tacks with a barb that prevents them from pulling apart. The ends are sealed with pressure-sensitive tape.

For larger piping it is common to use straight lengths of fiberglass, mitering the ends and securing them with a fiberglass jacket (lagging).

INSTALLING INSULATION FOR TANKS

Where fiberglass is specified, tanks are insulated using 2 ft × 4 ft boards in the thickness required. The boards are placed on the tank so they are similar in appearance to bricks. They are secured with metal bands. Over the bands wire is placed as a foundation for insulating cement applied over the tank to give a finished appearance.

Where rubber is specified, the tank is coated with adhesive and the rubber sheets are placed on the tank. The edges are coated with adhesive to seal it. Painting is not required.

PIPE SUPPORT METHODS

As the installation on a project progresses, a contractor must contend with different situations regarding the vapor barrier. Since the insulation system selected shall be protected against the migration of water vapor into the insulation, the integrity of the vapor barrier must be maintained. Where a hanger is installed directly on the pipe, the insulation must be placed over both the pipe and the hanger. Figure 5-1 illustrates a split-ring hanger attached directly on the pipe. This type of hanger is not recommended for use in chilled drinking water or other low-temperature lines.

Since low-density insulation is the type most often used, a situation arises wherein the primary considerations are keeping the vapor barrier intact and preventing the weight of the pipe from crushing the insulation. Figure 5-2 illustrates several high-density insert solutions for a clevis hanger supporting an insulated pipe.

The jacketing method shown in both figures can be used interchangeably with any type of insulation for which it is suited.

SELECTION OF INSULATION THICKNESS

There are four basic reasons for using insulation:

1. Controlling heat loss from piping or equipment.
2. Condensation control.
3. Personnel protection.
4. Economics.

Controlling Heat Loss

Increased concern about conservation and energy use has resulted in the insulation of piping to control heat loss becoming one of the primary

1. Pipe
2. Insulation (shown with factory-applied, non-metal jacket).
3. Overlap at logitudinal joints (cut to allow for hanger rod).
4. Tape applied at butt joints (Pipe covering section at hanger should extend a few inches beyond the hanger to facilitate proper butt joint sealing.)
5. Insulation altered to compensate for projections on split ring hangers (If insulation thickness is serverely altered and left insufficient for high temperature applications or condensation control, insulate with a sleeve of oversized pipe insulation.)
6. Insulation applied in like manner around rod on cold installations.

Source: MICA

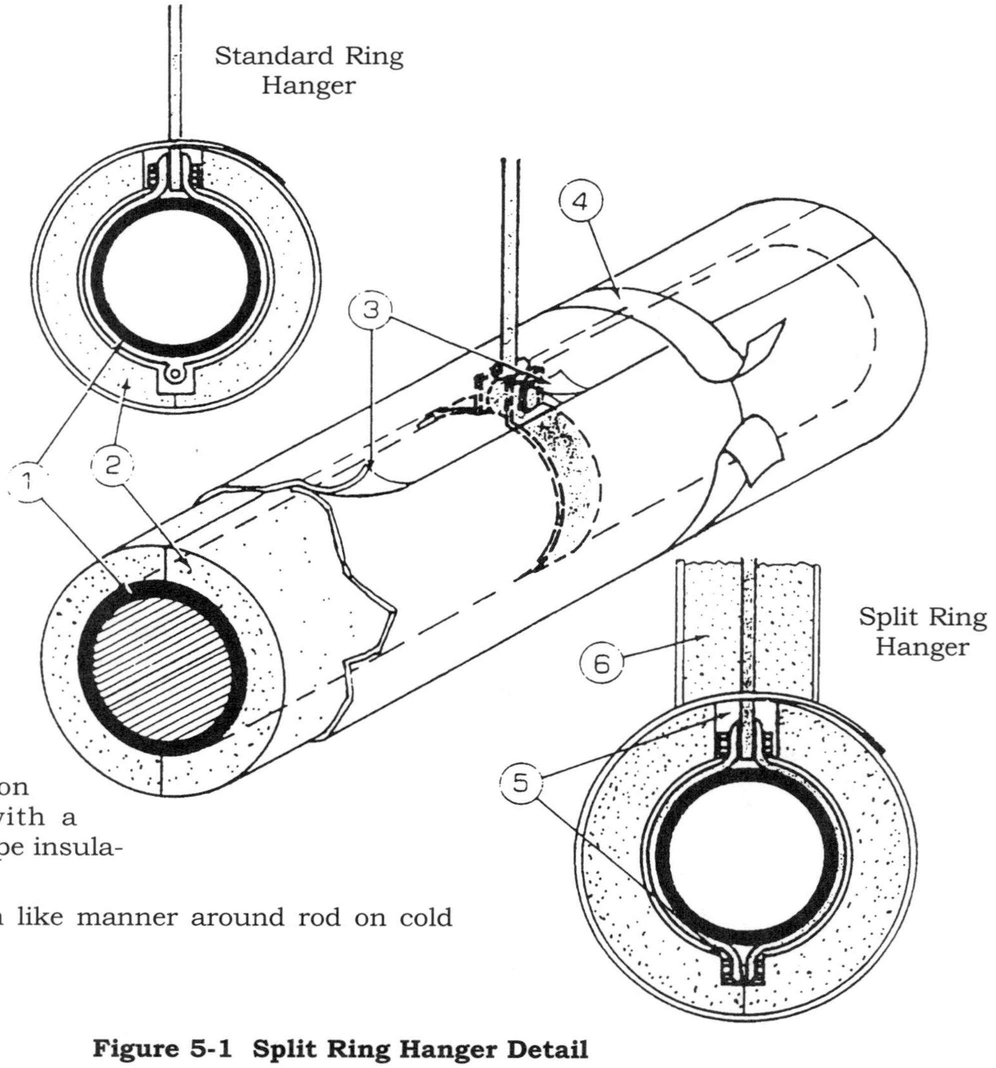

Figure 5-1 Split Ring Hanger Detail

considerations in design. Heat loss is basically an economic consideration, since the lessening of heat loss produces a more cost-efficient piping system. The proper use of insulation can have dramatic results.

Determining heat loss from insulated piping
The insulation installed on domestic hot water, hot water return, and chilled drinking water systems is intended to keep heat loss from the water to a minimum. Since fiberglass insulation is the type most often used, Table 5-1 is provided to give the heat loss through vertical and horizontal piping as well as the heat loss through bare pipe. Table 5-2 is given for piping intended to be installed outdoors.

When calculating the heat loss from round surfaces, such as a pipe, the plumbing engineer

should remember that the inside surface of the insulation has a different diameter than the outside. Therefore, a means must be found to determine the equivalent thickness that shall be used. This is done by the use of Table 5-3. To read this table, enter with the actual pipe size and insulation thickness then read the equivalent thickness of the insulation.

Condensation Control

As mentioned before, water vapor in the air will condense on a cold surface if the temperature of the cold surface is at or below the dew point. If the temperature is above the dew point, condensation will not form. The purpose of a vapor barrier is to minimize or eliminate such condensation. For this to be accomplished, the joints

1. Pipe
2. Insulation (type specified for the line).
3. High density insulation insert (Extend beyond the shield to facilitate proper butt joint sealing.)
4. Factory-applied vapor-barrier jacket securing two insulation sections together (cold application).
5. Jacketing (field-applied metal shown)
6. Metal shield
7. Wood block or wood dowel insert.
Source: MICA

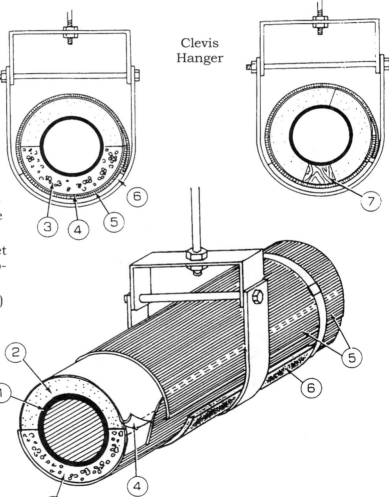

Figure 5-2 Clevis Hanger - High Density Inserts

and overlaps must be tightly sealed. This is done through one of three methods:

1. Rigid jackets such as metallic or plastic.
2. Membranes such as laminated foils or treated paper.
3. Mastics applied over the pipe, either emulsion or solvent type.

Table 5-4 shows the dry bulb, dew-point temperature at which condensation will form. Table 5-5 is provided to indicate the thickness of fiberglass insulation with water at 50°F (10°C) needed to prevent condensation.

Personnel Protection

When hot water flows through an uninsulated piping system, it is usually at a temperature that may cause the scalding of any person touching the pipe. Insulation is used to lower the surface temperatures of hot water pipes to prevent such harm. A surface temperature of 120°F (49°C) has been shown not to cause harm to a person coming in contact with the pipe. Table 5-6 gives the thickness of fiberglass insulation and the surface temperature of the insulation. The thickness shown in this table should be compared with that shown in Table 5-1 or 5-2 to see which thickness is greater. The greater thickness should be used.

Economics

The two factors involved are the cost of insulation and the cost of energy. To calculate the energy savings in financial terms, the following are needed:

1. Service temperature of the surface
2. Pipe size or flat
3. Btu difference between air and surface or flat (linear feet or square feet)
4. Efficiency of heating equipment
5. Annual operating hours
6. Cost of fuel.

If the plumbing designer wishes to make an economic comparison among various insulation systems, there are many formulas and computer programs available for the purpose. Discussion of these methods is beyond the scope of this chapter.

FREEZE PROTECTION

No amount of insulation will prevent the freezing of water (or sewage) in a pipeline that remains dormant over a period of time. Studies by the U.S. Army Cold Region Research and Engineering Laboratory (CRREL) have shown that the freezing of water in pipes is much more complicated and can be blocked much earlier than had been thought.

Table 5-1 Heat Loss in Btu/H/Ft Length of Fiberglass Insulation, ASJ Cover 150°F Temperature of Pipe

Horizontal

NPS / THK / BARE	½		¾		1		1¼		1½		2		2½		3		4		5		6		8	
HL	HL	ST																						
BARE	36		44		54		67		75		92		110		131		165		200		235		299	
½"	10	92	10	90	13	93	20	98	18	94	20	93	23	94	30	95	36	95	43	95	53	97	68	97
1"	7	86	8	87	9	86	11	88	11	87	13	87	15	88	18	88	22	88	27	89	32	89	38	89
1½"	5	84	6	84	7	84	8	84	9	85	10	85	10	84	14	85	17	86	20	86	23	86	28	8
2"	5	82	5	83	6	83	7	83	7	83	9	83	9	83	11	84	14	84	16	84	18	84	23	85

Vertical

THK / BARE	½		¾		1		1¼		1½		2		2½		3		4		5		6		8	
HL	HL	ST																						
BARE	32		40		49		61		69		84		100		120		152		185		217		277	
½"	9	92	10	90	13	93	19	99	18	95	20	94	23	94	30	96	35	96	43	96	52	97	67	98
1"	7	86	8	87	9	86	11	88	11	87	13	88	15	88	18	89	22	89	26	89	31	90	38	89
1½"	5	84	6	84	7	84	8	84	9	85	10	85	10	84	14	86	16	86	20	86	23	87	28	8
2"	5	83	5	83	6	83	7	83	7	83	9	83	9	83	11	84	14	84	16	85	18	85	23	85

Source: Courtesy of Owens/Corning.
Notes: 80°ambient temperature,
0 wind velocity,
0.85 bare surface emittance,
0.90 surface emittance

HL = heat loss (BTU/h/ft length)
ST = surface temperature (°F)
Bare = bare pipe, iron pipe size
THK = thickness

Table 5-2 Heat Loss from Piping

Insulation Type	Insulation Factor	Heat Loss per Inch Thickness, Based on K Factor @ 50°F Mean Temp. (Btu/h · °F · ft²)
Glass fiber (ASTM C547)	1.00	0.25
Calcium silicate (ASTM C533)	1.50	0.375
Cellular glass (ASTM C552)	1.60	0.40
Rigid cellular urethane (ASTM C591)	0.66	0.165
Foamed elastomer (ASTM C534)	1.16	0.29
Mineral fiber blanket (ASTM C553)	1.20	0.30
Expanded perlite (ASTM C610)	1.50	0.375

		IPS												
		½	¾	1	1¼	1½	2	2½	3	4	6	8	10	12
Insulation Thickness (in.)	ΔT, °F	\multicolumn{13}{Tubing Size (in.)}												
		¾	1	1¼	1½	2								
0.5	10	0.5	0.6	0.7	0.8	0.9	1.1	1.3	1.5	1.8	2.6	3.3	4.1	4.8
	50	2.5	2.9	3.5	4.1	4.8	5.5	6.5	7.7	9.6	13.5	17.2	21.1	24.8
	100	5.2	6.1	7.2	8.6	9.9	11.5	13.5	15.9	19.9	28.1	35.8	43.8	51.6
	150	8.1	9.5	11.2	13.4	15.5	17.9	21.0	24.8	31.9	43.8	55.7	68.2	80.2
	200	11.2	13.1	15.5	18.5	21.4	24.7	29.0	34.3	42.7	60.4	76.9	94.1	110.7
	250	14.6	17.1	20.2	24.1	27.9	32.2	37.8	44.7	55.7	78.8	100.3	122.6	144.2
1.0	10	0.3	0.4	0.4	0.5	0.6	0.6	0.7	0.8	1.0	1.4	1.8	2.2	2.6
	50	1.6	1.9	2.2	2.5	2.9	3.2	3.7	4.4	5.4	7.4	9.4	11.4	13.4
	100	3.4	3.9	4.5	5.2	5.9	6.8	7.8	9.1	11.2	15.5	19.5	23.8	27.8
	150	5.3	6.1	7.0	8.2	9.3	10.5	12.2	14.2	17.4	24.1	30.4	37.0	43.3
	200	7.4	8.4	9.7	11.3	12.8	14.6	16.8	19.6	24.0	33.4	42.0	51.2	59.9
	250	9.6	11.0	12.6	14.8	16.7	19.0	22.0	25.6	31.4	43.6	54.9	66.9	78.2
1.5	10	0.3	0.3	0.3	0.4	0.4	0.5	0.5	0.6	0.8	1.0	1.3	1.4	1.8
	50	1.3	1.5	1.7	1.9	2.2	2.4	2.8	3.2	3.9	5.3	6.6	8.0	9.3
	100	2.7	3.1	3.5	4.0	4.5	5.1	5.8	6.7	8.1	11.1	13.8	16.7	19.5
	150	4.3	4.8	5.5	6.3	7.1	7.9	9.1	10.4	12.6	17.2	21.5	26.0	30.3
	200	5.9	6.7	7.6	8.7	9.8	11.0	12.5	14.5	17.5	23.8	29.7	36.0	41.9
	250	7.8	8.7	9.9	11.4	12.8	14.4	16.4	18.9	22.8	31.1	38.9	47.1	54.8
2.0	10	0.2	0.2	0.3	0.3	0.4	0.4	0.4	0.5	0.6	0.8	1.0	1.2	1.4
	50	1.1	1.3	1.4	1.6	1.8	2.0	2.3	2.6	3.1	4.2	5.2	6.3	7.3
	100	2.4	2.7	3.0	3.4	3.8	4.2	4.8	5.5	6.5	8.8	10.9	13.1	15.2
	150	3.7	4.2	4.7	5.3	5.9	6.6	7.5	8.5	10.2	13.7	17.0	20.4	23.6
	200	5.2	5.8	6.5	7.4	8.2	9.1	10.3	11.8	14.1	19.0	23.5	28.2	32.7
	250	6.8	7.5	8.5	9.6	10.7	11.9	13.5	15.4	18.5	24.8	30.7	36.9	42.7
2.5	10	0.2	0.2	0.2	0.3	0.3	0.3	0.4	0.4	0.5	0.7	0.8	1.0	1.2
	50	1.0	1.1	1.3	1.4	1.6	1.8	2.0	2.3	2.7	3.6	4.4	5.2	6.0
	100	2.2	2.4	2.7	3.0	3.3	3.7	4.1	4.7	5.6	7.5	9.1	10.9	12.6
	150	3.4	3.7	4.2	4.7	5.2	5.8	6.5	7.3	8.7	11.5	14.2	17.0	19.6
	200	4.7	5.2	5.8	6.5	7.2	8.0	9.0	10.2	12.1	16.0	19.6	23.5	27.1
	250	6.1	6.8	7.5	8.5	9.4	10.4	11.7	13.3	15.8	20.9	25.7	30.7	35.4
3.0	10	0.2	0.2	0.2	0.3	0.3	0.3	0.3	0.4	0.5	0.6	0.7	0.9	1.0
	50	1.0	1.1	1.2	1.3	1.4	1.6	1.8	2.0	2.4	3.1	3.8	4.5	5.2
	100	2.0	2.2	2.4	2.7	3.0	33	3.7	4.2	4.9	6.5	7.9	9.4	10.8
	150	3.1	3.4	3.8	4.3	4.7	5.2	5.8	5.6	7.7	10.1	12.3	14.7	16.8
	200	4.3	4.8	5.3	5.9	6.5	7.2	8.0	9.0	10.7	14.0	17.0	20.3	23.3
	250	5.7	6.2	6.9	7.7	8.5	9.4	10.5	11.8	13.9	18.3	22.3	26.5	30.5

Source: RAYCHEM.

Notes: 1. Pipe heat loss (Q_B) is shown in watts per foot (W/ft). 2. Heat loss calculation is based on metal pipes insulated with glass fiber (ASTM C547) and located outdoors in a 20 mph wind. 3. A 10% safety factor has been included. 4. W/ft = Btu/ft x 0.293.

Table 5-3 Insulation Thickness–Equivalent Thickness (in.)

DN	NPS	½ L₁	½ A	1 L₁	1 A	1½ L₁	1½ A	2 L₁	2 A	2½ L₁	2½ A	3 L₁	3 A
15	½	0.76	0.49	1.77	0.75	3.12	1.05	4.46	1.31	—	—	—	—
20	¾	0.75	0.56	1.45	0.75	2.68	1.05	3.90	1.31	—	—	—	—
25	1	0.71	0.62	1.72	0.92	2.78	1.18	4.02	1.46	—	—	—	—
32	1¼	0.63	0.70	1.31	0.92	2.76	1.31	3.36	1.46	—	—	—	—
40	1½	0.60	0.75	1.49	1.05	2.42	1.31	4.13	1.73	—	—	—	—
50	2	0.67	0.92	1.43	1.18	2.36	1.46	3.39	1.73	4.43	1.99	—	—
65	2½	0.66	1.05	1.38	1.31	2.75	1.73	3.71	1.99	4.73	2.26	—	—
80	3	0.57	1.18	1.29	1.46	2.11	1.73	2.96	1.99	3.88	2.26	4.86	2.52
90	3½	0.92	1.46	1.67	1.73	2.46	1.99	3.31	2.26	4.22	2.52	5.31	2.81
100	4	0.59	1.46	1.28	1.73	2.01	1.99	2.80	2.26	3.65	2.52	4.68	2.81
115	4½	0.94	1.74	1.61	1.99	2.35	2.26	3.15	2.52	4.11	2.81	5.02	3.08
125	5	0.58	1.74	1.20	1.99	1.89	2.26	2.64	2.52	3.54	2.81	4.40	3.08
150	6	0.54	2.00	1.13	2.26	1.79	2.52	2.60	2.81	3.36	3.08	4.17	3.34
	7	—	—	1.11	2.52	1.84	2.81	2.54	3.08	3.27	3.34	4.25	3.67
200	8	—	—	1.18	2.81	1.81	3.08	2.49	3.34	3.39	3.67	4.15	3.93
	9	—	—	1.17	3.08	1.79	3.34	2.62	3.67	3.32	3.93	4.06	4.19
250	10	—	—	1.09	3.34	1.85	3.67	2.50	3.93	3.18	4.19	3.90	4.45
300	12	—	—	1.22	3.93	1.82	4.19	2.45	4.45	3.10	4.71	3.79	4.97
350	14	—	—	1.07	4.19	1.65	4.45	2.26	4.71	2.90	4.97	3.57	5.24
400	16	—	—	1.06	4.71	1.63	4.97	2.23	5.24	2.86	5.50	3.50	5.76
450	18	—	—	1.05	5.24	1.62	5.50	2.21	5.76	2.82	6.02	3.45	6.28
500	20	—	—	1.05	5.76	1.61	6.02	2.19	6.28	2.79	6.54	3.41	6.81
600	24	—	—	1.04	6.81	1.59	7.07	2.16	7.33	2.74	7.59	3.35	7.85

Source: Owens/Corning.
DN = nominal diameter
NPS = nominal pipe size
L₁ = equivalent thickness (in.)
$L_1 = r_2 \ln (r_2/r_1)$

where
r_1 = inner radius of insulation (in.)
r_2 = outer radius of insulation (in.)
ln = log to the base e (natural log)
A = square feet of pipe insulation surface per lineal foot of pipe

Table 5-4 Dew-Point Temperature

Dry-Bulb Temp. (°F)	Percent Relative Humidity 10	15	20	25	30	35	40	45	50	55	60	65	70	75	80	85	90	95	100
5	-35	-30	-25	-21	-17	-14	-12	-10	-8	-6	-5	-4	-2	-1	1	2	3	4	5
10	-31	-25	-20	-16	-13	-10	-7	-5	-3	-2	0	2	3	4	5	7	8	9	10
15	-28	-21	-16	-12	-8	-5	-3	-1	1	3	5	6	8	9	10	12	13	14	15
20	-24	-16	-11	-8	-4	-2	2	4	6	8	10	11	13	14	15	16	18	19	20
25	-20	-15	-8	-4	0	3	6	8	10	12	15	16	18	19	20	21	23	24	25
30	-15	-9	-3	2	5	8	11	13	15	17	20	22	23	24	25	27	28	29	30
35	-12	-5	1	5	9	12	15	18	20	22	24	26	27	28	30	32	33	34	35
40	-7	0	5	9	14	16	19	22	24	26	28	29	31	33	35	36	38	39	40
45	-4	3	9	13	17	20	23	25	28	30	32	34	36	38	39	41	43	44	45
50	-1	7	13	17	21	24	27	30	32	34	37	39	41	42	44	45	47	49	50
55	3	11	16	21	25	28	32	34	37	39	41	43	45	47	49	50	52	53	55
60	6	14	20	25	29	32	35	39	42	44	46	48	50	52	54	55	57	59	60
65	10	18	24	28	33	38	40	43	46	49	51	53	55	57	59	60	62	63	65
70	13	21	28	33	37	41	45	48	50	53	55	57	60	62	64	65	67	68	70
75	17	25	32	37	42	46	49	52	55	57	60	62	64	66	69	70	72	74	75
80	20	29	35	41	46	50	54	57	60	62	65	67	69	72	74	75	77	78	80
85	23	32	40	45	50	54	58	61	64	67	69	72	74	76	78	80	82	83	85
90	27	36	44	49	54	58	62	66	69	72	74	77	79	81	83	85	87	89	90
95	30	40	48	54	59	63	67	70	73	76	79	82	84	86	88	90	91	93	95
100	34	44	52	58	63	68	71	75	78	81	84	86	88	91	92	94	96	98	100
110	41	52	60	66	71	77	80	84	87	90	92	95	98	100	102	104	106	108	110
120	48	60	68	74	79	85	88	92	96	99	102	105	109	109	112	114	116	118	120
125	52	63	72	78	84	89	93	97	100	104	107	109	111	114	117	119	121	123	125

Source: MICA.

Table 5-5 Insulation Thickness to Prevent Condensation, 50°F Service Temperature and 70°F Ambient Temperature

DN	Nom. Pipe Size (in.)	20			50			70			80			90		
		THK	HG	ST	THK	HG	ST	THK	HG	ST	THK	HG	ST	THK	HG	ST
15	0.50				0.5	2	66	0.5	2	66	0.5	2	66	1.0	2	68
20	0.75				0.5	2	67	0.5	2	67	0.5	2	67	0.5	2	67
25	1.00				0.5	3	66	0.5	3	66	0.5	3	66	1.0	2	68
32	1.25				0.5	3	66	0.5	3	66	0.5	3	66	1.0	3	67
40	1.50				0.5	4	65	0.5	4	65	0.5	4	65	1.0	3	67
50	2.00	Condensation			0.5	5	66	0.5	5	66	0.5	5	66	1.0	3	67
65	2.50	control not			0.5	5	65	0.5	5	65	0.5	5	65	1.0	4	67
75	3.00	required for this			0.5	7	65	0.5	7	65	0.5	7	65	1.0	4	67
90	3.50	condition			0.5	8	65	0.5	8	65	0.5	8	65	1.0	4	68
100	4.00				0.5	8	65	0.5	8	65	0.5	8	65	1.0	5	67
125	5.00				0.5	10	65	0.5	10	65	0.5	10	65	1.0	6	67
150	6.00				0.5	12	65	0.5	12	65	0.5	12	65	1.0	7	67
200	8.00				1.0	9	67	1.0	9	67	1.0	9	67	1.0	9	67
250	10.00				1.0	11	67	1.0	11	67	1.0	11	67	1.0	11	67
300	12.00				1.0	12	67	1.0	12	67	1.0	12	67	1.0	12	67

Source: Courtesy Certainteed.
Notes: 25 mm = 1 in.
THK = Insulation thickness (in.).
HG = Heat gain/lineal foot (pipe) 28 ft (flat) (Btu).
ST = Surface temperature (°F).

Table 5-6 Insulation Thickness for Personnel Protection, 120°F Maximum Surface Temperature, 80°F Ambient Temperature

Nom. Pipe Size (in.)	250				350				450				550			
	TH	LF	SF	ST	TH	LF	SF	ST	TH	LF	SF	ST	TH	LF	SF	ST
0.50	0.5	25	51	109	1.0	30	40	104	1.0	48	64	118	1.5	55	52	113
0.75	0.5	25	41	104	0.5	42	68	120	1.5	45	43	107	1.5	64	61	118
1.00	0.5	34	55	112	1.0	37	40	105	1.0	60	66	120	1.5	69	58	117
1.25	0.5	37	49	109	1.0	47	51	112	1.5	55	42	107	1.5	77	59	118
1.50	0.5	46	61	117	1.0	48	46	109	1.5	62	47	110	2.0	70	40	106
2.00	0.5	50	55	114	1.0	56	47	110	1.5	70	48	111	2.0	84	48	112
2.50	0.5	59	56	115	1.5	45	26	97	1.5	72	41	107	1.5	102	59	119
3.00	0.5	75	64	120	1.0	76	52	114	1.5	93	53	115	2.0	110	55	117
3.50	1.0	43	25	96	1.0	71	41	107	1.5	93	46	111	2.0	112	49	113
4.00	0.5	89	61	119	1.0	90	52	114	1.5	112	56	117	2.0	131	58	119
5.00	1.0	67	33	102	1.0	110	55	117	1.5	134	59	120	2.5	131	46	112
6.00	1.0	79	35	103	1.0	130	57	119	2.0	124	44	110	2.5	150	48	114
8.00	1.0	95	33	103	1.0	157	55	118	2.0	153	45	112	2.5	177	48	114
10.00	1.0	121	36	105	1.5	136	37	106	2.0	179	45	112	2.5	215	51	117
12.00	1.0	129	32	103	1.0	212	54	118	2.0	207	46	113	2.5	248	52	118

Source: Certainteed.

Notes: TH = Thickness of insulation (in.)
HL = heat loss (Btu/h)
LF = Heat loss per lineal foot of pipe (Btu/h)
SF = Heat loss per square foot of outside insulation surface (Btu/h)
ST = Surface temperature of insulation (°F)

Table 5-7 Time for Dormant Water to Freeze

Fiberglass Insulation

Pipe or Tubing Size (in.)	Air Temp., °F (°C)	Water Temp., °F (°C)	Insulation Thickness, in. (mm)	Time to 32°F (0°C) DORMANT water (h)	Time to 32°F (0°C) Solid Ice (h) [a]	Flow [b]
⅝ OD CT	-10 (-23.3)	50 (10)	0.66 (N¾) (19.1)	0.30	3.10	0.33
1⅛ OD CT	-10 (-23.3)	50 (10)	0.74 (N¾) (19.1)	0.75	8.25	0.44
1⅝ OD CT	-10 (-23.3)	50 (10)	0.79 (N¾) (19.1)	1.40	14.75	0.57
3⅛ OD CT	-10 (-23.3)	50 (10)	0.88 (N¾) (19.1)	3.5	37.70	0.83
1 IPS	-10 (-23.3)	50 (10)	0.76 (N¾) (19.1)	0.75	8.25	0.48
2 IPS	-10 (-23.3)	50 (10)	0.85 (N¾) (19.1)	2.10	22.70	0.67
3 IPS	-10 (-23.3)	50 (10)	0.89 (N¾) (19.1)	3.60	38.40	0.90
5 IPS	-10 (-23.3)	50 (10)	0.95 (N¾) (19.1)	6.95	73.60	1.25

Foamed Plastic Insulation

Pipe or Tubing Size (in.)	Air Temp., °F (°C)	Water Temp., °F (°C)	Insulation Thickness, in. (mm)	Time to 32°F (0°C) DORMANT Water (h)	Time to 32°F (0°C) Solid Ice (h) [a]	Flow [b]
⅝ OD CT	-10 (-23.3)	50 (10)	1 (25.4)	0.60	6.20	0.16
1⅛ OD CT	-10 (-23.3)	50 (10)	1 (25.4)	1.30	13.70	0.26
1⅝ OD CT	-10 (-23.3)	50 (10)	1 (25.4)	2.35	24.75	0.32
3⅛ OD CT	-10 (-23.3)	50 (10)	1 (25.4)	5.55	58.65	0.52
1 IPS	-10 (-23.3)	50 (10)	1 (25.4)	1.50	15.75	0.25
2 IPS	-10 (-23.3)	50 (10)	1 (25.4)	3.80	40.15	0.39
3 IPS	-10 (-23.3)	50 (10)	1 (25.4)	6.05	64.20	0.53
5 IPS	-10 (-23.3)	50 (10)	1 (25.4)	11.15	118.25	0.78

[a] No way to calculate slush. 32°F (0°C) ice value higher due to heat of fusion.
[b] Flow is expressed as gal/h/ft of pipe (12.4 L/hr-m).
Example: For 100 ft. (30.5m) pipe run, multiply value shown by 100. This is the minimum continuous flow to keep water from freezing.
OD CT = outside diameter, copper tube
IPS = iron pipe size

Table 5-7 is provided as a direct reading table for estimating the time it will take for dormant water to freeze. For some installations it is not possible to have the water remain dormant. If the water is flowing, as it does in a drainage line, use Figure 5-3, a nomogram that gives the temperature drop of flowing water. If the contents cannot be prevented from freezing, the plumbing engineer can add hot water to raise the temperature, heat trace the line, or provide sufficient velocity to keep the contents from freezing.

To calculate the flow of water in a line to prevent freezing, use the following formula:

Equation 5-2

$$gpm = \frac{A_1 \times A_2 \times (0.5TW - TA + 16)}{40.1 \ D^2 \ (TW - 32)}$$

where

gpm	=	Flow rate (gpm)
A_1	=	Pipe flow area (ft²)
A_2	=	Exposed pipe surface area (ft²)
TW	=	Water temperature (°F)
TA	=	Lowest air temperature (°F)
D	=	Inside diameter of pipe (ft)

INSULATION DESIGN CONSIDERATIONS

1. Insulation will attenuate sound from the flow of pipe contents. Where sound is a problem, such as in theaters, adding an extra thickness of insulation will lessen the sound.

2. The health and safety involved with the storage and handling of the insulation and/or jacketing materials will be alleviated by proper

adherence to established safe storage and handling procedures.

3. The rate of expansion will affect the efficiency of the insulation over a long period of time. The difference between the expansion of insulation and the expansion of the pipe will eventually lead to gaps after numerous flexings.

4. Protect the insulation against physical damage by adding a strong jacket or delaying installation on a piping system. It has been found that workmen walking on the pipe pose the greatest danger.

5. If the insulation is to be installed in a corrosive atmosphere, the proper jacket shall be installed to withstand the most severe conditions.

6. Union regulations should be reviewed to ensure that the insulation contractor installs a jacket. Some metal jackets above a certain thickness are installed by the general contractor.

7. Space conditions may dictate the use of one insulation system over another to fit in a confined space.

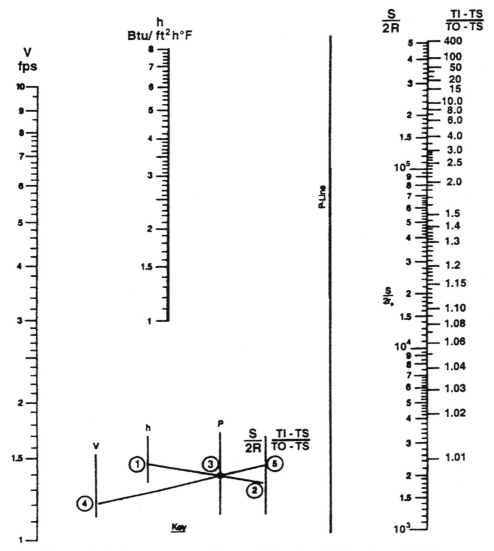

Figure 5-3 Temperature Drop of Flowing Water in a Pipeline

BIBLIOGRAPHY

1. American Society of Heating, Refrigerating, and Air-Conditioning Engineers (ASHRAE). Standard 90.1.

2. Frankel, M. 1988. Thermal insulation for plumbing systems. *Plumbing Engineer* July.

3. Frankel, M. 1996. *Facility piping systems handbook.* McGraw-Hill.

4. Kenny, T. M. 1991. Guard against freezing in water lines. *Chemical Engineering Progress* September.

5. Midwest Insulation Contractors Association. 1999. *Commercial and industrial insulation standards.*

6. O'Keefe, W. 1974. Thermal insulation. *Power Magazine.*

7. U.S. Army. *Depth of freeze and thaw in soils.* Technical Manual TM-5-852-6.

Hangers and Supports

INTRODUCTION

Hangers, supports, and anchors for piping systems require more than a simple specification for a hanger or support type suitable for holding in place a portion of piping or supporting a run of pipe. The plumbing engineer and designer not only need to create a specific performance specification applicable to the requirements and demands of the necessary general and basic piping systems within the project; they must also account for specific environmental considerations as well as the substances—including the amount and composition—expected to flow or pass through the various piping systems.

In the early 1900s, when simpler times and fewer complex environments prevailed, piping system supports and hangers were specified to help support or firmly anchor piping systems, prevent pipe runs from sagging, allow for some motion to help alleviate breakage, and provide for an adequate slope to accommodate drainage or flow. It was recognized that vibration within piping systems could have various effects, and early engingeering texts suggested that some soft material, such as felt, be used to help stop motion and deaden sound.

Given the litigious nature of today's society, a plumbing engineer can no longer take for granted that a piping system is "standard." What was once a simple performance and design standard that specified a simple device for attaching a pipe to a horizontal or vertical surface, holding a pipe in place, or supporting a long run of pipe has evolved to the need for the engineer to evaluate the total environment in which the pip-

ing system will function. The plumbing engineer must now be cognizant of structural components, chemical interactions, metal fatigue analysis, acoustic engineering, and even electric current transference.

The once simple pipe hanger and support has become a complex element in the overall design and specification of a piping and plumbing system. The plumbing engineer needs to consider the hangers and supports utilized within the overall piping and plumbing systems to be just one more element of the total system and must therefore be cognizant of a multitude of environmental and physical characteristics that may interact with and affect the overall system. The engineer often needs to go beyond the simple specifications for support types and hanger distances specified in basic plumbing codes. Indeed, he or she may need to consult with other engineering disciplines and with the pipe and pipe support manufacturers for the correct materials to specify for particular applications.

The engineer must not underestimate the importance of the hangers and supports used for the plumbing system. Supporting a pipe on a wall or from a ceiling seems simple enough—just find the right hanger for the job in the catalogue and leave the rest to the installers. Wrong! The right hanger is an integral part of the engineering and design of the plumbing system. Consider the Mother Goose rhyme:

> For want of a nail, the shoe was lost,
> For want of a shoe, the horse was lost,
> For want of a horse, the rider was lost,
> For want of a rider, the battle was lost,

For want of a battle, the kingdom was lost,
And all for the want of a horseshoe nail.

Don't lose a whole plumbing system for want of the right hangers and supports.

HANGER AND SUPPORT CONSIDERATIONS

A major element of the plumbing engineer's design role is to properly study, evaluate, and analyze not just the piping layout in relationship to the structure and equipment but also the totality of the piping systems that will be utilized and the surrounding environmental and physical characteristics that will come to bear on the overall performance of the completed system.

The plumbing engineer all too often treats pipe hangers and supports in a casual manner, overlooking the need for a more technical specification or performance characteristic. The most common hanger and support detail specified on plans is a simple statement that indicates that the piping shall be supported in a good and substantial manner in accordance with all local codes and ordinances. The detail may go on to specify the horizontal or vertical spacing of the supports.

The standard codes on plumbing systems provide little help to the plumbing engineer. Their admonishments are simple:

- All water piping shall be adequately supported to the satisfaction of the administrative authority.

- [Piping shall be] supported for the weight and the design of the material used.

- Supports, hangers, and anchors are devices for properly supporting and securing pipe, fixtures, and equipment.

- Suspended piping shall be supported at intervals not to exceed those shown in . . . .

- All piping shall be supported in such a manner as to maintain its alignment and prevent sagging.

- Hangers and anchors shall be of sufficient strength to support the weight of the pipe and its contents. Piping shall be isolated from incompatible materials.

HANGERS AND SUPPORTS AS PART OF THE PIPING SYSTEM

The plumbing engineer needs to consider a number of factors as he or she incorporates hangers, supports, and anchors into the design of an appropriate piping system. Given the wide variety of environmental and physical characteristics that a project will be designed around, it is not possible to provide an exhaustive listing of potential areas that need evaluation. Some basic considerations include the following.

Loads

What will be the total load of the piping system? Basic engineering requires that first and foremost there be a performance and load calculation conducted to determine the physical amount and weight of all the specific piping system elements. In this initial determination the engineer considers not only the weight of the piping itself but also that of all associated elements, including: valves; fittings; the bulk, weight, and flow characteristics of the substance to flow through or be carried within the pipe; and thermal or acoustical insulating or other pipe covering material.

In addition, depending on the piping system's location, other natural and manmade forces that may create an additional load on the piping system—such as rain, ice, and snow for piping systems exposed to natural weather conditions—must be considered. When a portion of the piping system will be exposed and relatively easy to reach, the engineer may want to give some consideration to the potential for unintended uses, such as people using exposed portions of the piping system to exercise from or to hang or use as supports for various items or devices (plants, lights, etc.).

The chosen hanger, support, and anchor system must, at a minimum, accommodate the piping system load. Moreover, the plumbing engineer needs to work closely with the structural engineer to ensure that the building structure will be able to handle the loading created by the attachment of the piping system. This load calculation may also incorporate other elements as indicated below.

Thermal Stresses

What stresses and accompanying limitations will be imposed on the piping system? A wide variety of thermal stresses need to be accommodated by the hangers, supports, and anchors for the piping system. What external influences need to be accommodated?

A number of external and internal influences may need to be considered as they relate to thermal effects and the accompanying movements that can occur within a system. Hangers and supports must provide for flexibility and axial (twisting), latitudinal, and longitudinal motions.

Thermal events subject the piping system to both internal and external influences resulting in contractions and expansions, which can be gradual or sudden in their movements. Here again, natural and manmade environments have to be taken into account. Whenever the piping system and its surrounding environment will be subject to any heating or cooling events, the hangers and supports must be able to accommodate the contraction and expansion effects that will affect the piping system. In addition, the hangers must also be able to accommodate the effects of heating and cooling events that affect the substances being carried within the piping system (e.g., certain liquids flow at different velocities under different temperatures).

Even in a piping system with thermal considerations accommodated by design elements, such as an expansion loop, the accompanying lateral movement should be accommodated by buttressing with the proper hangers and supports.

Pressure Fluctuations

Just as with thermal stresses, pressure fluctuations that occur because of the substance being transported within the piping system will be accompanied by contraction and expansion effects that need to be accommodated by the proper hangers and supports. These pressure fluctuations are often complex, as they involve the conduct of fluids, gases, and semisolids being transported in an enclosed environment, a pipe.

Changes in pressure can create unrealized stresses on the hangers and supports for the piping system. The condition referred to as "water hammer" can cause movement and vibration within a piping system that, if too firmly or rigidly anchored, will fail in the piping material or the supports, which will exacerbate the condition. Water hammer can occur within any piping system carrying liquids when there is a significant fluctuation of flow volume or pressure or when a contaminate substance, such as air, enters the piping system—not just in the typical domestic cold water piping system.

The plumbing engineer must not only design a piping hanger and support system to handle extreme pressure fluctuation but also ensure that the building structure it is attached to is able to handle the applied loads created by the movement of the piping system.

Structural Stresses

Perhaps the most obvious of all external influences on a piping system are the structural elements to which the piping system must be attached and must pass through. Wood, steel, glass—every natural and manmade material is subject to contraction and expansion due to internal and external effects. Many of these structural stresses must be accommodated by the plumbing engineer within the design of the hangers and supports for the piping system. Every building must itself be engineered to handle the stresses of the basic structural components: wood, metal, and concrete.

These building structural stresses must often be accommodated as the plumbing engineer designs the piping system. For example, the diameter of the metal dome of the Capitol in Washington, DC, is known to expand by up to 6 in. when heated by the sun during the summer months. Anchors and supports of piping systems that initially are attached to vertical metal structural components and transition to horizontal attachments to concrete structural components have to contend not only with the contraction and expansion of the piping system materials but also with the expansion and contraction of the structural elements.

Natural Environmental Conditions

The susceptibility of a piping system to natural conditions must be accounted for within the piping system and the accompanying hangers, supports, and anchors. The major effect of these natural environmental conditions is on the basic building structure. However, within structures designed to handle extreme natural phenomena, the piping system itself must be hardened, or conditioned.

Typical natural phenomena consist of seismic forces and sustainable periods of high winds, including hurricanes and typhoons. These types of phenomena create major stresses and loads on a building's structure; an extreme high-rise building, such as the Empire State Building in New York City, is known to move 4 to 12 in.

laterally in high winds. In zones of known natural phenomena, such as areas susceptible to earth movement, the plumbing engineer needs to engineer the piping and support systems to sustain the shocks, stresses, and loads inherent with and applied by these extreme forces.

While a plumbing system may not be expected to survive the complete destruction of a building's structure, it is expected to survive intact and working in the event that the building structure itself survives.

Reactivity and Conductivity Considerations

The plumbing engineer often needs to be an environmental and engineering detective as he/she designs a piping system for a building. The hangers and supports so vital to providing an integrity to the piping system often must also provide protection from unexpected natural and manmade activities, events, and phenomena totally unrelated to structure, stresses, loads, and similar engineering events.

Just as the engineer must consider the makeup and/or protection for the interior surfaces of piping material that will be used for carrying various substances, so too must he/she consider the exterior components of the piping system that will be subject to environmental and manmade conditions. The hangers and supports must also be factored into this reactive equation.

Reactive conditions can consist of chemical reactions between unlike materials or because of the introduction of a reactive substance or electrical conductivity that can occur between different materials or due to electrical "leakage" onto a piping system. These reactive and conductivity concerns can be unobtrusive and unexpected. Regardless, they can be the cause of unexpected failure in the hangers or supports of the piping system.

This type of failure can be especially acute in unexpected areas. Chemical fumes, salt water, and cleaning liquids can all cause a chemical reaction between two differing metals, one of the hanger or support and one of the pipe. Initial indicators of potential failure can be seen in corrosion or the compounds produced by chemical reaction that attach to the hangers and supports in inhospitable environments such as boiler rooms or in specialty gas and liquid systems.

It is vital that such reactive conditions be considered and that the engineer specify compatible pipe and support materials or provide for protective coatings or materials. It is especially important that the engineer ensure that the interior portions of hangers, supports, and clamps that come in contact with piping are also subject to the protective coatings; otherwise, they will be prone to failure as the material is destroyed from the inside out.

Similarly, the effects of electrical current seepage or leakage can cause unexpected but known effects between two dissimilar materials or when a chemical agent, such as calcium chloride, that may leach from wet concrete becomes a reactive agent. The plumbing engineer may need to evaluate the potential for this electrical leakage, especially in common raceways where piping and conduit will be placed side by side, and provide suitable protection via the hangers and supports.

Acoustics

For certain structures the engineer may need to consider various acoustical dimensions related to piping systems. In general, there are two significant types of acoustical annoyances the engineer must consider. The first is noise such as the sound of liquid rushing through a pipe or a harmonious resonance that starts a pipe "ringing." In these instances, the engineer must ensure that not only the piping system but also the accompanying supports receive proper insulation.

The second type of acoustic effect that needs to be considered is that created by vibration and movement within the piping system. This acoustic anomaly requires a hanger and support system that offers a combination of three-dimensional flexibility to account for lateral, longitudinal, and axial movements of the piping system and a sound and vibration insulating coating material or anchor integrated into the hanger.

Manmade Environmental Conditions

The plumbing engineer should also be cognizant of any manmade environmental conditions that can affect the piping system. These created conditions can cause uncalculated stresses and loads on the system and lead to premature failure. Created environmental conditions that can result in resonance or vibration affecting interior structural systems include major traffic arteries with significant automotive and truck traffic; airport takeoff and landing patterns; nearby rivers and canals; potential for nearby future construction; underground digging; and underground traffic, such as subways and railroad tunnels.

General

The old adage "The whole is only as strong as its individual parts" applies directly to piping hangers and supports. Myriad environmental and physical conditions can be considered when choosing the correct hanger, support, or anchor.

Nothing, however, substitutes for experience and knowledge. The engineer should work directly with a pipe's manufacturer regarding the proper spacing criteria and hanging methods for the pipe that is to be specified.

In the end, plumbing engineering is as much a science as an art. While there is almost no limit to the number of variables that can be examined in choosing hangers and supports for a plumbing system, practicality and resource limitations must also be taken into consideration.

HANGER AND SUPPORT SELECTION AND INSTALLATION

Hanger Types

Hangers, supports, and clamps come in a wide variety of materials, shapes, and sizes. (See Figure 6-1.) While the major purpose of the hangers shown is to support the loads and stresses imposed on a piping system, specification of the correct hanger is a vital component for the overall structural integrity of the building itself. Not only must the structure be able to handle the loads and stresses of the piping system, but the hanger and support system must be engineered to provide flexibility, durability, and structural strength.

Selection Criteria

To ensure proper hanger and support selection, the plumbing engineer must determine or be cognizant of the degrees of freedom that will be necessary within the piping system due to its operating characteristics. These degrees of freedom need to be considered in a three-dimensional space to account for lateral, horizontal, vertical, and axial movements and fluctuations.

To keep things simple and easy, the most typical selection criterion used is the one most closely associated with the type of pipe material and the temperature fluctuations with the system. This simple selection process requires that the correct hanger choice be made from Table 6-1, then, based on that hanger choice and the temperature of the overall piping system, Table 6-2 can be used to select the appropriate hanger.

While this selection process is the most prevalent one used, however, it relies on averages and standards. It does not take into account all the three-dimensional fluctuations and movements that, depending on the structure and all the associated or potential stresses and loads, will affect the overall plumbing system.

Tables 6-1 and 6-2 should be used as guidelines for selecting the most suitable type of hanger for the support requirement at each in

Table 6-1 Pipe Classification by Temperature

System	Class	Temperature Rating, °F (°C)
Hot	A-1	120 to 450 (49 to 232)
Hot	A-2	451 to 750 (233 to 399)
Hot	A-3	Over 750 (over 400)
Ambient	B	60 to 119 (16 to 48)
Cold	C-1	33 to 59 (1 to 15)
Cold	C-2	−20 to 32 (−29 to O)
Cold	C-3	−39 to −20 (−39 to −29)
Cold	C-4	−40 and below (−40 and below)

Table 6-2 Hanger and Support Selections

To find recommended hanger or support components.
1. Locate the system temperature and insulation condition in the two columns at left.
2. Read across the column headings for the type of component to be used.
3. Numbers in boxes refer to those types shown in Table 6-1.

Temp. Range °F(°C)	System	Insulation	Steel Clips (A)	Malleable Iron Rings (B)	Steel Bands (C)	Steel Clamps (D)	Cast Iron Hanging Rolls (E)	Cast Iron Supporting Rolls (F)	Steel Trapezes (G)	Steel Protection Saddles & Shields (H)	Steel or Cast Iron Stanchions (I)	Steel Welded Attachment (J)	Steel Riser Clamps 2 bolt (K)	Steel Riser Clamps 4 bolt (L)	Welded Attachments Steel (M)	Turn Buckles (N)	Swing Eyes (O)	Clevises (P)	Inserts (Q)	C-Clamps (R)	Beam Clamps (S)	Welded Attachments (T)	Brackets (U)
120(49) to 450(232)	HOT A-1	COVERED a	24 W/39	NONE	1,5,7,9,10 W/39 OR 40	2,3	41,43 W/39 OR 40	44,45,46 W/39 OR 40	59 W/39 OR 40	39,40	36,37,38 W/39 OR 40	35 c	8	42 c	c	13,15	16,17	14	18 e	19,23	20,21,25,27 28,29,30	22,57,58	31,32,33,34
		BARE	24,26	6,11,12	1,5,7,9,10	3,4	41,43	44,45,46	59	NONE	36,37,38												
451(233) to 750(399)	HOT A-2 34	COVERED a	24 W/39	NONE	1 W/39 OR 40	3	41 W/39 OR 40	44,45,46 W/39 OR 40	59 W/39 OR 40	39,40	36,37,38 W/39 OR 40	35 c	NONE	42 c	c	13,15	16,17	14	18 e	NONE	20,21,25,27 28,29,30	22,57,58	31,32,33
		BARE	24,26	6,11,12	1,5,7,9,10	3,4	41,43	44,45,46	59	NONE	NONE												
OVER 750(399)	HOT A-3	COVERED a	NONE	NONE	1 W/40	ALLOY 2,3	41,43 W/40 OR ALLOY 39	44,45,46 W/40 OR ALLOY 39	59 W/40 OR ALLOY 39	40 ALLOY 39	36,37,38 W/40 OR ALLOY 39	ALLOY 35 c	NONE	ALLOY 42 c	ALLOY 39 c	13	17	14	c,e	NONE	20,21,25,27 28,29,30	22,57,58 c	31,32,33,34
		BARE	NONE	NONE	NONE	ALLOY 2,3,4	NONE	NONE	c	NONE	NONE												
60(16) to 119(48)	AMBIENT B	COVERED a	24,26	NONE	1,5,7,9,10 W/39 OR 40	3,4	41,43 W/39 OR 40	44,45,46 W/39 OR 40	59 W/39 OR 40	39,40	36,37,38 W/39 OR 40	c	8	42 c	c	13,15	16,17	14	18 e	19,23	20,21,25,27 28,29,30	22,57,58	31,32,33,34
		BARE	24,26	6,11,12	1,5,7,9,10 W/40	3,4	41,43	44,45,46	59	NONE	36,37,38												
33(1) to 59(15)	COLD C-1	COVERED a	26 W/40	NONE	1,5,7,9,10 W/40	3,4 W/40	41,43 W/40 d	44,45,46 W/40 d	59 W/40	40	36,37,38 W/40	c	8	42 c	c	13,15	16,17	14	18 e	19,23	20,21,25,27 28,29,30	22,57,58	31,32,33,34
		BARE	24,26	6,11,12	1,5,7,9,10 W/40	3,4	41,43	44,45,46	c	NONE	36,37,38												
-19(-28) to 32(0)	COLD C-2	COVERED a	NONE	NONE	1,5,7,9,10 W/40	NONE	41,43 W/40 d	44,45,46 d	c,d W/40	40	36,37,38 W/40	c	8	42	c	13,15	16,17	14	18 e	19,23	20,21,25,27 28,29,30	22,57,58 c	31,33,34
		BARE	NONE	NONE	1,5,7,9,10 W/40	3,4	41,43	44,45,46	c	NONE	36,37,38												
BELOW -19(-28)	COLD C-3 & C4	COVERED a	NONE	NONE	b,c	NONE	41,43 W/40 d	44,45,46 W/40 d	b,c,d W/40	40	36,37,38 W/40	b,c	b,c	b,c	b,c	13,15	16,17	14	18 e	19,23	20,21,25,27 28,29,30	22,57,58 c	31,32,33,34
		BARE	NONE	NONE	NONE	b,c	NONE	NONE	b,c	NONE	b,c												

Source: From MSS SP-69-2002, *Pipe Hangers and Supports: Selection and Application,* reprinted with permission of Manufacturers Standardization Society.

aHangers on insulated systems shall incorporate protection saddles, shields, pipe clamps, or welded lugs which project through the insulation to provide external attachment.

bThe selection of type and material shall be made by the piping design engineer.

cThe design shall be in accordance with MSS SP-58 or as specified by the piping design engineer.

dFor shields used with rollers or subject to point loading, see MSS SP-69, Table 5.

eContinuous inserts, embedded plates, anchor bolts, and concrete fasteners may be used as specified by the piping design engineer.

cremental step of the design process. These tables offer the basics of hanger selection, i.e., they offer a variety of hanger choices and the material composition most suited for the temperature characteristics that will affect the piping system.

What these tables cannot do is substitute for the design engineering process that determines the proper hanger selection based on the environmental and physical influences that will affect the different elements of the piping system under varying conditions. The most instructive aspect of Table 6-2 is found in the notes at the end of the table (see Notes b, c, and e).

Hanger and Support Spacing

After the appropriate hanger components have been selected for the type of piping system and the type of building or structural support available, the plumbing engineer must "not" identify the spacing appropriate to the type of pipe used. Table 6-3 provides support criteria for some of

the most common pipe materials. The plumbing engineer must ensure that the design criteria are in compliance with local code requirements.

Again, just as with Table 6-2, it needs to be noted that Table 6-3 provides guidelines only, and the piping systems are presumed to exist under ideal circumstances with little environmental or physical influences. Therefore, these spacing guidelines are at the upper end of the specifications; that is, they should be considered the maximum spacing for hangers and supports.

For proper hanger spacing the engineer needs, once again, to evaluate and take into account the three-dimensional fluctuations and movements as well as the environmental and physical influences that will affect the entirety of the plumbing system. Proper spacing is a function of stress, vibration, and the potential for misuse (e.g., exposed piping used as a ladder, scaffolding, or exercise equipment). Spacing criteria are heavily dependent on pipe direction changes; structural attachment material and

Table 6-3 Maximum Horizontal Pipe Hanger and Support Spacing

	1		2		3		4		5	6	7	8	9	10
	Std Wt Steel Pipe				Copper Tube									
Nominal Pipe or Tube Size	Water Service		Vapor Service		Water Service		Vapor Service		Fire Protection	Ductile Iron Pipe	Cast Iron Soil	Glass	Plastic	Fiberglass Reinforced
in. (mm)	ft	(m)	ft	(m)	ft	(m)	ft	(m)						
¼ (6)	—	—	—	—	5	(1.5)	5	(1.5)	Follow requirements of the National Fire Protection Association.	20 ft (6.1 m) max spacing; min of one (1) hanger per pipe section close to the joint behind the bell and at change of direction and branch connections. For pipe sizes six (6) in. (150 mm) and under, installed on ASME B31 projects, that are subject to loading other than weight of pipe and contents, the span should be limited to the maximum spacing for water service steel pipe.	10 ft (3.0 m) max spacing; min of one (1) hanger per pipe section close to joint on the barrel, also at change of direction and branch connections.	8 ft (2.4 m) max spacing, follow pipe manufacturer's recommendations.	Follow pipe manufacturer's recommendations for material and service condition.	Follow pipe manufacturer's recommendations for material and service condition.
⅜ (10)	7	(2.1)	8	(2.4)	5	(1.5)	6	(1.8)						
½ (15)	7	(2.1)	8	(2.4)	5	(1.5)	6	(1.8)						
¾ (20)	7	(2.1)	9	(2.7)	5	(1.5)	7	(2.1)						
1 (25)	7	(2.1)	9	(2.7)	6	(1.8)	8	(2.4)						
1¼ (32)	7	(2.1)	9	(2.7)	7	(2.1)	9	(2.7)						
1½ (40)	9	(2.7)	12	(3.7)	8	(2.4)	10	(3.0)						
2 (50)	10	(3.0)	13	(4.0)	8	(2.4)	11	(3.4)						
2½ (65)	11	(3.4)	14	(4.3)	9	(2.7)	13	(4.0)						
3 (80)	12	(3.7)	15	(4.6)	10	(3.0)	14	(4.3)						
3½ (90)	13	(4.0)	16	(4.9)	11	(3.4)	15	(4.6)						
4 (100)	14	(4.3)	17	(5.2)	12	(3.7)	16	(4.9)						
5 (125)	16	(4.9)	19	(5.8)	13	(4.0)	18	(5.5)						
6 (150)	17	(5.2)	21	(6.4)	14	(4.3)	20	(6.1)						
8 (200)	19	(5.8)	24	(7.3)	16	(4.9)	23	(7.0)						
10 (250)	22	(6.7)	26	(7.9)	18	(5.5)	25	(7.6)						
12 (300)	23	(7.0)	30	(9.1)	19	(5.8)	28	(8.5)						
14 (350)	25	(7.6)	32	(9.8)										
16 (400)	27	(8.2)	35	(10.7)										
18 (450)	28	(8.5)	37	(11.3)										
20 (500)	30	(9.1)	39	(11.9)										
24 (600)	32	(9.8)	42	(12.8)										
30 (750)	33	(10.1)	44	(13.4)										

Source: From MSS SP-69-2002, *Pipe Hangers and Supports: Selection and Application*, reprinted with permission of Manufacturers Standardizaton Society.

Notes:

1. For spacing supports incorporating type 40 shields, see MSS SP–69-2002, Table 5.

2. Does not apply where span calculations are made or where there are concentrated loads between supports, such as flanges, valves, and specialties, or changes in direction requiring additional supports.

3. Unbalanced forces of hydrostatic or hydrodynamic origin (thrust forces) unless restrained externally can result in pipe movement and separation of joints if the joints of the system are not of a restrained joint design. (For pressure piping with joints not having a restraining design, other positive restraining means such as clamps, rods, and/or thrust blocking shall be used to maintain the integrity of the joints.)

points; additional plumbing system loadings, such as valves, flanges, filters, access ports, tanks, motors, drip, splash and condensate drainage, pipe shielding and insulation; and other specialty design requirements.

Anchoring

The strength, safety, and integrity of the plumbing system depends on the hangers or supports that the plumbing engineer specifies. How much additional design work is required as part of the plumbing system depends on the specification of the original proposal and the overall responsibilities of the plumbing engineer. It is not enough to specify a hanger or support—an important consideration is how it is anchored.

The plumbing system must be viewed as a complete entity. Thus, the designer may well need to be fully versed in the methodologies of anchoring hangers and supports in various structural elements and materials. At a minimum, the engineer needs to ensure close coordination between his/her engineered design and that of the other design engineers, including iron and concrete structural engineers, to ensure properly spaced and applied hangers, supports, and their anchors.

The anchoring of hangers and supports requires different methodologies depending on the structural elements and the transitions from vertical and horizontal surfaces and from differing materials (e.g., from steel to concrete). A hanger or support will perform only up to the capability of its attachment to a structural element.

Figure 6-1 shows some of the materials and devices often used for anchoring hangers and supports. The extent of detail required within the plumbing system design depends on the project parameters and the practicality and responsibility of the engineer to the overall building assembly.

Perhaps the most difficult hanger and support attachment requirement is that to concrete in an existing structure. It may well be necessary for the plumbing engineer to contact the original concrete designer or supplier. Depending on experience, it is wise to involve an experienced hanger manufacturer or contractor for the proper anchoring of hangers and supports.

Anchor Types

The types of anchors vary according to the structural elements and materials to be used for attachment. The basic attachment elements are shown in Figure 6-2. However, there is a wide variety of anchor bolts, screws, washers, nuts, rods, plates, and strengtheners. It may well be in the engineer's purview to establish loading, shear, and stress specifications for the hanger and support anchoring structure.

Depending on the elements and material of the structure, the requirements and specifications for the hanger and support anchors vary widely. Anchoring to wood is significantly different from anchoring to steel. In the later case, welding specifications may well need to be included as well as bonding material compatability ensured.

Anchoring to concrete requires the use of implanted anchors during the pouring of the concrete or subsequent attachment using anchor bolts and plates. Table 6-4 shows the pipe hanger rod size for a single rigid rod hanger. Care should be taken to observe the loading associated with special conditions that may induce a load beyond the hanger rod strength. Moreover, lateral stress and axial tension will affect the choice of rod size and material. See Table 6-5 for load ratings of threaded hanger rods and Table 6-6 for minimum design load ratings for rigid pipe hanger assemblies. These tables show acceptable standards for hanger materials. However, it is important to check a particular manufacturer's specifications as well. See Table 6-7(A) and (B), sample design load tables for manufacturer's concrete inserts. (See Figure 6-1 for referenced inserts.) In the overall engineered design, load and stress calculations for multiple hanger and support assemblies and the use of multiple anchor assemblies (such as concrete rod inserts) require additional evaluation and analysis to properly incorporate the effects of a distributed load.

Hangers, Supports, and Anchor Materials

There is an almost unlimited variety of materials that can be used for producing hangers, supports, and their anchors. With the increased use of plastic, fiberglass, and other lightweight and corrosion-resistant pipe materials, there are matching hangers and supports.

Table 6-4 Recommended Minimum Rod Diameter for Single, Rigid Rod Hangers

		Types of Pipe [a]			
		Steel Water Service Steel Vapor Service Ductile iron Pipe Cast Iron Soil		Copper Water Service Copper Vapor Service Glass, Plastic Fiberglass Reinforced	
Nominal Pipe or Tubing Size		Nominal Rod Diam.		Nominal Rod Diam.	
in.	(mm)	in.	(mm)	in.	(mm)
¼	(6)	⅜	(M10)	⅜	(M10)
⅜	(10)	⅜	(M10)	⅜	(M10)
½	(15)	⅜	(M10)	⅜	(M10)
¾	(20)	⅜	(M10)	⅜	(M10)
1	(25)	⅜	(M10)	⅜	(M10)
1¼	(32)	⅜	(M10)	⅜	(M10)
1½	(40)	⅜	(M10)	⅜	(M10)
2	(50)	⅜	(M10)	⅜	(M10)
2½	(65)	½	(M12)	½	(M12)
3	(80)	½	(M12)	½	(M12)
3½	(90)	½	(M12)	½	(M12)
4	(100)	⅝	(M16)	½	(M12)
5	(125)	⅝	(M16)	½	(M12)
6	(150)	¾	(M20)	⅝	(M16)
8	(200)	¾	(M20)	¾	(M20)
10	(250)	⅞	(M20)	¾	(M20)
12	(300)	⅞	(M20)	¾	(M20)
14	(350)	1	(M24)		
16	(400)	1	(M24)		
18	(450)	1	(M24)		
20	(500)	1¼	(M30)		
24	(600)	1¼	(M30)		
30	(750)	1¼	(M30)		

Source: From MSS SP-69-2002, *Pipe Hangers and Supports: Selection and Application*, reprinted with permission of Manufacturers Standardizaton Society.

Notes:

1. For calculated loads, rod diameters may be sized in accordance with Table 6-5 (MSS SP-58-2002, Table 3) provided the requirements of Table 6-6 (MSS SP-58-2002, Table 1) are satisfied. In addition, hanger rods shall be a minimum of ⅜ in. (9.6 mm) diameter and shall be limited to pipe or tubing NPS 4 (DN100) and less. For pipe and tubing NPS 4 (DN100) and greater, the rod diameter shall be not less than ½ in. (12.7 mm) and sized for loads per Table 6-5. In addition, the minimum rod diameter for rigid hangers must be sized for the loads shown in Table 6-6.

2. Rods may be reduced one size for double rod hangers. Minimum rod diameter shall be ⅜ in. (M10).

a See Table 6-3.

Table 6-5 Load Ratings of Carbon Steel Threaded Hanger Rods

Nominal Rod Diameter		Root Area of Thread		Max. Safe Load at Rod Temp. of 650°F (343°C)	
in.	(mm)	in.²	(mm²)	lb	(kg)
⅜	(9.6)	0.068	(43.8)	730	(3.23)
½	(12.7)	0.126	(81.3)	1,350	(5.98)
⅝	(15.8)	0.202	(130.3)	2,160	(9.61)
¾	(19.0)	0.302	(194.8)	3,230	(14.4)
⅞	(22.2)	0.419	(270.3)	4,480	(19.9)
1	(25.4)	0.551	(356.1)	5,900	(26.2)
1¼	(31.8)	0.890	(573.5)	9,500	(42.4)
1½	(38.1)	1.29	(834.2)	13,800	(61.6)
1¾	(44.4)	1.74	(1125)	18,600	(82.8)
2	(50.8)	2.30	(1479)	24,600	(109)
2¼	(57.2)	3.02	(1949)	32,300	(144)
2½	(63.5)	3.72	(2397)	39,800	(177)
2¾	(69.8)	4.62	(2980)	49,400	(220)
3	(76.2)	5.62	(3626)	60,100	(267)
3¼	(82.6)	6.72	(4435)	71,900	(320)
3½	(88.9)	7.92	(5108)	84,700	(377)
3¾	(95.2)	9.21	(5945)	98,500	(438)
4	(101.6)	10.6	(6844)	114,000	(505)
4¼	(108.0)	12.1	(7806)	129,000	(576)
4½	(114.3)	13.7	(8832)	146,000	(652)
4¾	(120.6)	15.4	(9922)	165,000	(733)
5	(127.0)	17.2	(11074)	184,000	(819)

Source: From MSS SP-58-2002, *Pipe Hangers and Supports: Materials, Design, and Manufacture*, reprinted with permission of Manufacturers Standardizaton Society.

Notes:

1. For materials other than carbon steel, see requirements of MSS SP-58-2002, Section 4.7 and Table 2.

2. Tabulated loads are based on a minimum actual tensile stress of 50 ksi (345 MPa) divided by a safety factor of 3.5, reduced by 25%, resulting in an allowable stress of 10.7 ksi. (The 25% reduction is to allow for normal installation and service conditions.)

3. Root areas of thread are based on the following thread series:

   diam. 4 in. and below: coarse thread (UNC)

   diam. above 4 in.: 4 thread (4-UN)

Table 6-6 Minimum Design Load Ratings for Pipe Hanger Assemblies

Applicable to all components of complete assembly, including pipe attachment, rod, fixtures, and building attachment.

Nominal Pipe or Tube Size		Min. Design Load Ratings at Normal Temp. Range [a]	
in.	(mm)	lb	(kg)
⅜	(10)	150	(0.67)
½	(15)	150	(0.67)
¾	(20)	150	(0.67)
1	(25)	150	(0.67)
1¼	(32)	150	(0.67)
1½	(40)	150	(0.67)
2	(50)	150	(0.67)
2½	(65)	150	(0.67)
3	(80)	200	(0.89)
3½	(90)	210	(0.93)
4	(100)	250	(1.11)
5	(125)	360	(1.60)
6	(150)	480	(2.14)
8	(200)	760	(3.38)
10	(250)	1120	(4.98)
12	(300)	1480	(6.58)
14	(350)	1710	(7.61)
16	(400)	2130	(9.47)
18	(450)	2580	(11.48)
20	(500)	3060	(13.61)
24	(600)	3060	(13.61)
30	(750)	3500	(15.57)

Source: From MSS SP-58-2002, *Pipe Hangers and Supports: Materials, Design, and Manufacture*, reprinted with permission of Manufacturers Standardizaton Society.

Notes:

1. See MSS SP-58-2002, Section 4, for allowable stresses and temperatures.

2. Minimum rod diameter restrictions: Hanger rods shall be a minimum of ⅜ in. (9.6 mm) diameter and shall be limited to pipe or tubing NPS 4 (DN100) and less. For pipe and tubing NPS 4 (DN100) and greater, the rod diameter shall be not less than ½ in. (12.7 mm) and shall be sized for loads per Table 6-5. In addition, the minimum rod diameter for rigid hangers must be sized for loads as shown above.

3. For loads greater than those tabluated, hanger component load ratings shall be established by the manufacturer. Design shall be in accordance with all criteria as outlined in MSS SP-58-2002.

4. Pipe attachment ratings for temperature ranges between 650 and 750°F (343 and 398°C) shall be reduced by the ratio of allowable stress at service temperature to the allowable stresses at 650°F (343°C).

5. For services over 750°F (398°C), attachments in direct contact with the pipe shall be designed to allowable stresses listed in MSS SP-58-2002, Tables 2 and A2.

a Normal temperature range is −20 to 650°F (−29 to 343°C) for carbon steel, −20 to 450°F (−29 to 231°C) for malleable iron, and −20 to 400°F (−29 to 204°C) for gray iron.

Table 6-7(A) Sample Design Load Tables for Manufacturer's Concrete Inserts

Design Load Chart for 3000 psi Hard Rock Concrete

Rod Size (in.)	Design Load Vertical (psi)				Design Load Shear (psi)				Design Load 45° (psi)		
	A	B	C	De [a] (in.)	A	B	C	De [a] (in.)	A	B	C
⅜	1207	457	457	1	675	675	675	2	612	364	385
½	2043	496	496	1.4	912	912	912	2	892	454	454
⅝	1690	532	532	1.7	1148	1148	1148	2	967	514	514
¾	2321	567	567	2	1368	1368	1368	2.5	1217	567	567
⅞	2321	878	878	4	1596	1596	1596	3	1338	801	801

Design Load Chart for Lightweight Concrete

Rod Size (in.)	Design Load Vertical (psi)				Design Load Shear (psi)				Design Load 45° (psi)		
	A	B	C	Min (in.)	A	B	C	De [a] (in.)	A	B	C
⅜	905	343	343	⅞	590	590	590	2	547	307	321
½	1632	372	372	⅞	590	590	590	2	828	323	374
⅝	1268	399	399	⅞	590	590	590	2	852	337	419
¾	1741	426	426	⅞	590	590	590	2½	1084	350	459
⅞	1741	656	656	⅞	590	590	590	3	1178	439	654

Table 6-7(B) Sample Design Load Tables for Manufacturer's Concrete Inserts

Rod Size (in.)	Design Load Vertical (psi)		Design Load Shear (psi)		Design Load 45° (psi)		"E"Embed- ment Depth (in.)	De [a] min. (in.)
	Hard Rock	Lt. Wt.	Hard Rock	Lt. Wt.	Hard Rock	Lt. Wt.		
⅜	1255	753	978	733	777	525	3½	2
½	2321	1392	978	733	980	679	3½	2
⅝	780	468	1278	958	688	445	4	2
¾	1346	806	1278	958	927	619	4	2½
⅞	2321	1392	1278	958	1166	803	4	6

Source: Table 6-7(A) and (B) courtesy of ⓣ**TOLCO**.

a De = distance to the edge of the concrete that must be maintained for the rod to meet the design load.

It is up to the plumbing engineer to match and coordinate the various materials available. Because of possible chemically reactive and galvanic effects, it is of special importance to match the hanger, support, and anchor material composition to the composition of the piping system material. Because of the mixing, matching, and use of differing materials and the different interactions possible, the plumbing engineer needs to be extremely aware of the proper spacing and anchoring of hangers and, where questionable, to confirm with the pipe, hanger, support, and anchor manufacturers the loads, stresses, and spacing criteria specifications.

Pipe Clamps

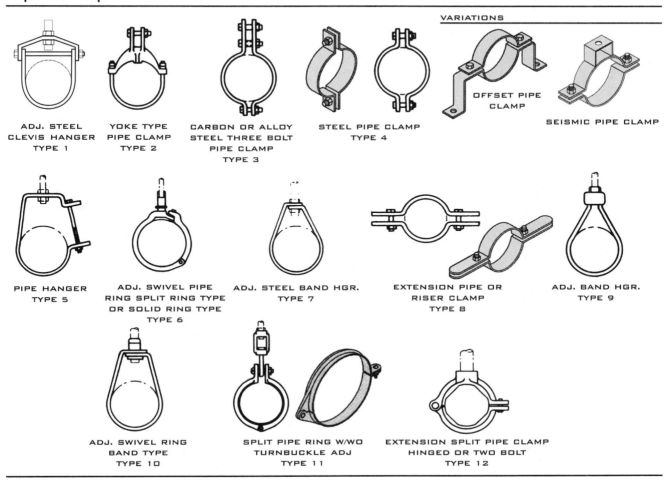

VARIATIONS

ADJ. STEEL
CLEVIS HANGER
TYPE 1

YOKE TYPE
PIPE CLAMP
TYPE 2

CARBON OR ALLOY
STEEL THREE BOLT
PIPE CLAMP
TYPE 3

STEEL PIPE CLAMP
TYPE 4

OFFSET PIPE
CLAMP

SEISMIC PIPE CLAMP

PIPE HANGER
TYPE 5

ADJ. SWIVEL PIPE
RING SPLIT RING TYPE
OR SOLID RING TYPE
TYPE 6

ADJ. STEEL BAND HGR.
TYPE 7

EXTENSION PIPE OR
RISER CLAMP
TYPE 8

ADJ. BAND HGR.
TYPE 9

ADJ. SWIVEL RING
BAND TYPE
TYPE 10

SPLIT PIPE RING W/WO
TURNBUCKLE ADJ
TYPE 11

EXTENSION SPLIT PIPE CLAMP
HINGED OR TWO BOLT
TYPE 12

Threaded Products

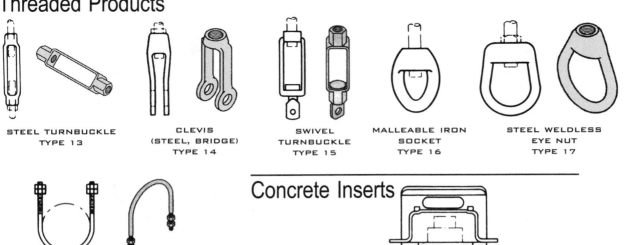

STEEL TURNBUCKLE
TYPE 13

CLEVIS
(STEEL, BRIDGE)
TYPE 14

SWIVEL
TURNBUCKLE
TYPE 15

MALLEABLE IRON
SOCKET
TYPE 16

STEEL WELDLESS
EYE NUT
TYPE 17

U-BOLT
TYPE 24

Concrete Inserts

STEEL OR MALLEABLE
CONCRETE INSERT
TYPE 18

Figure 6-1 Types of Hangers and Supports

Sources: Details of hanger and support types are from MSS SP-69-2002, *Pipe Hangers and Supports: Selection and Application*, reprinted with permission of Manufacturers Standardization Society; supplementary details are courtesy of TOLCO®.

Beam Clamps

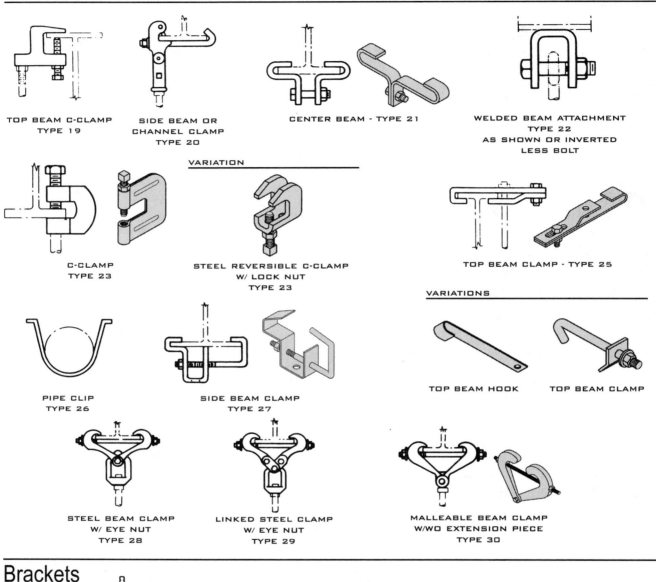

TOP BEAM C-CLAMP
TYPE 19

SIDE BEAM OR
CHANNEL CLAMP
TYPE 20

CENTER BEAM - TYPE 21

WELDED BEAM ATTACHMENT
TYPE 22
AS SHOWN OR INVERTED
LESS BOLT

C-CLAMP
TYPE 23

VARIATION

STEEL REVERSIBLE C-CLAMP
W/ LOCK NUT
TYPE 23

TOP BEAM CLAMP - TYPE 25

VARIATIONS

TOP BEAM HOOK   TOP BEAM CLAMP

PIPE CLIP
TYPE 26

SIDE BEAM CLAMP
TYPE 27

STEEL BEAM CLAMP
W/ EYE NUT
TYPE 28

LINKED STEEL CLAMP
W/ EYE NUT
TYPE 29

MALLEABLE BEAM CLAMP
W/WO EXTENSION PIECE
TYPE 30

Brackets

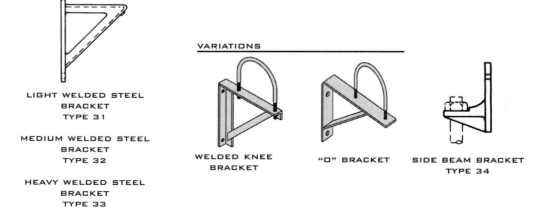

LIGHT WELDED STEEL
BRACKET
TYPE 31

MEDIUM WELDED STEEL
BRACKET
TYPE 32

HEAVY WELDED STEEL
BRACKET
TYPE 33

VARIATIONS

WELDED KNEE
BRACKET

"O" BRACKET

SIDE BEAM BRACKET
TYPE 34

(Figure 6-1 continued)

Pipe Slides, Supports, Anchors, and Shields

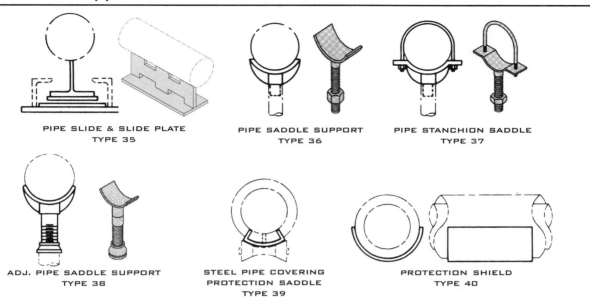

PIPE SLIDE & SLIDE PLATE
TYPE 35

PIPE SADDLE SUPPORT
TYPE 36

PIPE STANCHION SADDLE
TYPE 37

ADJ. PIPE SADDLE SUPPORT
TYPE 38

STEEL PIPE COVERING
PROTECTION SADDLE
TYPE 39

PROTECTION SHIELD
TYPE 40

Pipe Rollers

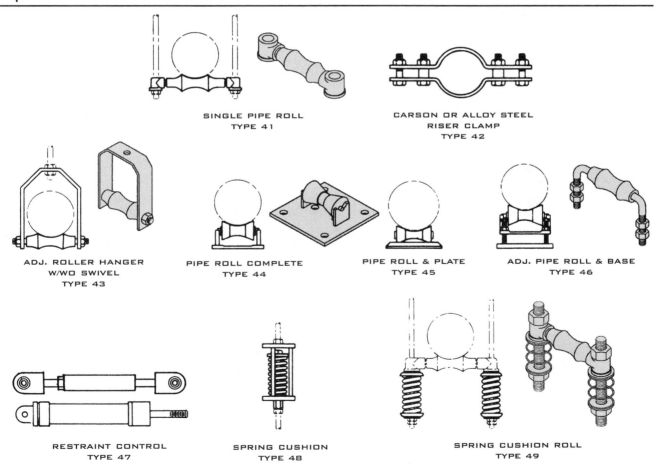

SINGLE PIPE ROLL
TYPE 41

CARSON OR ALLOY STEEL
RISER CLAMP
TYPE 42

ADJ. ROLLER HANGER
W/WO SWIVEL
TYPE 43

PIPE ROLL COMPLETE
TYPE 44

PIPE ROLL & PLATE
TYPE 45

ADJ. PIPE ROLL & BASE
TYPE 46

RESTRAINT CONTROL
TYPE 47

SPRING CUSHION
TYPE 48

SPRING CUSHION ROLL
TYPE 49

(Figure 6-1 continued)

Spring Hangers and Constant Supports

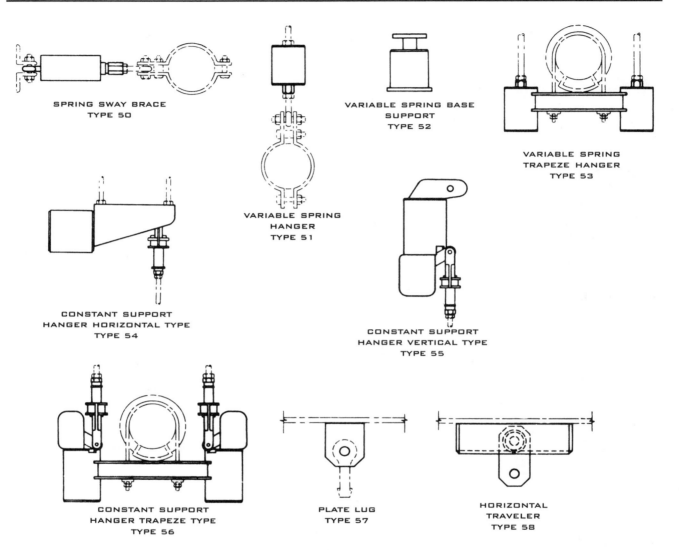

(**Figure 6-1 continued**)

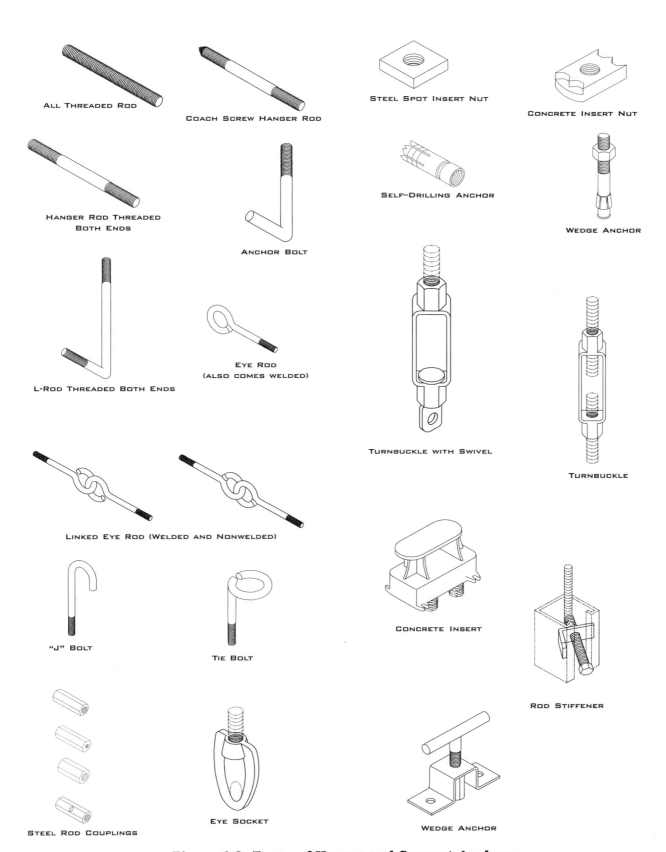

ALL THREADED ROD

COACH SCREW HANGER ROD

STEEL SPOT INSERT NUT

CONCRETE INSERT NUT

HANGER ROD THREADED BOTH ENDS

SELF-DRILLING ANCHOR

WEDGE ANCHOR

ANCHOR BOLT

L-ROD THREADED BOTH ENDS

EYE ROD (ALSO COMES WELDED)

TURNBUCKLE WITH SWIVEL

TURNBUCKLE

LINKED EYE ROD (WELDED AND NONWELDED)

"J" BOLT

TIE BOLT

CONCRETE INSERT

ROD STIFFENER

STEEL ROD COUPLINGS

EYE SOCKET

WEDGE ANCHOR

Figure 6-2 Types of Hanger and Support Anchors

Source: Anchor details courtesy of TOLCO®.

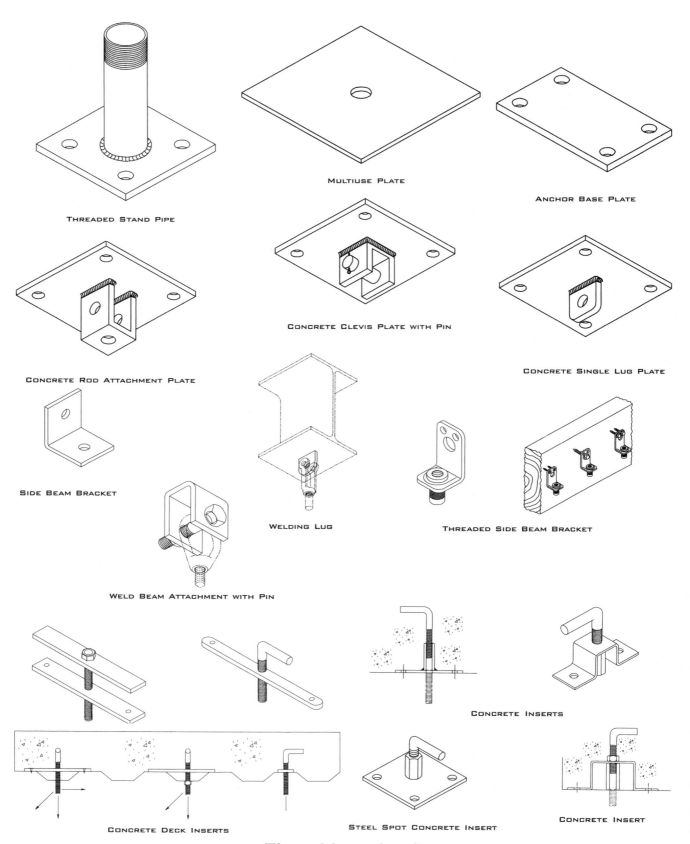

THREADED STAND PIPE

MULTIUSE PLATE

ANCHOR BASE PLATE

CONCRETE CLEVIS PLATE WITH PIN

CONCRETE ROD ATTACHMENT PLATE

CONCRETE SINGLE LUG PLATE

SIDE BEAM BRACKET

WELDING LUG

THREADED SIDE BEAM BRACKET

WELD BEAM ATTACHMENT WITH PIN

CONCRETE INSERTS

CONCRETE DECK INSERTS

STEEL SPOT CONCRETE INSERT

CONCRETE INSERT

(Figure 6-2 continued)

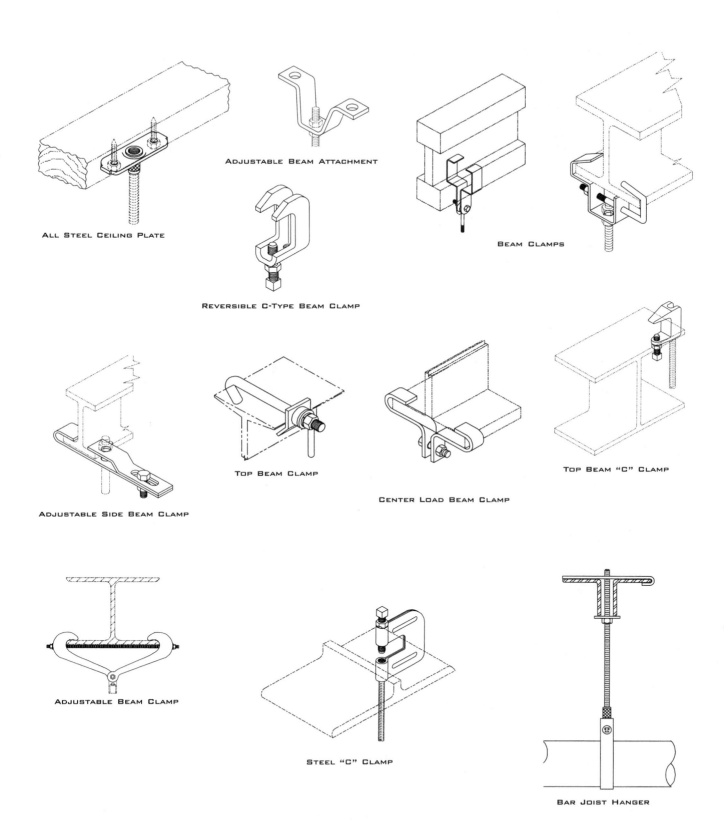

ALL STEEL CEILING PLATE

ADJUSTABLE BEAM ATTACHMENT

REVERSIBLE C-TYPE BEAM CLAMP

BEAM CLAMPS

ADJUSTABLE SIDE BEAM CLAMP

TOP BEAM CLAMP

CENTER LOAD BEAM CLAMP

TOP BEAM "C" CLAMP

ADJUSTABLE BEAM CLAMP

STEEL "C" CLAMP

BAR JOIST HANGER

(Figure 6-2 continued)

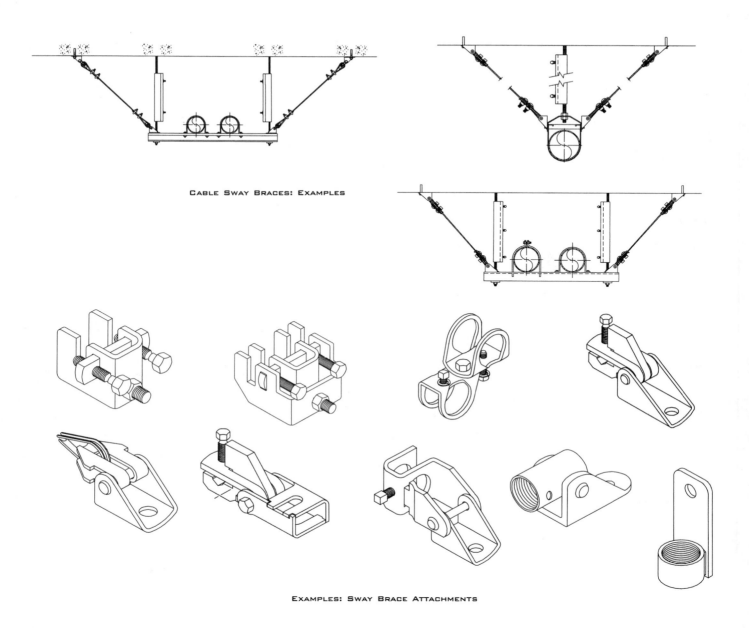

CABLE SWAY BRACES: EXAMPLES

EXAMPLES: SWAY BRACE ATTACHMENTS

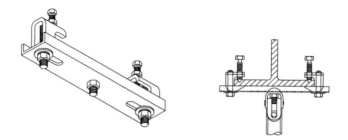

SWAY BRACE ATTACHMENTS: BAR JOISTS

(Figure 6-2 continued)

GLOSSARY[1]

Acceleration limiter A device, hydraulic, mechanical, or spring, used to control acceleration and control shock and sway in piping systems.

Access channel Conduit or channel that is cast in place within concrete structural elements and that provides for the passing through of pipe. Placed horizontally throughout a concrete structure to facilitate future access.

Access opening An opening or conduit that is cast in place within concrete structural elements and that provides for the passing through of pipe. Most typical usage is for short vertical conduit in concrete slabs to eliminate the subsequent drilling of core holes.

Accumulator A container, used in conjunction with a hydraulic cylinder or rotating vane device used for the control of shock or sway in piping systems, used to accommodate the difference in fluid volume displaced by the piston. Also serves as a continuous supply of reserve fluid.

Adjustable Mechanical or automated movement providing for linear adjustment capability (regardless of the plane or dimension). Adjustment may be mechanical, such as a threaded rod, or assisted with vacuum or air pressure.

Adjustment device Component(s) that provides for adjustablility. (See "adjustable.")

After cold pull elevation The mechanical drawing view incorporating additional piping elements during installation that will be necessary for thermal fluctuations once piping system is "hot" or operational.

Alloy A chrome-moly material (often less than 5% chrome) used as a material to resist the effects of high temperatures (750–1100°F [399–593°C]). Alloys are used as pipe, hanger, support, and anchor material.

Anchor 1. To fasten or hold a material or a device to prevent movement, rotation, or displacement at the point of application. 2. Also an appliance used in conjunction with piping systems to fasten hangers and supports to prevent movement, rotation or displacement.

Anchor bolt A fastener (e.g., bolt or threaded rod) that is used for attachment or connection of materials, devices, or equipment. Often refers to the bolt that is embedded in concrete or passed through an opening in steel that is used to attach a hanger or support to a concrete or steel structure.

As built Refers to the actual installation and configuration of construction or placement.

Assembly A preformed arrangement or a gathered collection of various appliances and components used to carry, hold, and/or restrain devices, equipment, or a piping system load in tension.

Auxiliary stop A supplemental restraint that temporarily locks or holds in place movable parts. Often used in conjunction with spring devices, such as a "spring hanger," to provide for a fixed position enabling a load to be transferred to a supporting structure in a desired placement during construction or installation.

Axial brace An assembly or bracket device used to resist twisting or to restrain a piping run in the axial direction.

Band or strap hanger An appliance or device used as a hanger or support for pipe that provides for vertical adjustment. Also used to connect pipe to a "hanger assembly."

Base support A device that carries a load from beneath and is used to carry a load's weight in compression.

Beam clamp A mechanical device used to connect, as a hanger or support, or to hold part of a piping system to a structural beam element (typically a steel beam; a clamp firmly holds multiple materials or devices together and does not require welding).

Bearing plate See "slide plate" and "roll plate."

Bent An assembly or frame consisting of two vertical members joined by one or more horizontal members used for the support of a piping system to a structural element.

---

[1]The basic word set for this glossary has been excerpted and/or adapted from MSS SP-90, 2000 edition, with permission from Manufacturers Standardization Society.

Bolting Use of bolts, studs, and nuts as fasteners.

Brace, brace assembly A preformed appliance or assembly consisting of various components and, depending on its location, used to hold and/or restrain a piping system from horizontal, vertical, and lateral forces.

Brace, hanger, or support drawing The mechanical drawing detailing the elements and components of an assembly or frame structure that incorporates a bill of material, load and movement data, and both general and specific identification.

Bracket A preformed support or fastener, usually constructed in a cantilevered manner, with or without additional diagonal structural members for load stability and designed to withstand a gravity load and horizontal and vertical forces.

C clamp A preformed appliance in a C shape that attaches to a flange or other part of a structural member and acts as an anchor for a hanger, support, or other device such as a threaded rod.

Cable A component used to brace structural assemblies and piping systems (also called "wire rope").

Cantilever A projecting structural element or member supported at only one end.

Center beam clamp A jaw type mechanical device used to connect, as a hanger or support, or used to hold part of a piping system to a structural beam element (typically a steel beam). Used with I-beams and wide flange beams to provide a centered beam connection.

Channel clamp A mechanical device with a channel adapter and hook rod, that provides an off-center attachment that attaches to the bottom flange of a channel beam and provides a connection for a hanger, support, or other part of a piping system.

Clamp A mechanical device used to connect, as a hanger or support, or used to hold part of a piping system to a structural beam element. (A clamp firmly holds multiple materials or devices together and does not require welding.) See "beam clamp," "C clamp," "channel clamp," "double bolt pipe," "three bolt clamp," "double bolt riser," "riser clamp," and "pipe clamp."

Clevis A connector device or metal shackle that has the ends drilled to receive a pin or bolt and that is used for attaching or suspending parts.

Clevis hanger A support device providing vertical adjustment consisting of a clevis type top bolted to a formed steel bottom strap.

Cold elevation See "design elevation" and "after cold pull elevation."

Cold hanger location The location of the pipe hangers, supports, and assemblies of the installed piping system in reference to the building structure and structural elements prior to the invoking of an operating environment.

Cold load The stress or loading put on a piping system prior to the occurrence of a normal or steady-state operating environment (as measured at ambient temperature). The cold load equals the operating load plus or minus load variations.

Cold setting The position at which a mechanical control device indicator, such as that on a "spring hanger," is set to denote the proper non-operating position installation setting of the unit.

Cold shoe A "T" section hanger or support with integrated insulation that has been designed for cold temperature piping system application.

Cold spring The act of prestressing a piping system during installation to condition it for minimal fluctuations, expansions, and other reactions when the finished piping system and related equipment are used in the designed operating environment.

Colored finish A generic term to describe various color finishes that are used as an identifier for product compatibility. For example, a copper colored finish on connectors or piping would denote the product was sized for copper tubing.

Commercial piping system A piping system located in a commercial building structure that generally includes fire protection, plumbing, heating, and cooling piping systems.

Component(s) Any individual item, appliance, or device that is combined with others to create an assembly or is part of a whole.

Concrete fastener A device installed in or attached to concrete by various means (often precast, drilled, or epoxied) to which a pipe hanger or support can be attached.

Concrete insert and concrete insert box An anchor device that is cast in place in a concrete structure and provides for a hanger, support, rod, or similar attachment. Insert provides load assist to a piping system and has nominal lateral adjustment.

Continuous insert An anchoring device in the form of a channel (which can be of varying lengths), that is cast in place in a concrete structure and provides for multiple hangers, supports, rods, or similar attachments. Insert provides load assist to a piping system and has the capability for lateral adjustments.

Constant support hanger A mechanical and spring coil device that provides a constant support for a piping system, while permitting some dimensional movement.

Constant support hanger indicator A device attached to the movable arm of a "constant support hanger" that measures vertical pipe movement.

Copper plating See "plating."

Corrosion The process that describes the oxidation of a metal that is weakened or worn down by chemical action.

Cut short The shortening or lengthening of a section of pipe to provide for reduced fluctuations, expansions, and other reactions when the finished piping system and related equipment are used in the designed operating environment.

DWV Drain, waste, and venting.

Deadweight load The combination of all stress or loading put on a piping system that takes into consideraton only the weight of the piping system including the pipe, hangers, and supports, insulation, and pipe contents.

Design elevation The overall mechanical drawing view of the piping system as designed.

Design load The combination of all stress or loading put on a piping system as defined in the "engineered drawing" or as part of the engineered design specificaton.

Deviation A measurement of difference often expressed as a percentage. Often used to describe the accuracy difference between actual and specified performance criteria.

Double acting A descriptor for a mechanical device that provides resistance in both tension and compression cycles.

Double bolt pipe clamp See "three bolt pipe clamp."

Drag The retarding force that acts on a portion of a hydraulic or mechanical device as it moves through fluid, gas, or other friction-generating substances. Also refers to the force required to extend and retract a hydraulic or mechanical element of a hanger or support device during activation at low velocity.

Dynamic force or dynamic loading The additional loading and stress conditions that must be taken into consideration over and above a steady-state condition.

Dynamic load The temporary stress or loading put on a piping system as the result of internal or external forces that create movement or motion in the system.

Elbow lug An elbow-shaped device with a pipe connector welded to it for use as an attachment.

Electrogalvanized A protective coating of electroplated zinc. See also "galvanized."

Electroplated Plating by using an electro deposition process. See also "plating."

Electrolysis The producing of chemical changes due to the differences in electrical potential between dissimilar materials, in the presence of moisture. See also "corrosion."

Elevation A mechanical drawing view that is a geometrical projection as seen on a vertical plane.

Embedded A device or fastener that is cast in place in a concrete structure, for example, an embedded attachment plate or rod.

Engineered drawing A mechanical drawing that details the elements and components of a piping system and incorporates a bill of material, load and movement data, location information, and both general and specific identitfication.

Engineered hanger assembly A mechanical drawing that details the elements and components of a hanger assembly and incorporates a bill of material, load and movement data, location information, and both general and specific identification. See also "semiengineered hanger assembly."

Erected elevation See "design elevation."

Extension riser clamp An attachment device for the support of vertical piping that provides for the transfer of the piping load to the bearing surface to which the clamp is attached.

Eye rod A bolt or rod with a circular or pear-shaped end that permits other components or devices to be attached by means of a bolt or pin. The eye may be forged, welded, or nonwelded.

Eye socket An appliance that provides for the attachment of a threaded bolt or rod to the bolt or rod of another component or device.

Fabrication A term used to refer to a part constructed or manufactured out of standard parts or raw materials.

Fabricated steel part A component that is constructed from standard shapes of steel plate.

Fabricator A business engaged in the fabrication of parts.

Forged clevis A connector device, a clevis, that has been formed as one piece, i.e., forged.

Four-way brace An assembly consisting of lateral and longitudinal bracing that is designed to control back and forth movement in four directions.

Framing steel A structural steel member, normally less than 10 ft in length, used between existing members as a means of providing for the attachment of a hanger or support for a piping system.

Friction load The stress or loading put on a piping system as the result of frictional forces that exist between different surfaces that are in contact with each other, such as moving or sliding surfaces.

Galvanized A zinc coating applied to steel for protection from oxidation and other chemical actions.

Gang hanger A hanger assembly utilizing a common cross member to provide support for parallel runs or banks of piping.

Guide A device used to permit pipe movement in a predetermined direction while restraining movement in other directions.

Hanger A device that is suspended from a structure and used to carry or support a load.

Hanger assembly A general term used to describe a series of assembled components that make up a device that is connected to or suspended from a structure and is used to carry or support a load in tension or carry a load under compression. The device may be designed to prevent, resist, or limit movement, or it may be used to permit movement in a predetermined direction while restraining movement in other directions.

Hanger drawing See "brace," "hanger," or "support drawing."

Hanger loads See "pipe hanger loads."

Hanger rod Round steel bar, normally threaded, used to connect components for hangers and supports.

Heavy bracket A bracket used for the support of heavy loads (see "bracket").

Hinged pipe clamp Also known as a "split ring," it is a hinged attachement device that permits installation before or after piping is in place and is primarily used on noninsulated piping.

Horizontal traveler A hanger or support device that will accommodate horizontal piping movement.

Hot dip galvanized A corrosion protection coating of zinc applied to steel or other metals.

Hot elevation The mechanical drawing view of the piping system as it will appear in its full operating environment.

Hot hanger location The location of the pipe hangers, supports, and assemblies of the installed piping system in reference to the building structure and structural elements within the operating environment.

Hot load The stress or loading put on a piping system as the result of a normal or steady-state operating environment. See "operating load."

Hot setting The position at which a mechanical control device indicator, such as that on a "spring hanger," is set to denote the proper operating position setting of the unit.

Hot shoe A "T" section hanger or support with integrated insulation that has been designed for hot temperature piping system application.

HVAC Heating, ventilation, and air conditioning.

Hydraulic snubber See "hydraulic sway brace."

Hydraulic sway brace A hydraulic cylinder or rotating vane device used for the control of shock or sway in piping systems, while allowing for normal thermal expansion.

Hydrostatic load The stress or loading put on a piping system as the result of hydrostatic testing. See "hydrostatic test load."

Hydrostatic lock The condition wherein a supplemental restraint temporarily locks or holds in place moveable parts during a hydrostatic test. Often used in conjunction with spring devices, such as a "spring hanger," to provide for a fixed position enabling a load to be transferred to a supporting structure in a desired placement during construction or installation.

Hydrostatic test A preoperational test whereby the piping system is subjected to a pressurized fluid test in excess of the specified operational pressure to ensure the integrity of the system.

Hydrostatic test load The temporary loading condition consisting of the total load weight of the piping (gravitational load), insulation, and test fluid for piping systems subjected to hydrostatic tests.

Industrial piping system A piping system located in an industrial complex that generally includes fire protection, plumbing, heating and cooling piping systems, and also incorporates process, vacuum, air, steam or chemical piping systems.

Insert An anchor device that is cast in place in a concrete structure and provides for a hanger, support, rod, or similar attachment. Insert provides load assist to a piping system and has nominal lateral adjustment.

Insert box See "concrete insert."

Insert nut A female threaded anchor device that is locked into position as part of an insert and that receives a threaded rod or bolt.

Institutional piping system A piping system located in an institutional environment or building structure that generally includes fire protection, plumbing, heating and cooling piping systems, and process, vacuum, air, or chemical gas piping systems.

Insulated pipe support A hanger or support with an integrated insulation insert designed for use with insulated pipe.

Insulation protection saddle A device used to prevent damage to the insulation on a pipe at the support point.

Integral attachment When connector pieces and devices have been welded together as hangers and supports or an assembly.

Intermediate anchor An attachment point used to control the distribution, loading, and movement on a flexible piping system.

Invert Drawing elevation view from the bottom or underneath.

Jacket A metal covering placed around the insulation on a pipe to protect it against damage.

Knee brace A diagonal structural member used to transfer load or provide stability.

Lateral brace A two-way brace designed to restrain a piping system against transverse loads.

Lateral stability The state or degree of control of a piping system transverse to the run of the pipe.

Light bracket A bracket used for the support of light loads (see "bracket").

Limit stop An internal device built into a mechanical device to prevent the overstressing of a spring coil, overtravel, or release of a load.

Liner Material placed between hangers, supports, or an assembly to protect a piping system from damage or other undesirable effects.

Load adjustment scale A scale used on a mechanical device to indicate the load adjustment.

Load bolt or pin A bolt or pin used to support the weight or load carried by a hanger or assembly.

Load coupling An adjustment device used to connect hanger and support components.

Load indicator A pointer, dial, or gauge for reading or determining the settings and changes of a device.

Load rated The rating of a particular size of component or assembly to withstand a specified force with a safety factor applied.

Load scale A measurement pointer, dial, or gauge attached to a device to provide a means of determining static or dynamic aspects of a supported load.

Load variation The difference in the elevations at a support point between the time of installation (cold) and actual operation (hot) environment.

Load See "pipe hanger load."

Location See "pipe hanger location."

Lock up The operational period when a hydraulic, mechanical, or spring device used for the control of shock and sway in piping systems is actuated.

Longitudinal brace A two-way brace designed to restrain a piping system against axial loads.

Lug A welded appliance to provide an attachment point to a structural member or piping.

Mechanical snubber See "mechanical sway brace."

Mechanical sway brace A mechanical device used for the control of shock or sway in piping systems, while allowing for normal thermal expansion.

Medium bracket A bracket used for the support of moderate loads (see "bracket").

Metric hanger A hanger or support that conforms to metric measurements and, where appropriate, contains a metric threaded connection.

Mill galvanized A corrosion protection coating of zinc applied at the point of fabrication.

Multiple support See "gang hanger."

Negligible movement The calculated minimum movement at a support point for a portion of a piping system where there is an inherent flexibility of the piping system.

Nominal size The identified size, which may vary from the actual size.

Nonintegral attachment When connector pieces and devices do not require being welded together as hangers and supports or an assembly.

Nut, insert See "insert nut."

Offset A relative displacement between a structural attachment point and a piping system that is incorporated into the design to accommodate movement.

Operating load The stress or loading put on a piping system as the result of a normal or steady-state operating environment.

Pipe attachment Any component or device used to connect a pipe to a hanger, support, or assembly.

Pipe brace See "brace."

Pipe channel Conduit or channel that is cast in place within concrete structural elements and that provides for the passing through of pipe. Placed horizontally throughout a concrete structure to facilitate future access.

Pipe clamp A bolted clamp attachment that connects a pipe to a hanger, support, assembly, or structural element.

Pipe clip An attachment appliance used to connect a pipe directly to a structural element, also referred to as a "strap" or a "pipe clamp."

Pipe covering protection saddle A protective covering used to prevent damage to insulation surrounding a pipe at hanger and support points.

Pipe elevations See "design elevation," "erected elevation," "after cold pull elevation," and "cold elevation."

Pipe hanger An appliance or device that is attached to, or suspended from, a structural element and that will be used to support a piping system load in tension.

Pipe hanger assembly An "assembly" used for a piping system.

Pipe hanger drawing A mechanical drawing that details the elements and components of a piping system and incorporates a bill of material, load and movement data, location information, and both general and specific identitfication. See also "engineered drawing" and "semiengineered drawing."

Pipe hanger load See specific load types: "cold load," "deadweight load," "design load," "dynamic load," "friction load," "hot load," "hydrostatic load," "operating load," "thrust load," "seismic load," "thermal load," "trip-out load," "wind load," and "water hammer load."

Pipe hanger location See location types: "cold hanger location" and "hot hanger location."

Pipe hanger plan and **pipe hanger plan location** The "engineered design" and "elevations" that fully detail the hangers, supports, and anchors of a piping system. Mechanical drawings include appropriate offsets as a result of movement and displacement expectations.

Pipe insulation shield A rigid insert appliance designed to protect pipe insulation passing through hangers, supports, and assemblies.

Pipe load See specific load types: "cold load," "deadweight load," "design load," "dynamic load," "friction load," "hot load," "hydrostatic load," "operating load," "thrust load," "seismic load," "thermal load," "trip-out load," "wind load," and "water hammer load."

Pipe opening An opening, conduit, or channel that is cast in place within concrete structural elements and that provides for the passing through of pipe. Most typical usage is for short vertical conduit in concrete slabs to eliminate the subsequent drilling of core holes.

Pipe rack A structural frame that is used to support piping systems. See "assembly."

Pipe roll A pipe hanger or support that utilizes a roller or bearing device to provide the ability for lateral axial movement in a piping system.

Pipe saddle support A pipe support that utilizes a curved section for cradling the pipe.

Pipe shoe A hanger or support (typically T shaped) attached to the pipe to transmit the load or forces to adjacent structural elements.

Pipe size Reference to nominal pipe size, unless otherwise specified.

Pipe sleeve An opening, conduit, or channel that is cast in place within concrete structural elements and that provides for the passing through of pipe. Most typical usage is for short vertical conduit in concrete slabs to eliminate the subsequent drilling of core holes. However, conduit or channel may be placed horizontally throughout a concrete structure to facilitate future access.

Pipe sleeve, pipe sleeve hanger or support An appliance or device that surrounds a pipe and connects to a hanger or support to provide for alignment and limited movement.

Pipe slide A hanger or support that incorporates a "slide plate" to accommodate horizontal pipe movement.

Pipe strap An attachment appliance used to connect a pipe directly to a structural element. See "pipe clip" and "pipe clamp."

Pipe support A device or "stanchion" by which a pipe is carried or supported from beneath. In this position the pipe load is in compression.

Pipe system load See specific load types: "cold load," "deadweight load," "design load," "dynamic load," "friction load," "hot load," "hydrostatic load," "operating load," "thrust load," "seismic load," "thermal load," "trip-out load," "wind load," and "water hammer load."

Plate lug See "lug."

Plating An electroplating process whereby a metalic coating (e.g., copper, crome, or zinc) is deposited on a substrate.

Point loading The point of application of a load between two surfaces; typically describes the load point between a curved and a flat surface.

Preset Prior installation adjustment of hangers, supports assemblies, equipment, and devices.

Protection saddle A "saddle" that provides a protective covering or coating to prevent damage to pipe or to the insulation surrounding a pipe at hanger and support points.

Protection shield An appliance, which may be rigid or flexible, designed to protect pipe or insulation at contact points with hangers and supports.

Random hanger A hanger or support that requires field fabrication and the exact location, shape, and type of which are left to the discretion of, and are to be determined by, the installer.

Reservoir An attachment or separate container used in conjunction with a fluid (or gas) using device (e.g., hydraulic) that provides a means to store or hold a supply of liquid (or gas) in order to provide for a reserve or otherwise ensure for an adequate or continuous supply of fluid (or gas).

Restraint Any appliance, device, or equipment that prevents, resists, or limits unplanned or random movement.

Restraining control device Any hydraulic, mechanical, spring, or other rigid or flexible hanger, support, or device used to control movement.

Resilient support A hanger, support, or device that provides for vertical, horizontal, lateral, or axial movement.

Retaining strap An appliance or device used in conjunction with clamps and other components to secure hangers and supports to structural elements.

Rigid brace A "brace" capable of controlling and limiting movement; provides restraint in both tension and compression, unlike a cable.

Rigid hanger A hanger or support that controls or limits vertical and horizontal movement.

Rigid support See "rigid hanger."

Rigging Appliances and devices, including chain, rope, and cable, used to erect, support, and manipulate.

Ring band An appliance or device consisting of a strap (steel, plastic, or other material) formed in a circular shape with an attached knurled swivel nut used for vertical adjustment.

Riser An upright or vertical member, structural or otherwise.

Riser clamp An appliance or device used to provide connections to and support for upright or vertical members, structural or otherwise.

Riser hanger A hanger or support used in conjunction with a "riser."

Rod A slender bar typically considered to have a circular cross section; available in a variety of materials. See "threaded rod."

Rod coupling An appliance or device used to join two rods. See "threaded rod coupling."

Rod hanger A hanger or support that has an integrated "rod" as part of its construction.

Rod stiffener An appliance or device used to provide additional rigidity to a "rod."

Roll stand A "pipe roll" mounted on a stand and used for support.

Roll and plate A combination of a "pipe roll" and a "slide plate" used for minimal lateral and axial movement where minimal or no vertical adjustment is required.

Roll hanger An appliance or device that utilizes a "pipe roll" for lateral and axial movement when used to carry a load in suspension or tension.

Roll plate A flat appliance, typically a steel or alloy plate, that will permit movement and/or facilitate a sliding motion. See "slide plate."

Roll trapeze A combination device utilizing a "pipe roll" and a "trapeze hanger."

Saddle A curved appliance or device designed to cradle a pipe and used in conjunction with a hanger or suppport.

Safety factor The ultimate strength of a material divided by the allowable stress. Also the ultimate strength of a device divided by the rated capacity.

Scale plate A device attached to hangers, supports, and asssemblies to detect changes in load or movement.

Seismic control device An appliance or device used to provide structural stability in the event of a change in the steady-state environment affecting a building's structure, such as would occur with a natural event such as an earthquake or other violent action.

Seismic load The temporary stress or loading put on a piping system as the result of a change in the steady-state environment affecting a building's structure, such as would occur with a natural event such as an earthquake or other violent action.

Semiengineered drawing A mechanical drawing that details the elements and components of a piping system and incorporates a bill of material, load and movement data, and other general identification.

Semiengineered hanger assembly A mechanical drawing that details the elements and components of a hanger assembly and incorporates a bill of material, load and movement data, and other general identification.

Service conditions Description of the operating environment and operating conditions, including operating pressures and temperatures.

Shear lug An appliance or device primarily to transfer axial stress (shear stress) and load to a support element.

Shield See "protection shield."

Side beam bracket A "bracket" designed to be mounted in a vertical position by attachment to a structural element. This bracket provides mounting capability for a hanger or support.

Side beam clamp A "beam clamp" that provides for an off-center attachment to the structural element.

Significant movement The calculated movement at a proposed support point for a hanger or support.

Single acting A descriptor for a mechanical device that provides resistance in either tension or compression cycles, but not both. See "double acting."

Single pipe roll A "pipe roll" used in a "trapeze hanger."

Sleeper A horizontal support, usually located at grade.

Slide plate A flat appliance, typically a steel or alloy plate, which will permit movement and/or facilitate a sliding motion.

Sliding support An appliance or device that provides for only frictional resistance to horizontal movement.

Slip fitting An appliance or device used to help align and provide for limited movement for a pipe. This device is used as an assembly component.

Snubber A hydraulic, mechanical, or spring device used for the control of shock and sway; a shock absorber.

Special component Any appliance or device that is designed and fabricated on an "as required" basis.

Spider guide An appliance or device used with insulated piping for maintaining alignment during axial expansion and contraction cycles.

Split ring See "hinged pipe clamp."

Spring cushion hanger A simple, noncalibrated, single rod spring support, used for providing a cushioning effect.

Spring cushion roll A pair of spring coils with retainers for use with a "pipe roll."

Spring hanger An appliance or device using a spring or springs to permit vertical movement.

Spring snubber See "spring sway brace."

Spring sway brace A spring device used for the control of vibration or shock or bracing against sway.

Stanchion A straight length of structural material used as a support in a vertical or upright position.

Stop An appliance or device used to limit movement in a specific direction.

Strap An attachment appliance used to connect a pipe directly to a structural element. See "pipe clip" and "pipe clamp."

Stress analysis An analytical report that evaluates material, structural, or component stress levels.

Strip insert See "continuous insert."

Structural attachment An appliance or device used to connect a hanger, support, or assembly to a structural element.

Strut A rigid tension/compression member.

Strut clamp An appliance or device used to secure a pipe to a strut.

Support A device that attaches to or rests on a structural element and is used to carry a load in compression.

Support drawing See "brace," "hanger," or "support drawing."

Suspension hanger See "pipe hanger."

Sway brace See "lateral brace" or "restraining control device."

Swivel pipe ring See "ring band."

Swivel turnbuckle An appliance or device that provides flexibility and linear adjustment capability; used in conjunction with hangers and supports. See "turnbuckle."

Thermal load The stress or loading put on or introduced to a piping system as the result of regular or abrupt changes in the steady-state temperature of the pipe contents or the surrounding environment.

Threaded rod A steel, alloy, plastic, or other material rod threaded along its full length. Threads may be rolled or cut.

Threaded rod coupling An appliance or device used to join two threaded rods.

Three bolt pipe clamp A "pipe clamp" normally used for horizontal insulated piping that utilizes bolts to attach the clamp to the pipe and a separate "load bolt" to transfer the piping weight to the remainder of the "pipe hanger assembly" from a point outside the insulation (previously known as a "double bolt pipe clamp").

Top beam clamp A mechanical device used to connect, as a hanger or support, or used to hold part of a piping system to the top of a structural beam element (typically a steel beam; a clamp firmly holds multiple materials or devices together and does not require welding).

Thrust load The temporary stress or loading put on a piping system as the result of a change in the steady-state operating environment of the pipe contents as a result of regular or abrupt changes associated with equipment or mechanical devices such as the discharge from a safety valve, relief valve, pump failure, or failure of some other mechanical device or element.

Transverse brace See "lateral brace."

Trapeze hanger A "pipe hanger" consisting of parallel vertical rods connected at their lower ends by a horizontal member that is suspended from a structural element. This type of hanger is often used when there is an overhead obstruction or where insufficient vertical space is available to accommodate a more traditional hanger or support.

Travel device A hanger or support device that will accommodate piping movement.

Travel indicator See "constant support hanger indicator" and "variable spring hanger indicator."

Travel scale A device attached to a spring unit to measure vertical movement.

Travel stop An appliance or device that temporarily locks moveable parts in a fixed position, enabling a load to be transferred to a supporting structural element during installation and testing phases.

Trip-out load The temporary stress or loading put on a piping system as the result of a change in the steady-state flow of the pipe contents as a result of the change associated with equipment or mechanical devices such as a turbine or pump.

Turnbuckle A device with one left-hand female threaded end and one right-hand female threaded end, used to join two threaded rods and provide linear adjustment.

Two-way brace A "brace" designed to control movement in two directions. See "lateral brace" and "longitudinal brace."

U-bolt A U-shaped rod with threaded ends that fits around a pipe and is attached to a structural element or a supporting member.

Vapor barrier An uninterrupted nonpermeable material used as a cover for insulated pipe to exclude moisture from the insulation.

Variability The "load variation" of a "variable spring hanger" divided by the "hot load" expressed as a percentage.

Variable spring hanger A spring coil device that produces varying support while permitting vertical movement.

Variable spring hanger indicator A device attached to a "variable spring hanger" that measures vertical pipe movement.

Velocity limited A term relating to "snubbers" in which velocity is the means of control.

Vibration control device An appliance used to reduce and/or control the transmission of vibration to structural elements.

Vibration isolation device See "vibration control device."

Water hammer load The temporary stress or loading put on a piping system as the result of a change, abrupt or otherwise, in the steady-state flow of the pipe contents.

Welded beam attachment A U-shaped flat bar appliance, normally welded to a steel beam and used to connect a hanger, support, or assembly.

Welded pipe attachment The use of a weld to attach a pipe to a hanger, support, or assembly.

Weldless eye nut A forged steel appliance that provides an attachment point for a threaded "hanger rod" to a bolt or pin connection.

Wire hook A type of hanger or support that is simply a bent piece of heavy wire.

Wind load The temporary or steady-state stress or loading put on or added to a piping system as the result of a change of environmental conditions such as increased steady state or alternating air movement. Usually refers to piping systems in environmentally exposed conditions.

Wire rope See "cable."

Vibration Isolation

During the past 40 years, vibration and noise problems have become more critical. In today's tall buildings, installation and operating economies often result from locating mechanical equipment on the upper levels of buildings, including machinery penthouses. This places the mechanical equipment in close proximity to high-priced space, where vibration and noise cannot be tolerated.

The pumps, compressors, and other associated equipment have become larger. This means that greatly increased power input is being applied to modern, lighter structures, further increasing the difficulty of achieving successful installations. To increase capacity and reduce costs, equipment speeds have been increased.

For the same amount of unbalance, doubling the equipment's revolutions per minute (rpm) quadruples the unbalanced force. Despite the efforts of equipment manufacturers to compensate for this through improved balance of rotating equipment, the net result has still been more vibration and noise generation.

Thick concrete floors and walls in the older buildings were stiffer and could withstand and absorb more machinery vibration and noise than the new structures utilizing steel, pan type floors, and curtain walls. The lighter structures have resonant frequencies that are much more readily excited by equipment vibration. In the past, a very critical installation on an upper floor could be achieved by allowing not more than 10% vibration transmission. Today, many installations must be designed for not more than 1 or 2% transmissibility.

People are no longer willing to tolerate vibration and noise. Installations that were satisfactory in the past are no longer acceptable by our more sophisticated modern standards. Noise levels must now be controlled to the extent that equipment noise does not add to the noise level of any building area. Furthermore, tests have been conducted to establish acceptable noise criteria for different types of use. These noise criteria (NC) curves take into consideration individuals' sensitivity to both loudness and frequency of noise. Similar criteria are available for vibration.

In summary, there are more, larger, and higher speed machines installed higher on lighter structures disturbing more sophisticated tenants. The only satisfactory solution is to analyze the structure and equipment, not just as individual pieces of equipment, but as a total system. Every element must be carefully considered to ensure a completely satisfactory job. It is impossible to separate vibration and noise problems.

THEORY OF VIBRATION CONTROL

A very simple equation applies to determining the transmission of steady-state vibration, the constantly repeating sinusoidal wave form of vibration generated by such equipment as compressors, engines, and pumps:

Equation 7-1

$$T = \frac{F_t}{F_d} = \frac{1}{(f_d^2/f_n) - 1}$$

where

T = Transmissibility

F_t = Force transmitted through the resilient mountings

F_d = Unbalanced force acting on the resiliently supported system

f_d = Frequency of disturbing vibration, cycles per minute (cpm) (hertz [Hz])

f_n = Natural frequency of the resiliently mounted system, cycles per minute (cpm) (Hz)

This equation is exact for steel springs because they have straight-line load deflection characteristics and negligible damping. When the equation is used for organic materials, the following corrections normally give conservative results: For rubber and neoprene, use 50% of the static deflection when calculating f_n. For cork, use f_n equal to one and one-half times the natural frequency determined by actual test.

The natural frequency of the resiliently mounted system (f_n) can be calculated using the following equation:

Equation 7-2

$$F_n = \frac{188}{(1/d)^{\frac{1}{2}}}$$

where

d = Static deflection of the resilient mounting, in. (mm)

When using Equation 7-2 in international standard (SI) units, the 188 multiplying factor should be changed to 947.5. The static deflection can be obtained from the expression:

Equation 7-3

$$d = \frac{W}{k}$$

where

W = Weight on the mounting, lb (kg)

k = Stiffness factor of the mounting of deflection, lb/in. (kg/mm)

The natural frequency (f_n) of a resiliently mounted system is the frequency at which it will oscillate by itself if a force is exerted on the system and then released. This can be illustrated by suspending a weight from a very long rubber band. The longer the rubber band, the more deflection the weight produces in it. If the weight is then pulled down slightly by hand and released, it will oscillate up and down at the natural frequency of the system. The more deflection in the system, the lower its natural frequency. The importance of this can be seen by examining Equation 7-1 rewritten in the following form:

Equation 7-4

$$F_t = F_d \left[\frac{1}{(f_d^2/f_n) - 1} \right]$$

A system may have up to six natural frequencies. It will be found that in the practical selection of machine mountings, if the vertical natural frequency of the system is made low enough for a low transmissibility, the horizontal and rotational natural frequencies will generally be lower than the vertical and can be disregarded, except on machines with very large horizontal unbalanced forces or with large unbalanced moments, such as horizontal compressors and large two-, three-, and five-cylinder engines.

Obviously, we want to minimize the transmitted force (F_t). Since the disturbing force (F_d) is a function of the machine characteristics and cannot be reduced, except by dynamic balancing of the machine—or by reducing the operating speed, which is seldom practical—the transmitted force can be reduced only by minimizing the function $1/[(f_d^2/f_n) - 1]$.

This can be accomplished only by increasing the frequency ratio (f_d/f_n). However, since the disturbing frequency (f_d) is fixed for any given machine and is a function of the rpm, it can seldom be changed. The only remaining variable is the mounting natural frequency (f_n). Reducing f_n by increasing the static deflection of the resilient mountings reduces the vibration transmission. This explains why the efficiency of machinery mountings increases as their resiliency and deflection increase.

Figure 7-1 shows the effect of varying frequency ratios on the transmissibility. Note that for f_d/f_n less than 2, the use of mountings actually increases the transmissibility above what would result if no isolation were used and the machine were bolted down solidly. In fact, if careless selection of the mount results in a mounting with the natural frequency equal to or nearly equal to the disturbing frequency, a very serious condition called "resonance" occurs. In Equation 7-4, the denominator of the transmissibility function becomes zero and the transmitted force (f_t) theoretically becomes infinite. As the ratio f_d/f_n increases beyond 2, the resilient mountings reduce the transmitted force.

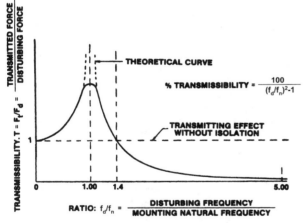

Figure 7-1 Transmissibility vs. Frequency Ratio

Note: This curve applies to steel spring isolators and other materials with very little damping.

Figure 7-2 shows a chart that can be used to select the proper resilient mountings when the following job characteristics are known: weight per mounting, disturbing frequency, and design transmissibility. The chart shows the limitations of the various types of isolation materials, data that are particularly helpful in selecting the proper media.

TYPES OF VIBRATION AND SHOCK MOUNTINGS

Cork

Cork was the original vibration and noise isolation material and has been used for this purpose for at least 100 years. The most widely used form of cork today is compressed cork, which is made of pure granules of cork without any foreign binder and compressed and baked under pressure with accurately controlled density. Cork can be used directly under machines, but its widest applications are under concrete foundations (see Figure 7-3). It is not affected by oils, acids normally encountered, or temperatures between 0 and 200°F (–17.8 and 93.3°C) and will not rot under continuous cycles of moistening and dryness, but it is attacked by strong alkaline solutions. Cork under concrete foundations still giving good service after 20 years indicates that the material has a long, useful life when properly applied. Cork is fairly good as a low-frequency shock absorber, but its use as a vibration isolator is limited to frequencies above 1800 cpm (Hz). Cork has good sound insulation characteristics. Because of the large amount of damping in cork, the natural frequency cannot be computed from the static deflection and must be determined in tests by vibrating the cork under different loads to find the resonance frequency, which establishes the natural frequency of the material. The limiting values for cork given in Figure 7-2 were determined in this manner.

Elastomers

Elastomers have very good sound insulation characteristics, are fairly good for low-frequency shock absorption, and are useful as vibration isolators for frequencies above 1200 cpm (Hz). Typical elastomer mountings are illustrated in Figure 7-4. The temperature range of natural rubber is 50 to 150°F (10 to 65.6°C), that of neoprene is 0 to 200°F (–17.8 to 93.3°C).

Neoprene Rubber

Neoprene rubber is recommended for applications where there is continuous exposure to oil. Special elastomer compounds are available to meet conditions beyond those cited. Elastomers tend to lose resiliency as they age. The useful life of elastomer mountings is about seven years

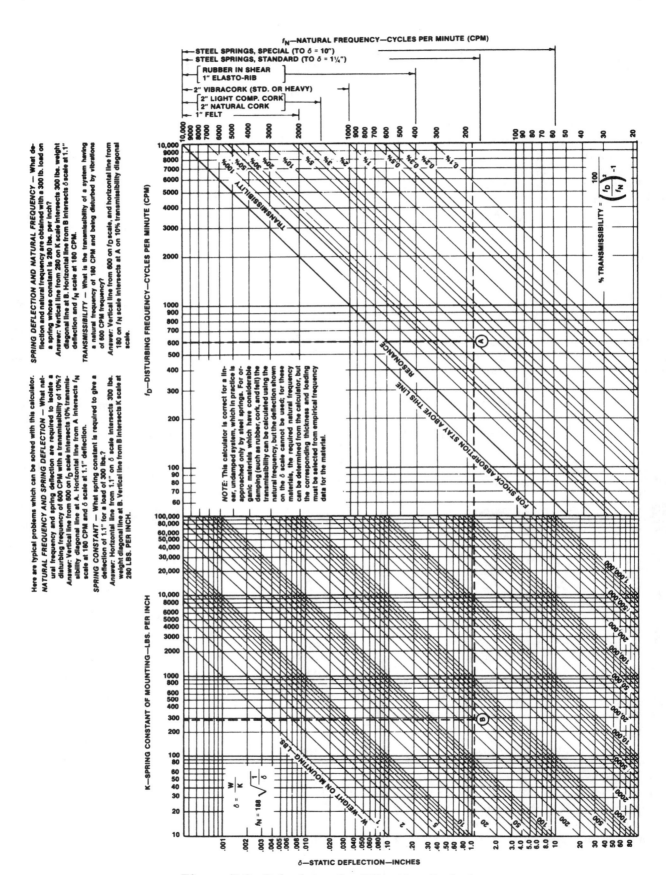

Figure 7-2 Calculator for Vibration Isolation

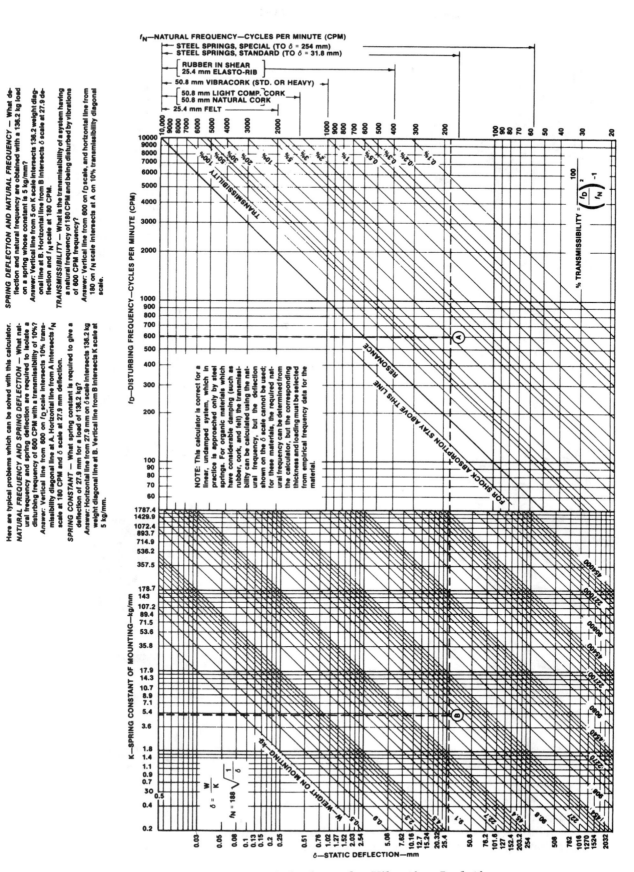

Figure 7-2(M) Calculator for Vibration Isolation

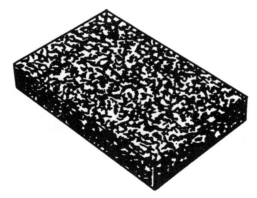

Figure 7-3 Typical Cork

under nonimpact applications and about five years under impact applications, though they retain their sound insulation value for much longer. Individual molded elastomer mountings are generally economical only with the light- and medium-weight machines, since heavier capacity mountings approach the cost of the more efficient steel spring isolators. Pad type elastomer isolation has no such limitations.

Steel Spring Isolators

Steel spring isolators provide the most efficient method of isolating vibration and shock, approaching 100% effectiveness. The higher efficiency is due to the greater deflections they provide. Standard steel spring isolators, such as those shown in Figure 7-5, provide deflections up to 5 in. (127 mm) compared to about ½ in. (12.7 mm) maximum for rubber and other materials, while special steel spring isolators can give deflections up to 10 in. (254 mm). Since the performance of steel springs follows very closely the equations of vibration control, their performance can be very accurately predetermined, eliminating costly trial and error, which is sometimes necessary in other materials. Most steel spring isolators are equipped with built-in leveling bolts, which eliminate the need for shims when installing machinery. The more rugged construction possible in steel spring isolators provides for a long life, usually equal to that of the machine itself. Since high-frequency noises sometimes tend to bypass steel springs, rubber sound isolation pads are usually used under spring isolators to stop such transmission into the floor on critical installations.

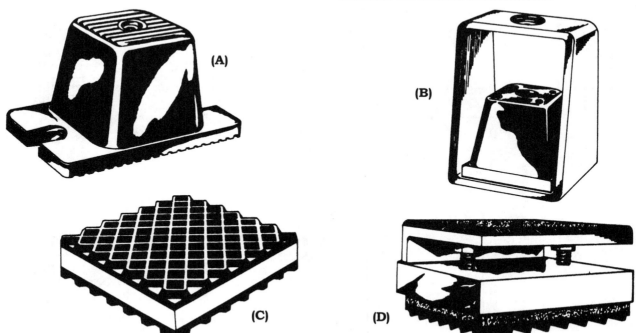

Figure 7-4 Typical Elastomer and Elastomer-Cork Mountings: (A) Compression and Shear Elastomer Floor Mountings Provide Up to ½ in. (12.7 mm) Deflection; (B) Elastomer Hangers for Suspended Equipment and Piping; (C) Elastomer/Cork Mountings Combine Characteristics of These Two Materials, Provide Nonskid Surface, Which Eliminates Bolting Machine Down; (D) Elastomer/Cork Mounting with Built-In Leveling Screw.

Figure 7-5 Typical Steel Spring Mounting

Table 7-1 tabulates the useful range of cork, rubber, and steel springs for different equipment speeds.

APPLICATIONS

Properly designed mountings now permit installation of the heaviest mechanical equipment in penthouses, on roofs directly over offices and sleeping areas. Such upper-floor installations permit certain operating economies and release valuable basement space for garaging automobiles. When heavy machinery is installed on upper floors, great care must be used to prevent vibration transmission, which often shows up many floors below when a wall, ceiling, or even a lighting fixture has the same natural frequency as the disturbing vibration. The result of such resonance vibration is a very annoying noise.

Efficient mountings permit lighter, more economical construction of new buildings and prevent difficulties when machinery is installed on the concrete-filled, ribbed, metal deck floors. They also permit installation of heavy machinery in old buildings which were not originally designed to accommodate such equipment.

Vibration and noise transmission through piping is a serious problem. When compressors are installed on resilient mountings, provision should be made for flexibility in the discharge and intake piping to reduce vibration transmission. This can be accomplished either through the use of flexible metallic hose (which must be of adequate length and very carefully installed in strict accordance with the manufacturer's specifications) or by providing for flexibility in the piping itself. This is often accomplished by running the piping for a distance equal to 15 pipe diameters, both vertically and horizontally, before attaching the piping to the structure. Additional protection is provided by suspending the piping from the building on resilient mountings.

Effective vibration control for machines is usually quite inexpensive, seldom exceeding 3% of the equipment cost. In many cases, resilient mountings pay for themselves immediately by eliminating special machinery foundations or the need to bolt equipment to the floor. It is much cheaper to prevent vibration and structural noise transmission by installing mountings when the equipment is installed than it is to go back later and try to correct a faulty installation. Resilient machinery mountings should not be considered a panacea for noise transmission problems. They have a definite use in the overall solution of noise problems and their intelligent use can produce gratifying results at low cost.

Table 7-1 The Relative Effectiveness of Steel Springs, Rubber, and Cork in the Various Speed Ranges

Range	RPM	Springs	Rubber	Cork
Low	Up to 1200	Required	Not recommended	Unsuitable except for shock[a]
Medium	1200–1800	Excellent	Fair	Not recommended
High	Over 1800	Excellent for critical jobs	Good	Fair to good

a For noncritical installations only; otherwise, springs are recommended.

8

Grease Interceptors

INTRODUCTION

The purpose of a grease interceptor is to trap and store suspended grease from the spent water passing through the device, thereby preventing deposition of the grease in the sanitary drainage system and ensuring a free flow at all times. Grease interceptors are installed in locations where the liquid wastes contain a large amount of grease. These devices are normally required in kitchen sinks, drains, and any other plumbing fixtures in restaurants, hotels, and institutions. Residential dwellings very seldom discharge the grease in such quantities as to warrant a grease interceptor. This chapter discusses the following aspects of the grease interceptor: its principle of operation, its design characteristics, existing custom-made and commercially available equipment, its applications, code requirements, operation and maintenance provisions, and economics.

PRINCIPLE OF OPERATION

Most currently available grease interceptors operate on the principle of separation by flotation. The design of the grease interceptors and their proper use, however, require a thorough understanding of the theory involved.

The particles in a still fluid of greater density will rise to the surface because of gravity. These particles will accelerate until the friction resistance is equal to the buoyant force. The final velocity for a spherical particle, known as its "floating velocity," may be calculated using Newton's equation for the frictional drag with the driving force, shown in Equation 8-1.

Equation 8-1

$$\frac{(C_d A \rho\ v^2)}{2} = (\rho_1 - \rho)\ g\ V$$

This yields the following mathematical relationship:

Equation 8-2

$$v = \sqrt{\frac{4}{3}\frac{g}{C_d}\frac{\rho_1 - \rho}{\rho}D}$$

where

C_d = Drag coefficient number

A = Projected area of the particle ($\pi D^2/4$ for a sphere)

v = Relative velocity between the particle and the fluid

ρ = Mass density of the fluid

ρ_1 = Mass density of particle

g = Gravitational constant, 32.2 ft/s/s

D = Diameter of the particle

V = Volume of the particle ($1\frac{1}{3}\pi r^3$ for a sphere) (r = radius of the particle)

Experimental values of the drag coefficient number have been correlated with the Reynolds number, a dimensionless term expressing the ratio of the inertia and viscous forces. The expression for the Reynolds number, $R = \rho v D/\mu$, contains, in addition to the parameters defined above, the absolute viscosity. The drag coefficient has been demonstrated to equal $24/R$ (Stokes law). When this value is substituted for C_d in Equation 8-2, the result is the following (Reynolds number < 1):

Equation 8-3

$$v = \frac{g\,(\rho_1 - \rho)\,D^2}{18\,\mu}$$

The relationship in Equation 8-3 has been verified by a number of investigators for spheres and fluids of various types.

Note: Equation 8-2 applies to particles with diameters 0.4 in. (10 mm) or smaller and involving Reynolds numbers less than 1. For larger diameters, there is a transition region; thereafter, Newton's law applies.

The effect of shape irregularity is most pronounced as the floating velocity increases. Since grease particles to be removed in sanitary drainage systems have slow floating velocities, particle irregularity is of small importance.

Figure 8-1 shows the settling velocities of discrete spherical particles in still water. The heavy lines are for settling values computed using Equation 8-3 and for drag coefficients depending on the Reynolds number. Below a Reynolds number of 1.0, the settlement is according to Stokes law. As noted above, as particle sizes and Reynolds numbers become larger, first there is a transition stage and then Newton's law applies. At water temperatures other than 50°F (10°C), the ratio of the settling velocities to those at 50°F (10°C) will be approximately as $(T + 10)/60$, where T is the water temperature in degrees Fahrenheit (degrees Celsius). Sand grains and heavy floc particles settle in the transition region; however, most of the particles significant in the investigation of water treatment settle well within the Stokes law region. Particles with irregular shapes settle somewhat more slowly than spheres of equivalent volume. If the volumetric concentration of the suspended particles exceeds about 1%, the settling is hindered to the extent that the velocities are reduced by 10% or more.

Flotation is the opposite of settling insofar as the densities and particle sizes are known.

DESIGN CHARACTERISTICS

Detention Period

The detention period, P, is the theoretical time that the water is held in the grease interceptors. The volume of the tank for the required detention period can be computed as follows:

Equation 8-4

$$V = \frac{QP}{7.48}$$

As an example of the use of Equation 8-4, for a detention period, P, equal to 2 minutes, and a flow rate, Q, of 35 gpm, the tank volume is:

$$V = \frac{35 \times 2}{7.48} = 9.36 \text{ ft}^3$$

Detention periods, unless otherwise indicated, are based on the average flow.

In International Standard (SI) units, the denominator in Equation 8-4 becomes approximately unity (1).

Flow-Through Period

The actual time required for the water (or sewage) to flow through an existing tank is called the "flow-through period." How closely this flow-through period approximates the detention period depends on the tank. A well-designed tank should provide a flow-through period of at least 30% of the theoretical detention period.

Factors Affecting Flotation in the Ideal Basin

The ideal flotation basin is one in which the direction of the flow is horizontal, and the velocity is uniform in all parts of the settling zone for a time equal to the detention period. The concentration of the suspended particles of each size is the same at all points of the vertical cross section at the inlet zone. A particle is removed when it reaches the top of the settling zone.

Figure 8-2, a longitudinal section through an ideal basin, shows the entrance and outlet zones where a turbulence in the influent and effluent will interfere with the flotation. The mat zone is that portion of the tank where the separated solids are stored before removal. L and H are the length and the liquid depth, respectively,

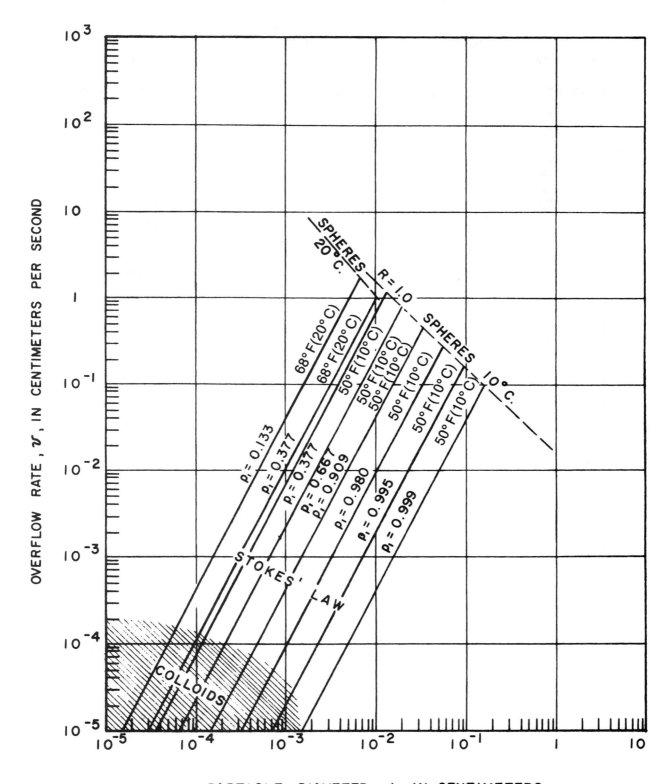

PARTICLE DIAMETER , d , IN CENTIMETERS

Figure 8-1 Rising Velocities in Still Water

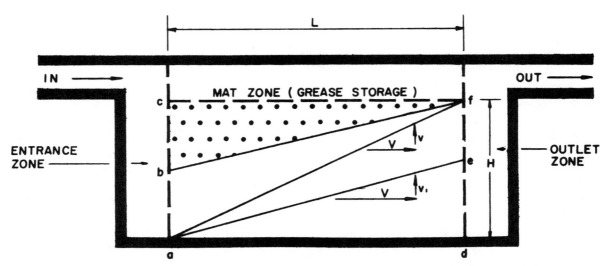

Figure 8-2 Longitudinal Section Through an *Ideal* Grease Interceptor

of the usable removal zone. V is the horizontal velocity of the water and v is the floating velocity of the smallest particle for which removal of all particles in the water is expected. Obviously, the detention period in the basin must be long enough to allow this smallest particle to float from the bottom to the top. In other words, L/V and H/v are both equal to the detention time. The line a-b is the path followed by a particle of settling value v that entered the floating zone at a. All others of the same and greater floating values will reach the top at the same time or sooner. Line a-f is the path of a rising particle with velocity v entering the interceptor at a.

A particle having a floating value v_1 (smaller than v), assuming a uniform distribution throughout the liquid, will not float to the top if it enters the basin below point b. The ratio of the removal of this size particle to the removal of a particle with a floating value v will be ab/ac. From similar triangles, the removal ratio will be v_1/v. The quantity of water flowing through the grease interceptor can be determined using the relations:

$$P = \frac{L}{V} = \frac{H}{v}$$

$$v = \frac{VH}{L}$$

$$\frac{v}{V} = \frac{H}{L}$$

interceptor liquid volume = QP

Equation 8-5

$$Q = BVH$$

Equation 8-6

$$\frac{V}{v} = \frac{L}{H}, \text{ or}$$

Equation 8-6a

$$V = \frac{1}{H} v$$

Substituting in Equation 8-5 yields the following:

Equation 8-7

$$Q = BLv, \text{ or}$$

Equation 8-7a

$$v = \frac{Q}{BL}$$

The ratio of removal of the particles having a floating velocity of v_1 and v will be as follows:

Equation 8-8

$$r = \frac{v_1}{v} = \frac{v_1 BL}{Q}$$

where

Q = Flow through the grease interceptor

V = Horizontal velocity

v = Floating velocity (overflow rate)

v_1 = Floating velocity less than v

L = Length of the grease interceptor

H = Liquid depth of the grease interceptor

B = Width of the grease interceptor

P = Detention period

r = Removal ratio

The velocity v is the overflow rate (or tank discharge) per unit of plan area. Consideration of this design parameter leads to the conclusion that, with a given Q, the greater the horizontal area of the tank, the smaller the v. The smaller the particles removed, the more efficient the tank. Theoretically, the depth has no effect on a tank's efficiency. This condition indicates that very shallow tanks are advisable; however, other considerations—which are discussed later—affect the tank depths as built in practice. Low overflow rates have been demonstrated experimentally as important design criteria. The importance of low values of v has led to the design of tanks that are subdivided horizontally, which effectively increases the surface area while retaining a fairly high V. Difficulty with grease removal, however, has prevented the use of this type of tank.

Figure 8-2 indicates that the entrance and exit zones should be small when compared with the floating zone. This condition would appear to favor the use of long, narrow tanks. The mat zone should also be small, which favors the use of tanks with a continuous (or frequent) grease removal over those that are cleaned after long intervals of time.

The principles of flotation discussed above are applicable strictly to particles that are separate and distinct. In strong concentrations of very small particles, as in turbid waters, hindered flotation takes place. This condition means that the faster-rising particles collide with the slower-rising particles with more or less agglomeration due to adhesion. The resulting larger particles float still faster. This condition is particularly noticeable where the suspended particles are highly flocculent, i.e., composed of masses of very finely divided material. A tank that is deep enough to permit agglomeration, therefore, will have a blanket (or mass) of flocculent material receiving the suspended solids from the material rising from below or from the currents passing through it and will lose masses of the agglomerated solids to the storage space above.

While varying floating rates among the particles is probably the most important factor in agglomeration, the varying liquid velocities throughout the tank will have a similar effect, causing the fast-moving particles to collide with the slower-moving particles. Since flocculation can be assumed to continue throughout the entire floating period, the amount of flocculation will depend on the detention period. Accordingly, with a given overflow rate, a tank of considerable depth should be more efficient than a shallow unit. On the other hand, a decrease in the overflow rate might have the same effect. Flotation tests might determine this point (the point of agglomeration) for a known water (or sewage).

Practical Design

While acquaintance with the theory of flotation is important to the engineer, several factors have prevented the direct application of this theory to the design of grease interceptors. Some turbulence is unavoidable at the inlet end of the tank. This effect is greatly reduced by good inlet design, including baffling, that will distribute the influent as uniformly as practicable over the cross section of the tank. There is also some interference with the streamline flow at the outlet, but this condition is less pronounced than the inlet turbulence and is reduced only by using overflow weirs or baffles. The density currents are caused by differences in the temperature and the density. Incoming water (or sewage) will have more suspended matter than the partially clarified contents of the tank. Therefore, there will be a tendency for the influent to form a relatively rapid current along the bottom of the tank, which may even extend to the outlet. This condition is known as "short circuiting" and occurs even though there is a uniform collection at the outlet end.

Flocculation of the suspended solids has been mentioned; its effects, however, are difficult to predict.

In general, the engineer depends upon experience as well as the code requirements of the various local health departments for the best detention and overflow rates. Many jurisdiction inlet and the outlet details vary with the ideas of the manufacturer. Length, width, depth, and inlet and outlet details enter into the design of a grease interceptor. Of these items, depth has already been discussed as having some effect on the tank's efficiency, the smaller depth giving a shorter path for the rising particles, a smaller overflow rate with a given detention period and, therefore, a greater efficiency. The tank's inlets and outlets require careful consideration by the designer. The ideal inlet reduces the inlet velocity in order to prevent the pronounced currents toward the outlet, distributes the water as uniformly as practical over the cross section of the tank, and mixes it with the water already in the tank to prevent the entering water from short circuiting toward the outlet.

EQUIPMENT

The removal of grease from a system may be accomplished with the use of manufactured grease interceptors currently available. Alternatively, a custom-made, poured-in-place or precast concrete grease interceptor may be used. Presently grease interceptors are available in various styles, categorized as manual, semiautomatic, and automatic units—see Figure 8-3(A–D)—and are designed and tested in conformance with nationally recognized standards.

Manually Operated Units

Existing conventional, manually operated manufactured grease interceptors are extremely popular and generally available up to 50 gallons per minute (gpm) (3.2 L/s) rated flow capacity for most applications. See Figure 8-3(A). For flow rates above 50 gpm (3.2 L/s), large capacity manufactured units are commonly used. The internal designs of these devices are similar. The

inlet baffles, usually available in various styles and arrangements, act to reduce the size of the entrance zone. Quiescent flow beyond this entrance point ensures at least a 90% efficiency of grease removal through the flotation process. Care should be taken to avoid long runs of pipe between source and interceptor to avoid grease accumulation prior to the interceptor.

Grease removal in the manually operated grease interceptors is completed by opening the access cover and pulling out a removable perforated bucket or manually skimming the accumulated grease from the water's surface.

Semiautomatic Units

A typical semiautomatic, manufactured grease interceptor is shown in Figure 8-3(B). This unit operates in the conventional, gravity separation manner with grease accumulation on the surface of the water in the interceptor. However, instead of an operator opening the cover for grease removal, the accumulated grease is removed by a process that may be termed "forced flotation." In this process the draw-off procedure for removing the grease from the interceptor is a simple operation.

Hot water from the plumbing fixture is discharged through the grease interceptor for a brief period of time to warm the unit and liquefy the congealed grease. The draw-off valve is closed to block the outlet.

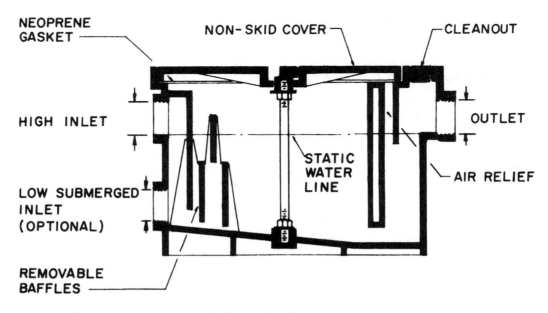

Figure 8-3(A) Typical Manually Operated Grease Interceptor

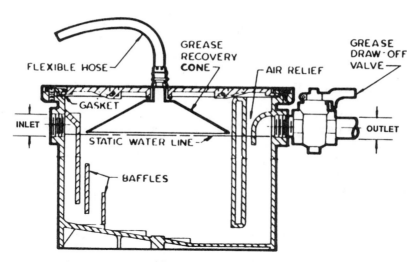

Figure 8-3(B) Typical Semiautomatic Grease Interceptor

A moderate flow of hot water is discharged into the grease interceptor to raise the water level and force the grease into the draw-off or recovery cone or pyramid and thence out through the attached draw-off hose to a grease disposal container. When the grease is completely discharged and clear water is observed exiting the hose, the draw-off valve is opened. The grease interceptor is now clean and ready for normal operation.

With this type of semiautomatic grease interceptor, no priming is required before the unit is placed in service. It must be noted, however, that all gravity separators (interceptors) must be filled with water to the static water line at all times to function.

Grease should be removed at least once a week. The most desirable time for grease removal from an interceptor is immediately after the unit has been put to its heaviest use.

Another variation of the semiautomatic grease interceptor is illustrated in Figure 8-3(C). In this arrangement, a skimming tray that is provided with the unit retains the accumulated grease. Cleaning becomes a matter of simply discharging the hot water through the device. The resultant heat liquefies the grease, which is then ejected through the nozzle at the push of the handle. The ejected grease may be collected in a bucket (or other container) for easy disposal. Any water that may enter the tray is directed back

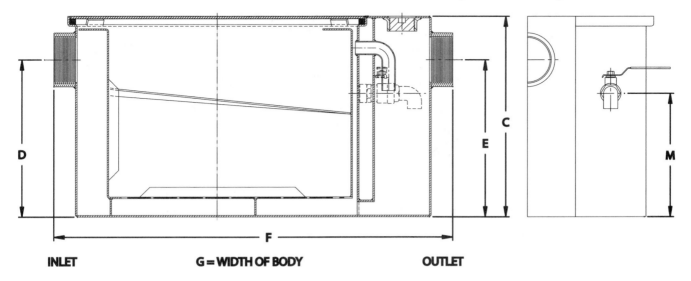

Figure 8-3(C) Construction Details, Cast-Iron Semiautomatic Grease Interceptor

Source: Courtesy of Zurn Plumbing Products.

into the intercepting chamber by means of a water discharge port incorporated into the design of the skimming tray.

Automatic Power-Operated Units

Another variation of grease interceptors currently on the market, described by manufacturers as automatic, are those that incorporate in their design electrically powered skimming devices. See Figure 8-3(D). In such units the grease is separated by gravity flotation in the conventional manner. Then the grease is skimmed from the surface of the water in the interceptor by a powered skimming device activated by a timer on a time or event-controlled basis.

The skimmed grease is essentially scraped or wiped from the skimmer surface and directed into a trough from which it drains via a conduit from the interceptor into a disposal container. Most automatic units are fitted with an electric immersion heater necessary to elevate the temperature in the interceptor to maintain the contained grease in a liquid state for skimming purposes. Such grease interceptors are generally referred to as automatic grease/oil recovery devices (GRDs).

It is recommended that when GRDs are considered for installation that the manufacturer be consulted regarding electrical, service, and maintenance requirements. Furthermore, owing to these requirements, it is essential that those responsible for operating automatic power-operated units be thoroughly trained in such operation.

Automatic Computer-Controlled Units

Interceptors falling into this recently introduced category are basically gravity separators with controlled grease recovery, sized and rated according to established procedures. According to their manufacturers, these interceptors employ computer-controlled sensors, which sense the presence of grease and automatically initiate the grease draw-off cycle at a predetermined percentage level of the interceptor's rated capacity. Grease is then drawn from the top of the grease layer in the interceptor. The draw-off cycle continues until the presence of water is sensor detected, stopping the cycle to ensure that only water-free grease is recovered. If required, an immersion heater is automatically activated at the onset of the draw-off cycle to liquefy grease in the interceptor.

Moreover, if either the unit's grease collection reservoir, where the recovered grease is stored pending removal, or the interceptor itself is near capacity, with potential overload sensed, warning measures and unit shutdown are automatically activated.

Manufacturers should be consulted regarding the particulars of construction, installation, operation, and maintenance of their units.

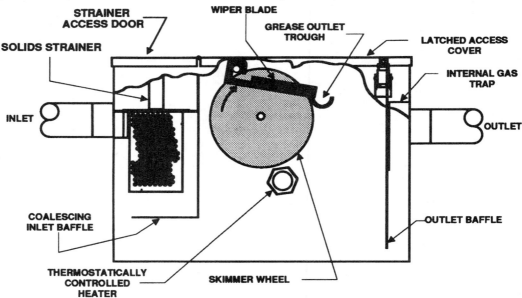

Figure 8-3(D) Construction Details, Automatic Grease Interceptor

Custom-Made Units

Custom-made grease interceptors are commonly made of 4-in. (101.6-mm) minimum thickness concrete walls and intermediate baffles to dampen the flow and retain the grease by flotation. Figure 8-4 shows a typical installation. Generally, these custom-made units are used outside buildings as in-ground installations rather than as inside systems adjacent to or within kitchen areas. These custom-made units do not generally include the specialized baffle, draw-off, or flow-control arrangements common to manufactured units. It is a common procedure to select a grease interceptor large enough to ensure a laminar flow and quiescent flotation at all times (due to the dampening volume of the liquid within the unit). If a custom-made unit is located in a traffic area, care must be taken to ensure that the access cover is capable of withstanding any possible traffic load. It is also important that the internal components be readily removable at all times to allow an easy cleanout procedure. This condition can be a problem if wood baffles are used, which may tend to swell in their guides and prevent removal for cleaning.

The following is a list of recommended installation provisions for grease interceptors located outside a building:

1. The unit should be installed as close to the source of grease as possible.

2. The influent should enter the unit at a location below the normal water level to keep the surface as still as possible.

3. The inlet and the outlet of the unit should be provided with cleanouts for unplugging both the sewers and the dip pipes.

4. The effluent should be drawn from near the bottom of the unit, via a dip pipe, to remove as much flotable grease and solids as possible.

5. A large manhole, or removable slab, should be provided for access to all chambers of the grease interceptor for complete cleaning of both the flotable and the settleable solids.

6. The top, or cover, should be gastight and capable of withstanding traffic weight.

7. A difference in elevation between the inlet and the outlet of 3 to 6 in. (76.2 to 152.4 mm) should be provided to ensure a flow

through the grease interceptor during surge conditions without the waste backing up in the inlet sewer. As the grease begins to accumulate, the top of the grease layer will begin to rise above the normal water level at a distance of approximately 1 in. (25.4 mm) for each 9 in. (228.6 mm) of grease thickness.

APPLICATIONS

Most local administrative authorities require, in their jurisdiction's codes, that spent water (from kitchen fixtures producing large amounts of grease) discharge into an approved grease interceptor before entering the municipality's sanitary drainage system. This code requirement normally includes multicompartment pot sinks, dishwashers, and grease-extracting hoods installed over frying or other grease-producing equipment; it can also include area floor drains.

If floor drains are connected to the grease interceptor, the engineer must give special consideration to other adjacent fixtures, such as dishwashers, which may be connected to a common line with the floor drain upstream of the grease interceptor. Unless flow control devices are used on high-volume fixtures upstream of the floor drain connection, flooding of the floor drain can occur. A common misapplication is the installation of a flow control device at the inlet to the grease interceptor, which may restrict the dishwasher discharge into the grease interceptor but floods the floor drain on the common branch. See Figure 8-5(A) and (B) for typical examples of single/multiple-fixture installations with and without flow control devices. Floor drains connected to a grease interceptor generally require a recessed (beneath-the-floor) grease interceptor design. See Figure 8-5(B) for a typical example.

An acceptable design concept is to locate the grease interceptors as close to the grease-producing fixture(s) as possible. Under-the-counter or above-slab interceptor installations are often possible adjacent to the grease-producing fixture(s). See Figure 8-5(C). This type of arrangement often avoids the individual venting of the fixture(s), with a common vent and trap downstream of the grease interceptor serving to vent the fixture(s) and the grease interceptor together. A p-trap, therefore, is not required on the fixture outlet.

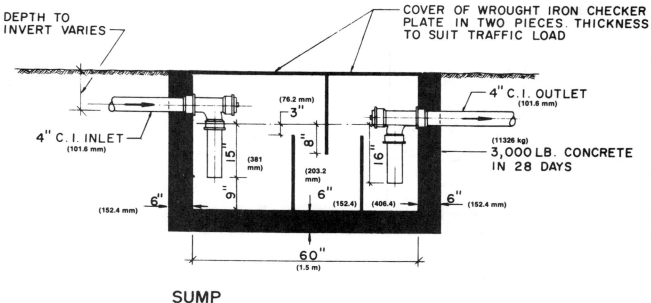

SUMP
SECTIONAL ELEVATION A-A

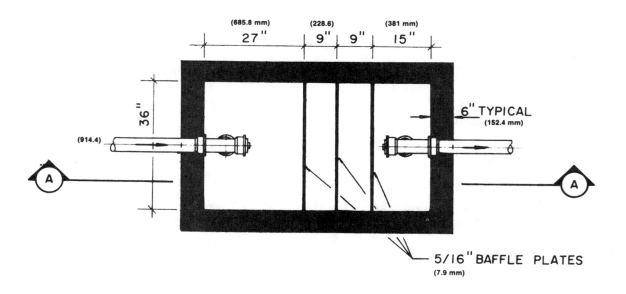

SUMP WITH COVER REMOVED
PLAN

NOTE: Dimensions shown are minimum. Large inside
        dimensions may be required depending on peak
        flow.   See design example.

Figure 8-4 Typical Custom-Made Grease Interceptor

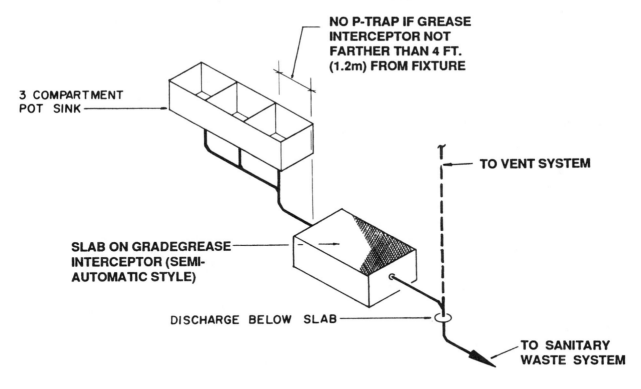

**Figure 8-5(A) Typical Schematic Grease Waste System Arrangement,
Single-Fixture Installation, No Flow Control**

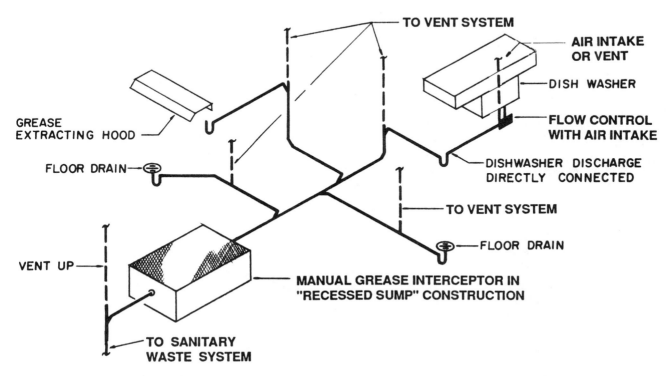

**Figure 8-5(B) Typical Schematic Grease Waste System Arrangement,
Multiple-Fixture Installation with Flow Control**

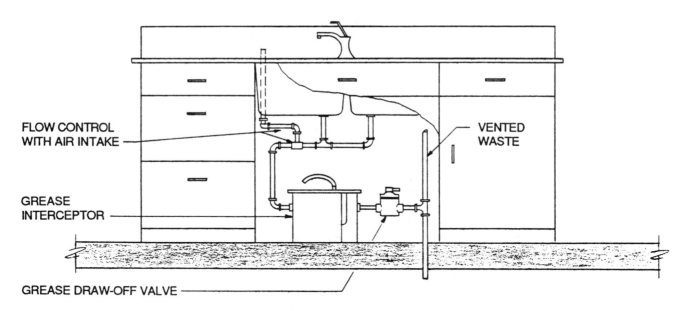

FLOW CONTROL
WITH AIR INTAKE

VENTED
WASTE

GREASE
INTERCEPTOR

GREASE DRAW-OFF VALVE

Figure 8-5(C) Typical Above-Slab Installation, Grease Draw–Off Valve

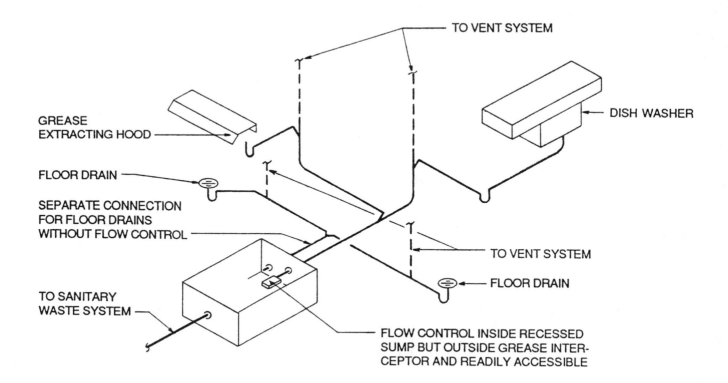

TO VENT SYSTEM

GREASE
EXTRACTING HOOD

DISH WASHER

FLOOR DRAIN

SEPARATE CONNECTION
FOR FLOOR DRAINS
WITHOUT FLOW CONTROL

TO VENT SYSTEM

FLOOR DRAIN

TO SANITARY
WASTE SYSTEM

FLOW CONTROL INSIDE RECESSED
SUMP BUT OUTSIDE GREASE INTER-
CEPTOR AND READILY ACCESSIBLE

**Figure 8-5(D) Typical Schematic Grease Waste System Arrangement,
Multiple-Fixture Installation, Alternate Hook-Up**

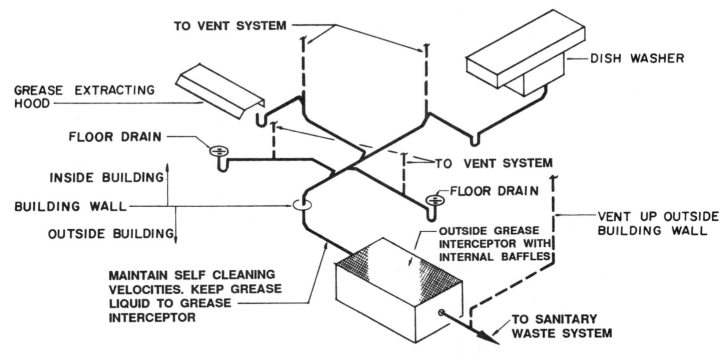

Figure 8-5(E) Typical Schematic Grease Waste System Arrangement, Multiple-Fixture Installation, Outside Grease Interceptor

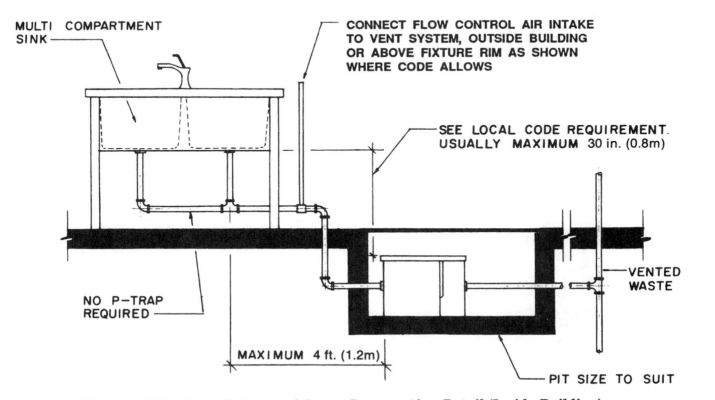

Figure 8-5(F) Typical Recessed Sump Construction Detail (Inside Building)

The location of a grease interceptor far from the fixtures it serves will allow the grease to cool and solidify in the waste lines upstream of the grease interceptor, causing clogging conditions. Some practical considerations are also important if a grease interceptor is to be located near the fixture(s) it serves. If the interceptor unit is an under-the-counter, above-the-slab device, the designer should make sure to allow enough space above the cover to allow the complete removal of the grease basket contents.

If the interceptor is in a below-slab installation, the designer should be sure that the coverplate is not located directly underneath where a kitchen worker may constantly stand. Because of the high temperatures of the liquid in the grease interceptor, such an arrangement can be very warm on the worker's feet. One way to avoid this problem is to recess the below-slab grease interceptor into a specially provided concrete recess in the floor slab. An aluminum checker plate access cover, or other similar material, can be installed at the finished slab level, thereby eliminating the warm cover problem.

Some local administrative authorities prohibit the discharge of food waste disposers through a grease interceptor because of the clogging effect of the ground-up particles. Some ordinances also require that grease interceptors not be installed where the surrounding temperatures under normal operating conditions are less than 40°F (4.4°C).

Flow Control

Flow control devices are generally best located at the outlet of the fixtures they serve. A few additional precautions, however, are also necessary for the proper application of flow control devices. The engineer should be sure that there is enough vertical space available if the flow control device is an angle pattern with a horizontal inlet and a vertical outlet. A common difficulty encountered is the lack of available height for an above-slab grease interceptor adjacent to the fixture served when the vertical height needed for the drain outlet elbow, the pipe slope on the waste arm from the fixture, the vertical outlet flow control fitting, and the height from the grease interceptor inlet to the floor are all allowed for.

The air intake (vent) for the flow control fitting may terminate under the sink back as high as possible to prevent overflow or terminate in a return bend at the same height and on the outside of the building. When the fixture is individually trapped and back vented, air intake may intersect the vent stack. All installation recommendations are subject to the approval of the code authority. The air intake allows air to be drawn into the flow control downstream of the orifice baffle, thereby promoting air entrained flow at the interceptor's rated capacity. The air entrained through the flow control also aids the flotation process by providing a lifting effect for the rising grease. Flow control fittings are not common for the floor drains or for the fixtures that would flood if their waste discharge is restricted (such as a grease-extracting hood during its flushing cycle). It is particularly important to install the grease interceptor close to the grease-discharging fixture when the flow control devices are used because of the lower flow in the waste line downstream of the flow control device. Such flow may not be enough to ensure self-cleaning velocities of 3 feet per second (fps) (0.9 m/s).

GUIDELINES FOR SIZING

The following recommended sizing procedure for grease interceptors may be used by the engineer as a general guideline for the selection of these units. The designer should consult the local administrative authority regarding variations in the allowable drain-down times acceptable under the approved codes. Calculation details and explanations of the decisionmaking processes have been included in full in the examples as an aid to the designer using these guidelines in specific situations.

Example 8-1 Single-fixture installation, manufactured unit, no flow control. Size the grease interceptor for a three-compartment pot (scullery) sink, each compartment 18 in. × 24 in. × 12 in. (457.2 mm · 609.6 mm · 304.8 mm).

Step 1 Determine the sink volume.

Cubic contents of one sink compartment = 18 × 24 × 12 = 5184 in.^{3}

Cubic contents of the 3 sink compartments = 3 × 5184 = 15,552 in.^{3}

Contents expressed in gal =

$\dfrac{15.552}{231}$ = 67.3 gal

$(457.2 \cdot 609.6 \cdot 304.8 = 84.95 \cdot 10^6$ mm^3 = $8.49 \cdot 10^4$ mL.

$3 \cdot 8.49 \cdot 10^4$ = $25.44 \cdot 10^4$ mL

Contents expressed in liters = 254.4 L)

Step 2 Determine the required size of grease interceptor. A sink (or fixture) is seldom filled to the brim, and dishes, pots, or pans displace approximately 25% of the water. Therefore, 75% of the actual fixture capacity should be used to establish the drainage load.

0.75 × 67.3 gal = 50.8 gal

(0.75 · 254.4 =190.8 L)

Step 3 Calculate the flow rate based on detention time. The most generally accepted drainage period is 1 minute. On any given project, however, conditions may exist whereby a longer drainage period could be considered. The flow rates are calculated using the following equation:

$$\frac{\text{Drainage load, in gal (L)}}{\text{Drainage load, in min (s)}} = \text{Flow rate, in gpm (L/s)}$$

Therefore, the flow rate for this example would be as follows: 50 gpm (3.15 L/s) for a 1-min total drainage or 25 gpm (1.58 L/s) for a 2-min total drainage (this condition provides a longer period, should one be desired).

Step 4 Select the grease interceptor.

A grease interceptor with a rated capacity of 50 gpm (3.15 L/s) for 1 min or 25 gpm (1.58 L/s) for 2 min should be selected. The local administrative authority having jurisdiction should be consulted. Choose an on-slab system, if possible, for ease of installation and accessibility if a semiautomatic device is used.

Example 8-2 Manufactured unit, multiple-fixture installation with flow control. Size the grease interceptor for the fixture sizes and the flow rates shown below:

1. A dishwasher with a 37-gal (140-L) power wash tank and a 7.5-gpm (0.5-L/s) final rinse consumption. The power wash tank is dumped after each meal serving, 3 times a day. The maximum final rinse consumption is 450 gph (0.5 L/s).

2. A grease-extracting hood 20 ft (6.1 m) long. Hood is a single section with a single drain washed automatically once per day on a 5-minute cycle.

3. The floor drains: 2 floor drains, each one 4 in. (101.6 mm) in size and rated at 50 gpm (3.15 L/s) flow capacity.

Step 1 Calculate the flow produced from each fixture.

1. *The dishwasher* The engineer should refer to the manufacturer's literature. Peak drain flow (initial rate) with full tank = 38 gpm (2.4 L/s). Use 40 gpm (2.5 L/s) as a conservative figure.

2. *The grease-extracting hood* The engineer should refer to the manufacturer's literature. The total water consumption is equal to the total water of the nozzles in the duct plus the total water consumption of the drain line preflush. Number of nozzles required in a 20-ft (6.1-m) long duct = 2L + 4 (from the manufacturer's literature), where L is equal to the length of the hood. Therefore, the total number of nozzles is equal to 2 (20) + 4 = 44.

From the manufacturer's literature, the flow rate per nozzle (at 50 psi [344.7 kPa] flowing pressure) is equal to 0.28 gpm (0.02 L/s) per nozzle.

Therefore, the total flow is equal to the number of nozzles multiplied by the flow rate per nozzle = 44 × 0.28 = 12.32 gpm (44 · 0.02 = 0.88 L/s).

Add flow from the preflushing line.

From the manufacturer's literature, the preflushing flow rate at 50 psi (344.7 kPa) flowing pressure = 1 gpm (0.06 L/s).

Therefore, the total water consumption and the maximum drain flow = 12.32 + 1.00 = 13.32 gpm (0.84 L/s).

As a conservative figure, the engineer should use 1 gpm per lineal foot (0.21 L/s per meter) of hood = 20 × 1 = 20 gpm (1.3 L/s).

3. The floor drains as listed, flow rate = 50 gpm (3.15 L/s) for each drain.

Step 2 Establish the expected maximum flow rate with diversity.

It is highly unlikely that the dishwasher, the grease-extracting hood, and the two floor drains will ever discharge simultaneously. It is possible, however, that the dishwasher and the grease-extracting hood may discharge simultaneously at the end of a day's operation. If this is the case, the peak flow would be 40 gpm (2.5 L/s) for the dishwasher plus 20 gpm (1.3 L/s) for the hood = 60 gpm (3.8 L/s).

Step 3 Decide whether separate units for each fixture or a single unit for multiple fixtures will be used.

The proximity of the grease interceptor to the grease-discharging fixture is very important for cost savings in venting and for ensuring that the discharge liquid temperature stays above 120°F (48.9°C) to maintain the grease in a liquid state into the interceptor. A single unit for multiple fixtures means a recessed grease interceptor because of the slope required between the fixture and the grease interceptor. On the other hand, a single unit is generally more economical as an overall installation. Use a single recessed unit to accommodate all fixtures whenever possible.

Step 4 Decide where the flow control devices are to be installed.

The dishwasher produces the largest waste flow from a single fixture. If a flow control device is included to limit the dishwasher discharge to 20 gpm (1.3 L/s), then the total flow will be 20 + 20 = 40 gpm (2.5 L/s). A flow control device cannot be used on the extractor hood because the hood might flood during the discharge if the flow control device limits the drain flow to less than the nozzles produce.

The flow control devices are not generally practical to use on the floor drains because of the difficulty of the location in the floor. It is best to install the dishwasher flow control device at the dishwasher above the floor. If the flow control device were located at the grease interceptor, there would be a chance of flooding the floor drain line because of the common connection to the grease interceptor.

An alternate solution would be to connect the floor drains separately to the grease interceptor and use a flow control device at the grease interceptor for the combined dishwasher and extractor hood line. A common discharge line will be used in this example.

Step 5 Size the grease interceptor.

The largest unrestricted flow rate will still be 50 gpm (3.2 L/s) from the floor drains rather than the 40 gpm (2.5 L/s) from the simultaneous discharge of 40 gpm (2.5 L/s) from the dishwasher and the extractor hood combined together. A 50 gpm (3.2 L/s) unit should be selected.

Step 6 Decide if the unit is to be manual or semiautomatic.

Step 7 Miscellaneous considerations.

In this example, it is very important that the cover does not become too hot to walk over and that the cast iron unit does not rust and corrode in the slab on the grade installation. A concrete recess should be provided to help avoid these problems.

Example 8-3 Outside custom-made unit, multiple-fixture installation, no flow control. Size the grease interceptor for the fixture sizes and the flow rates as in Example 8-2 and the particles of 0.01 in. (0.25 mm). Assume ρ_1 = 0.909.

From Example 8-2, the following data are obtained:

dishwasher flow = 40 gpm (2.5 L/s)

grease-extracting hood = 20 gpm (1.3 L/s)

floor drains = 50 gpm (3.2 L/s)

Step 1 Establish the expected maximum flow rate with diversity.

The diversity consideration will be the same as that shown in Example 8-2 except that no flow control is to be used in this example to ensure that all the grease-laden waste gets to the outside grease interceptor before solidifying. In this case, the peak flow rate with the fixtures discharging simultaneously will be 60 gpm (3.8 L/s).

Step 2 Calculate the required volume for the minimum detention period, P.

Assume the minimum detention period, P, to ensure the solidification of grease to be 5 minutes, which is also equal to the flow-through period. Then, the minimum volume is equal to 5 × 60 = 300 gal (1135.5 L).

Step 3 Select and check the tank size.

Assume the practical size for cleaning out the grease and accessibility to be 5 ft long, 2 ft wide and 5 ft liquid depth (1.5 m · 0.6 m · 1.5 m). The volume is equal to 50 × 7.48 = 374 gal (1415.6 L).

Step 4 Calculate the horizontal velocity.

$$V = \frac{L}{P} = \frac{5}{6.23} = 0.8 \text{ fpm (4.1 m/s)}$$

Step 5 Check the overflow rate.

$$\text{Overflow rate, } v = \frac{VH}{L} = 0.8 \times 5/5$$

$$= 0.8 \text{ fpm (4.1 m/s)}$$

This overflow rate provides 100% particle removal down to 0.1 in. (3.0 mm), which is not sufficient. However, we can improve the removal efficiency by lowering the overflow rate. This condition is accomplished by enlarging the plan area and reducing the depth because the depth has almost no dependence on the tank efficiency. Therefore, it is assumed a 5 ft long × 5 ft wide × 2 ft liquid depth (1.5 m · 1.5 m · 0.6 m).

The detention time and horizontal velocity remain the same but the overflow rate is now

$$0.8 \times 2/5 = 0.32 \text{ fpm (1.6 m/s)}$$

With an overflow rate of 0.32 fpm (1.6 m/s), a 100% removal efficiency of particles down to 0.01 in. (0.2 mm) is acceptable.

CODE REQUIREMENTS

The local administrative authority having jurisdiction will establish the need for a grease interceptor on a specific project and, therefore, should be consulted at the start of the design.

The following model plumbing codes should be viewed for provisions regarding grease interceptors:

Uniform Plumbing Code, promulgated by
    International Association of Plumbing
    and Mechanical Officials
    5001 E. Philadelphia St.
    Ontario, CA 91761

International Plumbing Code, promulgated
    by
    International Code Council
    5360 Workman Mill Rd.
    Whittier, CA 90601

National Standard Plumbing Code, promulgated by:
    National Association of Plumbing-
    Heating-Cooling Contractors
    180 S. Washington Street, Box 6808

Falls Church, VA 22046-1148

Table 8-1, Summary of Code Requirements, provides an itemized list incorporating the major provisions of the model plumbing codes reviewed and is included herein as an abbreviated design guide for the engineer when specifying sizing. It is important to review the applicable code in effect in the area for any variation from this generalized list.

OPERATION AND MAINTENANCE

Operational methods can create problems for the engineer even if all the design techniques for grease interceptors presented have been observed. Failing to scrape dinner plates and other food waste bearing utensils into the food waste disposer prior to loading them into dishwasher racks means that the liquid waste discharged from the dishwasher to the grease interceptor will also carry solid food particles into the grease interceptor unit. The grease interceptor is not a food waste disposer.

Another common problem is too long a period between grease removals. This period differs for each installation and is best left to the experience of the operating staff. It is possible, however, that if the flow rate of the unit is constantly exceeded (no flow control) with high-temperature water, such as a heavy discharge from a dishwasher, the grease in the unit may periodically be liquefied and washed into the drainage system downstream of the grease interceptor. In this case, the operator may never realize the unit needs cleaning because it never reaches its grease storage capacity. The only difficulty, of course, is that when the temperature of the grease-water mixture finally cools in the drainage system downstream of the grease interceptor, clogging will ultimately occur.

Adequate maintenance is critical to an efficient grease interceptor installation. One of the most common problems is the disposal of the accumulated grease. The grease removed must be disposed of in various ways depending on local requirements. Do not pour the grease down any other drain or in any sewer line or bury the grease in the ground. Dispose of grease through garbage pickup or some similar approved operation.

Table 8-1 Summary of Model Plumbing Code Requirements for Grease Interceptors

1. Grease interceptors are not required in individual dwelling units or residential dwellings.
2. Grease interceptors are limited to flow rates not less than 20 gpm (1.3 L/s) and not greater than 55 gpm (3.5 L/s).
3. Flow control devices are required at the drain outlet of each grease-producing fixture.
4. Flow control devices having adjustable (or removable) parts are prohibited.
5. Grease interceptors are required to have an approved rate of flow related to the total number and the capacity of the fixtures discharging into the unit as follows:

Total Number of Fixtures Connected	Maximum Capacity of Fixtures Connected, gal (L)	Required Rate of Flow, gpm (L/s)	Grease Retention Capacity, lb (kg)
1	50 (189.3)	20 (1.3)	40 (18.2)
2	65 (246.0)	25 (1.6)	50 (22.7)
3	90 (340.7)	35 (2.2)	70 (31.8)
4	125 (473.1)	50 (3.2)	100 (45.4)

6. Grease interceptors installed such that the inlet is more than 4 ft (1.2 m) in elevation below the outlet of the grease-producing fixture must have an approved rate of flow at least 50% greater than given above.
7. No more than 4 fixtures are to be connected to one grease interceptor.
8. Water-cooled grease interceptors are prohibited.
9. Food waste disposers are not to be connected through a grease interceptor.
10. Grease interceptors must be designed so that they will not become air-bound if tight covers are used.
11. An approved custom-made grease trap of concrete (or other approved material) must not require a flow control device.
12. The grease collected from a grease interceptor must not be introduced into any drainage piping or public or private sewer.
13. No grease interceptor may have any enzyme or other opening for similar chemicals.
14. Each grease interceptor and separator must be installed so that it is readily accessible so the cover can be removed for servicing and maintenance. Need to use ladders or move bulky objects to service the grease interceptors may constitute a violation of the accessibility requirement.
15. Grease interceptors and separators must be maintained in efficient operating condition by the periodic removal of accumulated grease.

ECONOMICS

Broadly speaking, a single grease interceptor is more economical than a multiple interceptor installation for any given grease waste system. The length and cost of the grease waste piping to transport waste to a single large interceptor must be compared to the cost of short lengths and more than one unit.

REFERENCE

1. Camp, Thomas R. 1946. Sedimentation and the design of settling tanks. In *Transactions of the American Society of Civil Engineers*, Vol. III, p. 895.

BIBLIOGRAPHY

1. American Society of Mechanical Engineers (ASME). 2000. *Grease interceptors*, ASME A112.14.3.

2. ———. 2001. *Grease recovery devices*, ASME A112.14.4.

3. Davis, Calvin V. 1952. *Handbook of applied hydraulics*. New York: McGraw-Hill.

4. Hardenberg, W. A., and E. R. Rodie. 1961. *Water supply and waste disposal*. Scranton, PA: International Textbook Company.

5. Hogan, Jerald R. 1975. Grease trap discussion. *Plumbing Engineer* May/June.

6. Plumbing and Drainage Institute. *Guide to grease interceptors*.

7. Plumbing and Drainage Institute. *Testing and rating procedure for grease interceptors*, Standard PDI-G101. South Easton, MA.

8. Steel, Ernest W. 1953. *Water supply and sewage*, 3d ed. New York: McGraw-Hill.

Cross-Connection Control

INTRODUCTION

Public health officials have long been concerned about cross-connections in plumbing systems and public drinking water distribution systems. Such cross-connections, which make possible the contamination of potable water, are ever-present dangers. One example of cross-connection occurred in Chicago in 1933, when contamination of a drinking water system happened because of old, defective fixtures and an improperly designed plumbing system. As a result, 1409 individuals contracted amoebic dysentery, which caused 98 deaths.

Cross-connections are the links through which contaminating matter can enter the potable water supply. In other words, they are the common point between a potable and a nonpotable system. The contaminant enters the potable water system when the pressure of the polluted source exceeds the pressure of the potable source. This action is called "back-pressure" or "backflow." Essentially, it is the reversal of the hydraulic gradient and can be produced by a variety of circumstances. Cross-connections may appear in many subtle forms and in unexpected places. The reversal of pressure in the water supply may also be freakish and unpredictable. The probability of contaminating a potable water supply system through a cross-connection in a single plumbing system may seem remote. However, when the multitude of similar systems is considered, the probability is greatly increased.

It can be argued that cross-connections exist because of three basic problems. First, plumbing is frequently installed by persons who are unaware of the possible dangers of cross-connections. Second, such connections are made as a simple matter of convenience without regard to the hazardous situation that might be created. And third, when the installer or designer does consider backflow prevention it is often done by providing inadequate protection, such as a single valve or other mechanical device.

To effectively combat the dangers posed by cross-connections, education in their recognition and prevention is needed. First, installers must know that hydraulic and pollution factors may combine to produce a sanitary hazard if a cross-connection is present. Second, they must understand that there are reliable and simple backflow prevention devices and methods that may be substituted for the convenient—but dangerous—direct connection. And third, it has to be clear that the hazards that may arise from direct connections greatly outweigh the convenience they afford.

This chapter does not describe all the possible cross-connections in piping systems. Rather, its primary purpose is to define, describe, and illustrate typical cross-connections and to suggest approved methods and appropriate devices by which they may be eliminated without interfering with the intended functions of the water supply distribution systems. The plumbing engineer should consult with the authority having jurisdiction to determine the acceptable methods and backflow prevention devices that are locally approved under the applicable health ordinances.

HEALTH AND SAFETY

The American Medical Association and state and local health department officials are cognizant of the risks that cross-connections pose to public health. Because of antiquated plumbing systems, defective equipment, and recurrent nonconformance to the plumbing codes, the chances for contaminating the public water supply through cross-connections are good. Enteric (gastrointestinal) infections caused by drinking water affected by cross-connection and contamination can occur anywhere, as noted in the EPA case studies given later in this chapter.

Some of the chemicals most commonly introduced inadvertently into the drinking water system are as follows:

- Paraquat, an agricultural herbicide
- Chlordane, an insecticide
- Heptachlor, an insecticide
- Hexavalent chromium, an anticorrosive agent and algicide
- Glycol, an antifreeze solution
- Sodium dichromate, a toxic rust inhibitor/ defoamant.

Since the consumer makes the assumption that the water that comes from the tap is pure and safe to drink, there is a joint responsibility on the part of the water supplier/purveyor and the building owner to maintain the safety of the product to the last free-flowing tap in the distribution system. When the water leaves the water treatment plant, it is safe to drink. It travels to the point of use in a protected environment or pipeline that maintains the safety and purity of the product—until the pipeline is broken or tapped into. Once the pipeline is tapped to provide service to the various consumers served by the system, the potential is created for the water in the pipeline to become contaminated or polluted. Hence, the water supplier must adopt a program that will protect the safety of the water distribution system from hazards that originate on the premises of his customers. Such a program is known as a "containment program" and involves the installation of a backflow preventer at the water meter or where the water enters the building.

It's the engineer's responsibility to advise his or her clients of any potential problems and specify the proper backflow prevention devices.

It's the building owner's responsibility to prevent such occurrences by properly maintaining building equipment and backflow prevention devices on a continual basis. To avoid cross-connections between the potable water system and the various mechanical and plumbing systems that require domestic water for proper operation and makeup purposes, the design engineers and the building owners must refer to the municipal codes and to the authorities having jurisdiction regarding regulations on backflow prevention and cross-connection control. A typical statement in the plumbing codes is "Direct connections between potable water systems and other systems or equipment containing water or unknown substances shall be prohibited, except when an approved backflow prevention device is installed, tested, and maintained to ensure proper operation on a continuing basis."

This should become an automatic concern for all engineers, building owners, maintenance engineers, and the like so that future cross-connections between potable and nonpotable water sources can be prevented, thus minimizing health-related infections and emergencies, costly repairs, and litigation.

THEORY OF BACK-PRESSURE AND BACK-SIPHONAGE

A cross-connection is the link, or channel, connecting a source of pollution with a potable water supply. The polluting substance, in most cases a liquid, tends to enter the potable water supply if the net force acting upon the liquid acts in the direction of the potable water supply. Two factors are, therefore, essential for backflow: First, there must be a link between the two systems, and, second, the resultant force must be toward the potable water supply.

To understand the principles of back-pressure and back-siphonage one must understand the terms frequently used in their discussion. Force, unless completely resisted, will produce motion. Weight is a type of force resulting from the earth's gravitational attraction. Pressure, P, is a force per unit area, such as pounds per square inch (psi). Atmospheric pressure is the pressure exerted by the weight of the atmosphere above the earth.

Pressure may be referred to using an absolute scale, as in pounds per square inch absolute (psia), or a gage scale, as in pounds per square inch gage (psig). Absolute pressure and gage pressure are related. Absolute pressure is equal to the gage pressure plus the atmospheric pressure. At sea level, the atmospheric pressure is 14.7 psia. Thus,

Equation 9-1

$$P_{absolute} = P_{gage} + 14.7 \text{ psi, or}$$

Equation 9-1a

$$P_{gage} = P_{absolute} - 14.7 \text{ psi}$$

In essence, then, absolute pressure is the total pressure. Gage pressure is simply the pressure read on a gage. If there were no pressure on the gage other than atmospheric, the gage would read zero. Then the absolute pressure would be equal to 14.7 psi, which is the atmospheric pressure.

The term "vacuum" indicates that the absolute pressure is less than the atmospheric pressure and that the gage pressure is negative. A complete or total vacuum would mean a pressure of 0 psia or –14.7 psig. Since it is impossible to produce a total vacuum, the term "vacuum" as used here means all degrees of partial vacuum. In a partial vacuum, the pressure ranges from slightly less than 14.7 psia (0 psig) to slightly greater than 0 psia (–14.7 psig).

Back-siphonage results in fluid flow in an undesirable or reverse direction. It is caused by atmospheric pressure exerted on a pollutant liquid, forcing it toward a potable water supply system that is under a vacuum. Backflow, although literally meaning any type of reversed flow, refers to the flow produced by the differential pressure existing between two systems, both of which are at pressures greater than atmospheric.

Water Pressure

For an understanding of the nature of pressure and its relationship to water depth, consider the pressure exerted on the base of a cubic foot of water at sea level. The average weight of a cubic foot of water is 62.4 lb (per ft³). The base may be subdivided into 144 in.², with each subdivision being subjected to a pressure of 0.433 psig. (See Figure 9-1.)

Suppose another cubic foot of water were placed directly on top of the first. The pressure on the top surface of the first cube, which was

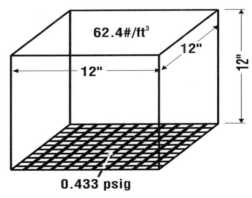

Figure 9-1 Pressure Exerted by 1 Ft of Water at Sea Level

originally atmospheric, or 0 psig, would now be 0.433 psig as a result of the superimposed cubic foot of water. The pressure of the base of the first cube would also be increased by the same amount, 0.866 psig, or two times the original pressure. (See Figure 9-2.)

If this process were repeated with a third cubic foot of water, the pressures at the base of the bottom, middle, and top cube would be 1.299 psig, 0.866 psig, and 0.433 psig, respectively. It is evident that pressure varies with depth below a free water surface. In general, each foot of elevation change within a liquid changes the pressure by an amount equal to the weight per unit area of 1 ft of the liquid. The rate of increase for water is 0.433 psi per ft of depth.

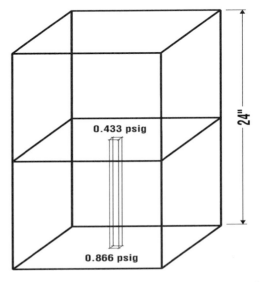

Figure 9-2 Pressure Exerted by 2 Ft of Water at Sea Level

Frequently, water pressure is referred to using the terms "pressure head" or just "head" and is expressed in units of feet of water. One foot of head would be equivalent to the pressure produced at the base of a column of water 1 ft in depth. One ft of head or 1 ft of water is equal to 0.433 psig. One hundred ft of head are equal to 43.3 psig.

Siphon Theory

Figure 9-3 depicts the atmospheric pressure on a water surface at sea level. An open tube is inserted vertically into the water; atmospheric pressure, which is 14.7 psia, acts equally on the surface of the water within the tube and on the outside of the tube.

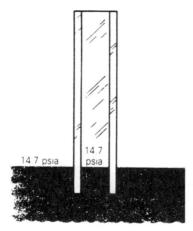

Figure 9-3 Pressure on the Free Surface of a Liquid at Sea Level

If, as shown in Figure 9-4, the tube is slightly capped and a vacuum pump is used to evacuate all the air from the sealed tube, a vacuum with a pressure of 0 psia is created within the tube. Because the pressure at any point in a static fluid is dependent upon the height of that point above a reference line, such as sea level, it follows that the pressure within the tube at sea level must still be 14.7 psia. This is equivalent to the pressure at the base of a column of water 33.9 ft high, and, with the column open at the base, water would rise to fill the column to a depth of 33.9 ft. In other words, the weight of the atmosphere at sea level exactly balances the weight of a column of water 33.9 ft in height. The absolute pressure within the column of water in Figure 9-4 at a height of 11.5 ft is equal to 9.7 psia. This is a partial vacuum with an equivalent gage pressure of –5.0 psig.

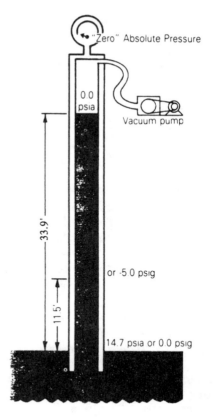

Figure 9-4 Effect of Evacuating Air from a Column

As a practical example, assume the water pressure at a closed faucet at the top of a 100-ft building to be 20 psig; the pressure on the ground floor would then be 63.3 psig. If the pressure at the ground were to drop suddenly due to a heavy fire demand in the area of 33.3 psig, the pressure at the top of the building would be reduced to –10 psig. If the building water system were airtight, the water would remain at the level of the faucet because of the partial vacuum created by the drop in pressure. If the faucet were opened, however, the vacuum would be broken and the water level would drop to a height of 77 ft above the ground. Thus, the atmosphere was supporting a column of water 23 ft high.

Figure 9-5 is a diagram of an inverted U-tube that has been filled with water and placed in two open containers at sea level. If the open containers are placed so that the liquid levels in each container are at the same height, a static state will exist and the pressure at any specified level in either leg of the U-tube will be the same. The equilibrium condition is altered by raising one of the containers so that the liquid level in

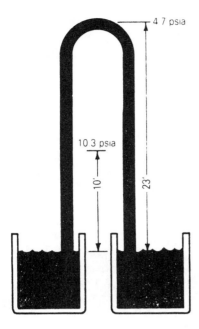

Figure 9-5 Pressure Relationships in a Continuous Fluid System at the Same Elevation

one container is 5 ft above the level of the other. Since both containers are open to the atmosphere, the pressure on the liquid surfaces in each container will remain at 14.7 psia.

If it is assumed that a static state exists, momentarily, within the system shown in Figure 9-6, the pressure in the left tube at any height above the free surface in the left container can be calculated. The pressure at the corresponding level in the right tube above the free

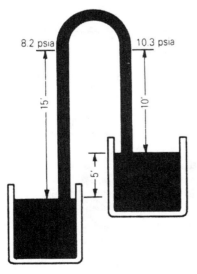

Figure 9-6 Pressure Relationships in a Continuous Fluid System at Different Elevations

surface in the right container may also be calculated. As shown in Figure 9-6, the pressure at all levels in the left tube would be less than that at corresponding levels in the right tube. In this case, a static condition cannot exist because fluid will flow from the higher pressure to the lower pressure; the flow would be from the right tank to the left tank. This arrangement will be recognized as a siphon. The crest of a siphon cannot be higher than 33.9 ft above the upper liquid level, since atmosphere cannot support a column of water greater in height than 33.9 ft.

Figure 9-7 illustrates how this siphon principle can be hazardous in a plumbing system. If the supply valve is closed, the pressure in the line supplying the faucet is less than the pressure in the supply line to the bathtub. Flow will occur, therefore, through siphonage, from the bathtub to the open faucet. The siphon actions cited have been produced by reduced pressures resulting from a difference in the water levels at two separated points within a continuous fluid system.

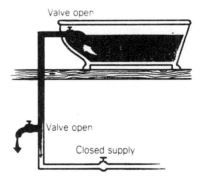

Figure 9-7 Back-Siphonage in a Plumbing System

Reduced pressure may also be created within a fluid system as a result of fluid motion. One of the basic principles of fluid mechanics is the principle of conservation of energy. Based upon this principle, it may be shown that as a fluid accelerates, as shown in Figure 9-8, the pressure is reduced. As water flows through a constriction such as a converging section of pipe, the velocity of the water increases; as a result, the pressure is reduced. Under such conditions, negative pressures may be developed in a pipe. The simple aspirator is based on this principle. If this point of reduced pressure is linked to a source of pollution, back-siphonage of the pollutant can occur.

Figure 9-8 Negative Pressure Created by Constricted Flow

One of the common occurrences of dynamically reduced pipe pressures is found on the suction side of a pump. In many cases similar to the one illustrated in Figure 9-9, the line supplying the booster pump is undersized or does not have sufficient pressure to deliver water at the rate at which the pump normally operates. The rate of flow in the pipe may be increased by a further reduction in pressure at the pump intake. This often results in the creation of negative pressure at the pump intake. This negative pressure may become low enough in some cases to cause vaporization of the water in the line. Actually, in the example in Figure 9-9, flow from the source of pollution would occur when pressure on the suction side of the pump was less than the pressure of the pollution source; but that is backflow, which is discussed under the under Back-Pressure later in this chapter.

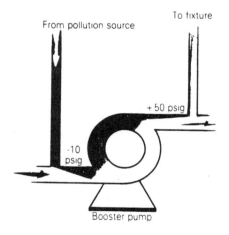

Figure 9-9 Dynamically Reduced Pipe Pressures

The preceding discussion described some of the means by which negative pressures may be created and which frequently occur to produce back-siphonage. In addition to the negative pressure or reversed force necessary to cause back-siphonage and backflow, there must also be the cross-connection or connecting link between the potable water supply and the source of pollution. Two basic types of connection may be created in piping systems: the solid pipe with valved connection and the submerged inlet.

Figures 9-10 and 9-11 illustrate solid connections. This type of connection is often installed where it is necessary to supply an auxiliary piping system from the potable source. It is a direct connection of one pipe to another pipe or receptacle. Solid pipe connections are often made to continuous or intermittent waste lines where it is assumed that the flow will be in one

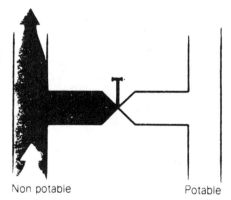

Figure 9-10 Valved Connection Between Potable Water and Nonpotable Fluid

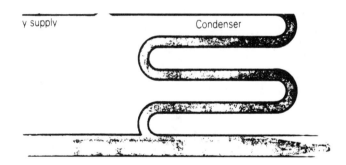

Figure 9-11 Valved Connection Between Potable Water and Sanitary Sewer

direction only. An example of this would be used cooling water from a water jacket or condenser, as shown in Figure 9-11. This type of connection is usually detectable, but creating a concern on the part of the installer about the possibility of reverse flow is often more difficult. Upon questioning, however, many installers admit that a solid connection was made because the sewer is occasionally subjected to back-pressure.

Submerged inlets are found on many common plumbing fixtures and are sometimes necessary features if the fixtures are to function properly. Examples of this type of design are si-phon-jet urinals, water closets, flushing rim slop sinks, and dental cuspidors. Old-fashioned bath-tubs and lavatories had supply inlets below the flood level rims, but modern sanitary design minimizes or eliminates this hazard in new fix-tures. Chemical and industrial process vats sometimes have submerged inlets where the wa-ter pressure is used as an aid in diffusion, dispersion, and agitation of the vat contents. Though the supply pipe may come from the floor above the vat, back-siphonage can occur, as it has been shown that the siphon action can raise a liquid, such as water, almost 34 ft. Some sub-merged inlets that are difficult to control are those that are not apparent until a significant change in the water level occurs or where a sup-ply may be conveniently extended below the liquid surface by means of a hose or auxiliary piping. A submerged inlet may be created in numerous ways, and its detection in some of these subtle forms may be difficult.

Back-Pressure

Any interconnected fluid system in which the pressure of one exceeds the pressure of the other may have flow from one to the other as a result of the pressure differential. The flow occurs from the zone of higher pressure to the zone of lower pressure. This type of backflow is of concern in buildings where two or more piping systems are maintained. The potable water supply is usu-ally under pressure directly from the city water main. Occasionally, a booster pump is used. The auxiliary system is often pressurized by a cen-trifugal pump, although back-pressure may be caused by gas or steam pressure from a boiler. A reversal in differential pressure may occur when pressure in the potable water system drops, for some reason, to a pressure lower than that in the system to which the potable water is connected.

The most positive method of avoiding this type of backflow is the total or complete separa-tion of the two systems. Other methods used involve the installation of mechanical devices. All methods require routine inspection and main-tenance. Dual piping systems are often installed for extra protection in the event of an emergency or possible mechanical failure of one of the sys-tems. Fire protection systems are an example. Another example is the use of dual water con-nections to boilers. These installations are

sometimes interconnected, thus creating a pos-sible health hazard.

PREVENTION OF BACK-PRESSURE AND BACK-SIPHONAGE

A wide choice of devices exists that can be used to prevent back-siphonage and back-pressure from adding contaminated fluids or gases to a potable water supply system. Generally, selec-tion of the proper device to use is based on the degree of hazard posed by the cross-connection. Additional considerations are piping size, loca-tion, and the potential need to periodically test the devices to ensure proper operation.

There are six basic types of device used to prevent cross-connections: air gaps, barometric loops, vacuum breakers (both atmospheric and pressure type), dual check with atmosphere vent, double-check valve assemblies, and reduced-pressure-principle devices. In general, the manufacturers of all these devices, with the ex-ception of the barometric loop, produce them to one or more of three basic standards, thus assur-ing the public that dependable devices are being utilized and marketed. The major standards in the industry are: American Society of Sanitary Engineers (ASSE), American Water Works Asso-ciation (AWWA), Canadian Standards Association (CSA), and the University of Southern Califor-nia Foundation for CrossConnection control and Hydraulic Research. (USC FCCC & HR) (see the Glossary).

Air Gaps

Air gaps are nonmechanical backflow preventers that are very effective devices to be used where either back-siphonage or back-pressure condi-tions may exist. Their use is as old as piping and plumbing itself, but only relatively recently have standards been issued that standardize their design. In general, the air gap must be twice the supply pipe diameter but never less than 1 in.

Although an extremely effective backflow preventer when used to prevent back-siphonage and back-pressure conditions, an air gap does interrupt the piping flow with corresponding loss of pressure for subsequent use (see Figure 9-12). Consequently, air gaps are primarily used at end-of-the-line service where reservoirs or stor-age tanks are desired. Other considerations for

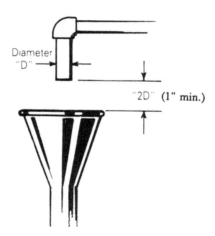

Figure 9-12 Air Gap

the plumbing engineer contemplating the use of an air gap are

1. In a continuous piping system, each air gap requires the added expense of reservoirs and secondary pumping systems.

2. The air gap may be easily defeated in the event that the 2 × diameter (2D) requirement is purposely or inadvertently compromised. Excessive splash may be encountered in the event that higher than anticipated pressures or flows occur. The splash may be cosmetic or a true potential hazard—the simple solution being to reduce the 2D dimension by thrusting the supply pipe into the receiving funnel. By so doing, however, the air gap is defeated.

3. At an air gap, the water is exposed to the surrounding air with its inherent bacteria, dust particles, and other airborne pollutants or contaminants. In addition, the aspiration effect of the flowing water can drag down surrounding pollutants into the reservoir or holding tank.

4. Free chlorine can come out of treated water as a result of the air gap and the resulting splash and churning effect as the water enters the holding tanks. This reduces the ability of the water to withstand bacteria contamination during long-term storage.

5 . For the above reasons, air gaps must be inspected as frequently as mechanical backflow preventers are. They are not exempt from an in-depth cross-connection control program requiring periodic inspection of all backflow devices.

Air gap protection may be fabricated from commercially available plumbing components or purchased as separate units and integrated into plumbing and piping systems. An example of the use of an air gap is shown in Figure 9-13.

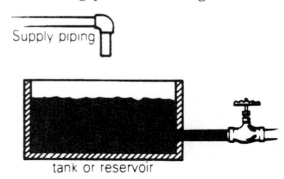

Figure 9-13 Air Gap in a Piping System

Barometric Loop

The barometric loop consists of a continuous section of supply piping that abruptly rises to a height of approximately 35 ft and then returns back down to the original level. It is a loop in the piping system that effectively protects against back-siphonage. It is not used to protect against back-pressure backflow.

Its operation, in the protection against back-siphonage, is based upon the principle that a water column, at sea level pressure, will not rise above 33.9 ft (see the discussion in Backflow and Back-Siphonage above and Figure 9-14).

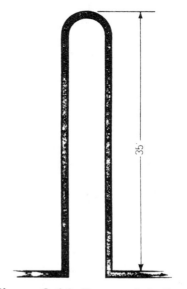

Figure 9-14 Barometric Loop

In general, barometric loops are locally fabricated and are 35 ft high.

Atmospheric Vacuum Breakers

These devices are among the simplest and least expensive mechanical types of backflow preventer. When installed properly, they can provide excellent protection against back-siphonage. They must not be utilized to protect against back-pressure conditions. Construction usually consists of a plastic or polymer float that is free to travel on a shaft and seal in the uppermost position against atmosphere with an elastomeric disc. Water flow lifts the float, which then causes the disc to seal. Water pressure keeps the float in the upward sealed position. Termination of the water supply causes the disc to drop down,

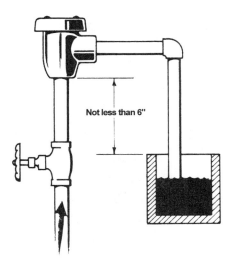

Figure 9-16 Atmospheric Vacuum Breaker— Typical Installation

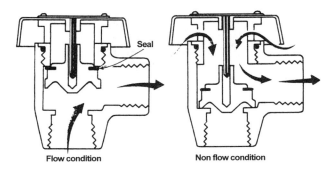

Figure 9-15 Atmospheric Vacuum Breakers

venting the unit to the atmosphere and thereby opening the downstream piping to atmospheric pressure, thus preventing back-siphonage. Figure 9-15 shows a typical atmospheric breaker.

In general, these devices are available in ½-through 3-in. size. They must be installed vertically, must not have shut-offs downstream, must be installed at least 6 in. higher than the highest outlet, and cannot be tested once they are installed in the plumbing system.

Figure 9-16 shows the generally accepted installation requirements. Note that there is no shut-off value downstream of the device that would keep the atmospheric vacuum breaker under constant pressure. Figure 9-17 shows a typical installation of an atmospheric vacuum breaker in a plumbing supply system.

Hose Bibb Vacuum Breakers

These small devices are a specialized application of the atmospheric vacuum breaker. They are generally attached to sill cocks which, in turn, are connected to hose-supplied outlets such as garden hoses, slop sink hoses, and spray outlets. They consist of a spring-loaded check valve that seals against an atmospheric outlet when water supply pressure is turned on. Typical construction is shown in Figure 9-18.

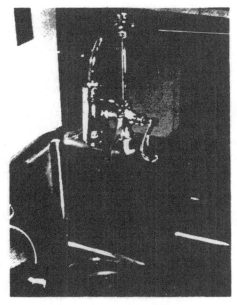

Figure 9-17 Atmospheric Vacuum Breaker in a Plumbing Supply System

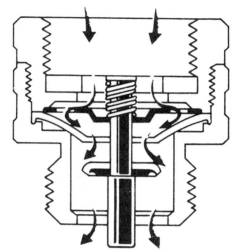

Figure 9-18 Hose Bibb Vacuum Breaker

When the water supply is turned off, the de-

**Figure 9-19 Hose Bibb Vacuum Breaker—
Typical Installation**

vice vents to atmosphere, thus protecting against back-siphonage conditions. These devices should not be used as back-pressure devices. Manual drain options are available, together with tamper-proof versions. A typical installation is shown in Figure 9-19.

Pressure Vacuum Breakers

This device is an outgrowth of the atmospheric vacuum breaker and evolved in response to a need to have an atmospheric vacuum breaker that could be utilized under constant pressure and tested in-line. A spring on top of the disc and float assembly, two added shut-off valves,

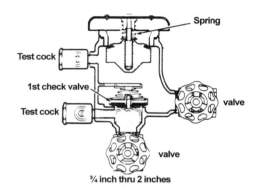

Figure 9-20 Pressure Vacuum Breaker

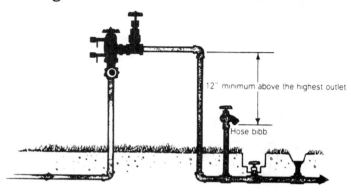

**Figure 9-21 Pressure Vacuum Breaker—
Typical Agricultural and Industrial
Applications**

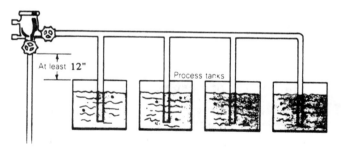

test cocks, and an additional first check provided the answer.

Again, these devices may be used under constant pressure but do not protect against back-pressure conditions. As a result, installation must be at least 12 in. higher than the existing outlet. See Figures 9-20 and 9-21.

Dual Check with Intermediate Atmospheric Vent

The need to provide a compact device in ½- and ¾-in. pipe size that protects against moderate hazards, is capable of being used under con-

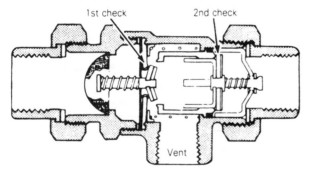

Figure 9-22 Dual-Check Valve with Atmospheric Vent

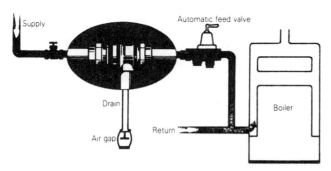

Figure 9-23 Dual-Check Valve with Atmospheric Vent—Typical Residential Use

stant pressure, and protects against back-pressure resulted in this unique backflow preventer. Construction is basically two check valves having an atmospheric vent located between the two checks. See Figure 9-22.

Line pressure keeps the vent closed, but positive supply pressure or back-siphonage will open the inner chamber to atmosphere. With this device, extra protection is obtained through the atmospheric vent capability. Figure 9-23 shows a typical use of the device on a residential boiler supply line.

Double-Check Valve Assemblies

A double-check valve is essentially two single-check valves coupled within one body and furnished with test cocks and two tightly closing shut-off valves.

The test capability feature gives this device a big advantage over the use of two independent check valves in that it can be readily tested to determine if either or both check valves are inoperative or fouled by debris. Each check is spring-loaded closed and requires approximately 1 psi to open.

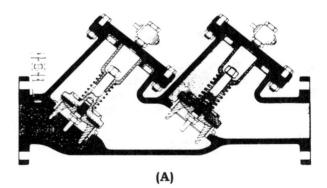

(A)

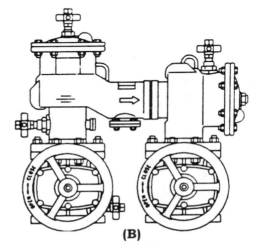

(B)

Figure 9-24 (A) Double-Check Valve, (B) Double-Check Valve Assembly

This spring loading provides the ability to "bite" through small debris and still seal, a protection feature not prevalent in unloaded swing check valves. Figure 9-24(B) shows a cross section of a double-check valve complete with test cocks. Double-check valves are commonly used to protect against low- to medium-hazard installations such as food processing steam kettles and apartment projects. They may be used under continuous pressure and protect against both back-siphonage and back-pressure conditions.

These devices must be installed in an accessible location to allow for testing and maintenance.

Double-Check Detector Valve Assemblies

This device is an outgrowth of the double-check valve and is primarily utilized in fire line installations. Its purpose is to protect the potable supply line from possible contamination from booster pump fire line back-pressure, stagnant "black water" that sits in fire lines over extended periods of time, the addition of "raw" water through outside fire pumper connections (siamese outlets), and the detection of any water movement in the fire line water due to fire line leakage or deliberate water theft. It consists of two spring-loaded check valves, a bypass assembly with water meter and double-check valve, and up to floor tightly closing shut-off valves. The addition of test cocks makes the device testable to ensure proper operation of both the primary checks and the bypass check valve. In the event of very low fire line water usage (possible theft of water), the lower pressure drop inherent in the bypass system permits the low flow of water to be metered through the bypass system. In a high flow demand, associated with flow fire capability, the main check valves open, permitting high-volume, low restricted flow through the two large spring-loaded check valves. See Figure 9-25.

Residential Dual-Check Valve Assemblies

The need to furnish inexpensive back-siphonage and back-pressure protection for individual residences resulted in the debut of the residential dual check. Protection of the main potable

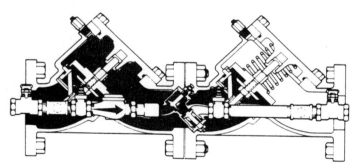

Figure 9-25 Double-Check Detector Check

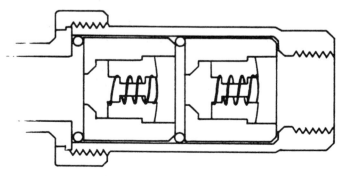

Figure 9-26 Residential Dual Check

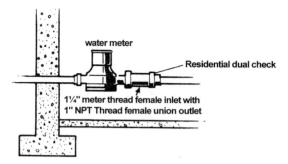

Figure 9-27 Residential Dual Check Installation

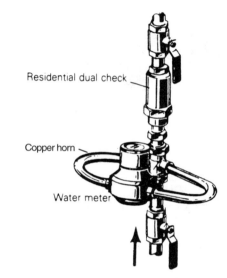

Figure 9-28 Residential Dual Check Installation

supply from household hazards reinforced a true need for such a device. Figure 9-26 shows a cutaway of the device.

It is sized for ½-, ¾-, and 1-in. service lines and is installed immediately downstream of the water meter. Typical installations are shown in Figures 9-27 and 9-28.

Reduced-Pressure-Principle Backflow Preventer

Maximum protection is achieved against back-siphonage and back-pressure conditions utilizing reduced-pressure-principle backflow preventers. These devices are essentially modified double-check valves with an atmospheric vent capability placed between the two checks and designed such that this "zone" between the two checks is always kept at least 2 lb less than the supply pressure. With this design criteria, the reduced-pressure-principle backflow preventer can provide protection again back-siphonage and back-pressure when both the first and second checks become fouled. They can be used under constant pressure and at high-hazard installations. Most codes prohibit the installation of these devices in pits or below grade. They are furnished with test cocks and shut-off valves to enable testing and are available in sizes ⅜ through 10 in.

Figure 9-29(A) shows typical devices representative of ¾- through 2-in. sizes and Figure 9-29(B) shows typical devices representative of 2½- through 10-in. sizes.

The principles of operation of a reduced-pressure-principle backflow preventer are as follows (see Figure 9-30): Flow from the left enters the intermediate chamber against the pressure exerted by loaded check valve 1. The supply pressure is reduced thereupon by a predetermined amount. The pressure in the central chamber is maintained lower than the incoming supply pressure through the operation of relief valve 3, which discharges to the atmosphere whenever the central chamber pressure approaches within a few pounds of the inlet

pressure. Check valve 2 is lightly loaded to open with a pressure drop of 1 psi in the direction of flow and is independent of the pressure required to open the relief valve. In the event that the pressure increases downstream from the device, tending to reverse the direction of flow, check valve 2 closes, preventing backflow. Because all valves may leak as a result of wear or obstruction, the protection provided by check valves is not considered sufficient. If some obstruction prevents check valve 2 from closing tightly, the leakage back into the central chamber would increase the pressure in this zone, the relief valve would open, and flow would be discharged to the atmosphere.

When the supply pressure drops to the minimum differential required to operate the relief valve, the pressure in the central chamber should be atmospheric. If the inlet pressure should become less than atmospheric pressure, relief valve 3 should remain fully open to the atmosphere to discharge any water that may be caused to backflow as a result of back-pressure and leakage of check valve 2.

Malfunctioning of one or both of the check valves or relief valve should always be indicated

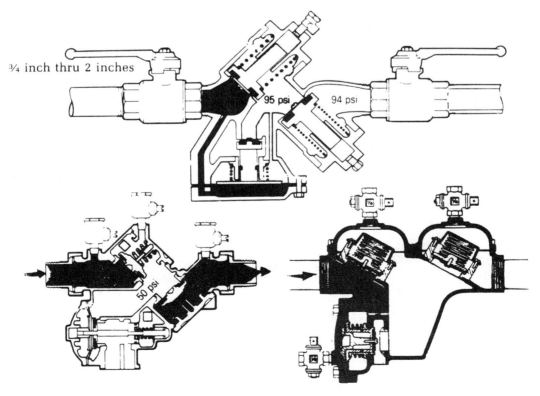

Figure 9-29 (A) Reduced-Pressure Zone Backflow Preventer (¾–2 in.)

2½ inch thru 10 inches

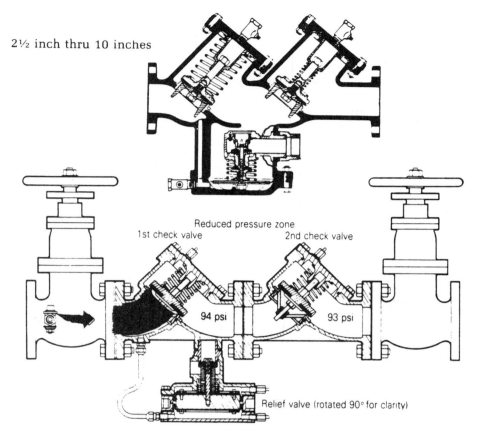

Reduced pressure zone
1st check valve   2nd check valve

94 psi   93 psi

Relief valve (rotated 90° for clarity)

Figure 9-29 (B) Reduced-Pressure Zone Backflow Preventer (2½ – 10 in.)

by a discharge of water from the relief port. Under no circumstances should plugging of the relief port be permitted because the device depends upon an open port for safe operation. The pressure loss through the device can be expected to average between 10 and 20 psi within the normal range of operation, depending upon the size and flow rate of the device. See Figure 9-30.

Reduced-pressure-principle backflow preventers are commonly installed on high-hazard installations such as plating plants, where they would protect against primarily back-sipho-

ACME PLATING

Meter

Reduced pressure principle backflow preventer   Water main

Figure 9-31 Plating Plant Installation

nage potential; car washes, where they would protect against back-pressure conditions; and funeral parlors, hospital autopsy rooms, etc. The reduced-pressure-principle backflow preventer forms the backbone of cross-connection control programs. Since it is utilized to protect against high-hazard installations, and high-hazard installations are the first considerations in protecting public health and safety, these devices are installed in large quantities over a broad

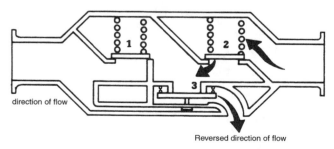

direction of flow

Reversed direction of flow

**Figure 9-30 Reduced-Pressure Zone
Backflow Preventer—Principle of Operation**

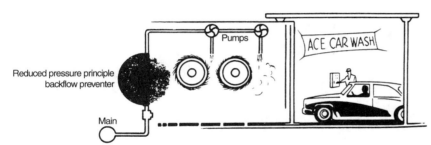

Figure 9-32 Carwash Installation

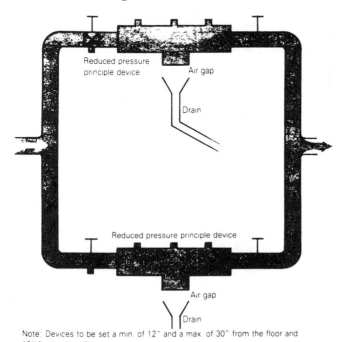

Note: Devices to be set a min. of 12" and a max. of 30" from the floor and 12" from any wall.

Figure 9-33 Reduced-Pressure Principle Devices—Typical Bypass Configuration

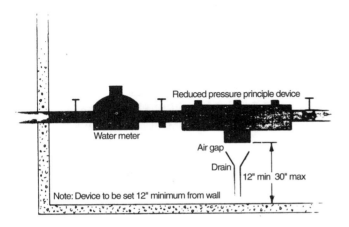

Figure 9-34 Reduced-Pressure Principle Device—Typical Installation

range of plumbing and water works installations. Figures 9-31 and 9-32 show typical installations of these devices on high hazard installations. See also Figures 9-33 and 9-34.

ADMINISTRATION OF A CROSS-CONNECTION PROGRAM

Under the provisions of the Safe Drinking Water Act of 1974, the federal government established, through the EPA, national standards of safe drinking water. States are responsible for the enforcement of these standards as well as the supervision of public water supply systems and the sources of drinking water. The water purveyor (supplier) is held responsible for compliance to the provisions of the act, including a warranty that water quality provided by his/her operation is in conformance with the EPA standards at the source and is delivered to the customer without the quality being compromised as a result of delivery through the distribution system. As specified in the *Code of Federal Regulations* (Vol. 40, Para. 141.2, Sect. c),

> Maximum contaminant level means the maximum permissible level of a contaminant in water which is delivered to the free flowing outlet of the ultimate user of a public water system, except in the case of turbidity where the maximum permissible level is measured at the point of entry to the distribution system. Contaminants added to the water under circumstances controlled by the user, except those resulting from corrosion of piping and plumbing caused by water quality, are excluded from this definition.

Figure 9-35 depicts several options that are open to a water purveyor considering cross-connection protection for commercial, industrial, and residential customers. The purveyor may elect to work initially on "containment" theory. This approach utilizes a minimum of backflow devices and isolates the customer from the water main. While it is recognized that containment does not protect the customer within his/her building, it does effectively prevent him/her from possibly contaminating the public water system.

If the water purveyor elects to protect his/her customers on a domestic internal protective

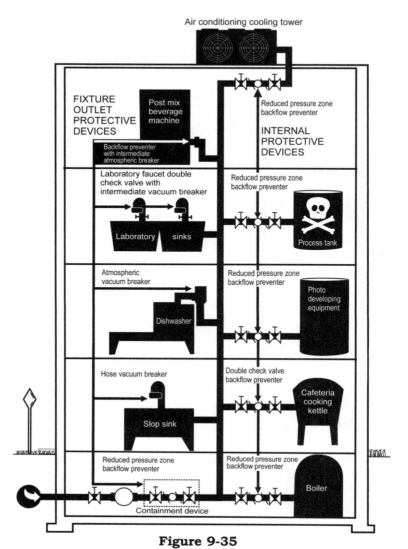

Figure 9-35

basis and/or "fixture outlet protective basis," then cross-connection control protective devices are placed at internal high-hazard locations as well as at all locations where cross-connections exist at the "last free-flowing outlet." This approach entails extensive cross-connective survey work on behalf of the water superintendent or his/her agent as well as constant policing of the plumbing within each commercial, industrial, and residential account. In large water supply systems, fixture outlet protection, cross-connection control is virtually impossible to achieve and police because of the quantity of systems involved, the complexity of the plumbing systems inherent in many industrial sites, and the fact that many plumbing changes are made within industrial and commercial establishments that do not require the water department's license or

otherwise endorsement or ratification when contemplated or completed. In addition, internal plumbing cross-connection control survey work is generally foreign to the average water purveyor and is not normally a portion of his/her job. While it is admirable for the water purveyor to accept and perform survey work, that person should be aware that in doing so he/she runs risks of additional liability in an area where he/she may be in conflict with plumbing inspectors, maintenance personnel, and other public health officials.

Even where extensive fixture outlet protection, cross-connection control programs are in effect through the efforts of an aggressive and thorough water supply cross-connection control program, the water authorities should also have an active containment program to address the many plumbing changes that are made and are inherent within commercial and industrial establishments. In essence, fixture outlet protection becomes an extension of the containment program.

For the supplier of water to provide maximum protection of the water distribution system, consideration should be given to requiring the owner of a premises (commercial, industrial, or residential) to provide, at his/her own expense, adequate proof that the internal water system complies with the local or state plumbing code(s). In addition, he/she may be required to install, have tested, and maintain all backflow protection devices that would be required—at his/her own expense!

The supplier of water should have the right of entry to determine degree of hazard and the existence of cross-connections in order to protect the potable water system. By so having, he can assess the overall nature of the facility and its potential impact on the water system (i.e., determine the degree of hazard), personally see actual cross-connections that could contaminate the water system, and take appropriate action to ensure the elimination of the cross-connection or the installation of required backflow devices.

To enable the water purveyor to fully administer a cross-connection control program, all public health officials, plumbing inspectors, building managers, plumbing installers, and maintenance people should participate and share in the responsibility to protect the public health and safety of individuals from cross-connections and contamination or pollution of the public water supply system.

Cross-Connection Control Work

Cross-connection control survey work should be performed only by personnel knowledgeable about commercial and industrial potential cross-connections as well as general industrial uses for both potable and process water. If containment is the prime objective of the survey, then only sufficient time to determine the degree of hazard inherent within the facility or operation need be spent in the facility.

Once this is determined, a judgment can be made by the cross-connection control inspector as to what type of backflow protective device is needed at the potable supply entrance or immediately downstream of the water meter. In the event that the cross-connection control program requires "total" protection to the last free-flowing outlet, then the survey must be conducted in depth to visually inspect for all cross-connections within the facility and make recommendations and requirements for fixture outlet protective devices, internal protective devices, and containment devices.

It is recommended that consideration be given to the following objectives when performing a cross-connection control survey:

1. Determine if the survey will be conducted with a prearranged appointment or unannounced.

2. Upon entry, identify yourself and the purpose of the visit and request to see the plant manager, owner, or maintenance supervisor to explain the purpose of the visit and why the cross-connection survey will be of benefit to him/her.

3. Ask what processes take place within the facility and for what purpose potable water is used, e.g, do the boilers have chemical additives? Are air-conditioning cooling towers in use with chemical additives? Do they use water savers with chemical additives? Do they have a second source of water (raw water from wells, etc.) in addition to the potable water supply? Does the processed water cross-connect with potentially hazardous chemical etching tanks, etc.?

4. Request "as-built" engineering drawings of the potable water supply to trace out internal potable lines and potential areas of cross-connection.

5. Initiate the survey at the potable entrance supply (the water meter, in most cases), then proceed with the internal survey in the event that total internal protective devices and fixture outlet protective devices are desired.

6. Survey the plant facilities with the objective of looking for cross-connections at all potable water outlets, such as

   A. Hose bibbs

   B. Slop sinks

   C. Washroom facilities

   D. Cafeterias and kitchens

   E. Fire protection and siamese outlets

F. Irrigation outlets

G. Boiler rooms

H. Mechanical rooms

I. Laundry facilities (hospitals)

J. Production floor

K. Air-conditioning cooling towers.

(See Appendix 9-B for an additional list of plumbing hazards.)

7. Make a sketch of all areas requiring backflow protection devices.

8. Review with the host what you have found and explain the findings. Inform him/her that he/she will receive a written report documenting the findings together with a written recommendation for corrective action. Attempt to answer all the questions at this time. Review the findings with the owner or manager if time and circumstances permit.

9. Document all findings and recommendations prior to preparing a written report. Include as many sketches with the final report as possible and specifically state the size and generic type of backflow preventer required at each cross-connection found.

10. Survey all commercial and industrial facilities and require appropriate backflow protection based on the containment philosophy and/or internal protection and fixture outlet protection. Follow up to ensure that the recommended devices are installed and tested both on an initial basis and per a periodic cross-connection control ordinance.

The surveys should be conducted by personnel experienced in commercial and industrial processes. The owners or owners' representatives should be questioned as to what the water is being used for in the facility and what hazards the operations may present to the water system (both within the facility and to the water distribution system) in the event that a back-siphonage or back-pressure condition exists concurrently with a nonprotected cross-connection. In the event that experienced survey personnel are not available within the water authority to conduct the survey, consideration should be given to having a consulting firm perform the survey on behalf of the water department.

CROSS-CONNECTION CONTROL ORDINANCE PROVISIONS

The successful promotion of a cross-connection and backflow connection control program in a municipality is dependent on legal authority to conduct such a program. Where a community has adopted a modern plumbing code, such as the *National Plumbing Code*, ASA A40.8-1955, or subsequent revisions thereof, provisions of the code will govern backflow and cross-connections. It then remains to provide an ordinance that will establish a program of inspection for elimination of cross-connections within the community. Frequently, authority for such a program may already reside with the water department or water authority. In such cases, no further document may be needed. A cross-connection control ordinance should have at least three basic parts:

1. Authority for establishment of a program

2. Technical provisions relating to eliminating backflow and cross-connections

3. Penalty provisions for violations.

Appendix 9-A describes a model program that is a suggested example for municipalities to use who desire to adopt (or create) a cross-connection control ordinance. Communities adopting ordinances should check with state health officials to ensure conformance with state codes. The form of the ordinance should comply with local legal requirements and receive legal adoption from the community.

APPENDIX 9-A SAMPLE WATER DEPARTMENT CROSS-CONNECTION CONTROL PROGRAM/ORDINANCE

[WATER DEPARTMENT NAME] CROSS-CONNECTION CONTROL PROGRAM/ORDINANCE

I. Purpose

a. To protect the public potable water supply served by the [ ] Water Department from the possibility of contamination or pollution by isolating, within its customers' internal distribution system, such contaminants or pollutants which could backflow or back-siphon into the public water system.

b. To promote the elimination or control of existing cross-connections, actual or potential, between its customers' in-plant potable water system, and nonpotable systems.

c. To provide for the maintenance of a continuing program of cross-connection control, which will effectively prevent the contamination or pollution of all potable water systems by cross-connection.

II. Authority

a. The Federal Safe Drinking Water Act of 1974, and the statutes of the State of [ ] Chapters [ ], the water purveyor has the primary responsibility for preventing water from unapproved sources, or any other substances, from entering the public potable water system.

b. [ ] Water Department, Rules and Regulations, adopted.

III. Responsibility

The Director of Municipal Services shall be responsible for the protection of the public potable water distribution system from contamination or pollution due to the backflow or back-siphonage of contaminants or pollutants through the water service connection. If, in the judgment of the Director of Municipal Services, an approved backflow device is required at the city's water service connection to any customer's premises, the Director, or his delegated agent, shall give notice in writing to said customer to install an approved backflow prevention device at each service connection to his premises. The customer shall, within ninety (90) days, install such approved device, or devices, at his own expense, and failure or refusal, or inability on the part of the customer to install said device or devices within ninety (90) days shall constitute a ground for discontinuing water service to the premises until such device or devices have been properly installed.

IV. Definitions

a. Approved

Accepted by the Director of Municipal Services as meeting an applicable specification stated or cited in this regulation, or as suitable for the proposed use.

b. Auxiliary Water Supply

Any water supply, on or available; to the premises other than the purveyor's approved public potable water supply.

c. Backflow

The flow of water or other liquids, mixtures or substances, under positive or reduced pressure in the distribution pipes of a potable water supply from any source other than its intended source.

d. Backflow Preventer

A device or means designed to prevent backflow or back-siphonage. Most commonly categorized as air gap, reduced-pressure principle device, double-check valve assembly, pressure vacuum breaker, atmospheric vacuum breaker, hose bibb vacuum breaker, residential dual check, dual check with intermediate atmospheric vent, and barometric loop.

d.1. Air Gap

A physical separation sufficient to prevent backflow between the free-flowing discharge end of the potable water system and any other system. Physically defined as a distance equal to twice the diameter of the supply side pipe diameter but never less than one (1) inch.

d.2. Atmospheric Vacuum Breaker

A device that prevents back-siphonage by opening an atmospheric vent when there is either a negative pressure or sub-atmospheric pressure in a water system.

d.3. Barometric Loop

A fabricated piping arrangement rising at least thirty-five (35) feet at its topmost point above the highest fixture it supplies. It is utilized in water supply systems to protect against back-siphonage.

d.4. Dual-Check Valve Assembly

An assembly of two (2) independently operating spring-loaded check valves with tightly closing shut-off valves on each side of the check valves, plus properly located test cocks for the testing of each check valve.

d.5. Double-Check Valve with Intermediate Atmospheric Vent

A device having two (2) spring-loaded check valves separated by an atmospheric vent chamber.

d.6. Hose Bibb Vacuum Breaker

A device that is permanently attached to a hose bibb and that acts as an atmospheric vacuum breaker.

d.7. Pressure Vacuum Breaker

A device containing one (1) or two (2) independently operated spring-loaded check valves and an independently operated spring-loaded air inlet valve located on the discharge side of the check or checks. Device includes tightly closing shut-off valves on each side of the check valves and properly located test cocks for the testing of the check valve(s).

d.8. Reduced-Pressure Principle Backflow Preventer

An assembly consisting of two (2) independently operating approved check valves with an automatically operating differential relief valve located between the two (2) check valves, tightly closing shut-off valves on each side of the check valves plus properly located test cocks for the testing of the check valves and the relief valve.

d.9. Residential Dual Check

An assembly of two (2) spring-loaded, independently operating check valves without tightly closing shut-off valves and test cocks. Generally employed immediately downstream of the water meter to act as a containment device.

e. Back-Pressure

A condition in which the owner's system pressure is greater than the supplier's system pressure.

f. Back-Siphonage

The flow of water or other liquids, mixtures or substances into the distribution pipes of a potable water supply system from any source other than its intended source caused by the sudden reduction of pressure in the potable water supply system.

g. Commission

The State of [ ] Water Supply and Pollution Control Commission.

h. Containment

A method of backflow prevention that requires a backflow prevention preventer at the water service entrance.

i. Contaminant

A substance that will impair the quality of the water to a degree that it creates a serious health hazard to the public leading to poisoning or the spread of disease.

j. Cross-Connection

Any actual or potential connection between the public water supply and a source of contamination or pollution.

k. Department

City of [ ] Water Department.

l. Director of Municipal Services

The Director, or his delegated representative, in charge of the Department of Municipal Services is invested with the authority and responsibility for the implementation of a cross-connection control program and for the enforcement of the provisions of the Ordinance.

m. Fixture Isolation

A method of backflow prevention in which a backflow preventer is located to correct a cross-connection at an in-plant location rather than at a water service entrance.

n. Owner

Any person who has legal title to, or license to operate or habituate in, a property upon which a cross-connection inspection is to be made or upon which a cross-connection is present.

o. Permit

A document issued by the Department that allows the use of a backflow preventer.

p. Person

Any individual, partnership, company, public or private corporation, political subdivision or agency of the State Department, agency or instrumentality or the United States or any other legal entity.

q. Pollutant

A foreign substance that, if permitted to get into the public water system, will degrade its quality so as to constitute a moderate hazard or impair the usefulness or quality of the water to a degree that does not create an actual hazard to the public health but that does adversely and unreasonably affect such water for domestic use.

r. Water Service Entrance

That point in the owner's water system beyond the sanitary control of the District; generally considered to be the outlet end of the water meter and always before any unprotected branch.

V. Administration

1. The Department will operate a cross-connection control program, to include the keeping of necessary records, that fulfills the requirements of the Commission's Cross-Connection Regulations and is approved by the Commission.

2. The Owner shall allow his property to be inspected for possible cross-connections and shall follow the provisions of the Department's program and the Commission's Regulations if a cross-connection is permitted.

3. If the Department requires that the public supply be protected by containment, the Owner shall be responsible for water quality beyond the outlet end of the containment device and should utilize fixture outlet protection for that purpose.

He may utilize public health officials, or personnel from the Department, or their delegated representatives, to assist him in the survey of his facilities and to assist him in the selection of proper fixture outlet devices, and the proper installation of these devices.

VI. Requirements

A. Department

1. On new installations, the Department will provide on-site evaluation and/or inspection of plans in order to determine the type of backflow preventer, if any, that will be required, will issue permit, and perform inspection and testing. In any case, a minimum of a dual-check valve will be required in any new construction.

2. For premises existing prior to the start of this program, the Department will perform evaluations and inspections of plans and/or premises and inform the owner by letter of any corrective action deemed necessary, the method of achieving the correction, and the time allowed for the correction to be made. Ordinarily, ninety (90) days will be allowed, depending upon the degree of hazard involved and the history of the device(s) in question.

3. The Department will not allow any cross-connection to remain unless it is protected by an approved backflow preventer for which a permit has been issued and which will be regularly tested to ensure satisfactory operation.

4. The Department shall inform the Owner, by letter, of any failure to comply by the time of the first reinspection. The Department will allow an additional fifteen (15) days for the correction. In the event the Owner fails to comply with the necessary correction by the time of the second reinspection, the Department will inform the Owner, by letter, that the water service to the Owner's premises will be terminated within a period not to exceed five (5) days. In the event that the Owner informs the Department of extenuating circumstances as to why the correction has not been made, a time extension may be granted

by the Department but in no case will exceed an additional thirty (30) days.

5. If the Department determines at any time that a serious threat to the public health exists, the water service will be terminated immediately.

6. The Department shall have, on file, a list of Private Contractors who are certified backflow device testers. All charges for these tests will be paid by the Owner of the building or property.

7. The Department will begin initial premises inspections to determine the nature of existing or potential hazards, following the approval of this program by the Commission, during the calendar year [ ]. Initial focus will be on high-hazard industries and commercial premises.

B . Owner

1. The Owner shall be responsible for the elimination or protection of all cross-connections on his premises.

2. The Owner, after having been informed by a letter from the Department, shall, at his expense, install, maintain, and test, or have tested, any and all backflow preventers on his premises.

3. The Owner shall correct any malfunction of the backflow preventer that is revealed by periodic testing.

4. The Owner shall inform the Department of any proposed or modified cross-connections and also any existing cross-connections of which the Owner is aware but has not been found by the Department.

5. The Owner shall not install a bypass around any backflow preventer unless there is a backflow preventer of the same type on the bypass. Owners who cannot shut down operation for testing of the device(s) must supply additional devices necessary to allow testing to take place.

6. The Owner shall install backflow preventers in a manner approved by the Department.

7. The Owner shall install only backflow preventers approved by the Department or the Commission.

8. Any Owner having a private well or other private water source, must have a permit if the well or source is cross-connected to the Department's system. Permission to cross-connect may be denied by the Department. The Owner may be required to install a backflow preventer at the service entrance if a private water source is maintained, even if it is not cross-connected to the Department's system.

9. In the event the Owner installs plumbing to provide potable water for domestic purposes which is on the Department's side of the backflow preventer, such plumbing must have its own backflow preventer installed.

10. The Owner shall be responsible for the payment of all fees for permits, annual or semiannual device testing, retesting in the case that the device fails to operate correctly, and second reinspections for noncompliance with Department or Commission requirements.

VII. DEGREE OF HAZARD

The Department recognizes the threat to the public water system arising from cross-connections. All threats will be classified by degree of hazard and will require the installation of approved reduced-pressure principle backflow prevention devices or double-check valves.

VIII. PERMITS

The Department shall not permit a cross-connection within the public water supply system unless it is considered necessary and that it cannot be eliminated.

a. Cross-connection permits that are required for each backflow prevention device are obtained from the Department. A fee of [$XX.XX] dollars will be charged for the initial permit and [$XX.XX] dollars for the renewal of each permit.

b. Permits shall be renewed every [ ] year(s) and are nontransferable. Permits are subject to revocation and become immediately revoked if the Owner should so change the type of cross-connection or degree of hazard associated with the service.

c. A permit is not required when fixture isolation is achieved with the utilization of a nontestable backflow preventer.

IX. EXISTING IN-USE BACKFLOW PREVENTION DEVICES

Any existing backflow preventer shall be allowed by the Department to continue in service unless the degree of hazard is such as to supersede the effectiveness of the present backflow preventer, or result in an unreasonable risk to the public health. Where the degree of hazard has increased, as in the case of a residential installation converting to a business establishment, any existing backflow preventer must be upgraded to a reduced-pressure principle device, or a reduced-pressure principle device must be installed in the event that no backflow device was present.

X. PERIODIC TESTING

a. Reduced-pressure principle backflow devices, double-check valve devices and pressure vacuum breakers should be tested and inspected at least semiannually or as required by the administrative authority.

b. Periodic testing shall be performed by the Department's certified tester or his delegated representative. This testing will be done at the Owner's expense.

c. The testing shall be conducted during the Department's regular business hours. Exceptions to this, when at the request of the Owner, may require additional charges to cover the increased costs to the Department.

d. Any backflow preventer that fails during a periodic test will be repaired or replaced. When repairs are necessary, upon completion of the repair, the device will be retested at the Owner's expense to ensure correct operation. High-hazard situations will not be allowed to continue unprotected if the backflow preventer fails the test and cannot be repaired immediately. In other situations, a compliance date of not more than thirty (30) days after the test date will be established. The Owner is responsible for spare parts, repair tools, or a replacement device. Parallel installation of two (2) devices is an effective means of the Owner ensuring uninterrupted water service during testing or the repair of devices and is strongly recommended when the owner desires such continuity.

e. Backflow prevention devices will be tested more frequently than specified in "a." above, in cases where there is a history of test failures and the Department feels that due to the degree of hazard involved, additional testing is warranted. Cost of the additional tests will be borne by the Owner.

XI. RECORDS AND REPORTS

a. Records

The Department will initiate and maintain the following:

1. Master files on customer cross-connection tests and/or inspections

2. Master files on cross-connection permits

3. Copies of permits and permit applications

4. Copies of lists and summaries supplied to the Commission.

b. Reports

The Department will submit the following to the Commission:

1. Initial listing of low-hazard cross-connections to the State

2. Initial listing of high-hazard cross-connections to the State

3. Annual update lists of items 1 and 2 above

4. Annual summary of cross-connection inspections to the State.

XII. FEES AND CHARGES

The Department will publish a list of fees or charges for the following services or permits:

1. Testing fees

2. Retesting fees

3. Fee for reinspection

4. Charges for after-hours inspections or tests.

ADDENDUM

1. Residential Dual Check

Effective the date of the acceptance of this Cross-Connection Control Program for the Town of [ ], all new residential buildings will be required to install a residential dual-check device immediately downstream of the water meter. Installation of this residential dual-check device on a retro-fit basis on existing service lines will be instituted at a time and at a potential cost to the home-owner as deemed necessary by the Department.

The Owner must be aware that installation of a residential dual-check valve results in a potential closed plumbing system within his resi-dence. As such, provisions may have to be made by the Owner to provide for thermal expansion within his closed loop system, i.e., the installa-tion of thermal expansion devices and/or pressure-relief valves.

2. Strainers

The Department strongly recommends that all new retrofit installations of reduced-pressure principle devices and double-check valve backflow preventers include the installation of strainers located immediately upstream of the backflow device. However, the use of strainers may not be acceptable by the Fire Protection authority having jurisdiction. The installation of strainers will preclude the fouling of backflow devices due to both foreseen and unforeseen cir-cumstances occurring to the water supply system such as water main repairs, water main breaks, fires, periodic cleaning and flushing of mains, etc. These occurrences may "stir up" debris within the water main that will cause fouling of backflow devices installed without the benefit of strainers.

APPENDIX 9-B POTENTIAL PLUMBING SYSTEM HAZARDS (PARTIAL LIST)

Fixtures with Direct Connections

Description

Air conditioning, air washer
Air conditioning, chilled water
Air conditioning, condenser water
Air line
Aspirator, laboratory
Aspirator, medical
Aspirator, weedicide and fertilizer sprayer
Autoclave and sterilizer
Auxiliary system, industrial
Auxiliary system, surface water
Auxiliary system, unapproved well supply
Boiler system
Chemical feeder, pot type
Chlorinator
Coffee urn
Cooling system
Dishwasher
Fire standpipe or sprinkler system
Fountain, ornamental
Hydraulic equipment
Laboratory equipment
Lubrication, pump bearings
Photostat equipment
Plumber's friend, pneumatic
Pump, pneumatic ejector
Pump, prime line
Pump, water-operated ejector
Sewer, sanitary
Sewer, storm
Swimming pool

Typical Fixtures with Submerged Inlets

Description

Baptismal font
Bathtub
Bedpan washer, flushing rim
Bidet
Brine tank
Cooling tower
Cuspidor
Drinking fountain
Floor drain, flushing rim
Garbage can washer
Ice maker
Laboratory sink, serrated nozzle
Laundry machine
Lavatory
Lawn sprinkler system
Photo laboratory sink
Sewer flushing manhole
Slop sink, flushing rim
Slop sink, threaded supply
Steam table
Urinal, siphon jet blowout
Vegetable peeler
Water closet, flush tank, ball cock
Water closet, flush valve, siphon jet

APPENDIX 9-C AMERICAN WATER WORKS ASSOCIATION STATEMENT OF POLICY

The American Water Works Association recognizes that the water purveyor has a responsibility to provide its customers at the service connection with water that is safe under all foreseeable circumstances. Thus, in the exercise of this responsibility, the water purveyor must take reasonable precaution to protect the community distribution system from the hazards originating on the premises of its customers that may degrade the water in the community distribution system.

Cross-connection control and plumbing inspections on the premises of water customers are regulatory in nature and should be handled through the rules, regulations and recommendations of the health authority or the plumbing-code enforcement agencies having jurisdiction. The water purveyor, however, should be aware of any situation requiring inspection and/or reinspection necessary to detect hazardous conditions resulting from cross-connections. If, in the opinion of the utility, effective measures consistent with the degree of hazard have not been taken by the regulatory agency, the water purveyor should take such measures as he deems necessary to ensure that the community distribution system is protected from contamination. Such action would include the installation of a backflow prevention device, consistent with the degree of hazard at the service connection or discontinuance of the service.

In addition, customer use of the water from the community distribution system for cooling or other purposes within the customer's system and later return of the water to the community distribution system is not acceptable and is opposed by AWWA.

Appendix 9-D Application of Backflow Prevention Devices

Standard Number	Device or Method	Type of Protection[a]	Hazard	Installation Dimensions and Position	Pressure Condition[b]	Comments	Use
ANSI A 112.2.1	Air Gap	BS & BP	High	Twice effective opening — not less than 1 inch above flood level rim	C		Lavatory, sink or bathtub spouts, Residential dishwasher (ASSE 1006) and clothes washers (ASSE 1007)
ASSE 1001	Pipe Applied Vacuum Breaker	BS	Low	• 6 inches above highest outlet • Vertical position only	I		Goosenecks and appliances not subject to back pressure or continuous pressure
ASSE 1011	Hose Bibb Vacuum Breaker	BS	Low	• Locked on hose bibb threads • At least 6 inches above grade	I	Freeze proof type required	Hose bibbs, hydrants, and sillcocks
ASSE 1012[c]	Dual Check Valve with Atmospheric Vent	BS & BP	Low to Moderate	• Any position • Drain piped to floor	C	• Air gap required on vent outlet • Vent piped to suitable drain	• Residential boilers, spas, hot tubs and swimming pool feedlines • Sterilizers • Food processing equipment • Photo lab equipment • Hospital equipment • Commercial dishwashers • Water cooled HVAC • Landscape hose bibb • Washdown racks • Makeup water to heat pumps
ASSE 1013	Reduced Pressure Zone Backflow Preventer	BS & BP	High	• Inside building • 18 inches to 48 inches (centerline to floor) • Outside building — 18 inches to 24 inches (centerline to floor) • Horizontal only	C	• Testing annually (minimum) • Overhaul five (5) yrs. (minimum) • Drain	• Chemical tanks • Submerged coils • Treatment plants • Solar systems • Chilled water • Heat exchangers • Cooling towers • Lawn irrigation (Type II) • Hospital equipment • Commercial boilers, swimming pools, spas • Fire sprinkler (high hazard as determined by commission)
ASSE 1015	Double Check Valve Assembly	BS & BP	Low	• Inside building —18 inches to 24 inches (centerline to floor) • Outside building — 18 inches to 24 inches (centerline to floor) • Horizontal only • 60 inches required above device for testing	C	• Testing annually (minimum) • Overhaul five (5) yrs. (minimum)	• Fire sprinkler systems (Type II low hazard) • Washdown racks • Large pressure cookers and steamers
ASSE 1020	Pressure Type Vacuum Breaker	BS	High	• Twelve (I2) inches to 60 inches above highest outlet • Vertical only	C	• Testing annually (minimum) • Overhaul rive (5) yrs. (minimum)	• Degreasers • Laboratories • Photo tanks • Type I lawn sprinkler systems and swimming pools (must be located outdoors)
ASSE 1024[c]	Dual Check Valve	BS & BP	Low	Any position	C		• Fire sprinkler systems Type I building • Outside drinking fountains • Automatic grease recovery device
ASSE 1035	Atmospheric	BS	Low	Six (6) inches above flood level per manufacturer	I/C		• Chemical faucets • Ice makers • Dental chairs • Miscellaneous faucet applications • Soft drink, coffee and other beverage dispensers • Hose sprays on faucets not meeting standards
ASSE 1056	Spill Proof Indoor Vacuum Breaker	BS	High	Twelve (12) inches to 60 inches above highest outlet Vertical Only	C	Testing annually (minimum) over haul five (5) yrs. (minimum)	• Degreasers • Laboratories • Photo Tanks • Type 1 Lawn Sprinkler systems and swimming pools (must be located outdoors)

a BS = Back-siphonage; BP = Back-pressure.

b I = Intermittent; C = Continuous.

c A tab shall be affixed to all ASSE 1012 and 1024 devices indicating:

   a. Installation date.

   b. The following statement: "FOR OPTIMUM PERFORMANCE AND SAFETY, IT IS RECOMMENDED THAT THIS DEVICE BE REPLACED EVERY FIVE (5) YEARS."

Appendix 9-E The Safe Drinking Water Act—Maximum Contaminant Levels

PRIMARY CONTAMINANTS	Maximum Contaminant Level (MCL)
Metals:	
Arsenic	0.05 mg/L
Barium	2.0 mg/L
Cadmium	0.005 mg/L
Chromium	0.1 mg/L
Copper	1.3 mg/L
Lead [a]	0.015 mg/L
Mercury	0.002 mg/L
Selenium	0.05 mg/L
Nonmetals:	
Fluoride	4 mg/L
Nitrate	10.0 mg/L
Volatile Organic Chemicals:	
Total Trihalomethanes	0.10 mg/L
Benzene	0.005 mg/L
Vinyl chloride	0.002 mg/L
Carbon tetrachloride	0.005 mg/L
1,2-Dichloroethane	0.005 mg/L
Trichloroethylene (TCE)	0.005 mg/L
1,4-Dichlorobenzene	0.075 mg/L
1,1-Dichloroethylene	0.007 mg/L
1,1,1-Trichloroethane	0.2 mg/L
o-Dichlorobenzene	0.6 mg/L
cis- 1,2-Dichloroethylene	0.07 mg/L
trans- 1,2-Dichloroethylene	0.1 mg/L
1,2-Dichloropropane	0.005 mg/L
Ethylbenzene	0.7 mg/L
Monochlorobenzene	0.1 mg/L
Styrene	0.1 mg/L
Toluene	1.0 mg/L
Xylenes	10.0 mg/L
Tetrachloroethylene	0.005 mg/L
Herbicides, Pesticides, PCBs:	
Chlordane	0.002 mg/L
Endrin	0.0002 mg/L
Heptachlor	0.0004 mg/L
Hexachlorobenzene	0.001 mg/L
Lindane	0.0002 mg/L
Methoxychlor	0.04 mg/L
Toxaphene	0.003 mg/L
PCBs	0.0005 mg/L
2,4-D	0.07 mg/L
2,4,5-TP Silvex	0.05 mg/L
Alachlor	0.002 mg/L
Atrazine	0.003 mg/L
Carbofuran	0.04 mg/L

PRIMARY CONTAMINANTS	Maximum Contaminant Level (MCL)
1,2-Dibromo-3-Chloropropane (DBCP)	0.0002 mg/L
Ethylene dibromide (EDB)	0.00005 mg/L
Heptachlor epoxide	0.0002 mg/L
Phenols:	
Pentachlorophenol	0.001 mg/L
Physical Parameters:	
Turbidity (in turbidity units)	5 TU
Radioactivity	15 picocuries
Microbiology:	
Coliform bacteria	0 per 100 mL

SECONDARY CONTAMINANTS	
Iron	0.3 mg/L
Manganese	0.05 mg/L
Zinc	5.0 mg/L
Chloride	250 mg/L
Sulfate	250 mg/L
Total dissolved solids	500 mg/L
Color	15 units
Corrosivity	none
Foaming agents	0.5 mg/L
Odor	3 T.O.N.
pH	6.5-8.5

Note: For these purposes, mg/L = milligrams per liter; parts per million = ppm; 1 ppm = 1,000 ppb; ppb = parts per billion; micrograms per liter = µg/L

[a] Level that requires action.

Appendix 9-F Index of Water Treatment Equipment/Water Problems

Problem and/or Pollutant

Equipment Options [a]	Aluminum	Arsenic	Asbestos	Barium	Cadmium	Chloride	Chlorine [b]	Chromium	Color	Copper	Endrin	Fluroide	Giardia Cysts	Hardness	Iron (Fe²)	Iron (Fe³)	Lead [c]	Lindane	Manganese	Mercury	Methoxychlor	Nitrate	Particulates	Pesticides, Herbicides, PCBs	Radium	Radon	Selenium	Silver	Sulfate	Tannic Acids	Taste & Ordor	Total Dissolved Solids	Total Trihalomethanes (TTHMs)	Toxaphene	Turbidity	VOCs	Zinc	2,4-D	2,4,5-TP Silvex
Carbon							•		•		•							•	•		•			•		•				•	•		•	•	•	•		•	•
Filtration			•						•				•		•								•												•				
Reverse osmosis	•	•	•	•	•	•	•	•	•	•	•		•	•	•	•	•	•		•	•	•	•		•		•	•	•			•			•		•	•	
Distillation	•	•		•	•	•		•		•		•	•	•	•	•	•	•	•	•		•	•		•		•	•	•	•		•			•		•		
Cation exchange					•	•				•				•	•				•						•														
Mineral bed														•																									
Activated alumina		•										•					•										•												
Anion exchange						•																•							•										

[a] Some equipment may reduce additional contaminants because of its unique design and/or combinations of technology. Ask for proof of performance.

[b] Not all reverse osmosis units are effective for chlorine reduction. Ask for proof of performance.

[c] Not all carbon units are effective for lead reduction. Ask for proof of performance.

APPENDIX 9-G CASE STUDIES OF CROSS-CONTAMINATION

The following documentation outlines cases of cross-connection incidents registered with the EPA that illustrate and emphasize how actual cross-connections have compromised and continue to compromise the drinking water quality and the public health.

1. Human Blood in the Water System

Health Department officials cut off the water supply to a funeral home located in a large city after it was determined that human blood had contaminated the fresh water supply. City water and plumbing officials said they did not think that the blood contamination had spread beyond the building; however, inspectors were sent into the neighborhood to check for possible contamination. The chief plumbing inspector had received a telephone call advising that blood was coming from drinking fountains within the building. Plumbing and county health department officials and inspectors went to the scene and found evidence that the blood had been circulating in the water system within the building. They immediately ordered the building cut off from the water system at the meter. Investigation revealed that the funeral home had been using a hydraulic aspirator to drain fluids from bodies of human remains as part of the embalming process. The aspirator directly connected to the water supply system at a faucet outlet located on a sink in the preparation (embalming) room. Water flow through the aspirator created suction that was utilized to draw body fluids through a hose and needle attached to the suction side of the aspirator.

The contamination of the funeral home potable water supply was caused by a combination of low water pressure in conjunction with the simultaneous use of the aspirator. Instead of the body fluids flowing into the sanitary system drain, they were drawn in the opposite direction into the potable water supply of the funeral home. (See Figure 9-G1)

2. Burned in the Shower

A resident of a small town in Alabama jumped into the shower at 5 A.M. one morning in October 1986, and when he got out his body was covered with tiny blisters. "The more I rubbed

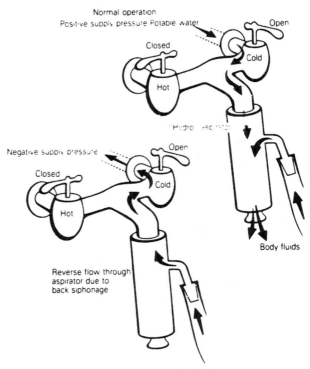

Figure 9-G1

it, the worse it got," the 60-year-old resident said. "It looked like someone took a blow torch and singed me." He and several other residents received medical treatment at the emergency room of the local hospital after it was discovered that the water system was contaminated with sodium hydroxide, a strong caustic solution. Other residents claimed that "it [the water] bubbled up and looked like Alka Seltzer. I stuck my hand under the faucet and some blisters came up." One neighbor's head was covered with blisters after she washed her hair and others complained of burned throats or mouths after drinking the water.

The incident began after an 8-in. water main that fed the town broke and was repaired. While repairing the water main, one workman suffered leg burns from a chemical in the water and required medical treatment. Measurements of the pH of the water were as high as 13 in some sections of the pipe.

Investigation into the cause of the problem led to a nearby chemical company that distributes chemicals such as sodium hydroxide as a possible source of the contamination. The sodium hydroxide was brought to the plant in liquid form in bulk tanker trucks and transferred to a holding tank and then dumped into 55-gal drums. When the water main broke, a truck driver was adding water from the bottom of the tank truck instead of the top, and sodium hydroxide back-siphoned into the water main. (See Figure 9-G2)

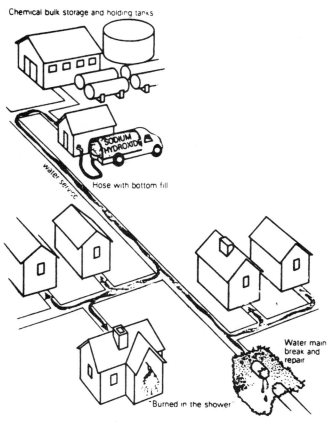

Chemical bulk storage and holding tanks

SODIUM HYDROXIDE

Hose with bottom fill

water service

Water main break and repair

"Burned in the shower"

Figure 9-G2

3. Propane Gas in the Water System

Hundreds of people were evacuated from their homes and businesses on an August afternoon in 1982 as a result of propane entering a city's water supply system. Fires were reported in two homes and the town water supply was contaminated. One five-room residence was gutted by a blaze resulting from propane gas "bubbling and hissing" from a bathroom toilet. In another home a washing machine explosion blew a woman against a wall. Residents throughout the area reported hissing, bubbling noises coming from washing machines, sinks, and toilets. Faucets sputtered out small streams of water mixed with gas and residents in the area were asked to evacuate their homes.

This near disaster occurred when the gas company initiated immediate repair procedures in one 30,000-gal capacity liquid propane tank.

To start the repair, the tank was purged of residual propane using water from one of two private fire hydrants located on the property. Water purging is the method of purging preferred over carbon dioxide, since it is more positive and will float out any sludge as well as any gas vapors. The purging consisted of hooking up a hose to one of the private fire hydrants located on the property and initiating flushing procedures.

Since the vapor pressure of the propane residual in the tank was 85 to 90 psi and the water pressure was only 65 to 70 psi, propane gas back-pressure backflowed into the water main. It was estimated that the gas flowed into the water mains for about 20 min and about 2000 ft^3 of gas was involved. This was enough gas to fill approximately 1 mile of an 8-in. water main. (See Figure 9-G3)

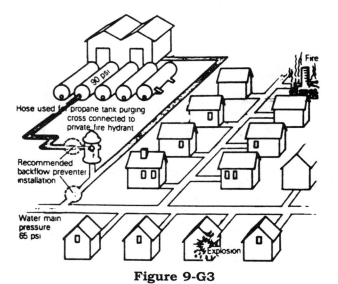

Fire

90 psi

Hose used for propane tank purging cross connected to private fire hydrant

Recommended backflow preventer installation

Water main pressure 65 psi

Explosion

Figure 9-G3

4. Boiler Water Enters High School Drinking Water

A high school was closed for several days in June 1984 when a home economics teacher noticed the water in the potable water system was yellow. City chemists determined that the samples taken contained levels of chromium as high as 700 parts per million, "astronomically higher than the accepted levels of 0.05 parts per million." The head chemist said that it was miraculous that no one was seriously injured or killed by the high levels of chromium. The chemical was identified as sodium dichromate, which is used in heating system boilers to inhibit corrosion of the metal parts.

No students or faculty were known to have consumed any water; however, area physicians and hospitals advised that if anyone had consumed those high levels of chromium, the symptoms would be nausea and burning of the mouth and throat. Fortunately, the home economics teacher, who saw the discolored water before school started, immediately covered all water fountains with towels so that no one would drink the water.

Investigation disclosed that chromium used in the heating system boilers to inhibit the corrosion of metal parts entered the potable water supply system as a result of backflow through leaking check valves on the boiler feed lines. (See Figure 9-G4)

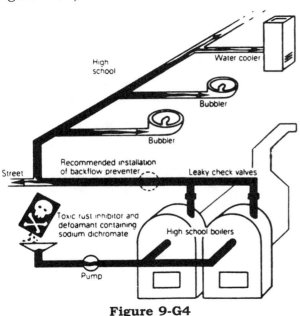

Figure 9-G4

5. Carwash Water in the Water Main

This carwash cross-connection and back-pressure incident, which occurred in February 1979, resulted in backflow chemical contamination of approximately 100 square blocks of water mains.

Because of prompt response by the water department a potentially hazardous water quality degradation problem was resolved without a recorded case of illness.

Numerous complaints of gray-green and "slippery" water were received by the water department from the same general area of town. A sample brought to the water department by a customer confirmed the reported problem and preliminary analysis indicated contamination

with what appeared to be a detergent solution. While emergency crews initiated flushing operations, further investigation within the contaminated area signaled that the problem was probably caused by a carwash or laundry, because of the soapy nature of the contaminant. The source was quickly narrowed down to a carwash and the proprietor was very cooperative, admitting to the problem and explaining how it had occurred. The circumstances leading up to the incident were as follows:

On Saturday, February 10, 1979, a high-pressure pump had broken down at the carwash. This pump recycled reclaimed wash and rinse water and pumped it to the initial scrubbers of the carwash. A potable water connection is not normally made to the carwash's scrubber system.

After the pump broke down, the carwash owner was able to continue operation by temporarily connecting a 2-in. hose section between the potable water supply within the carwash and the scrubber cycle piping.

On Monday, February 12, 1979, the owner repaired the high-pressure pump and resumed normal carwash operations. The 2-in. hose connection (cross-connection) was not removed!

Because of the cross-connection, the newly repaired high-pressure pump promptly pumped a large quantity of the reclaimed wash/rinse water out of the carwash and into a 12-in. water main in the street. This in turn was delivered to the many residences and commercial establishments connected to the water main.

Within 24 hours of the incident, the owner of the carwash had installed a 2-in. reduced-pressure principle backflow preventer on his water service and all carwash establishments in his town that used a wash water reclaim system were notified of the state requirement for backflow prevention. (See Figure 9-G5)

6. Shipyard Backflow Contamination

Water fountains at an East Coast shipyard were marked "No Drinking" as workers flushed the water lines to eliminate raw river water that had entered the shipyard following contamination from incorrectly connected water lines between ships at the pier and the shipyard. Some third shift employees drank the water before the pol-

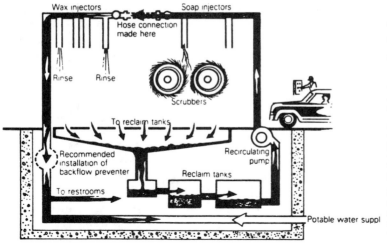

Figure 9-G5

lution was discovered and later complained of stomach cramps and diarrhea.

The cause of the problem was a direct cross-connection between the on-board salt water fire protection water system and the fresh water connected to one of the ships at the dock. While the shipyard had been aware of the need for backflow protection at the dockside tie-up area, the device had not been delivered and installed prior to the time of the incident. As a result, the salt water on-board fire protection system, being at a greater pressure than the potable water supply, forced the salt water, through back-pressure, into the shipyard's potable water supply system.

Fortunately, a small demand for potable water at the time of the incident prevented widespread pollution in the shipyard and the surrounding areas. (See Figure 9-G6)

7. Hexavalent Chromium in the Drinking Water

In July 1982, a well-meaning maintenance mechanic, attempting to correct a fogging lens in an overcooled laser machine, installed a tempering valve in the laser cooling line and inadvertently set the stage for a back-pressure backflow incident that resulted in hexavalent chromium contaminating the potable water of a large electronic manufacturing company employing 9000 people. Quantities of 50 parts per million hexavalent chromium were found in the drinking water, which is sufficient to cause severe vomiting, diarrhea, and intestinal sickness.

Maintenance crews working during the plant shutdown were able to eliminate the cross-connection and thoroughly flush the potable water system, thereby preventing a serious health hazard from occurring. The incident occurred as follows:

Laser machine lenses were kept cool by circulating chilled water that came from a large refrigeration chiller. The water used in the chiller was treated with hexavalent chromium,

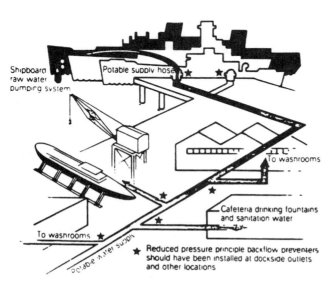

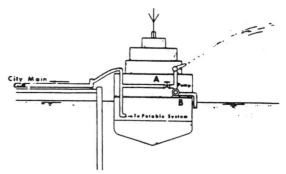

A. *Contact Point:* A valve connection exists between the potable and nonpotable systems aboard the ship.

B. *Cause of Reverse Flow:* While the ship is connected to the city water supply system for the purpose of taking on water for the potable system, the valve between the potable and nonpotable systems is opened, permitting contaminated water to be pumped into the municipal supply.

C. *Suggested Correction:* Each pier water outlet should be protected against backflow. The main water service to the pier should also be protected against backflow by an air gap or reduced-pressure principle backflow preventer.

Figure 9-G6

a chemical additive used as an anticorrosive agent and an algicide. As a result, the chilled water presented a toxic, nonpotable substance unfit for human consumption but very acceptable for industrial process water. No health hazard was present as long as the piping was identified, kept separate from potable drinking water lines and not cross-connected to the potable water supply.

A maintenance mechanic correctly reasoned that by adding a tempering valve to the chilled water line he could heat up the water and eliminate fogging of the laser lenses resulting from the chilled water being too cold. The problem with the installation of the tempering valve was that a direct cross-connection had been inadvertently made between the toxic chilled water and the potable drinking water system.

Periodic maintenance to the chiller was performed in the summer requiring that an alternate chiller feed pump be temporarily installed. This replacement pump had an outlet pressure of 150 psi and promptly established an imbalance of pressure at the tempering valve, thereby over pressurizing the 60 psi potable water supply. Back-pressure backflow resulted and pushed the toxic chilled water from the water heater and then into the plant potable drinking water supply system. Yellowish green water started pouring out of the drinking fountains, the washroom, and all the potable water outlets. (See Figure 9-G7)

8. Dialysis Machine Contamination

Ethylene glycol, an antifreeze additive to air-conditioning cooling tower water, inadvertently entered the potable water supply system in a medical center in September 1982, and two of six dialysis patients succumbed as a direct or indirect result of the contamination. The glycol was added to the air-conditioning water, and the glycol water mix was stored in a holding tank that was an integral part of the medical center's air-conditioning cooling system. Pressurized makeup water for the holding tank was supplied by a medical center potable water supply line and fed through a manually operated control valve. With this valve open, or partially open , potable makeup water flowed slowly into the glycol/water mixture in the holding tank until it filled to the point where the pressure in the closed tank equalled the pressure in the potable water supply feed line. As long as the potable feed line

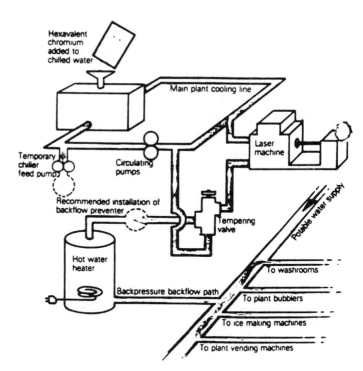

Figure 9-G7

pressure was equal to or greater than the holding tank pressure, no backflow could occur. However, the stage was set for disaster. It was theorized that someone in the medical center flushed a toilet or turned on a faucet, which in turn dropped the pressure in the potable water supply line to the air-conditioning holding tank. Since the manually operated fill valve was partially open, this allowed the glycol/water mixture to enter the medical center's potable water pipelines and flowed into the dialysis equipment. The dialysis filtration system takes out trace chemicals such as those used in the city water treatment plant, but the system could not handle the heavy load of chemicals that it was suddenly subjected to.

The effect upon the dialysis patients was dramatic: Patients became drowsy and confused and fell unconscious and were promptly removed to intensive care where blood samples were taken. The blood samples revealed a buildup of acid and the medical director stated that "something has happened in dialysis." Dialysis was repeated on the patients a second and third time.

Tests of the water supply to the filtration system quickly determined the presence of "an undesirable chemical in the water purification system." It was found that the partially open fill valve had permitted the glycol/ water mix to drain from the air-conditioning holding tank into the medical center's potable water supply lines and then into the dialysis filtration system equipment. (See Figure 9-G8)

These and other occurrences could have been and can be avoided by properly maintained equipment and the use of approved backflow prevention devices and vacuum breakers in all applications where cross-connections are prevalent.

GLOSSARY

Absolute pressure The sum of the indicated gauge pressure (psig) plus the atmospheric pressure. Hence, gauge pressure plus atmospheric pressure equals absolute pressure.

Air gap An air gap is a separation between the free flowing discharge end of a water pipe or faucet and the floor level rim of a plumbing fixture, tank, or any other device that it supplies. To be acceptable, the separation between the discharge end of the pipe and the upper rim of the receptacle it supplies must be at least twice the diameter of the pipe, and the separation must be a minimum of 1 in.

Atmospheric pressure At sea level this is equal to 14.7 psig.

Atmospheric vacuum breaker Should be used to protect against nontoxic back-siphonage only. This device contains a moving float check and internal air passage. Air is allowed to enter the passage when gauge pressure is zero or less. These devices should not be installed with shutoff valves downstream since this could subject the device to constant pressure, which could result in its failure.

Backflow The unwanted reversal of flow of water, or other liquids, gases, or substances into the safe or potable water supply. There are two types of backflow: back-siphonage and back-pressure.

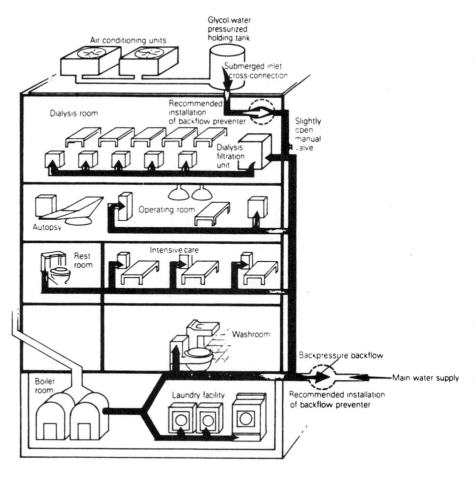

Figure 9-G8

Backflow preventer A device that complies with one or more recognized national standards, such as those of ASSE, AWWA, CSA or USC FCCC & HR, and with the requirements of the local regulatory agency. It is designed to prevent reversal of flow, or backflow.

The four types of mechanical backflow preventer are (1) the reduced-pressure principle device, (2) the double-check valve, (3) the pressure vacuum breaker, and (4) the atmospheric vacuum breaker.

The airgap is a nonmechanical backflow preventer.

Back-pressure backflow Backflow that occurs as a result of a pump or other pressure-producing piece of equipment creating pressures in the system that exceed the incoming water supply pressure. Back-pressure backflow also occurs when the incoming water supply pressure falls below the pressure in the system. Water always flows from a high-pressure zone to a zone of low pressure.

Back-siphonage backflow Backflow that occurs when the pressure in the incoming water supply piping falls to 0 psig or lower.

Containment A means of backflow prevention that requires the installation of a backflow preventer at the water meter or service entrance to the building. Before installation of a containment device, consideration should be given to the effect the backflow device will have on the hydraulics of the system. Prior to installation of such a device, a system survey is required.

Cross-connection A connection or potential connection that joins two separate piping systems, one containing safe or potable water, the other containing water or liquid of unknown purity or quality, steam, gas, chemicals, or substances other than safe, potable water.

Cross-connection control A two-point program consisting of both containment and point-of-use fixture isolation. The containment program requires an air gap or mechanical backflow prevention device to be installed at the point where water leaves the domestic water system or on the consumer side of the water meter.

An isolation program requires an ongoing survey to ensure there have been no alterations, changes, or additions to the system that may have created or re-created a hazardous condition. Fixture isolation is necessary to ensure that all those on the consumer's property are adequately protected.

Double-check valve assembly A device that consists of two independently acting spring-loaded check valves. They are typically supplied with test cocks and ball valves or gate valve shutoffs on the inlet and outlet side of the device to facilitate testing and maintenance. If special tools are required to maintain this device, it should be required that the tools be furnished with and permanently secured to the device (See "Special Tool.")

These devices protect against both types of potential backflow; however, they should be installed only for nontoxic applications. Consult local codes for specific application and installation requirements.

Fixture isolation Requires the elimination of cross-connection or installation of backflow prevention devices at the fixture or piece of equipment where a cross-connection exists or there is the potential one may be created. Such a program also requires periodic surveying to ensure that no cross-connections have been re-created or no new cross-connections have been created.

Flood level rim The point at which water overflows the rim of its receptacle or basin.

Flushometer valve A mechanism energized by water pressure that allows a measured flow of water for the purpose of flushing fixtures.

Free water surface When the pressure of a water surface is equal to the atmospheric pressure it is said to be a free water surface.

Indirect waste pipe A drainpipe that empties into the drainage system via an airbreak into a receptacle, interceptor, a venter trap or a properly vented and trapped fixture.

Joint responsibility The responsibility shared by the supplier or purveyor of water and the building owner for assuring and maintaining the safety of the consumer's drinking water. The supplier is responsible for protecting the safe drinking water supply from hazards that originate on the building owner's premises. It is the building owner's responsibility to ensure that his/her system complies with the plumbing code as a minimum standard and with existing reasonable industry standards when no code exists or is enforced. He/she is also responsible for the ongoing testing and maintenance of any backflow devices required to protect the water supply from any cross-connections found on his/her premises.

Negligent act An act that results from a failure to exercise reasonable care to prevent foreseeable backflow incidents from occurring or when correcting a potential problem another is created. For example, if a closed system is created by requiring a containment device without considering how such a device will alter the hydrodynamics within the system, and if this causes the rupture of a vessel such as a water heater, this could be considered negligent.

Plumbing The act or practice of installing, maintaining, or altering the pipes, valves, fittings, and fixtures that comprise the water supply, sanitary storm drainage, and venting of same in a building structure or piping system.

Plumbing code The legal minimum requirement for the safe installation, maintenance, and repair of plumbing systems, including the water system. When there is no applicable code, what is considered "good plumbing practice" should be applied by following reasonable industry standards.

Potable water The water that is furnished by the supplier of water with an implied warranty that it is pure and safe to drink. The public is allowed to make the assumption that it is safe to drink by the water supplier or regulatory agency having jurisdiction.

Pressure vacuum breaker A device that contains two independently operating valves, a spring-loaded check valve and a spring-loaded air inlet valve. The device has test cocks for in-line testing and two tightly sealing shutoff valves to facilitate maintenance and testing. It is used only to protect against back-siphonage.

Consult local codes for specific installation and applications.

Professional An individual who, because of his/her training and experience is held to a higher standard of care than the untrained individual or layman. The professional is exposed to liability for his/her action and/or inaction.

Reasonable care Working to standards that are known and accepted by the industry and applying those standards in practical ways to prevent injury or harm via predictable and foreseeable circumstances.

Reduced-pressure principle backflow preventer A device consisting of two separate and independently acting spring-loaded check valves, with a differential pressure-relief valve situated between the check valves. Since water always flows from a zone of high pressure to a zone of low pressure, this device is designed to maintain a higher pressure on the supply side of the backflow preventer than is found downstream of the first check valve. This ensures the prevention of backflow. An artificial zone of reduced pressure between the check valves is created by the tension on the first check valve spring. Pressure on the inlet side of the device is intended to remain a minimum of 2 psi higher than the pressure in the reduced-pressure zone.

Should the pressure in the zone rise to within 2 psi of the supply pressure, the relief valve will open to atmosphere to ensure that differential is maintained. These devices are designed to be in-line testable and maintainable. Many codes require that these devices be tested upon initial installation and semiannually or annually thereafter. They are typically supplied with test cocks and ball valves or gate valve shutoffs on the inlet and outlet side of the device to facilitate testing and maintenance. The device should be installed in a manner that allows testing and maintenance as required by the local code.

If special tools are required to service and maintain the device, the specification should require those tools to be furnished with and permanently secured to that device (see "Special Tool"). These devices provide effective protection against both types of backflow and from toxic and nontoxic substances. Consult local codes for specific application and installation requirements.

Special tool A tool peculiar to a specific device and necessary for the service and maintenance of that device. If such tools are required, the manufacturer must provide a warning in both the installation and the maintenance instructions and in the form of a warning label that must be permanently affixed to the assembly. The warning should alert the owner and his/her agent to the fact that special tools are required for the safe service and maintenance of this device. For your own safety and protection do not attempt to service this device without the required special tools.

Survey A premises inspection performed by a professional within the industry, such as an engineer or licensed plumbing contractor who has completed a survey course at a cross-connection survey school. The purpose of the inspection is to determine if a water system is in compliance with the plumbing code and other industry standards having to do with the protection of the safe drinking water supply.

Vacuum When atmospheric exceeds absolute pressure a vacuum is said to exist.

Vacuum breaker A device that prevents back-siphonage by allowing air to enter the water system. There are two types of vacuum breaker, the atmospheric and pressure types.

Water supply system All necessary service and distributing pipes, valves, and/or fittings needed to supply water in or next to the building served or its premises.

BIBLIOGRAPHY

1. *The Safe Drinking Water Act of 1974.*

2. US Environmental Protection Agency. n.d. *Cross-connection manual.* Washington, DC.

RESOURCES

1. American Society of Sanitary Engineering (ASSE).

2. American Water Works Association (AWWA).

3. National Sanitation Foundation International (NSF), 3475 Plymouth Road, Ann Arbor, MI 48105.

4. University of Southern California (USC) Foundations for Cross-connection Control and Hydraulic Research.

5. Washington Suburban Sanitary Commission (WSSC), Laurel, MD 20707.

10 Water Treatment

Surface water may contain disease-producing organisms, atmospheric gases, suspended matter, or organic substances. Groundwater, while less likely to contain pathogenic organisms, may contain dissolved minerals and have undesirable tastes and odors. Water provided by public and private utilities is regarded to be potable—adequately pure for human consumption according to the standards of the local health official. However, it may not be pure enough for certain industrial, medical, or scientific purposes. This chapter reviews the principles of basic water treatment, provides information on additional treatment (including a section on the selection and sizing of water softeners), and finally gives an overview of specialized treatment techniques.

CHEMICAL NAMES AND FORMULAE

The common chemical compounds used in connection with water softeners are tabulated in Table 10-1.

NEED AND PURPOSE FOR WATER TREATMENT

Damage by Untreated Water

Impure water damages the piping and equipment by scoring, scaling, and corroding. Water containing particles in suspension will, under certain conditions, erode the piping and score moving parts. Water containing dissolved acidic chemicals in sufficient quantities dissolves the metal surfaces it comes in contact with. Pitted pipe and tank walls are common manifestations of the phenomenon called "corrosion."

Scaling occurs when calcium or magnesium compounds in the water (in a condition commonly known as "water hardness") become separated from the water and adhere to the piping and equipment surfaces. This separation is usually induced by a rise in temperature (as these minerals become less soluble as the temperature increases). In addition to restricting flow, scaling causes damage to heat-transfer surfaces by decreasing the heat-exchange capabilities. The result of this condition is the overheating of tubes, followed by failures and equipment damage. Table 10-2 can be used to identify solutions to listed impurities and constituents found in water.

External and Internal Treatment

Changing the chemical composition of the water by means of mechanical devices (filters, softeners, demineralizers, deionizers, and reverse osmosis) is called "external treatment" because such treatment is outside the equipment into which the water flows. Neutralizing the objectionable constituents by adding chemicals to the water as it enters the equipment is referred to as "internal treatment." Economic considerations usually govern the choice between the two methods.

BASIC WATER TYPES

Following are the basic types of water:

1. *Raw water* is received from a well, municipal supply, etc.
2. *Tower water* is monitored and controlled for pH, algae, and total dissolved solids.

Table 10-1 Chemical Names, Common Names and Formulas

Chemical Name	Common Name	Formula
Bicarbonate (ion)	—	HCO_3^-
Calcium (metal)	—	Ca^{2+}
Calcium bicarbonate	—	$Ca(HCO_3)_2$
Calcium carbonate	Chalk, limestone, marble	$CaCO_3$
Calcium hypochlorite	Bleaching powder, chloride of lime	$Ca(ClO)_2$
Chlorine (gas)	—	Cl_2
Calcium sulfate	—	$CaSO_4$
Calcium sulfate	Plaster of paris	$CaSO_4 \cdot \frac{1}{2}H_2O$
Calcium sulfate	Gypsum	$CaSO_4 \cdot 2H_2O$
Carbon	Graphite	C
Carbonate (ion)	—	CO_3^{2-}
Carbon dioxide	—	CO_2
Ferric oxide	Burat ochre	Fe_2O_3
Ferruous carbonate	—	$FeCO_3$
Ferrous oxide	—	FeO
Hydrochloric acid	Muriatic acid	HCl
Hydrogen (ion)	—	H^+
Hydrogen (gas)	—	H_2
Hydrogen sulfide	—	H_2S
Iron (ferric ion)	—	Fe^{3+}
Iron (ferrous ion)	—	Fe^{2+}
Magnesium bicarbonate	—	$Mg(HCO_3)_2$
Magnesium carbonate	Magnesite	$MgCO_3$
Magnesium oxide	Magnesia	MgO
Magnesium sulfate	—	$MgSO_4$
Magnesium sulfate	Epsom salt	$MgSO_4 \cdot 7H_2O$
Manganese (metal)	—	Mn
Methane	Marsh gas	CH_4
Nitrogen (gas)	—	N_2
Oxygen (gas)	—	O_2
Potassium (metal)	—	K
Potassium permanganate	Permanganate of potash	$KMnO_4$
Sodium (metal)	—	Na
Sodium bicarbonate	Baking soda, bicarbonate of soda	$NaHCO_3$
Sodium carbonate	Soda ash	Na_2CO_3
Sodium carbonate	Sal soda	$Na_2CO_3 \cdot 10H_2O$
Sodium chloride	Salt	NaCl
Sodium hydroxide	Caustic soda, lye	NaOH
Sodium sulfate	Glauber's salt	$Na_2SO_4 \cdot 10H_2O$
Sulfate (ion)	—	SO_4^{2-}
Sulfuric acid	Oil of vitrol	H_2SO_4
Water	—	H_2O

Table 10-2 Water Treatment—Impurities and Constituents, Possible Effects and Suggested Treatments

Constituents	Possible Effects[a]							Treatment							
	Scale	Corrosion	Sludge	Foamin	Priming	Embrittlement	None (Inert)	Setting, coagulation, filtration, evaporation	Setting, coagulation, filtration, evaporation, ion exchange	Softening by chemicals, ion exchange materials, evaporators	Softening by heaters, chemicals, ion exchange materials, evaporators	Neutralizing, followed by softening or evaporation	Evaporation and demineralization by ion-exchange material	De-aeration	Coagulation, filtration, evaporation
Suspended solids	X		X	X	X			X							
Silica — SiO_2	X								X						
Calcium carbonate — $CaCO_3$	X									X					
Calcium bicarbonate — $Ca(HCO_3)_2$	X										X				
Calcium Sulfate — $CaSO_4$	X	X								X					
Calcium chloride — $CaCl_2$	X									X					
Magnesium carbonate — $MgCO_3$	X									X					
Magnesium bicarbonate — $Mg(HCO_3)_2$	X									X					
Magnesium chloride — $MgCl_2$	X	X								X					
Free acids — HCl, H_2SO_4		X										X			
Sodium chloride — $NaCl$							X						X		
Sodium carbonate — Na_2CO_3				X	X	X							X		
Sodium bicarbonate — $NaHCO_3$				X	X	X							X		
Carbonic acid — H_2CO_3		X												X	
Oxygen — O_2		X												X	
Grease and oil		X	X	X	X										X
Organic matter and sewage		X	X	X	X										X

[a] The possibility of the effects will increase proportionately to an increase in the water temperature.

3. *Potable water* is filtered, chlorinated, and/or otherwise treated to meet the local health department's standards for drinking water.

4. *Soft water* meets additional requirements of hardness.

5. *Deionized water* is specified in ranges of conductivity.

6. *Purified water* meets the requirements of local health officials.

7. *Distilled water* meets the requirements of local health officials on water for injection.

"Pure water" is a relative term used to describe water mostly free from particulate matter and dissolved gases that may exist in the potable water supply. Pure water is generally required in pharmacies, central supply rooms, laboratories, and laboratory glassware-washing facilities.

There are two basic types of pure water:

1. *Biopure water*, which is free from particulate matter, minerals, bacteria, pyrogens, organic matter and most dissolved gases

2. *High-purity water,* which is free from minerals, dissolved gases, and most particulate matter.

Water purity is most easily measured as specific resistance, in ohm-centimeters (Ω-cm), or expressed as parts per million (ppm) of ionized salt (NaCl). The theoretical maximum specific resistance of pure water is 18.3 megaohm-centimeters ($M\Omega$-cm) at 25°C, a purity that is nearly impossible to produce, store, and distribute. It is important to note that the specific resistance of water is indicative only of the mineral content and in no way indicates the level of bacterial, pyrogenic, or organic contamination.

Methods of Producing High-Grade Water

The four basic methods of producing high-grade or pure water are distillation, demineralization, reverse osmosis, and filtration. Depending upon the type of pure water required, one or more of the methods described below will be needed. Under certain conditions, a combination of methods may be required. These processes are explained in detail later in the chapter.

Distillation produces biopure water that is free from particulate matter, minerals, organics, bacteria, pyrogens, and most of the dissolved gases and has a minimum specific resistance of 300,000 Ω-cm. The important consideration here is that it is free from bacteria and pyrogen contaminations that are dangerous for the patient, particularly where intravenous solutions are concerned. Biopure water is needed in the pharmacy, central supply room, and any other area where there may be patient contact. Biopure water may also be desired in specific laboratories at the owner's request and as a final rinse in a laboratory glassware washer.

The typical water distillation system consists of an evaporator section, an internal baffle system, a water-cooled condenser, and a storage tank. The best material of construction is a pure block tin coating for both the still and the tank. The heat sources, in order of preference based on economy and maintenance, are steam, electricity, and gas. Gas is a very poor choice. The still may be operated manually or automatically. The distilled water may be distributed from the tank by gravity or by a pump. A drain is required. On stills larger than 50 gph, a cooling tower should be considered for the condenser water.

Demineralization, sometimes called "deionization," produces high-purity water that is free from minerals, most particulate matter, and dissolved gases. Depending upon the equipment, it can have a specific resistance of 50,000 Ω to nearly 18 MΩ. However, it can be contaminated with bacteria, pyrogens, and organics, as these can be produced inside the demineralizer itself. Demineralized water can be used in most laboratories, in the laboratory glassware washing facilities as a final rinse, and as pretreatment for still feed water.

The typical demineralizer apparatus consists of either a two-bed unit with a resistivity range of 50,000 Ω to 1 MΩ or a mixed-bed unit with a resistivity range of 1 MΩ to nearly 18 MΩ. The columns are of an inert material filled with a synthetic resin that removes the minerals by an ionization process. Since the unit runs on pressure, a storage tank is not required, nor is it recommended as bacteria may grow in it. A demineralizer must be chemically regenerated periodically, during which time no pure water is being produced. If a continuous supply of water is needed, a backup unit should be considered, as the process takes several hours. The regeneration can be done manually or automatically. An atmospheric, chemical-resistant drain is needed. Note that higher-pressure water is required for backwash during regeneration.

Service deionized water (SDI) If deionized water is required in a small amount and the facility does not want to handle the regenerant chemicals and/or the regenerant waste water, it may contract with a deionized water service provider to supply the facility with the quality and quantity of deionized water required. The SDI provider will provide the facility with service deionized water exchange tanks to furnish the quality, flow rate, and quantity of water required. When the tanks are exhausted, the SDI provider will furnish a new set of tanks. The SDI provider takes the exhausted tanks back to its facility for regeneration.

Reverse osmosis (RO) produces a high-purity water that does not have the high resistivity of demineralized water and is not biopure. Under certain conditions, it can offer economic advantages over demineralized water. In areas that have high mineral content, it can be used as a pretreatment for a demineralizer or still when large quantities of water are needed. Reverse osmosis is used primarily in industrial applications and in some hospitals and laboratories for specific tasks.

There are several types of reverse osmosis units available. Basically, they consist of a semipermeable membrane in either a roll form or a tube containing numerous hollow fibers. Water is forced through the semipermeable membrane under high pressure. A drain is required. A storage tank is also required with this system.

Filtration Various types of filter are available to remove the particulate matter from water as a pretreatment. The types of filter can range from a backwashable filter to filter cartridge housing. Depending upon the type of filter, a drain may be required.

Nanofiltration is a membrane system similar to reverse osmosis but with a looser membrane that will reject most polyvalent ions while allowing the monovalent ions of sodium and chloride to pass through. It is also called a "softening membrane."

Ultrafiltration is a membrane system that is still looser and is generally used to separate oil and water.

WATER CONDITIONS AND RECOMMENDED TREATMENTS

Turbidity

Turbidity is caused by suspended insoluble matter, including coarse particles that settle rapidly in standing water. Amounts range from almost zero in most groundwater and some surface supplies to 60,000 ppm in muddy, turbulent river water. Turbidity is objectionable for practically all water uses. The standard maximum for drinking water is 1–5 turbidity units (TU) (accepted by industry).

Generally, if turbidity can be seen easily, it will clog the pipes, damage the valves seats, and cloud the drinking water. For nonprocess water, if turbidity cannot be seen, it will present few or no problems.

Turbidity that is caused by suspended solids in the water may be removed from such water by coagulation, sedimentation, and/or filtration.

In extreme cases, where a filter requires frequent cleaning due to excessive turbidity, it is recommended that engineers use coagulation and sedimentation upstream of the filter. Such a device can take the form of a basin through which the water can flow at low velocities to let the turbidity causing particles settle naturally.

For applications where the water demand is high and the space limited, a mechanical device such as a clarifier utilizing chemical coagulant may possibly be more practical. This device mixes the water with a coagulant (such as ferric sulphate) and slowly stirs the mixture in a large circular container. The coarse particles will drop to the bottom and be collected in a sludge pit, while the finer particles will coagulate and also drop to the bottom of the container. The clarified water then leaves the device ready for use or further treatment.

Hardness

The hardness of water is due mainly to the presence of calcium and magnesium cations. These salts, in order of their relative average abundance in water, are bicarbonates, sulfates, chlorides, and nitrates. They all produce scale.

Calcium salts are about twice as soluble as magnesium salts in natural water supplies. The presence of bicarbonates of calcium and magnesium produces a condition in the water called "temporary hardness" because these salts can be easily transformed into a calcium or magnesium precipitate plus carbon dioxide gas.

The noncarbonic salts (sulfates, chlorides, and nitrates) constitute "permanent hardness" conditions.

Hardness is most commonly treated by the sodium-cycle ion exchange process, which exchanges the calcium and magnesium salts responsible for the hardness of the water for the very soluble sodium salts. Only calcium and magnesium (hardness ions) in the water are affected by the softening process. This process produces water that is nonscale forming. If the oxygen or carbon dioxide contents of the water are relatively high, the water may be considered aggressive.

The carbonic acid may be removed by aeration or degassification and the remaining acids may be removed by neutralization. Neutralization by blending hydrogen and sodium cation exchanger water is one of the methods for obtaining water with the desired alkalinity level.

Another method of neutralizing the acid in water is by adding alkali. The advantage of the alkali neutralization method is that the cost of the sodium cation exchange softener is eliminated. However, the engineer may want to weigh the cost of chemicals against the cost of the sodium ion exchange unit.

Aeration and Deaeration

As hardness in the water is objectionable because it forms scale, high oxygen and carbon dioxide contents are also objectionable because they corrode iron, zinc, brass, and several other metals.

Free carbon dioxide (CO_2) can be found in most natural water supplies. Surface waters have the lowest concentration, although some rivers may contain as much as 50 ppm. In groundwater, the CO_2 content varies from almost zero to concentrations so high that the carbon dioxide bubbles out when the pressure is released.

Carbon dioxide will also form when the bicarbonates are destroyed by acids, coagulants, or high temperatures. The presence of CO_2 will accelerate oxygen corrosion.

Carbon dioxide can be removed from the water by an aeration process. Aeration is simply a mechanical process for mixing the air and the water intimately. It can be done with spray nozzles, cascade aerators, pressure aerators, or forced draft units.

With this aeration process complete, there is water that is relatively free of CO_2 gas. But there is also water with a high oxygen content that is extremely corrosive at *elevated* temperatures.

Oxygen can be removed from the water by a deaeration process. Oxygen becomes less and less soluble as the water temperature increases; thus, it is easily removed from the water by bringing the water to its boiling point.

There are pressure and vacuum deaerators available. When it is necessary to heat the water, as in boilers, steam deaerators are used. Where the water will be used for cooling or other purposes where heating is not desired, vacuum units may be employed.

With aerators and deaerators in tandem, water free of CO_2 and O_2 is produced.

Minerals

Pure water is never found in nature. Natural water contains a series of dissolved inorganic solids, which are largely mineral salts. These mineral salts are introduced into the natural water by a solvent action as the water passes through (or across) the various layers of the earth. The types of mineral salt absorbed by the natural water depends upon the chemical content of the soil through which the natural water passes before it reaches the consumer; this may vary from area to area. Well water differs from river water and river water differs from lake water. Two consumers separated by a few miles may have water supplies of very dissimilar characteristics. Even the concentration and types of minerals may vary with the changing seasons in the same water supply.

Many industries can benefit greatly by being supplied with high-grade pure water. These industries are finding that they must treat their natural water supplies in various ways to achieve this condition. The recommended type of water treatment depends upon the chemical content of the water supply and the requirements of the particular industry. High-grade pure water results in greater economy of production and better products.

Before the advent of the demineralization process, the only method used to remove the mineral salts from natural water was a distillation process. Demineralization has a practical advantage over distillation: The distillation process involves removing the natural water from the mineral salts (or the larger mass from the smaller mass). Demineralization processes are the reverse of the distillation process as they remove the mineral salts from the natural water. This renders demineralization the more economical method of purifying natural water in most cases. Many industries today are turning to demineralization as the answer to their water problems.

The stringent quality standards for makeup for modern boilers are making demineralizers and reverse osmosis a must for these users. Modern plating practices also require the high quality that demineralization produces.

ION EXCHANGE—THEORY AND PRACTICE

According to chemical theory, compounds such as mineral salts, acid, and bases break up into ions when they are dissolved in water. Ions are simply atoms, singly or in groups, that carry an electric charge. They are of two types: the "cation" (which is positively charged) and the "anion" (which is negatively charged). For example, when dissolved in water, sodium chloride ($NaCl$) splits into the cation Na^+ and the anion Cl^-. Similarly, calcium sulfate ($CaSO_4$) in solution is present as the cation Ca^{2+} and the anion SO_4^{2-}. All the mineral salts in water are in their ionic form.

Synthetic thermal-setting plastic materials, known as "ion exchange resins," have been developed to remove these objectionable ions from the solution and to produce water of very high purity. These resins are small beads (or granules) usually of phenolic, or polystyrene, plastics. They are insoluble in water and their basic nature is not changed by the process of ion exchange. These beads (or granules) are very porous and they have readily available ion exchange groups on all their internal and external surfaces. The electrochemical action of these ion exchange groups draws one type of ion out of the solution and puts a different one in its place. These resins are of three types: (1) the cation exchanger (which exchanges one positive ion for another), (2) the anion exchanger (which exchanges one negative ion for another), and (3) the acid absorber (which absorbs complete acid groups on its surface).

A demineralizer consists of the required number of cation tanks and anion tanks (or, in the case of monobeds, combined tanks) with all the necessary valves, pipes, and fittings required to perform the steps of the demineralization process for the cation resin; an acid dilution tank material for the cation resin; and an acid dilution tank, as the sulfuric acid is too concentrated to be used directly. If hydrochloric acid is to be used as a cation regenerant, this mix tank is unnecessary since the acid is drawn in directly from the storage vessel. A mixing tank for soda ash or caustic soda, used in the anion regeneration, is always provided.

Since calcium and magnesium in the raw regenerant water will precipitate the hydroxide (or carbonate) salts in the anion bed, the anion resin must be regenerated with hardness-free water. This condition may be accomplished either with a water softener (which may be provided for this purpose) or by use of the effluent water from the cation unit to regenerate the anion resin. The use of a softener cuts down the regeneration time considerably, as both units may be regenerated simultaneously rather than separately.

Provided with each unit is a straight reading volume meter, which indicates gallons per run as well as the total volume put through the unit. Also provided with each unit is a conductivity/resistivity indicator used to check the purity of the effluent water at all times. This instrument is essentially a meter for measuring the electrical resistance of the treated water leaving the unit. It consists of two principal parts: the conductivity cell (which is situated in the effluent line) and the instrument box (to which the conductivity cell is connected).

The conductivity cell contains two electrodes, across which an electric potential is applied.

When these poles are immersed in the treated water, the resistance to the flow of the electricity between the two poles (which depends on the dissolved solids content of the water) is measured by a circuit in the instrument. The purity of the water may be checked by reading the meter. When the purity of the water is within the specific limits, the green light will glow. When the water becomes too impure to use, the red light will glow. In addition to this, a bell may be added which will ring when the red light glows to provide an audible as well as a visible report that the unit needs regeneration. This contact can also close an effluent valve, shift operation to another unit if desired, or put the unit into regeneration.

Controls

Several types of control are currently available to carry out the various steps of regeneration and return to service. Common arrangements are

- Type A—Completely automatic, conductivity meter initiation of regeneration, individual air- or hydraulic-operated diaphragm valves controlled by a sequence timer. Any degree of automation can be provided, if desired.

  This arrangement provides maximum flexibility in varying amounts and concentrations of regenerants, length of rinsing, and all other steps of the operating procedure. The diaphragm valves used are tight seating, giving maximum protection against leakage and thus contamination with a minimum of maintenance.

- Type B—Manually operated individual valves. This system combines maximum flexibility and minimum maintenance with an economical first cost. It is used on larger installations.

Internal Arrangements

The internal arrangements of the vessels are similar for all types of control. The internal arrangement used on medium to large units is shown in Figure 10-1. Smaller units have simpler arrangements since the distribution problems are simpler. The positive and thorough distribution of regenerants, rinse, and wash waters to achieve maximum efficiency is one of the secrets of the superior economy and reliability.

Ion Exchange Water Softeners

A typical hydrogen-sodium ion exchange plant is shown in Figure 10-2. This process combines sodium-cycle ion exchange softening with hydrogen-cycle cation exchange.

The sodium ion exchange process is exactly the same as a standard ion exchange water soft-

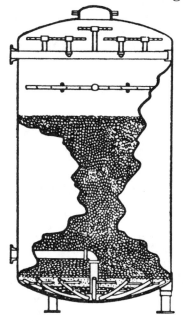

Figure 10-1 Ion Exchange Vessel—Internal Arrangements

ener. The hardness (calcium and magnesium) is replaced with sodium (nonscaling). The alkalinity (bicarbonates) and other anions remain as high as in the raw water.

The cation exchanger is exactly the same as the ones used with demineralizers and its effluent therefore contains carbon dioxide, sulfuric acid, and hydrochloric acid. The sodium ion exchange units are operated in parallel and their effluents are combined. The mineral acids in the hydrogen ion exchange effluent neutralize the bicarbonates in the sodium ion exchange effluent. The proportions of the two processes are varied to produce a blended effluent having the desired alkalinity. The carbon dioxide is removed by a degasifier. The effluent of this plant is soft and reduced in solids and has an alkalinity as low as is desired.

In a sodium ion exchange softener plus acid addition (Figure 10-3), the acid directly neutralizes the bicarbonate alkalinity to produce a soft, low-alkalinity water. The carbon dioxide produced is removed by a degasifier. The chief disadvantages of this process are that the total dissolved solids are not reduced and control of the process is somewhat more difficult.

In a sodium ion exchange softener plus chloride dealkalizer process, water passes first through the sodium ion exchange softener, which removes the hardness, and then through a chloride dealkalizer. The chloride dealkalizer is an ion exchanger that operates in the chloride cycle. The bicarbonates and sulfates are replaced by chlorides. The resin is regenerated with sodium chloride (common salt). The equipment is the same as that for sodium ion softeners. This process produces soft, low-alkalinity water. Total dissolved solids are not reduced, but the chloride level is increased. The chief advantages of this process are the elimination of acid and the extreme simplicity of the operation. No blending or proportioning is required.

In some cases, the anion resin can be regenerated with salt and caustic soda to improve capacity and reduce leakage of alkalinity and carbon dioxide.

BASIC WATER TREATMENT

The water provided by the municipalities is usually low enough in turbidity and organic constituents to preclude the use of filters, clarifiers, or chlorinators. As always, however, there are exceptions to the rule. When dealing with health and safety or with the operating efficiency of machinery, the occasional exception must always be considered by the engineers.

Chlorination

Chlorination of the water is most commonly used to destroy the organic (living) impurities therein. Organic impurities fall into two categories: *pathogenic* (which cause disease, such as typhoid and cholera) and *nonpathogenic* (which cause algae and slime that clog pipes and valves, discolor water, and produce undesirable odors).

These pathogenic and nonpathogenic organisms can be safely controlled by chlorine with scientifically engineered equipment to ensure

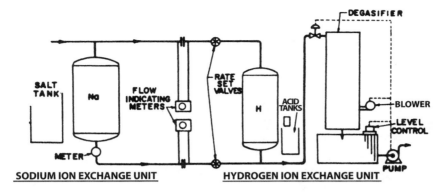

Figure 10-2 Hydrogen-Sodium Ion Exchange Plant

constant and reliable applications. An intelligent choice of the treatment necessary cannot be made until a laboratory analysis of the water has determined its quality and the quantities of water to be used are known. If there are microorganisms in objectionable amounts, a chlorination system is required.

When chlorine is added to the water, *hypochlorous* and *hydrochloric* acids are formed. Hydrochloric acid is neutralized by carbonates, which are naturally present in the water. It is the hypochlorous acid that provides the disinfecting properties of chlorine solutions. Part of the hypochlorous acid is used quickly to kill (by the oxidation process) the bacteria in the water. The remaining acid keeps the water bacteria free until it reaches the point of ultimate use.

This residual hypochlorous acid can take two forms. It may combine with the ammonia present in almost all waters. This *combined residual*, or *chloramine*, takes a relatively long time to kill the bacteria, but it is very stable. Thus, when a water system is large, it is desirable to keep a combined residual in the system to ensure safety from the treatment point to the farthest supply point.

If enough chlorine is added to the system, there will be more hypochlorous acid than can combine with the ammonia present in the water. The excess hypochlorous acid is called *free residual.* It is quite unstable, but it kills the organic matter very quickly. So, though the time it takes for this water to pass from the treatment plant to the point of ultimate use is short, only free residual can ensure that all bacteria will be killed. Maintaining an adequate free residual in the water is the only way to ensure that the water is safe. Its presence proves that enough chlorine was originally added to disinfect the water. If there is no residual, chances are that not all the bacteria in the water were killed; therefore, more chlorine must be added.

Chlorine gas or hypochlorite solutions can be readily and accurately added to the water at a constant rate or by proportional feeding devices offered by a number of suppliers.

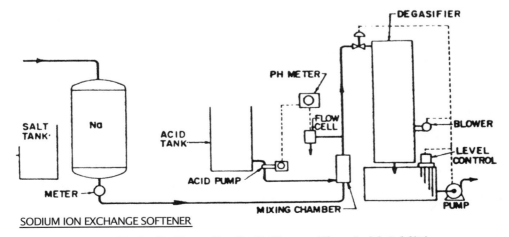

Figure 10-3 Sodium Cycle Softener Plus Acid Addition

Large municipal or industrial plants use chlorine gas because it is less expensive (hypochlorite solutions can be three to five times as expensive as chlorine gas) and convenient. Chlorinators, such as the one shown in Figure 10-4, inject chlorine gas into the water system in quantities proportional to the water flow.

For the treatment of small water supplies, hypochlorite solutions are sometimes found to be more advantageous. In feeding hypochlorite solutions, small proportioning chemical pumps, such as the one illustrated in Figure 10-5, may be used for injecting the hypochlorite soution directly into the pipelines or the reservoir tanks.

Clarification

Turbid water has insoluble matter suspended in it. The more turbidity in the water, the more clouded the water looks, the less potable it is, and the more likely it is to clog the pipes and valves.

Particles that are heavier than the fluid in which they are suspended will tend to settle, due to gravity, according to Stoke's law:

Equation 10-1

$$v = \frac{kd^2 (S_1 - S_2)}{z}$$

where

v = Settling velocity of the particle

k = Constant (usually 18.5)

d = Diameter of the particle

S_1 = Density of the particle

S_2 = Density of the fluid

z = Viscosity of the fluid

From Equation 10-1, it can readily be seen that the settling velocity of the particle decreases as the density (S_2) and the viscosity (z) of the fluid increase. Because the density and the viscosity of the water are functions of its temperature, it is readily understood why, for example, the rate of the particle settling in the water at a temperature of 32°F is only 43% of its settling rate at 86°F. Therefore, the removal of water turbidity by subsidence is most efficient in the summer months.

Where the water turbidity is high, filtration alone may be impractical due to the excessive requirements for backwash and media replacement. Subsidence is an acceptable method for the clarification of water that permits the settling of suspended matter.

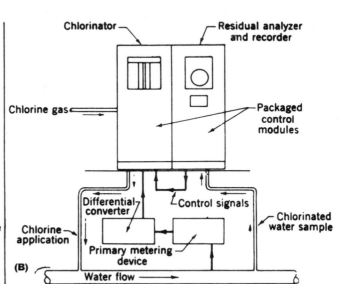

Notes: The system illustrated in (A) maintains a given residual where the flow is constant or where it changes only gradually. The direct residual control is most effective on recirculated systems, such as condenser cooling water circuits and swimming pools. The desired residual is manually set at the analyzer. The flow is chlorinated until the residual reaches a set upper limit. The analyzer starts the chlorinator and keeps it operating until the residual again reaches the established upper limit. In (B) the compound loop controls the chlorinator output in accordance with two variables, the flow and the chlorine requirements. Two signals (one from the residual analyzer and another from the flow meter), when simultaneously applied to the chlorinator, will maintain a desired residual regardless of the changes in the flow rates or the chlorine requirements.

Figure 10-4 Automatic Chlorinators

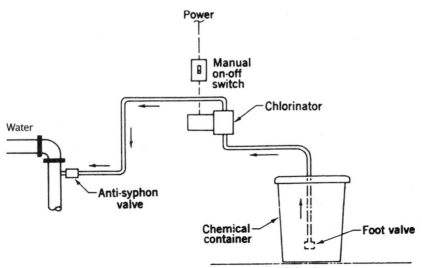

Figure 10-5 Manual Control Chlorinator

Although water flow in a horizontal plane will not seriously affect the particle settling velocity, an upward flow in a vertical plane prevents particle settling. The design of subsidence basins should, therefore, keep such interferences to a minimum. For practical purposes, the limit for removal of solids by subsidence is particles of 0.01 mm or larger diameter. Small particles have such a low rate of settling that the time required is greater than can be allowed. Figure 10-6 shows a typical design of a settling basin. Obviously, when large volumes of water are to be handled, the settling basins occupy a large amount of space. Also, they can present safety and vandalism problems if not properly protected.

Where space is limited, a more practical approach might be the use of a mechanical clarifier that employs chemical coagulants (see Figure 10-7). Such devices can be purchased as package units with simple in-and-out connections. There are currently many chemical coagulants available from which the designer can choose, including aluminum sulphate, sodium aluminate, ammonium alum, ferric sulfate, and ferric chloride. Each coagulant works better than the others in certain types of waters.

There are no simple rules to guide the engineer in the choice of the proper coagulant, the coagulant dosages or the coagulant aids. The water analysis, the temperature of the water, the type of clarification equipment, the load conditions, and the end use of the treated water are some of the factors that influence selection of the proper coagulant and that, therefore, must be considered by the engineer when selecting the coagulant. A few tests con-

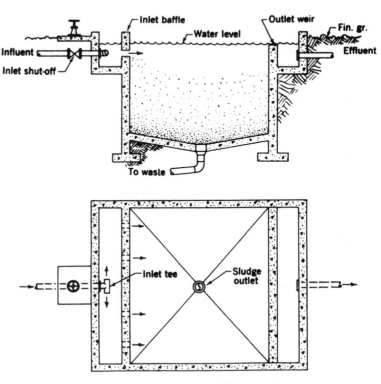

Figure 10-6 Settling Basin

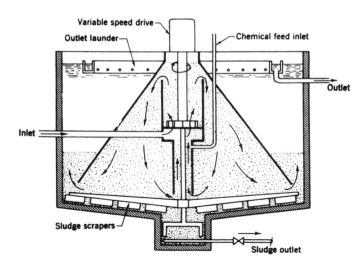

Notes: The turbid water enters the central uptake mixed with the coagulant and is forced toward the bottom of the unit. Some water and the suspended precipitates enter the lower end of the uptake for recirculation and contact with the incoming chemicals and the water. New coagulation is encouraged by contact with these previously formed precipitates. The water then enters the outer settling section. The clarified water rises to the outlet flume above. The heavier particles settle and are moved along the bottom to the sludge pit.

Figure 10-7 Mechanical Clarifier

ducted under actual operating conditions can assist the designer in achieving the best results.

Water leaves the settling basin on the mechanical clarifier at atmospheric pressure. Thus, the designer should bear in mind that the outputs must be pumped into the water distribution system.

Filtration

Filtration is the process of passing a fluid through a porous medium to remove the suspended solids *mechanically*. Where a clarifier of the type described above precedes the filters, the heavier, coagulated particles are removed from the water, and only the smaller, lighter particles reach the filter *bed.*

As the suspended particles lodge between the grains of the filter medium, flow is restricted. The coagulated particles build up on the surface of the filter bed. Penetration of the filter medium by the coagulated particles is achieved at the surface in the first device or 2 in. of the bed. This coagulated mat then acts as a fine filter for smaller particles.

The filter medium should be selected to provide a top layer coarse enough to allow some penetration of the top few inches of the bed by the coagulated material. Where a clarifier employing a chemical coagulant is placed ahead of the filters, a separate coagulant feed should be used to form a mat on the filter bed surface. Alum is commonly used for this purpose at a rate of about 1/10 lb for each square foot of filter bed surface. This coagulant mat should be replaced after each backwash.

The filters are of either the gravity or the pressure type.

Gravity filters As their name implies, the flow of water through gravity filters is achieved by gravity only.

The filter vessel may be rectangular or circular in configuration and made of steel or concrete. The filter most commonly used is the rectangular concrete unit illustrated in Figure 10-8. This unit has a very basic design. In its more sophisticated form, the gravity filter has storage wells for the clarified water, wash troughs for even collection of the backwash, and compressed air systems for agitation of the sand during backwash.

The advantages of the gravity filter over the pressure filter are that the filter sand can be easily inspected and the application of a coagulant is usually more easily controlled. The disadvantages are the initial pressure loss, requiring repumping of the water to pressurize the distribution system; the additional space re-

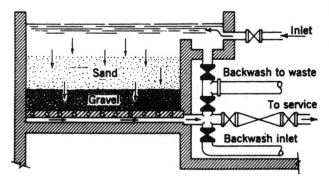

**Figure 10-8 Gravity Sand Filter
(Rectangular shaped, material)**

quired for installation; and the possibility of outside bacterial contamination.

Pressure filters Pressure filters are more widely favored in industrial and commercial water conditioning applications. These units have an advantage in that they may be placed in the line under pressure, eliminating the need to repump the water.

The design of the pressure filter is similar to that of a gravity filter with respect to the filter medium, the gravel bed, the underdrain system, and the control devices. The filter vessel is usually a cylindrical steel tank.

Vertical pressure sand filters, such as the one shown in Figure 10-9 range in diameter from 1 to 10 ft with capacities from 210 to 235 gpm at an average filter rate of 3 gpm/ft^2.

Multimedia depth filters are replacing single-media pressures filters. The depth filter has four layers of filtration media, each of a different size and density. The media become finer and denser in the lower layers. Particles are trapped throughout the bed, not in just the top few inches. That

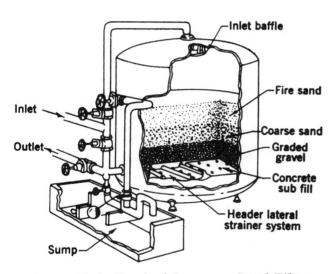

Figure 10-9 Vertical Pressure Sand Filter

allows a depth filter to run longer and use less backwash water.

Horizontal pressure sand filters, usually about 8 ft in diameter and 18–30 ft in length, have a water flow rate range of 218–570 gpm. The industry trend in recent years has been back to the horizontal pressure sand filters, which provide the advantages of a vertical filter with frequently a lower installed cost. When the filter tank is used in its horizontal position, a larger bed area can be obtained, thus increasing the flow rate available from a given tank size.

As with any mechanical device, proper operation and maintenance is the key to continued high operating efficiency.

Chemical pretreatment is often used to enhance filter performance, particularly when the turbidity includes fine colloidal particles.

Normal water flow rates for most gravity and pressure filters are 3 gpm/ft^2 of filter area. Recent design improvements in coagulation have enabled flow rates as high as 5–6 gpm for gravity filters.

High-rate pressure filters, with filtration rates of 20 gpm/ft^2, have proven to be very efficient in many industrial applications. The design overcomes the basic problem of most sand and other single-medium filters, which provide a maximum filtering efficiency only in the top few inches of the filter bed. The high-rate depth filters work at a maximum efficiency throughout the entire filter bed.

Backwashing As the filter material accumulates the suspended particles removed from the water, it should be cleaned to avoid any excessive pressure drops at the outlet and the carry-over of turbidity.

The need for cleaning, particularly in pressure filters, is easily determined through the use of pressure gages, which indicate the inlet and outlet pressures. Generally, when the pressure drop exceeds 5 psi, backwashing is in order. (See Figure 10-10.)

Cleaning is most commonly achieved through the process known as "backwashing." In this process, the filtered water is passed upward through the filter at a relatively high flow rate of 10–20 gpm/ft^2. The bed should expand at least 50%, as illustrated in Figure 10-11. This process keeps

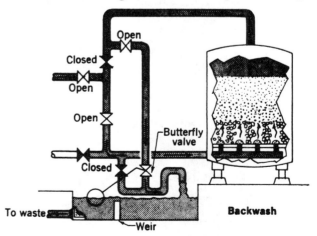

Figure 10-10 Backwashing

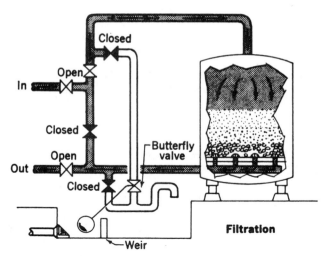

**Figure 10-11 Filtration and
Backsplash Cycles**

the grains of the filter medium close enough to
rub each other clean, but it does not lift them so
high that they are lost down the drain.
Backwashing can be automated by employing
pressure differential switches (electronically, hydraulically, or pneumatically) activating the
diaphragm or control valves that initiate the
backwash cycle at a given pressure drop.

Some problems connected with filter beds are
illustrated in Figures 10-12 through 10-14. Extremely turbid water or insufficient backwashing
causes accumulations called "mudballs." (See
Figure 10-12.) If not removed, they result in un-
even filtration and shorter filter runs and
encourage fissures. When the filter bed surface
becomes clogged with these deposits and simple
backwashing does not remove them, the filter
may have to be cut out of service and drained
and the deposits have to be removed by hand
skimming or the filter must be rebedded.

When fissures occur in the sand bed, the
cause can usually be traced to one or a combination of three items: (1) inlet water is not being
evenly distributed or is entering at too high a
velocity; (2) backwash water is not being evenly
distributed or is entering at too high a velocity;
(3) mudballs have stopped the passage of water
through certain areas and raised velocities in
others. The filter must be drained, opened, and
the filter medium cleaned and reoriented. (See
Figure 10-13.)

Ungravel upheaval is usually caused by violent backwash cycles where water is unevenly
distributed or velocities are too high. (See Figure 10-14.) If not corrected, fissures will be
encouraged or, worse, filter media will be allowed

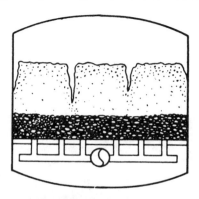

Figure 10-13 Fissures

to pass into the distribution system where they
may cause serious damage to valves and equipment as well as appear in potable water.

Diatomaceous earth filters The use of diatomaceous earth as a water filtering medium
achieved prominence during the 1940s as a result of the need for a compact, lightweight, and

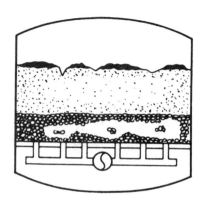

Figure 10-12 Mudballs

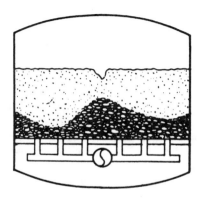

Figure 10-14 Ungravel Upheaval

portable filtering apparatus.

The water enters the filter vessel and is drawn through a porous supporting base that has been coated with diatomaceous earth. Filter cloths, porous stone tubes, wire screens, wire wound tubes and porous paper filter pads are some of the support base materials most commonly used today. Figure 10-15 illustrates a typical leaf design filter.

Diatomaceous earth, or silica (SiO_4), is produced from mineral deposits formed by diatoms, a fossilized plant that is similar to algae. Deposits of diatoms have been found as much as 1400 ft in thickness. Commercial filter aids are pro-

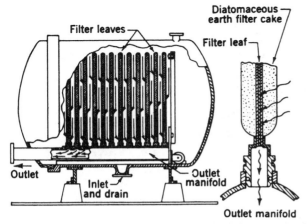

Figure 10-15 Leaf Design, Diatomaceous Earth Filter

duced from the crude material by a milling process that separates the diatoms from one another. The finished product is in the form of a fine powder.

When diatomaceous earth forms a cake on the support base, a filter of approximately 10% solids and 90% voids is achieved. The openings in this filter are so small that even most bacteria are strained out of the water.

The openings in the support base are not small enough initially to prevent the passage of individual diatomite particles. Some of these diatomite particles pass through the support base during the precoating operation. However, once the formation of the coating is complete, the interlocked mass of diatomite particles prevents any further passage of the particles.

Commercial diatomaceous earth is manufactured in a wide range of grades with differing filtration rates and differences in the clarity of the filtered water. The advantages of diatoma-

ceous earth filters, as compared to pressure sand filters, are (1) a considerable savings in the weight and required space, (2) a higher degree of filtered water clarity and purity in the outgoing water, and (3) the use of coagulants is not required. Its disadvantages are (1) only waters of relatively low turbidity can be efficiently used (it is not advisable to use these filters where the incoming water turbidities exceed 100 ppm since low-efficiency short filter runs will result), (2) the initial and operating costs usually far exceed those of the conventional sand filters, and (3) the incidence of high-pressure drop across the unit (as much as 25 to 50 psi) and the intermittent flows cause the filter cake to detach from the support base.

ADDITIONAL WATER TREATMENT

Water Softening

The engineer should not overlook the fact that water softening is required for practically all commercial and industrial building water usage. Generally, the engineer is cognizant of the water softening needs only when designing power plants, industrial laundries, and other similar applications. The result is usually that the owner has a water softener installed after occupancy, at greater cost than if it had been done in the original construction.

Generally speaking, almost any building supplied with water having a hardness of 3.5 grains per gallon (gpg) or more should have a water softener. This is true even if the only usage of the water other than for domestic purposes is for heating. Most water heater manufacturers recognize this fact and have stated that the principal threat to water heater life and performance is hard water. Approximately 85% of the water supplies in the United States have hardness values above the 3.5 gpg level. Thus, geographically speaking, the engineer should recognize that the need for water softening is almost universal.

Many engineers specify a water softener to supply the heating equipment only and completely disregard the softening needs for the balance of the cold water usage in the building. A typical example of this condition is in a college dormitory. There are many fixtures and appliances in a dormitory in addition to the hot water heater that require soft water, such as the piping itself, the flush valve toilets, the shower stalls, the basins, and the laundry rooms. Many fixtures and appliances that use a blend of hot and cold water will experience scale buildup and staining, even with the hot water softened.

One of the most common reasons for installing water softening equipment is to prevent the hardness scale buildup in piping systems, valves, and other plumbing fixtures. Scale builds up continually and at a faster rate as the temperature increases. The graph in Figure 10-16 illustrates the degree of scale deposit and the rate increase as the temperature of the water is elevated on water having a hardness of 10 gpg. For water of 20 gpg hardness, the scale deposit values can be multiplied by two. Although the rate of scale deposit is higher as the temperature increases, there is a significant scale buildup with cold water. Thus, the cold water scale, while taking a longer period of time to build up, is nevertheless significant.

Water softener selection The factors the designer should consider in sizing water softeners

include the following: the flow rate, the softener capacity, the frequency of regeneration, single vs. multiple systems, space requirements, cost, and operating efficiency.

Flow rate After determining the total flow rate requirements for the building, including all equipment, the engineer can consider the size of the water softener. The water softener selected should not restrict the rate of water flow beyond the pressure loss that the building can withstand, based on the pressures available at the source and the minimum pressure needed throughout the entire system.

With the rate of flow and the pressure drop known, a water softener that will meet both requirements can be selected by the designer. Standard softener units are designed for a pressure differential of approximately 15 psi, the most common differential acceptable for building design. Thus, for general usage, a water softener may be selected from a manufacturer's catalog.

The softener system should be capable of providing the design flow rates within the desired pressure drop. This means not only that the pipe and valve sizes must be adequate but that the water softener tank and its mineral must be capable of handling the flows while providing the soft water. The water softener design should be based on hydraulic and chemical criteria.

Good design practices for general use dictate that service flow rates through the water softener be approximately 10 gpm/ft^2 with mineral bed depths of 30 in. or more. Based on these accepted practices, the water softener is generally able to handle the peak flows for short periods of time.

The engineer should give more detailed consideration to the selection of water softeners where especially low-pressure losses are

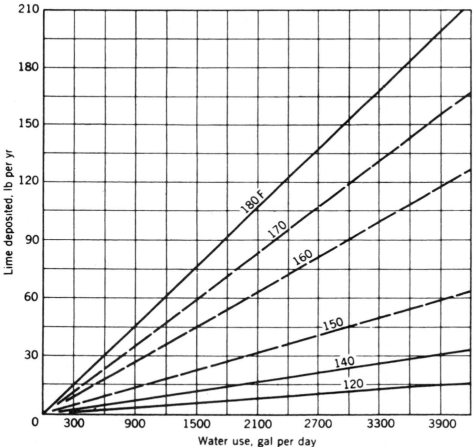

Figure 10-16 Lime Deposited from Water of 10 Grains Hardness as a Function of Water Use and Temperature

needed. Many equipment manufacturers offer complete pressure drop curves for their equipment, allowing the selection of components to fit any flow-pressure drop conditions desired.

Softener capacity Once the basic size of the water softener is selected based on flow rate, the designer should consider the length of the service run.

For each standard size water softener, a nominal quantity of softening mineral is used. This amount is based on the recommended depths of mineral (normally 30–36 in.) and the proper free-board space above the mineral (the space required for the proper expansion of the mineral during backwashing). Thus, from the unit initially selected, a standard capacity is known.

The capacity of a water softener is its total hardness exchange ability, generally expressed in terms of grains exchange. The normal capacity of available softening mineral (resins) is 30,000 gr for each cubic foot of mineral. Thus, the total capacity for the water softener is obtained by multiplying this value by the number of cubic feet of mineral in the water softener. The hardness of the raw water must be ascertained. By dividing the water hardness (grains per gallon) (expressed as $CaCO_3$ equivalent) into the total softener capacity (grains), the designer can determine the number of gallons of soft water that the unit will produce before requiring regeneration.

Knowing (or estimating) the total gallons of water used per day will indicate the frequency of regeneration. Most often, it is best to have a slight reserve capacity in order to accommodate any small increases in water usage.

Softening is not really a form of water purification since the function of a softener is to remove only the hardness (calcium and magnesium) from the water and substitute, by ion exchange, the softer element of sodium. Softeners are frequently used in hard water areas as pretreatment to distillation to simplify maintenance. They are often necessary as a pretreatment to deionizers and reverse osmosis, depending on the analysis of the feed water and the type of deionizer. The following steps should be taken prior to selecting a water softener:

1. Have a water analysis performed.

   A. Analyze water with portable test kit.

   B. Check with local authorities for water analysis.

   C. Send a water sample to a qualified water testing lab.

2. Determine water consumption.

   A. Use sizing charts.

   B. Use consumption figures from water bills (if bills are in cubic feet, multiply by 7.5 to convert to gallons).

   C. Take water meter readings.

3. Determine continuous and peak flow rates.

   A. Use the fixture count flow rate estimating guide to determine the required flow rate.

   B. Obtain flow rate figures for equipment to be serviced. (If flow rate data are given in pounds per hour, divide by 500 to convert to gallons per minute.)

   C. Take water meter readings during peak periods of water consumption.

4. Determine the water pressure.

   A. If there is a well supply, check the pump start and stop settings.

   B. Install a pressure gage.

5. Determine the capacity. Gallons per day × grains per gallon = grains per day.

6. Select the smallest unit that will handle the maximum capacity required between regenerations with a low salt dosage. Avoid sizing equipment with the high dosage unless there is reason to do so, such as a high-pressure boiler.

Example 10-1

Capacity required: 300,000 gr

- A 300,000-gr unit will produce this capacity when regenerated with 150 lb of salt.

- A 450,000-gr unit will produce this capacity when regenerated with 60 lb of salt.

  The 450,000-gr unit would be the better selection to remove 300,000 gr. Salt consumption will be 75 lb per regeneration as opposed to 150 lb on the smaller unit, a 50% salt consumption saving. It should be noted that while a salt saving is realized in using the lower salting rate on the larger unit, there will be an increase in hardness leakage. If minimum hardness leakage is required, such as for boiler feed water, the maximum salting rate (15 lb/ft^3) should be used.

7. Will the unit selected deliver the required flow rate?

   A. When sizing to a continuous flow rate, subtract the pressure drop from line pressure. At least 30 psi should be left for working pressure.

   B. When sizing to a peak flow rate, subtract the pressure drop from line pressure. At least 20 psi should be left for working pressure.

   C. If A or B has less than the minimum allowable working pressure, select a larger model that has a higher flow rate.

   D. The water softener requires a dynamic pressure of 35 psi to draw brine.

8. Available space. Compare the dimensions of the unit selected with the space available for installation.

9. Door ways. Make sure both softener and brine tank will fit through all doors and hallways to the installation area. If not, a twin unit or smaller brine tank may be used.

10. Make sure a drain is available that will handle the backwash flow rate of the unit selected. Refer to the specification sheet for backwash flow rates.

Fixture count flow rate estimating guide for water conditioners

This guide is for estimating "average" and "maximum" flow rate requirements (in gallons per minute) for both private and public buildings and is based on fixture flow rates and probability of use. It is to be used when actual continuous and peak flow rates are not known.

The average rates may be used when line pressure less the conditioner pressure drop is at least 30 psi at the highest point of use in the building.

The maximum rates are equal to the fixture count figures commonly used to size water lines and are applicable especially in low-water-pressure areas where pressure drop is critical.

The following is a step-by-step procedure for estimating fixture count flow rates.

1. Count and list each "type of fixture" used

intermittently. Multiply the total of each type by its private or public unit weight. Private or public unit weights must be determined by the use of the fixture. For example, lavatories in an apartment house are private. Lavatories in a restaurant are public. Add the products of each type of fixture to determine the "total fixture count weight."

2. From the "intermittent flow rate chart," select total fixture count, or the next highest fixture count, determined in 1.

3. Add to the flow rate determined in 2 any continuously used flow rates in gallons per minute. These additional requirements may include commercial dishwashers, garbage disposals that run continually in busy water, boiler makeup water, swimming pool makeup water, etc. In some cases, these additional requirements are seasonal and used separately. For example, if boilers are shut down during the summer months, use the additional requirement of the boiler or the air-conditioning system, whichever is greater. For example, the flow rate for a 10-unit apartment can be estimated as follows:

Example 10-2   10-unit apartment house

Type and Number of Fixtures		Private Unit Weight		Total Weight
10	Kitchen sink	× 2	=	20
10	Bathtub/shower	× 2	=	20
10	Lavatory	× 1	=	10
10	Tank type toilet	× 3	=	30
3	Washing machines	× 2	=	6
1	Air conditioner with 5 gpm makeup			86 Total

Fixture count weight	=	Average gpm
86		31

For a total of 86 fixture units, the corresponding flow rate is 31 gpm.

Add 31 gpm to 5 gpm for the air conditioner: 31 + 5 = 36 gpm

Select the smallest unit that has a continuous flow rate of 36 gpm.

4. Select the smallest water conditioner the continuous flow rate of which is equal to or greater than the total flow rate requirement in 3.

Line pressure less the pressure drop of the selected unit must be at least 30 psi to handle the peak flow rate periods.

If it is less than 30 psi:

A. Repeat Step 2 using the "maximum" column on the intermittent flow rate chart.

B. Add to A the additional requirements of Step 3.

C. Select a water conditioner the continuous flow rate of which is equal to or greater than the new total flow rate requirement.

When the maximum figures are used, line pressure less the conditioner pressure drop must be 20 psi minimum.

Note: When water conditioners are installed in series, such as an iron filter in a water softener, the 30 psi and 20 psi minimum pressures must be maintained after both units. Select combinations of conditioners with a total pressure drop, when subtracted from line pressure, of 30 psi minimum when using the average figures, or 20 psi when using the maximum figures.

Water consumption guide Where measurements of water consumption are not possible—for instance, where water meter records are not available—the following information can be used to estimate the amount of water consumed in several establishments. (**Note**: For more accurate figures, take meter readings during average or peak periods—a week or a month. Water bills may be used to determine daily water consumption.)

Apartments:

One-bedroom units—1.75 people/apartment; 2-bedroom units—3 people/apartment; 3-bedroom units—5 people/apartment;

Full line—60 gallons per day (gpd)/person; hot only—25 gpd/person;

One bath—1.5 gpm/apartment; 2 bath—2.5 gpm/apartment.

Barber shops:

75 gpd/chair.

Beauty shops:

300 gpd/station.

Bowling alleys:

75 gpd/lane.

Factories (not including process water):

With showers—35 gpd/person/shift; without showers—25 gpd/person/shift.

Farm animals:

Dairy cow—35 gpd; beef cow—12 gpd; hog—4 gpd; horse—12 gpd; sheep—2 gpd; chickens—10 gpd/100 birds; turkeys—18 gpd/100 birds.

Hospitals:

225 gpd/bed; estimate air conditioning and laundry separately.

Motels:

Full line—100 gpd/room; hot only—40 gpd/room.

Estimate the restaurant, bar, air conditioning, swimming pool, and laundry facilities separately, and add these to the room gallonage for total consumption.

Mobile home courts:

Estimate 3.75 people/home; estimate 60 gpd/person. (Outside water for sprinkling, washing cars, etc., should be bypassed.)

Restaurants:

Total (full line)—8 gal/meal;

Food preparation (hot and cold)—3 gal/meal; food preparation (hot only—1.5 gal/meal; cocktail bar—2 gal/patron.

Rest homes:

175 gpd/bed; estimate laundry separately.

Schools:

Full line—20 gpd/student; hot only—8 gpd/student.

Trailer parks:

100 gpd/space.

If manually operated equipment is desired, longer periods between regenerations may be desired to reduce the attention that an operator must give to the water softener. Thus, larger capacity units would have to be selected.

Single or multiple systems A single-unit softener will bypass the hard water during periods of regeneration (normally 1.5 h). This is the danger in a single-unit softener. If soft water requirements are critical and adequate soft water storage is not available, a twin or duplex water softener is needed.

Space needs Many times a softener system is selected without much concern for space needs. Generally, there is sufficient floor space available, although this factor should not be overlooked for storage. More commonly overlooked is the actual height of the softener tank and the additional height required (24 in.) for access through the top manhole opening for loading the unit. If height in the room is critical, the upper manhole can be located on the upper side shell of the softener tank (if so specified).

Severe room height restrictions normally require specifying a larger diameter, more squat softener tank with the same specified quantity of softening mineral. Further consideration must be given to the floor space around the equipment, particularly around the salt tanks, for loading purposes and accessibility for servicing the units.

Where water softeners are being installed in existing buildings, the door openings should be checked for passage of the softener equipment to the final loading.

Cost Technical advances in the water softening industry and increasing labor costs are for the most part responsible for the fact that almost all the equipment produced is operated automatically.

For budget estimating purposes, automatic water softening costs range from $15.00–40.00/1000 gr of exchange capacity, depending upon the degree of sophistication. This estimate is based on the total capacity of all units.

Operating efficiency Most water softeners are alike in terms of their operation. Their basic operating cost is the salt consumption. Practically all use a high-capacity, resinous mineral. The mineral can exchange 30,000 gr of hardness per cubic foot of mineral when regenerated with 15 lb of salt, which is the nominal standard rating currently used in industry.

As salt is the basic commodity that effects the operating cost, it is the only area where reduced costs may be considered. Fortunately, the softening mineral can be regenerated at different salt levels, yielding actual cost savings on the salt consumption. As indicated, with a 15-lb salt level, 30,000 gr/ft^3 can be obtained. With a salt dosage of 10 lb, a resulting capacity yield of

date _____

Project name

Location _____

Type of facility _____

What is water being used for? _____

Water analysis: (express in gr./ gal. or ppm as $CaCo_3$)

Total hardness _____

Sodium _____

Total dissolved solids _____

Sodium to hardness ratio _____

Iron _____

Flow rate (gpm) peak _____ Normal _____ Average _____

Allowable pressure loss _____ System inlet pressure _____

Operating hours/day _____ Gallons/day _____

Influent header pipe size _____

Electrical characteristics _____

Type of operation _____

Special requirement or options (ASME, lining, accessories) _____

Space limitation L _____ W _____ H _____

Figure 10-17 Water Softener Survey Data

25,000 gr/ft^3 and with 6 lb, a capacity of 20,000 gr/ft^3 is obtained.

Thus, approximately a 40% salt rating can be effected at the lower salt level. The lower salt levels can be used effectively on general applications, resulting in lower operating costs. However, where very high-quality soft water is required in an area where very high hardness water exists, this approach is not recommended.

Sizing Figure 10-17 will assist the engineer in developing the data required to size the basic softening equipment. The final selection of a system for specification should be made using this information. In many cases, the importance of the water softening equipment justifies calling on manufacturers' representatives for their recommendations. Their specialized knowledge can help in the design of a reliable, economical water softener system. Figure 10-18 provides a step-by-step procedure for selecting the water softener equipment.

Distillation

The principles of distillation are quite simple. The water passes through two phase changes, from liquid to gas and back to liquid (see Figure 10-19). All the substances that are not volatile remain behind in the boiler and are removed either continuously or intermittently. Water droplets are prevented from coming up with the water vapor by proper design of the still, which takes into account the linear velocity, and by use of an appropriate system of baffles.

It should be understood that, although the nonvolatile substances can be taken care of, the volatile substances in the feed water cause more problems. These, mainly CO_2, which are already present in the feed water or are formed by the decomposition of bicarbonates, can be removed by keeping the distillate at a relatively high temperature. The solubility of CO_2 at higher temperatures is much lower than at normal temperatures.

NH_3 is much more soluble in water than CO_2 and its tendency to redissolve is much higher too. Moreover, the ionization constant of NH_4OH is much greater than that of H_2CO_3, which means that equal amounts of NH_3 and CO_2 show different conductivities, (that for NH_3 is much higher than that for CO_2).

The purity of the distillate is usually measured with a conductivity meter, and a resistivity of 1 MΩ—or a conductivity of 1 microsiemens (μS)—is equivalent to approximately 0.5 ppm of NaCl. There is not much NaCl in the distillate! Most of the conductivity is accounted for by the presence of CO_2 (and NH_3) and not by dissolved solids. The question arises, do we really want 1 MΩ resistivity, or a maximum concentration of dissolved solids? It is quite possible that a distillate with a resistivity of 500,000 Ω (a conductivity of 2 μS) contains fewer dissolved solids than a distillate with a resistivity of 1,000,000 Ω (1 μS).

A problem in distillation can be scale formation. Scale forms either by the decomposition of soluble products of insoluble substances or because the solubility limit of a substance is reached during the concentration. There are several solutions to this problem:

1. A careful system of maintenance, descaling at regular intervals.

2. Softening of the feed water, that is, removing all Ca^{2+} and Mg^{2+} ions; this, however, does not remove the silica, which then may give a hard, dense scale that is very difficult to remove.

3. Removal of the alkalinity (HCO_3^-); sulfate and silica when originally present, will still form a harder scale than a carbonate scale.

4. Removal of all or most of the dissolved substances. This can be done by demineralization with ion exchangers or by reverse osmosis.

It may sound foolish to remove the impurities from the water before distilling the water off. However, keep in mind that distillation is the only process that will produce water guaranteed to be free of bacteria, viruses, and pyrogens. It may pay to have a pretreatment before a still to cut down on maintenance (descaling), downtime, and energy consumption, and to have better efficiency, capacity, and quality. It may require a higher initial investment, but in the long run you may be much better off, as long as you deal with a supplier who has the experience and technology in all water treatment systems to give you unbiased advice—that is, to give you a systems approach instead of pushing only one method.

Distilled water is often called "hungry" water. This refers to the fact that distilled or deionized water will absorb in solution much of the matter, in any phase, with which it comes in contact. It becomes important, therefore, to se-

Date _____

Project name _____

Location _____

Step 1. Operating conditions
    A. Operating hours per day _____
    B. Can regeneration take place once each day?   Yes _____   No _____
    C. If "B" is No, state days between regenerations _____
    D. Is a twin unit required?   Yes _____   No _____
    E. Type of operation:
        Time clock _____   Alarm meter _____   Auto reset meter _____
    F. Allowable pressure loss _____ psi.

Step 2. Flow rate (gpm) _____ (peak, average, continuous)

Step 3. Water usage per day:

_____ × 60 min./hr. × _____ GPM = _____
  Operating hr/day   Average flow rate   gal/day

Step 4. Required exchange capacity:

_____ × _____ = _____
Gal/day water usage   Water hardness (gr/gal)   Required exchange capacity (gr/day)

Step 5. Select resin capacity & salt dosage per cu ft.:
    (_____) 32,000 gr @ 15# (_____) 29,000 gr @ 10# (_____) 21,000 gr @ 6#

Step 6. One day of operation per regeneration (step no. 1-B)

_____ ÷ _____ = _____
  Required exch. cap (gr/day)   Resin cap (gr/ft^3)   Required resin (ft^3/day)

Note: If more than one day between regenerations is required, use step no. 7 instead of step no. 6.

Step 7. More than one day of operation per regeneration (step no. 1-B)
    Cubic feet of resin required:

_____ × _____ ÷ _____ = _____
  Required exch. cap. (gr/day) Number of days/regn. Resin cap. (gr/ft^3) Resin required (ft^3)

Step 8. Salt consumption per regeneration:

_____ × _____ = _____
  Required resin (ft^3 /regn.)   Salt dosage (lb/ft^3)   Salt regeneration (lb)

Step 9. System selection:
    (If auto-reset operation is desired, refer to step no. 10.)
    A. Select from the manufacturer's specification table, a single unit that meets the flow rate (step no. 2).
    B. Check that selected unit meets the allowable pressure loss at the flow rate (step no. 1-F).
    C. If a single unit will not meet both steps no. 9-A and 9-B, then a multiple unit is required (refer to step no. 10).
    D. Check that selected unit contains the required cubic feet of resin (step no. 6 or 7).
    E. If single unit will not meet step no. 9-D, then a multiple unit is required. (refer to step no. 10).
    F. Select a standard system that meets, or exceeds by no more than 10%, step nos. 9-A, 9-B, and 9-D. If a good balance is not available, refer to step no. 10.
    G. Check that brine-tank salt storage is sufficient to provide a minimum of two regenerations before requiring refill (step no. 8).

Step 10. Multiple systems:
    The following procedure should be followed for a twin unit.
    A. Select either auto-reset meter initiation or time clock to start regeneration. Refer to the appropriate subtitle.
    Auto-reset meter-initiated regeneration.
    B. Select, from the specification table, a tank size that meets the *flow rate* (step no. 2) and the *allowable pressure loss* (step no. 1-F). Each tank in the system must meet these conditions.
    C. Divide the required cu. ft. of resin (step no. 6 or 7) by two to determine the required cubic feet of resin contained in the tanks selected in step no. 10-B. Select a tank large enough to match the required cu. ft. resin/tank.
    D. Check that the brine tank salt storage is sufficient to provide a minimum of four regenerations per tank.
    Time clock regeneration
    E. Divide the *flow rate* (step no. 2) by 2 to determine the *flow rate per tank*. Select a tank size that meets this flow rate. (Both tanks will be on line during the operating period.)
    F. Check that the tank selected meets the *allowable pressure loss* (step no. 1-F) at the *flow rate per tank*.
    G. Follow step no. 10-C to determine the required cubic feet of resin per tank.
    H. Follow step no. 10-D to determine the brine tank to be used.

Step 11. Using this data, select a standard system from the softener specifications that most closely matches all the data. If none is available, a detailed specification should be developed which will allow the manufacturer to match the system requirements.

Step 12. Select options such as ASME code tanks, lining, and materials of construction, as required.

Figure 10-18 Water Softener Sizing Procedure

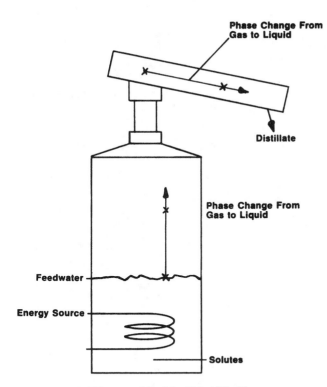

Phase Change From Gas to Liquid

Distillate

Phase Change From Gas to Liquid

Feedwater

Energy Source

Solutes

Figure 10-19 Distillation

lect a practical material for the production, storage, and distribution of distilled water. This, by itself, could be the subject of a lengthy article, but here we shall confine ourselves to a few brief summaries.

Years of experience and research have shown that pure tin is the most practical material for the production, storage, and distribution of distilled water due to its inert characteristic. It is the least soluble. (Other materials, such as gold, silver, and platinum, have equal or superior qualities but.are not considered for obvious reasons.) A secondary but almost equal advantage of tin is its relatively low porosity, which virtually eliminates the possibility of particle entrapment and growth in pores. In a good water still, therefore, all the surfaces that come in contact with the pure vapors and distillate should be heavily coated with pure tin. The storage tank, likewise, should be heavily coated or lined with pure tin on all interior surfaces. Tinned stills and storage tanks are not significantly more expensive than glass ones in all but the smallest sizes.

Titanium is being strongly considered as a promising material for distillation equipment. Although some stills have been made of it, it is more expensive than tin and has not yet been proven superior.

Distillation equipment applications and selection The use of distilled water was limited to hospitals and some pharmaceutical applications until recent advances in industry. Now, in virtually every hospital, in schools with science departments, in laboratories, and in industries other than pharmaceuticals, distilled water is vital to many operational functions.

In the construction of buildings requiring distilled water, the selection of the appropriate equipment to furnish it is usually the responsibility of the plumbing engineer. Before the proper equipment can be selected, the following factors should be considered:

1. The quantity of distilled water that will be required per day (or per week) by each department.

2. The purity requirements of each department and how critical these requirements are.

3. The space available for the equipment.

4. The availability of power.

Regarding the first two items, the engineer should obtain the anticipated quantity and purity requirements from all department heads who require distilled water.

In this section, it is assumed that less than 1000 gpd of distilled water is required for applications. The single-effect still operated at atmospheric pressure is generally the most practical and widely used still. For the consumption of larger quantities of distilled water, consideration may be given by the engineer to other types of stills (such as the multiple-effect and vapor-compression still). These stills have advantages and disadvantages that should be studied when the conditions warrant. See Figure 10-20 for an illustration of typical distillation equipment.

Centralized vs. decentralized stills The designer's choice between central distillation equipment and individual stills in each department is a matter of economics. In the case of central distillation, the factors to consider are the distances involved in piping the water to the various departments, hence, the cost of the appropriate piping and, possibly, the pumping requirements. For individual stills in each department, the original and maintenance costs of multiple stills can be high. In the majority of installations, the use of one or two large, centrally located stills with piped distribution systems has proven more practical and economi-

Still and tank combination produces 50 gpm, stores 500 gal of distilled water at Jimmy Fund Building, Children's Hospital, Boston, Massachusetts.

Typical still tank with automatic starting, stopping, and flushing controls. Controller allows only water that is above the desired standard to enter storage tank. Still is 30 gph size, storage tank is 200 gal.

Immersion type, ultraviolet equipment protects water in storage against bacteria for as long as 30 days. Ultraviolet source can be replaced with contaminating water in the storage tank.

Figure 10-20 Typical Distillation Equipment

cal than a number of smaller, individual stills.

Example 10-3

Assume that a total of 400 gpd of distilled water is required by all departments. A fully automatic still and storage tank combination should be used in this application. Fully automatic controls stop the still when the storage tank is full and start the still when the level in the storage tank reaches a predetermined low level. In addition, the evaporator is flushed out each time it stops. A 30-gph still (with a 300-gal storage tank) produces more than the desired 400 gpd. Because the still operates on a 24-h basis, as the storage tank calls for distilled water (even if no distilled water is used during the night) 300 gal are on hand to start each day. As water is withdrawn from the storage tank, the still starts and replenishes the storage tank at a rate of 30 gph.

In the foregoing example, the storage tank volume, in gallons, is ten times the rated gallons-per-hour capacity of the still. This is a good rule of thumb for a fully automatic still and storage tank combination. A closer study of the pattern of the anticipated demands may reveal unusual patterns, which may justify a larger ratio.

Still construction Due to the amount of heat required in the operation to change the water

into steam, it is impractical to make large-capacity, electrically heated and gas heated stills. All stills larger than 10 gph, therefore, should be heated by steam. For each gallon per hour of a still's rated capacity, steam heated stills require approximately ⅓ boiler horsepower, electrically heated stills need 2600 W, and gas fired stills need 14,000 Btu/h.

The still must be well designed and baffled to effect an efficient vapor separation without the possibility of carry-over of the contaminants and to ensure optimum removal of the volatile impurities. It is equally important that the materials used in construction of the still, the storage reservoir, and all components coming in contact with the distilled water do not react with the distilled water.

Distribution systems Cost can be a significant factor in the distribution system, particularly if it is extensive. The distribution system can consist of 316 stainless steel, PVC Schedule 80, and polyvinylidene fluoride (PVDF). The fittings, likewise, should be of the same material.

The purity requirements should be considered and a careful investigation made of the properties and characteristics of the materials being considered. Many plastics have a relatively porous surface, which can harbor organic and inorganic contaminants. With some metals, at least trace quantities may be imparted to the distilled water.

Types of stills and accessories While a well-designed still can produce pure distilled water for most purposes, the distilled water to be used by a hospital for intravenous injections or by a pharmaceutical company manufacturing a product for intravenous injections must be free of pyrogens (large organic molecules that cause individuals to go into shock). For such uses, a still with special baffles to produce pyrogen-free distilled water must be specified.

There are other types of stills designed to meet various purity requirements. The recommendations of the manufacturer should be obtained as to the proper type of still to specify for a specific application.

Storage reservoir The storage reservoir used for distilled water should be made of a material that is suited for the application and sealed with a tight cover so that contaminants from the atmosphere can not enter the system. As the distilled water is withdrawn from the storage tank, air must enter the system to replace it. In order to prevent airborne contamination, an efficient filter should be installed on the storage tank so that all air entering the tank may be filtered free from dust, mist, bacteria, and submicron particulate matter, as well as carbon dioxide.

Figure 10-21 illustrates a typical air filter. This air filter (both hydrophilic and hydrophobic) removes gases and airborne particles down to 0.2 μ. Purified air leaves at the bottom. The rectangular chamber is a replaceable filter cartridge. A and B are intake breather valves; C is an exhaust valve.

As a further safeguard against any possible contamination of the distilled water by biological impurities, an ultraviolet light can be attached to the inside of the cover (less effecive) and/or immersed in the distilled water (also less effective) or in the flow stream to effectively maintain its sterility. Ultraviolet lighting should be given strong consideration for hospital and pharmaceutical installations, as well as for any other applications where sterility is important.

Purity monitor One frequently used accessory is the automatic purity monitor. This device tests the purity of the distilled water coming from the still with a temperature compensated conduc-

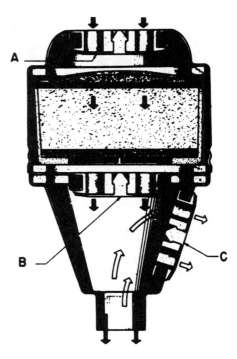

Figure 10-21 Typical Air Filter (See text for identification of parts.)

tivity cell. This cell is wired to a resistivity meter that is set at a predetermined standard of distilled water commensurate with the capability of the still. If, for any reason, the purity of the distilled water is below the set standard, the substandard water does not enter the storage tank and is automatically diverted to waste. At the same time, a signal will alert personnel that the still is producing substandard water so that an investigation may be made as to its cause. Simple wiring may be used to make the alarm signal visual or audible at any remote location, such as the plant engineer's office. The advantages of this automatic purity monitor are obvious, particularly ahead of large storage tanks (as one slug of bad water can ruin a whole tank).

Feed water

Pretreated feed water In the conventional or basic operation of a still, city water is used to condense the pure vapors from the evaporator and is heated. Part of this preheated water enters the evaporator as feed water, while the greater part goes to the drain. A well designed still has the intrinsic features to retard the formation of scale in the evaporator. These features include a frequent, automatic flushing and a bleeder valve that continuously deconcentrates the buildup of the impurities in the evaporator.

As a further aid in reducing the maintenance of a still in areas having exceptionally hard water, it is often desirable (but not essential) to demineralize (with a deionizer or reverse osmosis), soften, or otherwise pretreat the feed water. Demineralizing the feed water practically eliminates the need for cleaning the evaporator. For this purpose, the demineralizing process is relatively expensive; however, it does contribute to a higher purity of the distilled water.

Because water softening is less expensive than the demineralizing process, it is used more often as a method of pretreatment. It does not have the advantages of demineralized water—eliminating cleaning and contributing to a higher purity — but it does eliminate hard scale formation in the evaporator.

When any kind of pretreated feed water is used, an adequate preheater (for pretreated water) and a float feeder valve should be specified by the designer. With these devices, the raw water is used only as cooling water for the condenser and the pretreated feed water is piped separately to the still, eliminating the waste of the pretreated water. When the float feeder valve is used on any still equipped with an automatic drain, an automatic shut-off valve to the float feeder valve should also be specified so that the supply of pretreated water will stop at the same time the drain valve opens. Specifications prepared by the designer should give the type of pretreated water to be used.

Condensate as feed water Another method of reducing maintenance on a steam heated still is to use the condensed boiler steam as feed water to the still. Here again, the raw water is used only as condenser cooling water. The condensate from the steam trap is cooled then passed through an ion exchange cartridge and an organic removal filter. These cartridges remove any traces of scale forming salts, ionized amines, traces of odor, or taste impurities present in the original condensate and organics that may be given off by the ion exchange cartridge.

This type of system is commonly referred to as the "feedback purifier." This design contributes to a higher purity of the distillate and virtually eliminates the need to clean the still (since scale forming hardness has been eliminated from the feed water).

It is important for the engineer to determine the characteristics of the steam condensate when considering the feedback purifier system. If amines are used as the treatment for the boiler feed water in an excessive amount, this method should not be used. However, most condensates are satisfactory for this purpose.

Distribution pressure Whenever possible, it is best to locate the still and the storage tank where gravity can be employed to provide an adequate pressure to operate the distribution system. When this condition is not possible, centrifugal pumps of the appropriate size must be used. Along with the circulation pump, an orificed bypass back to the storage tank should be installed so that the pump can be operated continuously, maintaining adequate pressure in the distribution system. Then the distilled water will be available in any outlet all the time. The bypass relieves the pressure on the circulating pump when the water is not being drawn at its outlets.

A low-water cutoff should also be installed on the storage tank to shut off the pump if the storage tank runs dry. This pump arrangement is simpler in construction, more efficient to operate, and less expensive than a pressurized tank.

SPECIALIZED WATER TREATMENT

Chlorination

Chlorination has traditionally been used for the disinfection of drinking water. However, the initial investment required to properly chlorinate a potable water supply has, in many cases, restricted its use to the larger water consumer or to cities, which have the adequate financial support and sufficient manpower to properly maintain the chlorination system. This situation has forced smaller water consumers either to go to the expense of purchasing an automatic chlorination system or possibly to consume contaminated water from a poorly disinfected water supply.

The chlorination process has other drawbacks as a disinfectant beside finances. The transportation and handling of a gas chlorination system are potentially dangerous. When the safety procedures are followed, however, there are fewer problems than with either liquid or solid products. Chemically, chlorine is the most reactive halogen and is also known to combine with nitrogenous and organic compounds to form weak bacteriocidal compounds. These compounds (chloramines) require an extended period of contact time to effectively kill pathogenic microorganisms.

Chlorine combines with hydrocarbons to form *potentially* carcinogenic compounds (trihalomethanes).

Ozone Treatment

Ozone is a compound in which three atoms of oxygen are combined to form the ozone molecule O_3. It is a strong, naturally occurring, oxidizing and disinfecting agent. The unstable ozone (O_3) compound can be generated by the exposure of oxygen molecules (O_2) to ultraviolet radiation or high-energy electrical discharge in manufactured ozone generators.

Ozone can react with any oxidizable substance, such as certain forms of inorganic material like iron and manganese, many organic materials, and microorganisms. In an oxidation reaction, energy is transferred from the ozone molecule, leaving a stable oxygen (O_2) and a highly reactive oxygen atom (O_1). The molecule being oxidized then bonds with the loose oxygen atom creating an oxidized product or a derivation of the substance. Bacterial cells and viruses are literally split apart (lysed) or inactivated through oxidation of their DNA and RNA chains by ozone in water and waste-water treatment applications. Ozone is the most powerful oxidizer that can be safely used in water treatment.

Ozone is frequently used to treat waste water and as a disinfectant and oxidant for bottled water, ultrapure waters, swimming pools, spas, breweries, aquariums, soft drinks, cooling towers, and many other applications. Ozone is not able to produce a stable residual in a distribution system. However, ozone can lower the chlorine demand and thus the amount of chlorine required and the chlorine byproducts.

Ultraviolet Light Treatment

Ultraviolet light is electromagnetic radiation, or radiant energy, traveling in the form of waves. When ultraviolet light of a sufficient energy level is absorbed into matter it causes a chemical or physical change. In the case of microorganisms, ultraviolet light is absorbed to a level that is just enough to physically break the bonds in DNA to prevent life reproduction. Therefore, ultraviolet light is a mechanism capable of the disinfection of water. The most widely used source of this light is low-pressure mercury vapor lamps emitting a 254-nanometer (nm) wavelength. However, 185 nm can be used for both disinfection and total oxidizable carbon (TOC) reduction. The dosage required to destroy microorganisms is the product of light intensity and exposure time. The exposure requirements for different microorganisms are well documented by health agencies. Ultraviolet bulbs are considered to give 8000 h of continuous use and not to degrade to more than 55% of their initial output.

When ultraviolet equipment is sized, the flow rate and quality of incoming water must be taken into consideration. It is generally necessary to filter the water before the ultraviolet equipment. Sometimes it may be necessary to filter downstream of the ultraviolet equipment with 0.2-μ absolute filter cartridges to remove dead bacteria and cell fragments.

Ultraviolet equipment is often used in drinking water, beverage water, pharmaceuticals, ultrapure rinse water, and other disinfection applications.

Reverse Osmosis

Reverse osmosis (RO) is a water purification method that, over the past several years, has become an alternative to the more traditional techniques of distillation and deionization. This process is proving itself to be very practical and economical in a growing number of applications. Technical innovations and good design have handled many of the earlier limitations of the RO technology.

RO is a relatively simple concept. In normal osmosis, the water diffuses through a membrane and dilutes the more concentrated of the two solutions (Figure 10-22). If a pressure is applied to the concentrated solution, however, the flow can be reversed and hence the term "reverse osmosis" (see Figure 10-23). When this condition happens, the dissolved salts, organics, and colloidal solids are *rejected* by the membrane, thus resulting in a higher quality of water.

In practice, however, only a certain percentage of the incoming water is allowed to permeate this membrane. The concentrate is diverted to the drain, carrying with it the rejected contaminants. The continuous flushing process of the

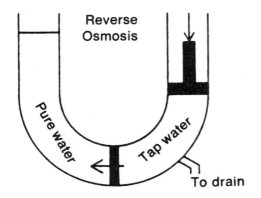

Figure 10-22 Reverse Osmosis Process

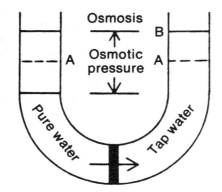

Figure 10-23 Osmotic Pressure

membrane prevents a phenomenon known as "concentration polarization," which is a buildup of the polarized molecules on the membrane surface that would further restrict flow in a short period of time.

Note: When equal volumes of water are separated by a semipermeable membrane, osmosis occurs as pure water permeates the membrane to dilute the more concentrated solution. The amount of physical pressure required to equalize the two volumes again, after equilibrium has been reached, is called the "osmotic pressure" (see Figure 10-22).

Note: If physical pressure is applied in excess of the osmotic pressure, reverse osmosis occurs as water passes back through the membrane, leaving contaminant concentrated upstream. In practice, the concentrate is diverted to drain, thus rejecting contaminants from the system altogether (see Figure 10-23).

In this section, the technology of RO and its use for producing quality water from tap water for research institutions, universities, hospitals, and laboratories is reviewed. RO is also applicable for large-scale production in the

pharmaceutical, chemical, electronics, food, and beverage industries. The following items are discussed:

1. The current technology and history of the reverse osmosis process,

2. A comparison of the RO water quality with that produced by other purification technologies,

3. The capital and operating costs of RO,

4. Applications for RO water,

5. Typical RO equipment for small- and large-scale production,

6. Combining RO and deionization equipment in applications requiring various grades of water quality.

Current technology and history of RO The current technology of RO developed rapidly as one specific application of the larger technology of synthetic membranes. Several code requirements had to be met before these membranes could be considered practical or economical for water purification processes.

First, the membrane had to be selective, i.e., it had to be capable of rejecting contaminants and yet still be highly permeable to water. This condition meant that it had to have a consistent polymeric structure with a pore size in the range of the smallest contaminant molecules possible.

Second, the membrane had to be capable of sustained high flux rates in order to be economical and practical in water application. The condition meant that the membrane had to be thin and yet durable enough for long-term use.

The original cellulose-acetate membranes developed proved to be highly permeable to the water. However, later developments led to a membrane with a *thin skin* (approximately 0.05 μ) cast on the top of a porous support structure (100 μ thick). This resulted in high flux rates, selectivity, and structural strength. The resulting RO membrane proved to be highly resistant to chemical and microbial degradation. It could also maintain the required water quality and flow rates under a sustained high pressure. Such a membrane could also be incorporated into a system with relatively low capital, equipment, and operating costs. These attributes were combined successfully and the resulting membrane achieved a flow rate or 20 gal/ft^2/day at 800 psi with 95% removal of salt.

RO water quality The term "high purity" is very often applied to a type of water that may be exceptionally free of one class of contaminant and yet may contain large amounts of another. The key, of course, is the application involved. For injectable pharmaceutical preparations, the particles and pyrogens are a major concern. In atomic absorption spectrophotometry or high-pressure liquid chromatography; however, even parts-per-billion traces of heavy metals or organics can present serious problems. One useful distinction is between *reagent-grade water* and *laboratory-grade water.*

Reagent-grade water means that all classes of contaminants have been removed from the water. There are several nationally recognized standards for reagent-grade water, including those published by the American Standard for Testing and Material (ASTM) and the College of American Pathologists (CAP). The minimum resistivity for reagent-grade water is 10 MΩ-cm at 25°C. The production of reagent-grade water always requires more than one stage of treatment. It should be produced at the point of use to minimize (or eliminate) transportation and storage, which invariably degrade the regeant water purity. A system for producing reagent-grade water might, for example, use the RO process to produce laboratory-grade water, plus a combination of activated carbon, deionization, and 0.20-μ membrane filtration. Only the laboratory-grade water would be accumulated and stored. The reagent water would be produced at high-flow rates as needed, thus eliminating the need to store it.

Laboratory-grade water is less rigorously defined, but it still refers to the water from which one or more types of contaminants have been removed. This definition should be distinguished from other processes that exchange one contaminant for another, such as water softening (in which calcium and magnesium salts are removed by exchanging them with sodium salts). The reverse osmosis, deionization, and distillation processes are all capable of producing laboratory-grade water.

The quality of the laboratory-grade water produced by several methods of central-system water production is shown in Table 10-3. The RO and distillation processes remove 99+% of all bacteria, pyrogens, colloidal matter, and organics above molecular weight 200. These methods remove the dissolved inorganic material, such as multivalent ions, calcium, magnesium, carbonates, and heavy metals to the level of 98%, while monovalent ions, such as

Table 10-3 Comparison of Laboratory-Grade Water Quality Produced by Centralized Systems

Contaminant	Tap, Typical	Reverse Osmosis Actual	Percent Removal	Distilled Actual	Percent Removal	Deionized Actual	Percent Removal
Microorganism/ mL	100	1	>99	1	>99	1000 [a]	none
Particles 5 μm/mL	10,000	1	>99	200	>97	10,000	none
Pyrogens	Variable	—	>99	—	>99	Variable	none
Dissolved organics ppm	12	1	>95	1	>95	12 [b]	none
Dissolved inorganics ppm $CaCO_3$	170	1–17	>90–98	1–8	>95–99	1–8	>95–99
Monovalent ions [c]	—	—	>90	—	>97	—	>97
Multivalent ions [d]	—	—	>97	—	>97	—	>97
Conductivity, μS, 25°C	333	2–40	—	2–10	—	2–10	—
Specific resistance MΩ/cm, 25°C	0.003	0.025–0.5	—	0.1–0.5	—	0.1–0.5	—
Silicates ppm	1	0.1	>90	0.1	>90	0.1	>90
Heavy metals ppm	1	0.1	>97	0.1	>97	0.1	>90
pH	7.5	6. 8	—	4–7. 5	—	7.0	—

[a] Bacteria often multiply in large deionizing (D.I.) resin beds used directly on tap water.

[b] Large D.I. resin beds also contribute organics from the resin beds.

[c] Monovalent ions: Singly charged ions such as Na^+, K^+, Cl^-

[d] Multivalent ions: Multiply charged ions such as Ca^{2+}, Mg^{2+}, CO_3^{2-}, SO_4^{2-}

sodium, potassium, and chloride, are removed to the level of 90–94% by RO and 97% by distillation processes.

Large-scale deionization processes achieve similar levels of inorganic ion removal, but they do not remove bacteria, pyrogens, particles, and organics. Bacteria, in fact, can multiply on the resins, resulting in an increase of biological contaminants over normal tap water.

It should be stressed at this time that the degrees of water purity shown in Table 10-3 are obtainable only from well cleaned equipment that is performing to its original specifications. Maintaining this condition for the deionization process means that the resins must be replaced (or regenerated) regularly and that the internal components of the still must be thoroughly cleaned. If a still is not properly and regularly cleaned, the residual contaminants can cause the pH value of the end product water to fall as low as pH 4. Reverse osmosis is the only one of the three methods that uses a reject stream to continuously remove the residual contaminants. Regularly scheduled prefilter changes and system maintenance are, of course, necessary to maintain the desired water quality.

For dependable long-term performance, the construction of the RO equipment for large-volume applications should be of all stainless steel fittings and bowls. Such a system should use solid state controls (with simple indicator lights and gauges) plus a conductivity meter that reads the tap and permeates water quality. High-pressure relief devices and low-pressure switches protect the membrane and the pump from any prefilter blockage and accidental feed-water shutoff. A water saver device that completely shuts off water flow when the storage tank is full but allows an hourly washing of the membrane is essential.

There are basically three types of semipermeable membranes manufactured from organic substances: the tubular membrane, the cellulose-acetate sheet membrane, and the polyamide-hollow fiber membrane. They may be used for similar applications, assuming that the proper pretreatment for each is furnished.

With the type of RO equipment described above and the feed water within production specifications, RO membranes may last two or three years.

Applications for RO The quality and cost of RO water make RO a strong competitor for distillation and deionization in many applications. Table 10-4 compares the three methods of water purification for several research and industrial applications.

Frequently, the user needs both laboratory-grade and reagent-grade waters to meet a wide range of needs. Figure 10-24 shows two ways of approaching this situation. Alternative A consists of a central RO system from which the water is piped to a point-of-use *polishing system* to be upgraded to reagent-grade water. This approach utilizes the economics of a large central RO system while ensuring the highest reagent-grade

Table 10-4 Applications of RO Water

Water Use	Method of Purification		
	RO	Distilled	Deionized
1. General process use	Yes	Yes	Yes
2. General lab use (buffers, chemical mfg.)	Yes	Yes	Yes (except for pyrogens, bacteria, and organics)
3. Dishwasher final rinse	Yes	Yes	Yes
4. Critical lab use (reagents, tissue culture, etc.)	Post-treatment necessary		
5. USP XXIII water for injection	Yes (Must meet purified water standard)	Yes	No
6. Hemodialysis	Yes	No	Yes (except for pyrogens, bacteria, and organics)

purity at those use points that require it. Alternative B employs smaller point-of-use RO systems, with point-of-use *polishing* and eliminates the lengthy distribution piping, a potential source of recontamination. Both alternatives include a final *polishing* by activated carbon, mixed-bed deionization, and 0.22-μ membrane filtration. In each case, laboratory-grade water is readily available directly from the RO system. Moreover, the transportation and storage of the reagent-grade water is avoided.

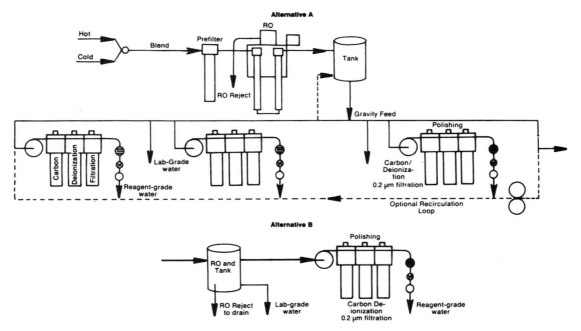

Figure 10-24 Approaches to Providing Laboratory-Grade and Reagent-Grade Water: (A) RO Water Purified Centrally and Transported by Pipe to Points of Use Then Polished, (B) RO System Coupled with Deionization System Totally at the Point of Use, Eliminating Piping.

Nanofiltration

Nanofiltration (NF) is a membrane filtration system that removes particles in the 300–1000 molecular weight range, rejecting selected ionic salts and most organics. Nanofiltration rejects the dissociated inorganic salts that are polyvalent, such as calcium, magnesium, and sulfate, while passing monovalent salts, such as sodium and chloride. Therefore, nanofiltration is often called a "softening membrane system." Nanofiltration operates at lower feed pressures. The equipment is similar to that for reverse osmosis.

Ultrafiltration

Ultrafiltration (UF) is a membrane filtration system of separating liquids and solids. It provides filtration in the range of 0.0015–0.1 μ or approximately 1000 to 100,000 molecular weight. Ultrafiltration is often used to separate oil and water as in cutting solutions, mop water, and coolants.

GLOSSARY

The following is a list of common terms used in connection with water conditioners. A thorough knowledge of these terms and their applications will enable the designer to offer more complete service. The following should not be used as the official definitions of such terms. The designer is referred to the Plumbing Terminology section of *ASPE Data Book*, Vol. 1, Chapter 1, "Formulae, Symbols and Terminology," (1999) or other acceptable definition sources.

Absorption The process of taking up a substance into the physical structure of a liquid or solid by a physical or chemical action but without a chemical reaction.

Adsorption The process by which molecules, colloids, and/or particles adhere to the surfaces by physical action but without a chemical reaction.

Algae A microscopic plant growth that may be found in some well waters in certain areas of the country. This plant growth may collect on the resin in the water conditioner and result in poor operation because of a restricted water flow.

Chlorination and dechlorination will control this problem and protect the plumbing lines and fixtures.

Alkalinity The capacity to neutralize acid, usually because of the presence of bicarbonate or carbonate ions.

Anion Negatively charged ion in a solution.

Automatic softener A fully automatic water softener regenerates at regular intervals, without attention, to provide a continuous supply of soft, conditioned water.

Backwashing After the ion exchange capacity of the water softener resin is exhausted, it is necessary to regenerate the resin so that its original capacity may be restored. A very important step in this process is called "backwashing," which is accomplished by reversing the flow of the water through the resin. This upward flow of water carries out to the drains any dirt and oxidized iron collected on top of the resin bed. Backwashing also prevents the resin from becoming packed or channeled.

Bacteria Tiny organisms occurring naturally in waters. Pathogenic (disease-causing) bacteria cause illnesses, such as typhoid, dysentery, and cholera.

Bacteriological examination New wells and private water supplies should be tested at periodic intervals to determine if the water is safe to drink. This bacteria test should be conducted by an official representative for the state board of health in accordance with accepted practice and local standards. A water softener, iron remover, clarifier, or neutralizer does not purify the water.

Bed depth In every water conditioner, there is a material for a specific purpose. In the water softener, it is called "high-capacity resin" or "ion exchange mineral." Depending upon the size of the tank, this material is measured in inches of depth in the tank. This measurement is called the "bed depth."

Biological oxygen demand (BOD) A measurement of the amount of oxygen required for the biochemical degradation of organic material in water.

Bleed through When all of the iron is not removed during the service cycle of a water softener (or iron remover), the iron remaining in the effluent of treated water is usually referred to as the "bleed through."

Brine A solution of sodium chloride (common salt) used for regenerating water softeners.

Brine tank A separate tank in the system employed to store the water and salt (sodium chloride) to form a brine solution.

Bypass A connection, or a valve system, that allows the hard water to supply the system while the water softener is being regenerated or serviced.

Calcium As one of the principal elements that constitutes the earth's crust, calcium compounds, when dissolved in water, making the water hard. The presence of calcium in the water is one of the major factors contributing to the formation of scale and insoluble soap curds, which are two ways of easily identifying hard water. Often it is expressed as calcium carbonate ($CaCO_3$).

CAP College of American Pathologists, which has set water purification standards for laboratory use.

Capacity The ability of certain size water conditioners to remove a specific quantity of hardness minerals, iron, or manganese from the water going through the water conditioner.

Carbon dioxide (CO_2) A gas that is produced from the air when water falls as rain or by the decaying action of organic matter in the earth.

Cartridge filter A filter device, usually disposable, with a wide range of micron sizes.

Cation Positively charged ions in solutions.

Chemical oxygen demand (COD) A measurement of the amount of oxygen required to oxidize chemicals in water.

Chloride (Cl) An element commonly found in most natural groundwaters and generally combined with other minerals, such as sodium chloride ($NaCl$).

Clarifier A device that removes turbidity, which is defined as sand, clay, silt or other undissolved foreign matter. (See "Turbidity.")

Coagulant A chemical added to water and waste-water applications to form flocs that adsorb, entrap, and bring together suspended matter so that it can be removed.

Coalescing The separation of immiscible fluids (such as oil and water) with different specific gravities.

Cocurrent regeneration During regeneration of a water conditioner, the flow is in the same direction of the service flow in all steps in the regeneration cycle except the backwash.

Concentrate In cross-flow filtration, reverse osmosis, nanofiltration, and ultrafiltration, concentrate is that amount of feed stream that does not permeate (go through) the membrane and thus concentrate the ions, suspended solids, and organics in the waste stream.

Conductivity The ability of water to conduct electricity. Conductivity is the inverse of resistivity. It is measured with a conductivity meter and described as microsiemens per centimeter (μS/cm), which is the same as micromhos per centimeter (μmho/cm), which was used in the past.

Control valve A device on a water conditioner that may be manually or automatically operated and used to direct (or control) the flow of the water in a certain direction.

Conversion formula—parts per million to grains per gallon Hardness minerals, calcium and magnesium, are measured in parts per million (ppm) or grains per gallon (gpg). The accepted conversion factor is 17.1 ppm = 1 gpg, i.e., 10 gpg of hardness = 171 ppm.

Corrosion The attack by water on any part of a water system causing the wasting away of metal parts.

Countercurrent regeneration During the regeneration of a water conditioner, all steps in the regeneration cycle, the flow is in the opposite direction of the service flow.

Cross-flow membrane filtration The separation of components of a fluid by a semipermeable membrane such as reverse osmosis, nanofiltration, ultrafiltration, and microfiltration.

Cubic foot of mineral The high-capacity resin or ion exchange mineral used in a water softener is measured and rated in cubic foot (ft^3)

lots. For example, 1 ft^3 of high-capacity resin will remove approximately 30,000 gpg of hardness minerals (calcium and magnesium) before a regeneration of the material is required.

Cycle The cycle of a water softener is generally defined as the length of time it will operate without a backwashing and/or regeneration.

Cycle operation Usually the sequence of valve operations on automatic water softeners. A two-cycle valve is a device in which upflow brining is combined with the backwash cycle, sacrificing the performance on both the backwashing and the brining. The five-cycle valve, such as the one fully automatic softeners feature, performs each essential regeneration step separately, therefore, under optimum conditions, this type of valve provides a longer life, a more efficient service, and a better performance.

Diatome An organism commonly found in waters and considered by health officials to be nonharmful. Diatomes may occasionally impart objectionable odors and their calcified skeletons make chalk and provide a diatomite powder used for swimming pool features.

Dissolved iron In water treatment, iron is usually described as being dissolved in water. The dissolved, or ferrous, iron is highly soluble in most waters and the undissolved, or ferric, iron is almost always insoluble in water.

Dissolved solids The residual material remaining after the solution evaporates to a dry state.

Distributor Sometimes this device is called a "strainer"; it is used within a softener tank to distribute the flow of the water throughout the tank and to prevent the resin from escaping into the lines.

Down flow Usually designates the down direction in which the water flows. For example, during the brine cycle of the manual and semi-automatic water softeners, the direction of the water flow is in the down direction.

Drain valve (drain line) A valve or line employed to direct or carry the backwash water, the used regenerant, and the rinse water to the nearest drain of the waste system.

Effluent The water moving away from, or out of, a water conditioner (see "Influent").

Endotoxin A heat-resistant pyrogen found in the cell walls of viable and nonviable bacteria. Expressed as EDU units.

Exhaustion In water softening or ion exchange, the point where the resin can no longer exchange additional ions of the type the process was designed for.

Ferric iron The insoluble form of iron. Ferrous iron in the water is readily converted to ferric iron by exposure to oxygen in the air.

Ferrous iron The soluble form of iron. (See "Ferric Iron.")

Filter-ag A mineral used in the clarifier to physically separate the suspended matter in some water supplies. This ceramic-like granular material is insoluble and it backwashes freely with less water than sand and other similar filter materials.

Filtration The process of passing a fluid through a filter material for the purpose of removing turbidity, taste, color, or odor.

Floc The suspended particles in the water that have coagulated into larger pieces and may form a mat on the top of the mineral or resin bed in a water conditioner and reduce or impair the efficient operation of the equipment.

Flow rate In water treatment, this term refers to the quantity of water flowing, given in gallons per minute (gpm) or gallons per hour (gph).

Flow regulator A mechanical or automatic device used in water treatment equipment to regulate the flow of the water to a specified maximum flow rate.

Flux In cross-flow filtration, the unit membrane throughput, expressed as volume per unit of time per area, such as gallons per day per square foot.

Free board The space above a bed of ion exchange resin or mineral in a water softener tank that allows for the unobstructed expansion of the bed during the backwash cycle.

Grains capacity The amount of hardness mineral (calcium or magnesium) that will be removed by a water softener mineral or resin within a specified length of time or by a specific quantity of the resin (see "High-Capacity Resin").

Grains per gallon (gpg) A common basis of reporting water analysis. One grain per gallon (gpg) equals 17.1 parts per million (ppm). One grain is 1/7000 of a pound.

Hardness The compounds of calcium and magnesium that are usually present in hard water.

Hardness leakage The presence of hardness minerals (calcium and magnesium) after the water has passed through the softener. Hardness leakage is encountered primarily because of hardness retained in the resin bed from the previous service run. This is normal, as a point of diminishing return is realized in salt consumed versus percentage of original new capacity. In normal practice, 15 lb of salt/ft^3 of resin is considered the practical upper limit for a regeneration. The amount of leakage expected in a properly operating system is directly proportional to the salt rate and the total dissolved solids (TDS) in the incoming water. The greater the TDS and the lower the skating rate (5 lb/ft^3 is generally considered minimum), the greater the hardness leakage. While some leakage is normal, as explained above, excessive leakage usually indicates faulty regeneration.

High-capacity resin This term applies to the manufactured material, in the form of beads or granules, that can be described as having the power to take hardness-forming ions and give up softness-forming ions and the reverse cycle thereof. This material is sometimes called ion exchange resin.

High purity A term describing highly treated water with attention to microbiological reduction or elimination, commonly used in the electronic and pharmaceutical industries.

Hose bib An outside plumbing connection for attaching a hose.

Hydrogen sulfide A highly corrosive gas that is often found in the water supplies. Water containing hydrogen sulfide gas has a characteristic boiled or rotten egg odor. A water softener is not designed to correct this condition.

Influent The water moving toward, or into, a water softener (see "effluent").

Inlet or outlet valve A gate valve on the inlet or outlet piping of a water conditioner.

Installation sequence In water treatment applications, it is sometimes necessary to install more than one piece of water treatment equipment to properly condition the untreated water. When this situation is necessary, it is imperative for the water treatment equipment to be installed in the proper sequence to ensure a satisfactory operation.

Ion An electrically charged particle. For example, one particle of salt is composed of approximately 100 million molecules and each molecule of sodium chloride (salt) is composed of one sodium atom and one chlorine atom. The chlorine and sodium atoms in a sodium chloride molecule are separated by dissolving the molecule in water in a process known as "ionization." However, the ions retain the electrostatic charge present in the original salt molecule.

Ion exchange The replacement of one ion by another. In the softening process, the sodium in the softener resin is exchanged for calcium, magnesium, iron, and manganese (if present).

Iron An element common to most underground water supplies, though not present in the large quantities that calcium and magnesium can be. Even small amounts of iron are highly objectionable in the water system. Iron removal from water is accomplished in two ways: the small amounts of the dissolved iron may be removed (1) by an ion exchange process or (2) by precipitation and filtration processes. For the latter method, an iron remover is used.

Limestone A common rock of the earth composed primarily of calcium. It combines with carbon dioxide present in groundwater to form calcium carbonate and causes hardness of water.

Magnesium An element that, along with calcium, is responsible for the hardness of water.

Natural water Water containing dissolved inorganic solids, which are largely mineral salts. These salts are introduced into the water by a solvent action, as the water passes through, or across, various layers of the earth. The type of mineral salts absorbed depends on the chemical contents of the soil through which the water passes. *Note*: Pure water (no impurities) is never found in nature.

Nitrate Something that is sometimes found in natural water, but in trace amounts. It is becoming more of a concern, as nitrate contamination from sewage or predominantely concentrated nitrogen fertilizers in the groundwater table is surfacing in some areas of the country. High nitrate levels, generally 10 ppm or more, can cause a condition known as "blue baby," a condition that inhibits the transfer of oxygen through the lung tissue to the bloodstream, resulting in oxygen starvation. Pregnant women and young children are cautioned in this regard; pregnant women are cautioned in regard to their unborn child as opposed to their own physical well-being. Adults do not normally suffer any effect at these levels. In animals, such as cattle and horses, high nitrate levels can cause stillborn offspring and miscarriages, as well as a high mortality rate of the newly born.

Ohm A unit of measurement. One ohm (1 Ω) is equals 0.5×10^{-6} ppm or 10^{-6} microsiemens (μS).

Parts per million (ppm) A common method of reporting water analyses. 17.1 ppm equals 1 grain per gallon (gpg). Parts per million is commonly considered equivalent to milligrams per liter (mg/L).

pH value A number denoting the alkaline or acid nature of the water (or solution). The pH scale ranges from 0 to 14, 7.0 being the accepted neutral point. A pH value below 7.0 indicates acidity in the water (or solution). Values for pH above 7.0 indicate alkalinity of the water (or solution).

Precipitate A solid residue formed in the process of removing certain dissolved chemicals out of a solution.

Pressure drop A decrease in the water pressure, measured in pounds per square inch (psi).

Regeneration Complete regeneration of a water softener, consisting of a backwash cycle, addition of sodium chloride (salt), and rinsing the sodium chloride solution through the ion exchange resin to exchange the hardness ions collected in the resin and prepare the solution for a service cycle.

Resin A synthetic polystyrene ion exchange material (often called a "high-capacity resin").

Rinse Part of the regeneration cycle of a water softener where fresh water is passed through a water softener to remove the excess salt (sodium chloride) prior to placing the water softener into service.

Salt A high-grade sodium chloride of a pellet or briquette type used for regenerating a water softener.

Service run The operating cycle of a water softener, during which the hard water passes through the ion exchange resin and enters the service lines as soft water.

Sodium (Na⁺) An element usually found in water supplies (depending on local soil conditions) that is a basic part of common salt (sodium chloride).

Soft water Water without hardness material, which has been removed either naturally or through ion exchange.

Sulphate (SO₄²⁻) A compound commonly found in waters in the form of calcium sulphate ($CaSO_4$) or magnesium sulphate ($MgSO_4$).

Suspension The foreign particles carried (but not dissolved) in a liquid, like rusty iron in water.

Tannin An organic color or dye, not a growth, sometimes found in waters. (The latter is the result of decomposition of wood buried underground.)

Titration A laboratory method of determining the presence and amount of chemical in a solution, such as the grains hardness (calcium and magnesium) of water.

Total dissolved solids (TDS) All dissolved materials in the water that cannot be removed by mechanical filtration, generally expressed in terms of parts per million (ppm).

Turbidity A term used to define the physical appearance of water. Laboratory analysis shows the turbidity (in ppm). All undissolved materials, such as clay, silt, or sand, are taken into consideration. If the turbidity is high and the water is unacceptable for use, a clarifier is recommended.

Up flow The up direction in which the water flows through the water conditioner during any phase of the operating cycle.

Virus A tiny organism that is smaller than bacteria and is resistant to normal chlorination. Viruses cause diseases, such as poliomyelitis and hepatitis (both of which are transmitted primarily through water supplies). Cross-connections or polluted waters are the primary means of transmission.

BIBLIOGRAPHY

1. Black, A.P., et al. 1963. The chemistry, technology and physiology of iodine in water disinfection. Paper presented at the 29th Annual Educational Conference of the National Association of Sanitarians.

2. Loeb, S., and S. Sourirajan.(1962). *Advanced Chem* 38, 117.

3. Lonsdale, H, and T. Podall, eds. 1972. *Reverse osmosis membrane research.* New York: Plenum Press.

4. Reid, D., and E. J. Breton. 1959. *Applied Polymer Science* 1, 133 .

5. Water Quality Association. 1999. *Ozone* 1–2.

6. Wattle, E., and C. T. Butterfield. 1944. Relative resistance of *Escherichin coli* and Eberthella thyphosa to chlorine and chloramines. *Public Health Report* 59, 1661.

11

Thermal Expansion

All piping materials undergo dimensional changes due to temperature variations in a given system. The amount of change depends on the material characteristics (the linear coefficient of thermal expansion or contraction) and the amount of temperature change. The coefficient of expansion or contraction is defined as the unit increase or decrease in length of a material per 1°F increase or decrease in temperature. Coefficients of thermal expansion or contraction for a number of commonly used pipe materials are shown in Table 11-1. These coefficients are determined in accordance with ASTM D-696 and are based on completely unrestrained specimens.

Table 11-1 Linear Coefficients of Thermal Expansion or Contraction

Material	Coefficient in/in °F	Expansion or Contraction in/100 ft/10°F
Steel	6.5×10^{-6}	0.078
Cast iron	5.6×10^{-6}	0.067
Copper	9.8×10^{-6}	0.118
Brass	10.4×10^{-6}	0.125
ABS	5.5×10^{-5}	0.66
PVC type I (PVC 1120 and 1220)	3.0×10^{-5}	0.36
PVC type II (PVC 2110, 2112, 2116, and 2120)	4.5×10^{-5}	0.54
PB	7.5×10^{-5}	0.90
PE	8.0×10^{-5}	0.96
CPVC	3.5×10^{-6}	0.42
SR	6.0×10^{-5}	0.72

Notes: ABS = acrylonitrile butadiene styrene; PVC = polyvinyl chloride; PB = polybutylene; PE = polyethylene; CPVC = chlorinated polyvinyl chloride; SR = Styrene Rubber.

If the coefficients of thermal expansion or contraction are known, the total changes in length may be calculated as follows:

Equation 11-1

$$L_2 - L_1 = \alpha L_1 (T_2 - T_1)$$

where

L_1 = Original pipe length, ft

L_2 = Final pipe length, ft

T_1 = Original temperature, °F

T_2 = Final temperature, °F

α = Coefficient of expansion or contraction, ft/ft-°F

A typical range of temperature change in a hot-water piping system is from 40°F entering water to 120°F distribution water, for an 80°F temperature differential. Total linear expansion or contraction for a 100-ft length of run when subject to an 80°F change in temperature can be calculated for the usual piping materials in a hot-water system. A typical range of temperature in a drain, waste, and vent (DWV) system is from 100°F (the highest temperature expected) to 50°F (the lowest temperature expected), for a 50°F temperature differential.

ABOVEGROUND PIPING

Two examples of aboveground piping are hot-water pipe that carries hot water intermittently with a gradual cooling inbetween, and drain, waste, and vent pipe into which water ranging from 50 to 100°F is intermittently discharged. These greater temperature changes are offset by the fact that most aboveground piping involves short runs with several changes in direction. Thus, for many installations, such as one- or two-family dwellings, no special precautions need to be taken. Of particular concern are hot water and DWV systems in high-rise buildings.

Pressure Piping

Aboveground pressure piping incorporating short runs and several changes in direction will normally accommodate expansion or contraction. Precaution should be taken to ensure that pipe hangers or clamps will allow longitudinal movement of the pipe and that the 90° bends are not butted against a wall or similar structure that will restrict movement.

If runs in excess of 20 ft are required, flexural offsets or loops should be provided. In order not to exceed the maximum allowable strain in the piping, the developed length that should be provided in the offset or loop can be calculated from the following equation:

Equation 11-2

$$\Delta = \frac{PL^3}{3\,EI}$$

where

Δ = Maximum deflection at the end of a cantilever beam, in.

P = Force at end, lb

L = Length of pipe subjected to flexible stress, in.

E = Flexural modulus of elasticity, psi

I = Moment of inertia, in.[4]

For pipes in which the wall thickness is not large with respect to the outside diameter, the moment of inertia and the sectional modulus can simply be calculated as follows:

$I = \pi R^3 t$ and

$Z = \pi R^2 t$

where

R = Outside radius, in.

t = Wall thickness, in.

Z = Section modulus, in.[3]

For thin-walled pipes, the maximum allowable stress and the maximum allowable strain can be calculated as follows:

$$S = \frac{4PL}{\pi D^2 t}$$

$$\varepsilon = \frac{\pi D^2 S t}{4L}$$

where

S = Maximum fiber stress in bending = M/Z, psi

M = Bending moment = PL, in-lb

D = Outside diameter, in.

ε = Strain

Substituting the maximum allowable stress and the maximum allowable strain into Equation 11-2, the development length of piping can be estimated by Equations 11-3 and 11-4, respectively.

Equation 11-3

$$L = \left(\frac{3ED\Delta}{2\,S}\right)^{\frac{1}{2}}$$

Equation 11-4

$$L = \left(\frac{3\,D\Delta}{2\,\varepsilon}\right)^{\frac{1}{2}}$$

Equation 11-3 is used when the maximum allowable stress is fixed, and Equation 11-4 when the maximum allowable strain is fixed. When Equation 11-4 is used, the flexural modulus of elasticity needs to be known. In cases where the modulus of the specific compound is not available, the following approximately average values are usually adequate:

Compound	E at 73°F, psi	Hydrostatic Design Stress for Water at 73°F, S
Copper	15.6 x 10⁻⁶	6000
Steel	30 x 10⁻⁶	
Cast iron		
Brass		
PVC 1120	400,000	2000
PVC 2110	340,000	1000
ABS 1210	240,000	1000
ABS 1316	340,000	1600
PE 2306	90,000	630

Equation 11-3 can be factored to yield the following equation:

Equation 11-5

$$L = \frac{3E}{2S} (D\Delta)^{\frac{1}{2}}$$

where

E and S = Constants for any given material

Using the values for E and S in the above table, Equation 11-3 or 11-5 reduces to the following table:

Compound	Equation 11-3, in.
Steel pipe	$L = 6.16 (D\Delta)^{\frac{1}{2}}$ [a]
Brass pipe	$L = 6.83 (D\Delta)^{\frac{1}{2}}$
Copper pipe	$L = 7.40 (D\Delta)^{\frac{1}{2}}$
PVC 1120	$L = 17.3 (D\Delta)^{\frac{1}{2}}$
PVC 2110	$L = 22.8 (D\Delta)^{\frac{1}{2}}$
ABS 1210	$L = 19.0 (D\Delta)^{\frac{1}{2}}$
ABS 1316	$L = 17.9 (D\Delta)^{\frac{1}{2}}$
PE 2306	$L = 14.6 (D\Delta)^{\frac{1}{2}}$
PE 3306	$L = 16.9 (D\Delta)^{\frac{1}{2}}$

[a] L = Developed length of piping used to absorb movement, ft.
D = Outside diameter of pipe, in.
Δ = Amount of movement to be absorbed, in.

Provisions must be made for the expansion and contraction of all hot-water and circulation mains, risers, and branches. If the piping is restrained from moving, it will be subjected to compressive stress on a temperature rise and to tensile stress on a temperature drop. The pipe itself can usually withstand these stresses, but failure frequently occurs at pipe joints and fittings when the piping cannot move freely.

There are two methods commonly used to absorb pipe expansion and contraction without damage to the piping:

1. Expansion loops and offsets.

2. Expansion joints.

Often the total movement to be absorbed by any expansion loop or offset is limited to a maximum of 1½ in. for metallic pipes. Thus, by anchoring at the points on the length of run that produce 1½-in. movement and placing the expansion loops or joints midway between the anchors, the maximum movement that must be accommodated is limited to ¾ in. The piping configuration used to absorb the movement can be in the form of a U-bend; a single-elbow offset; a two-elbow offset; or a three-, five-, or six-elbow swing loop. In the great majority of piping systems, the loop or joint can be eliminated by taking advantage of the changes in direction normally required in the layout.

Table 11-2 gives the total developed length required to accommodate a 1½-in. expansion. (The developed length is measured from the first elbow to the last elbow.)

Table 11-2 Developed Length of Pipe to Accommodate 1½-In. Movement

Pipe Size, in.	Steel Pipe, ft	Brass Pipe, in.	Copper Pipe, ft
0.5	7.7	7.7	8.3
0.75	8.7	8.6	9.3
1	9.8	9.6	10.4
1.25	10.4	10.8	11.7
1.5	11.5	11.5	12.5
2	12.8	12.7	13.8
2.5	14.2	14.2	15.4
3	16.0	15.7	17.0
4	16.0	17.7	19.2

Note: mm = in. x 25.4,
m = ft x 0.3048.

If a maximum allowable strain of 0.01 in./in. for plastic pipes is used, Equation 11-4 reduces to

$$L = 12.2 (D\Delta)^{\frac{1}{2}}$$

Use of the factors given in the table for Equation 11-3 or 11-5 above indicates that a strain of less than 0.01 in./in. will result.

Computer programs are available that readily solve these equations as well as address the various installation configurations.

Drain, Waste, and Vent Piping

Expansion or contraction does not usually present a problem in DWV installations in one- and two-family dwellings due to the short lengths of piping involved. It does create problems in high-rise buildings where long stacks are installed. Three methods of accommodating expansion or contraction are described below:

1. To accommodate expansion and contraction in building drains and drainage stacks, offsets may be provided. The developed length of the offset that should be provided can be calculated in accordance with the appropriate formula. For example, for a 50°F temperature differential in the straight run, the amount to be accommodated at the branch connection is approximately ⅜ in. To

accommodate this amount of expansion, the branch pipe must have sufficient development length to overcome a bending twist without being subjected to excessive strain.

2. Where allowed by applicable codes, expansion joints may be used. There are two types of expansion joint: the slip type and the bellows type. The slip type joint with an elastomeric seal requires packing and lubrication. Guides must be installed in the lines to prevent the pipes from bending in the joint. The bellows type expansion joint is satisfactory for the 1½-in. design limitation in movement. It should be guided or in some other way restrained to prevent collapse. An expansion joint should be installed every 30 ft according to the manufacturer's recommendations. Normally the expansion joint is installed in the thermal neutral position so that it can move in either direction to absorb either expansion or contraction. On vertical piping, the pipe should be anchored by side inlets or clamps at or near the joint.

3. Engineering studies have shown that by restraining the pipe every 30 ft to prevent movement, satisfactory installations can be made. Tensile or compressive stresses developed by contraction or expansion are readily absorbed by the piping without any damage. Special stack anchors are available and should be installed according to the manufacturer's recommendations.

UNDERGROUND PIPING

Underground piping temperature changes are less drastic because the piping is not exposed to direct heating from solar radiation, the insulating nature of the soil prevents rapid temperature changes, and the temperature of the transported medium can have a stabilizing effect on the pipe temperature.

Contraction or expansion of flexible pipe can be accommodated by snaking the pipe in the trench. An approximate sine wave configuration with a displacement from the centerline and a maximum offset as shown in Table 11-3 will accommodate most situations. The installation should be brought to the service temperature prior to backfilling. After increased length is taken up by snaking, the trench can be backfilled in the normal manner.

Up to 3 in. nominal size, rigid pipe can be handled by snaking in the same manner used for flexible pipe. Offsets and loop lengths under specific temperature variations are shown in Table 11-3. For distances of less than 300 ft, 90° changes in direction will take up any expansion or contraction that occurs.

For larger sizes of pipe, snaking is not practical or possible in most installations. The pipe is then brought to within 15°F of the service temperature and the final connection is made. This can be accomplished by shade backfilling, allowing the pipe to cool at night and then connecting early in the morning, or cooling the pipe with water. The thermal stresses produced by the final 15°F service temperature will be absorbed by the piping.

EXPANSION TANKS

Introduction

When you heat water, it expands. If this expansion occurs in a closed system, dangerous water pressures can be created. A domestic hot-water system can be a closed system. When hot-water fixtures are closed and the cold-water supply piping has backflow preventers, or any other device that can isolate the domestic hot-water system from the rest of the domestic water supply, a closed system can be created. See Figure 11-1(A).

These pressures can quickly rise to a point at which the relief valve on the water heater will unseat, thus relieving the pressure but at the same time compromising the integrity of the relief valve. See Figure 11-1(B). A relief valve installed on a water heater is not a control valve but a safety valve. It is not designed or intended for continuous usage. Repeated excessive pressures can lead to equipment and pipe failure and personal injury.

When properly sized, an expansion tank connected to the closed system provides additional system volume for water expansion while ensuring a maximum desired pressure in a domestic hot-water system. It does this by utilizing a pressurized cushion of air. See Figure 11-2.

The objectives of this section are to show the designer how to size an expansion tank for a domestic hot-water system and to explain the theory behind the design and calculations. The following discussion is based on the use of a diaphragm or bladder type expansion tank, which

Table 11–3

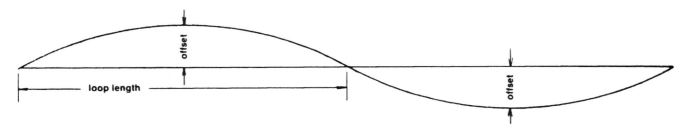

Flexible Pipe
Maximum Temperature Variation (Between Installation and Service), °F

Loop Length, ft	10	20	30	40	50	60	70	80	90	100
					Offset for Contraction, in.					
20	3	4	5	6	7	8	9	10	11	12
50	7½	10	12½	15	17½	20	22½	25	27½	30
100	15	20	25	30	35	40	45	50	55	60

Rigid Pipe
Maximum Temperature Variation (Between Installation and Service), °F

Loop Length, ft	10	20	30	40	50	60	70	80	90	100
					Offset for Contraction, in.					
20	1½	2	2½	3	3½	4	4½	5	5½	6
50	3¾	5	6¼	7½	8¾	10	11¼	12½	13¾	15
100	7½	10	12½	15	17½	20	22½	25	27½	30

Note: °C = (F – 32) /1.8
  mm = in. x 25.4
  m = ft x 0.3048

is the type most commonly used in the plumbing industry. This type of expansion tank does not allow the water and air to be in contact with each other.

Expansion of Water

A pound of water at 140°F has a larger volume than the same pound of water at 40°F. To put it another way, the specific volume of water increases with an increase in temperature. Specific volume data show the volume of 1 lb of water for a given temperature and are expressed in ft³/lb. If the volume of water at each temperature condition is known, the expansion of water can be calculated:

$$Vew = Vs_2 - Vs_1$$

where

Vew = Expansion of water, gal

Vs_1 = System volume of water at temperature 1, gal

Vs_2 = System volume of water at temperature 2, gal

Vs_1 is the initial system volume and can be determined by calculating the volume of the domestic hot-water system. This entails adding the volume of the water heating equipment with the volume of piping and any other part of the hot-water system.

Vs_2 is the expanded system volume of water at the design hot-water temperature. Vs_2 can be expressed in terms of Vs_1. To do that we look at the weight of water at both conditions.

The weight (W) of water at temperature 1 (T_1) equals the weight of water at T_2, or $W_1 = W_2$. At

T_1, $W_1 = Vs_1/vsp_1$, and similarly at T_2, $W_2 = Vs_2/vsp_2$, where vsp equals specific volume of water at the two temperature conditions (see Table 11-4 for specific volume data). Since $W_1 = W_2$, then

$$Vs_1/vsp_1 = Vs_2/vsp_2$$

Solving for Vs_2:

$$Vs_2 = Vs_1 \left(\frac{vsp_2}{vsp_1}\right)$$

Earlier it was stated that

$$Vew = Vs_2 - Vs_1$$

Substituting Vs_2 from above, we can now say that, since

$$Vs_2 = Vs_1 \left(\frac{vsp_2}{vsp_1}\right), \text{ then,}$$

$$Vew = Vs_1 \left(\frac{vsp_2}{vsp_1}\right) - Vs_1, \text{ or}$$

Equation 11-6

$$Vew = Vs_1 \left(\frac{vsp_2}{vsp_1} - 1\right)$$

Example 11-1

A domestic hot-water system has 1000 gal of water. How much will the 1000 gal expand from a temperature of 40°F to a temperature of 140°F?

Solution

From Table 11-4,

$vsp_1 = 0.01602$ (at 40°F)

$vsp_2 = 0.01629$ (at 140°F)

Utilizing Equation 11-6,

$$Vew = 1000 \left(\frac{0.01629}{0.01602} - 1\right)$$

$Vew = 16.9$ gal

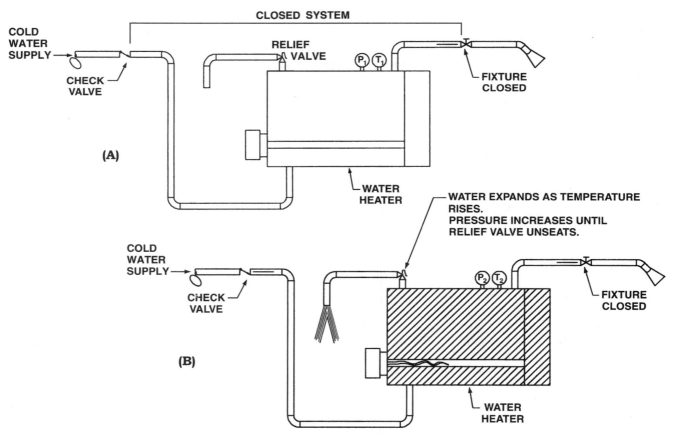

Figure 11-1 A Closed Hot Water System Showing the Effects as Water and Pressure Increase from (A) P_1 and T_1 to (B) P_2 and T_2

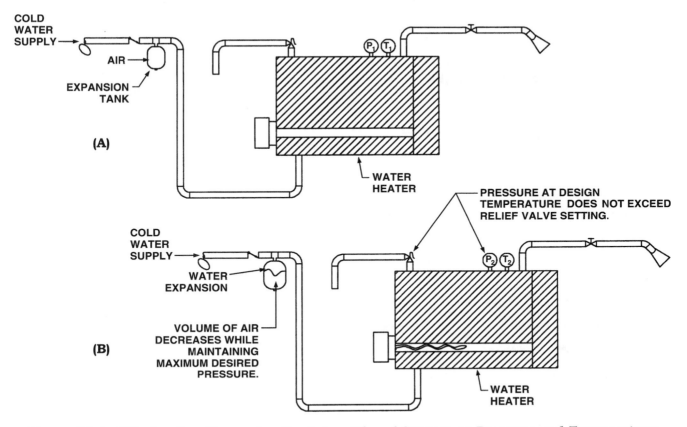

Figure 11-2 Effects of an Expansion Tank in a Closed System as Pressure and Temperature Increase from (A) P_1 and T_1 to (B) P_2 and T_2

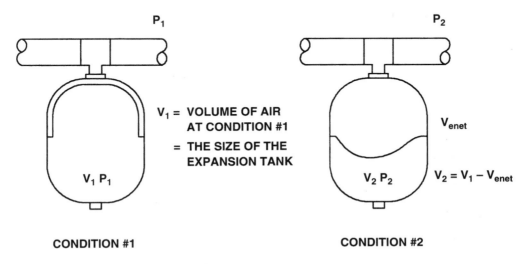

NOTE: PRESSURE OF WATER = PRESSURE OF AIR

Figure 11-3 Sizing the Expansion Tank

Please note that this is the amount of water expansion and should not be confused with the size of the expansion tank needed.

Table 11-4 Thermodynamic Properties of Water at a Saturated Liquid

Temp., °F	Specific Volume, ft^3/lb
40	0.01602
50	0.01602
60	0.01604
70	0.01605
80	0.01607
90	0.01610
100	0.01613
110	0.01617
120	0.01620
130	0.01625
140	0.01629
150	0.01634
160	0.01639

Expansion of Material

Will the expansion tank receive all the water expansion? The answer is no, because not just the water is expanding. The piping and water-heating equipment expand with an increased temperature as well. Any expansion of these materials will result in less of the water expansion being received by the expansion tank. Another way of looking at it is as follows:

$$Venet = Vew - Vemat$$

where

    Venet = Net expansion of water received by the expansion tank, gal

    Vew = Expansion of water, gal

    Vemat = Expansion of material, gal

To determine the amount of expansion each material will experience per a certain change in temperature one looks at the coefficient of linear expansion for that material. For copper, the coefficient of linear expansion is 9.5×10^{-6} in./in.°F; for steel it is 6.5×10^{-6} in./in.°F. From the coefficient of linear expansion, we can determine the coefficient of volumetric expansion of material. The coefficient of volumetric expansion is three times the coefficient of linear expansion:

$$ß = 3\alpha$$

where

$ß$ = Volumetric coefficient of expansion

α = Linear coefficient of expansion

The volumetric coefficient for steel, then, is 19.5×10^{-6} gal/gal°F, and for copper it is 28.5×10^{-6} gal/gal°F. The material will expand proportionally with an increase in temperature.

Equation 11-7

$$Vemat = Vmat \times ß\,(T_2 - T_1)$$

Making the above substitution and solving for Venet,

Equation 11-8

$$Venet = Vew - [Vmat_1 \times ß_1\,(T_2 - T_1) + Vmat_2 \times ß_2\,(T_2 - T_1)]$$

Table 11-5 Nominal Volume of Piping

Pipe Size, in.	Volume of Pipe, gal/linear ft of pipe
½	0.02
¾	0.03
1	0.04
1¼	0.07
1½	0.10
2	0.17
2½	0.25
3	0.38
4	0.67
6	1.50
8	2.70

Example 11-2

A domestic hot-water system has a water heater made of steel with a volume of 900 gal. It has 100 ft of 4-in. piping, 100 ft of 2-in. piping, 100 feet of 1½-in. piping, and 300 ft of ½-in. piping. All the piping is copper. Assuming that the initial temperature of water is 40°F and the final temperature of water is 140°F, (1) how much will each material expand, and (2) what is the net expansion of water that an expansion tank will see?

Solution

1. Utilizing Equation 11-7 for the steel (material no. 1),

$Vmat_1$ = 900 gal

$Vemat_1$ = 900 $(19.5 \times 10^{-6})(140 - 40)$

= 1.8 gal

For the copper (material no. 2), we first look at Table 11-5 to determine the volume of each size of pipe.

4-in.:	100 × 0.67 =	67 gal
2-in.:	100 × 0.17 =	17 gal
1½-in.:	100 × 0.10 =	10 gal
½-in.:	300 × 0.02 =	6 gal
Total volume of copper piping:		100 gal

Utilizing Equation 11-7 for copper,

$Vmat_2$ = 100 gal

$Vemat_2$ = 100 $(28.5 \times 10^{-6})(140 - 40)$

= 0.3 gal

2. The initial system volume of water (Vs_1) equals $Vmat_1$ + $Vmat_2$, or 900 gal + 100 gal. In Example 11-1, we already determined that 1000 gal of water going from 40 to 140°F will expand 16.9 gal. So, utilizing Equation 11-8, we find that Venet = 16.9 – (1.8 + 0.03) = 15 gal. This is the net amount of water expansion that the expansion tank will see. Once again, please note that this is not the size of the expansion tank needed.

Boyle's Law

We have determined how much water expansion will be seen by the expansion tank. Now it is time to look at how the cushion of air in an expansion tank allows us to limit the system pressure.

Boyle's law states that at a constant temperature, the volume occupied by a given weight of perfect gas (including for practical purposes atmospheric air) varies inversely as the absolute pressure (gage pressure + atmospheric pressure). It is expressed by

Equation 11-9

$$P_1V_1 = P_2V_2$$

where

P_1 = Initial air pressure, psia

V_1 = Initial volume of air, gal

P_2 = Final air pressure, psia

V_2 = Final volume of air, gal

How does this law relate to sizing expansion tanks in domestic hot-water systems? The air cushion in the expansion tank provides a space for the expanded water to go into. The volume of air in the tank will decrease as the water expands and enters the tank. As the air volume decreases the air pressure increases.

Utilizing Boyle's law, we can determine that the initial volume of air (i.e., the size of the expansion tank) must be based on (1) the initial water pressure, (2) the desired maximum water pressure, and (3) the change in the initial volume of the air. To utilize the above equation, we realize that the pressure of the air equals the pressure of the water at each condition and we make the assumption that the temperature of the air remains constant at condition 1 and condition 2. This assumption is reasonably accurate if the expansion tank is installed on the cold-water side of the water heater. Remember, in sizing an expansion tank you are sizing a tank of air, not a tank of water.

Referring to Figure 11-3, at condition 1, the tank's initial air pressure charge, P_1, equals the incoming water pressure on the other side of the diaphragm. The initial volume of air in the tank, V_1, is also the size of the expansion tank we are solving for. The final volume of air in the tank, V_2, also can be expressed as V_1 less the net expansion of water (Venet). The pressure of the air at condition 2, P_2, will be the same pressure as the maximum desired pressure of the domestic hot water system at the final temperature, T_2. P_2 should always be less than the relief valve setting on the water heater.

Utilizing Boyle's law,

$$P_1V_1 = P_2V_2$$

Since

$$V_2 = V_1 - Venet, \text{ then}$$

$$P_1V_1 = P_2(V_1 - Venet)$$

$$P_1V_1 = P_2V_1 - P_2Venet$$

$$(P_2 - P_1)V_1 = P_2Venet$$

$$V_1 = \frac{P_2 Venet}{P_2 - P_1}$$

Multiplying both sides of the equation by $(1/P_2)/(1/P_2)$, or by "1," the equation becomes:

Equation 11-10

$$V_1 = \frac{Venet}{1 - P_1/P_2}$$

where

V_1 = The size expansion tank required to maintain the desired system pressure, P_2, gal

Venet = Net expansion of water, gal

P_1 = Incoming water pressure, *psia* (*Note*: Absolute pressure is gage pressure plus atmospheric pressure, e.g., 50 psig = 64.7 psia.)

P_2= Maximum desired pressure of water, *psia*

Example 11-3

Looking again at the domestic hot-water system described in Example 11-2, if the cold water supply pressure is 50 psig and the maximum desired water pressure is 110 psig, what size expansion tank is required?

In Example 11-2 we determined that Venet equals 15 gal. Converting the given pressures to absolute and utilizing Equation 11-10 we can determine the size of the expansion tank needed:

V_1 = 15/(1 – 64.7/124.7)
     = 31 gal

Note: When selecting the expansion tank, make sure the tank's diaphragm or bladder can accept 15 gal of water (Venet).

Summary

Earlier in this section, the following were established:

Equation 11-6

$$Vew = Vs_1 \left(\frac{vsp_2}{vsp_1 - 1} \right)$$

Equation 11-8

$$Venet = Vew - [Vmat_1 \times ß_1 (T_2 - T_1) + Vmat_2 \times ß_2 (T_2 - T_1)]$$

In Equation 11-6, Vs_1 was defined as the system volume at condition 1. Vs_1 can also be expressed in terms of Vmat:

$$Vs_1 = Vmat_1 + Vmat_2$$

Making this substitution and combining the equations, we get the following two equations:

Equation 11-11

$$Venet = (Vmat_1 + Vmat_2)\left(\frac{vsp_2}{vsp_1} - 1\right) - [Vmat_1 \times ß_1(T_2 - T_1) + Vmat_2 \times ß_2(T_2 - T_1)]$$

Equation 11-10

$$V_1 = \frac{Venet}{1 - P_1/P_2}$$

where

Venet = Net expansion of water seen by the expansion tank, gal

Vmat = Volume of each material, gal

vsp = Specific volume of water at each condition, ft^3/lb

ß = Volumetric coefficient of expansion of each material, gal/gal°F

T = Temperature of water at each condition, °F

P = Pressure of water at each condition, psia

V_1 = Size of expansion tank required, gal

These two equations are required to properly size an expansion tank for a domestic hot water system.

BIBLIOGRAPHY

1. Copper Development Association, Inc. "Copper Tube," *Copper Brass Bronze Product Handbook*.

2. Steele, Alfred. 1982. *Engineered Plumbing Design*, 2d ed. Construction Industry Press, Elmhurst, IL.

3. *Thermal Expansion and Contraction of Plastic Pipe*, PPI-TR 21-Nov., 1974.

12 Water Coolers: Potable Water Coolers and Central Water Systems

UNITARY COOLERS

A mechanically refrigerated drinking-water cooler consists of a factory-made assembly in one structure. This cooler uses a complete, mechanical refrigeration system and has the primary functions of cooling potable water and providing such water for dispensing by integral and/or remote means.

Water coolers differ from water chillers. Water coolers are used to dispense potable water, whereas water chillers are used in air-conditioning systems for residential, commercial, and industrial applications, and in cooling water for industrial processes.

The capacity of a water cooler is the quantity of water cooled in 1 h from a specified inlet temperature to a specified dispensing temperature; it is expressed in gallons (liters) per hour. (See the section on ratings, which follows, and Table 12-1.) Standard capacities of water coolers range from 1 to 30 gph (3.8 to 114 L/h).

Types

The three basic types of water cooler are as follows:

1. A *bottle water cooler* (see Figure 12-1) uses a bottle, or reservoir, for storing the supply of water to be cooled and a faucet or similar means for filling glasses, cups, or other containers. It also includes a waste-water receptacle.

2. A *pressure type water cooler* (see Figure 12-2) is supplied with potable water under

pressure and includes a waste-water receptacle or means of disposing water to a plumbing drainage system (see Figure 12-3). Such coolers can use a faucet or similar means for filling glasses or cups, or a valve to control the flow of water as a projected stream from a bubbler so that water may be consumed without the use of glasses or cups.

Figure 12-1 Basic Bottled Drinking-Water Cooler

Note: This chapter was reprinted, with adaptations, by permission of the American Society of Heating, Refrigerating and Air-Conditioning Engineers, Inc., Atlanta, GA.

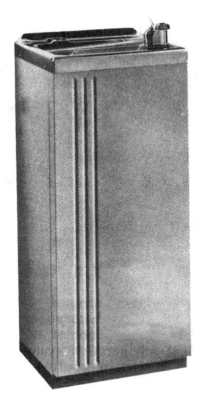

Figure 12-2 Pressure Type Water Cooler (Floor Mounted)

3. A *remote type cooler* is a factory-assembled single structure that uses a complete, mechanical refrigeration system and has the primary function of cooling potable water for delivery to a separately installed dispensing means.

In addition to these basic descriptions, coolers are described by: (1) specialized conditions of use, (2) additional functions they perform, or (3) the type of installation.

1. Specialized uses include the following:

A. An *explosion-proof water cooler* is constructed for safe operation in hazardous locations, as classified in Article 500 of the *National Electrical Code.*

B. A *cafeteria type cooler* is one that is supplied with water under pressure from a piped system and is intended primarily for use in cafeterias and restaurants for dispensing water rapidly and conveniently into glasses or pitchers. It includes a means for disposing waste water to a plumbing drainage system.

C. A *drainless water cooler* is a pressure type cooler supplied by ¼-in. tubing from an available source and does not have a waste connection. As with the bottle water cooler, a drip cup sits on a pressure switch to activate a solenoid valve on the inlet supply to shut off the supply by the weight of the water in the cup.

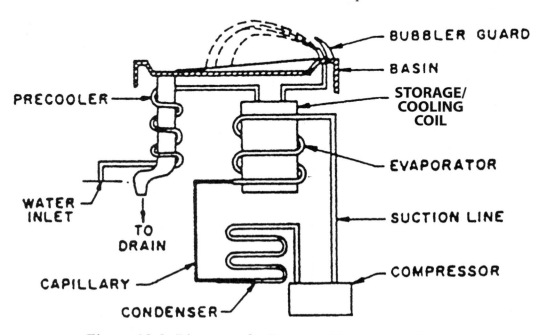

Figure 12-3 Diagram of a Pressure Type Water Cooler

D. *Water coolers for wheelchair use* are in four styles, as follows. [*Note*: For additional information, refer to ASPE *Data Book*, Volume 1, Chapter 6, "Plumbing for Physically Challenged Individuals," (1998); or the Americans with Disabilities Act (1990) and the Appendix (1994).]

a. The original design (see Figure 12-4) had the chilling unit mounted behind the back splash and a surface-mounted bubbler projecting 14 in. from the wall, enabling a person in a wheelchair to roll under.

Figure 12-5 Chilling Unit Mounted Below Level of Basin

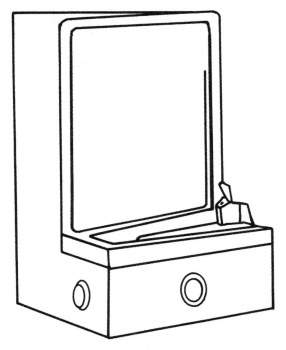

Figure 12-4 Chilling Unit Mounted Behind the Back splash

b. More commonly used at this time is one with a chilling unit below the level of the basin (see Figure 12-5) and the bubbler projecting from the wall at such a height that a person in a wheelchair can roll under.

c. The dual-height design is similar to that shown in Figure 12-5, but with a dual-height configuration. In some states there is a "child" ADA law. It is suggested that the designer check local codes carefully.

d. There is a fully recessed design with the chilling unit mounted above the dispenser (see Figure 12-6) and a recess under the fountain. When using this style, the designer should be sure the grill vanes go upward and the recess is of sufficient depth and width for a person in a wheelchair's use. It is suggested that some thought be given to the option of adding a glass or pitcher filler and possibly a cup dispenser.

2. Additional functions include the following:

A. A water cooler may also have a *refrigerated compartment*, with or without provisions for making ice (see Figure 12-7).

B. A water cooler may also include a means for *heating and dispensing potable water* for making instant hot beverages and soups (see Figure 12-7).

3. Types of installation include (see Figure 12-8)

A. Free-standing (Figure 12-9)

B. Flush to wall (Figure 12-10)

C. Wall hung (Figure 12-11)

D. Semirecessed (Figure 12-12)

E. Fully recessed (Figure 12-13).

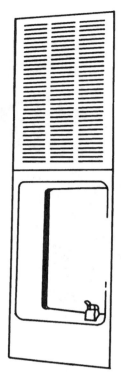

**Figure 12-6 Recess Chilling Unit
Mounted above Dispenser**

**Figure 12-7 Water Cooler with a
Refrigerator**

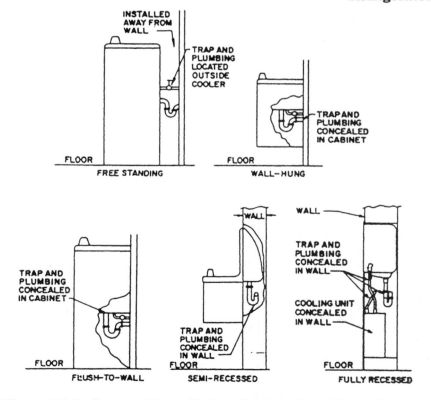

Figure 12-8 Types of Installation for Drinking-Water Coolers

Figure 12-9 Free-Standing Water Cooler

Figure 12-11 Wall-Hung Water Cooler

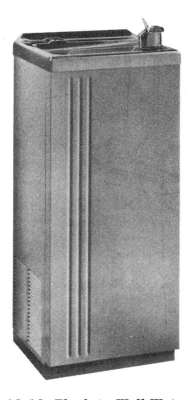

Figure 12-10 Flush-to-Wall Water Cooler

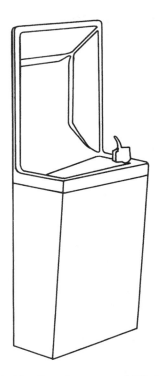

Figure 12-12 Semirecessed Water Cooler

Figure 12-13 Fully Recessed Water Cooler

Refrigeration Systems

Hermetically sealed motor compressors are commonly used for alternating current (AC) applications, both 50 and 60 Hz. Belt-driven compressors are generally used only for direct current (DC) and 25-Hz supply. The compressors are similar to those used in household refrigerators and range from 0.08 to 0.5 hp (0.06 to 0.37 kW).

Forced-air-cooled condensers are most commonly used. In coolers rated less than 10 gph (38 L/h), natural convection, air-cooled (static) condensers are sometimes included. Water-cooled condensers of tube-on-tube construction are used on models intended for high ambient temperatures or where lint and dust in the air make air-cooled types impractical.

Capillary tubes are used almost exclusively for refrigerant flow control in hermetically sealed systems.

Pressure-type coolers are often equipped with precoolers to transfer heat from the supply water to waste water. When drinking from a bubbler stream the user wastes about 60% of the cold water down the drain. In a precooler, there is an arrangement in which the incoming water is put in a heat exchange relationship with the waste water. Sometimes the cold waste water is also used to subcool liquid refrigerant. A precooler with this arrangement is termed an "economizer." Coolers intended only to dispense water into cups are not equipped with precoolers since there is no appreciable quantity of waste water.

Most water coolers manufactured today have the evaporator formed by refrigerant tubing bonded to the outside of a water circuit. The water circuit is usually a tank or a coil of large tubing. Materials used in the water circuit are usually nonferrous or stainless steel. Since the coolers dispense water for human consumption, sanitary requirements are essential. [See Underwriters' Laboratory (UL) 399.]

Water coolers that also provide a refrigerated storage space, commonly referred to as "compartment cooler," have the same control compromises common to all refrigeration devices that attempt two-temperature refrigeration using a single compressor.

Most bottle type compartment coolers are provided with the simplest series system, one in which the refrigerant feeds first to a water-cooling coil and then through a restrictor device to the compartment. When the compressor operates, both water cooling and compartment cooling take place. The thermostat is usually located to be more affected by the compartment temperature, so the amount of compressor operation and water cooling available depends considerably on the usage of the compartment.

Some compartment coolers, generally pressure types, are equipped with more elaborate systems, ones in which separate thermostats and solenoid valves are used to switch the refrigerant flow from a common high side to either the water-cooling evaporator or the compartment evaporator. A more recently developed method of obtaining the two-temperature function uses two separate and distinct systems, each having its own compressor, high side, refrigerant flow metering device, and controls.

Stream Regulators

Since the principal function of a pressure type water cooler is to provide a drinkable stream of cold water from a bubbler, it is usually provided with a valve to maintain a constant stream height, independent of supply pressure. A flow rate of 0.5 gpm (0.03 L/s) from the bubbler is generally accepted as giving an optimum stream for drinking.

Water Conditioning

Many older buildings have lead in the solder of the piping system. Because of concerns about lead, some manufacturers offer different methods of avoiding or removing the lead before it enters the water for the cooler.

1. *Bottle water*, which can be purchased from a reliable source.

2. *Lead-absorbent filter*, for installing on incoming water to the cooler.

3. *Reverse osmosis (RO) system*, which can be built into the water cooler.

Ratings

Water coolers are rated on the basis of their continuous flow capacity under specified water temperature and ambient conditions. Air-Conditioning and Refrigeration Institute (ARI) Standard 1010-2002, *Drinking Fountains and Self-Contained Mechanically-Refrigerated Drinking Water Coolers*, gives the generally accepted rating conditions and references test methods as prescribed in ASHRAE Standard 18-1987, *Methods of Testing for Rating Drinking-Water Coolers with Self-Contained Mechanical Refrigeration Systems*.

Standards and Codes

In addition to ARI Standard 1010-2002 and ASHRAE Standard 18-1987, reaffirmed in 1997, UL Standard 399 covers safety and sanitation requirements. Federal Specifications, WWP–541, and General Services, Federal, AA–2590; AA1154–B, AA–1153–B, and AA–1151–B, are usually prescribed by government purchasers.

Many local plumbing codes apply directly to water coolers. Primarily these codes are directed toward eliminating any possibility of cross-connection between the potable water system and the waste-water (or refrigerant) system. Most coolers are made with double-wall construction to eliminate the possibility of conflict with any code.

Installation

A supply stop should be used so that the unit may be serviced or replaced without having to shut down the water system.

Table 12-1 Standard Rating Conditions

| | Temperature, °F (°C) | | | | |
Type of Cooler	Ambient	Inlet Water	Cooled Water	Heated Potable Water[a]	Spill (%)
Bottle type	90 (32.2)	90 (32.2)	50 (10)	165 (73.9)	None
Pressure type					
Utilizing precooler (bubbler service)	90 (32.2)	80 (26.7)	50 (10)	165 (73.9)	60
Not utilizing precooler	90 (32.2)	80 (26.7)	50 (10)	165 (73.9)	None
Compartment type cooler	During the standard capacity test, there shall be no melting of ice in the refrigerated compartment, nor shall the average temperature exceed 46°F (7.8°C).				

Source: ARI Standard 1010, reprinted by permission.

Note: For water-cooled condenser water coolers the established flow of water through the condenser shall not exceed 2.5 times the base rate capacity, and the outlet condenser water temperature shall not exceed 130°F (54.4°C). The base rate capacity of a pressure water cooler having a precooler is the quantity of water cooled in 1 h, expressed in gallons per hour, at the standard rating conditions, with 100% diversion of spill from the precooler.

a   This temperature shall be referred to as the "standard rating temperature" (heating).

CENTRAL SYSTEMS

A central, chilled, drinking-water system is normally designed to provide water at 50°F (10°C) to the drinking fountains. Water is cooled to 45°F (7.2°C) at the central plant, thus allowing for a 5°F (2.8°C) increase in the distribution system. System working pressures are limited normally to 125 psig (861 kPa). (The designer should check the local code for the maximum pressure allowed.) A central, chilled, drinking-water system should be considered in any building, such as a multistory office building, where there are eight or more drinking fountains stacked one above the other.

A central, chilled, drinking-water system consists of (1) the chilling unit, (2) the distribution piping, (3) drinking fountains, and (4) controls.

Chillers

The chiller may be a built-up or factory-assembled unit; most installations now use factory-assembled units. In either case, the chiller consists of the following:

1. A semihermetic, direct-driven compressor using HFC-134a.

2. A condenser of the shell-and-tube or shell-and-coil type. It may be water or air cooled.

3. A direct-expansion type water cooler of the shell-and-tube type, with a separate field-connected storage tank or an immersion type coil installed in the storage tank. If a separate tank is used, a circulating pump is normally needed to circulate the water between the evaporator and the tank. Evaporator temperatures of 30 to 34°F (1.1°C) are used.

4. An adequately sized storage tank to accommodate the fluctuating demands of a multiple-outlet system. Without a tank, or with a tank that is too small, the fluctuations will cause overloading or short cycling, causing excessive wear on the equipment. The tank must be of nonferrous construction. The evaporator mounted in the tank should be of the same construction as the tank to reduce galvanic action.

5. Circulating pumps are normally of the bronze-fitted, close-coupled, single-stage type with mechanical seals. For the systems designed for 24-h operation, duplex pumps are installed, with each pump being used 12 h/day.

6. Controls consist of high- and low-pressure cutouts, freeze protection, and thermostatic control to limit the temperature of water leaving the chiller. A flow switch or differential pressure control should also be provided to stop the compressor when there is no flow through the cooler. Another desirable item is a time switch that can be used to operate the plant during periods of building occupancy.

Distribution Piping System

The distribution piping delivers chilled water to the drinking fountains. Systems can be upfeed or downfeed, as shown in Figures 12-14 and 12-15. The piping can be galvanized steel, copper, or brass designed for a working pressure of 125 psig (861 kPa).

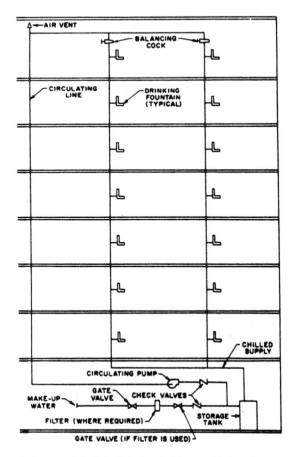

Figure 12-14 Upfeed Central System

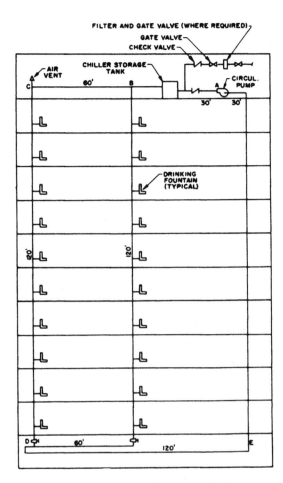

Figure 12-15 Upfeed Central System

Drinking-Water Coolers and Central Systems

The makeup cold-water lines are made of the same material as the distribution piping. When the water supply has objectionable characteristics, such as high iron or calcium content, or contains odoriferous gases in solution, a filter should be installed in the makeup water line.

Insulation is necessary on all the distribution piping and the storage tanks. The insulation should be glass fiber insulation—such as is normally used on chilled-water piping, with a conductivity, k, of 0.22 (32) at a 50°F (10°C) mean temperature, and with a vapor barrier jacket—or equal. All valves and piping, including the branch to the fixture, should be insulated. The waste piping from the drinking fountain, including the trap, should be insulated. This insulation is the same as is recommended for use on cold-water lines.

Drinking Fountains

Any standard drinking fountain can be used on a central drinking-water system. Usually drinking fountains are made of vitreous china or stainless steel. It is important, however, that the automatic volume or stream regulator provided with the fountain be capable of providing a constant stream height from the bubbler with inlet pressures up to 125 psig (861 kPa).

System Design

Refrigeration For an office building, a usage load of 5 gph (19 L/h) per fountain for an average corridor and office is normal. The water consumption for other occupancies is given in Table 12-2. Table 12-3 is used to convert the usage load in gph (L/h) to the refrigeration load in Btu/h (W). The heat gain from the distribution piping system is based on a circulating water temperature of 45°F (7.2 °C). Table 12-4 lists the heat gains for various ambient temperatures. The length of all lines must be included when calculating the heat gain in the distribution piping. Table 12-5 tabulates the heat input from variously sized circulating pump motors.

The total cooling load consists of the heat removed from the makeup water, the heat gains from the piping, the heat gains from the storage tank, and the heat input from the pumps. A safety factor of 10 to 20% is added before selecting a condensing unit. The size of the safety factor is governed by usage. For example, in a building having weekend shutdown, the higher factor of safety would provide for pickup on reopening the building Monday morning when the total volume of water in the system would need to be cooled down to the operating temperature. Since the water to the chiller is a mixture of makeup and return water, the chiller selection should be based on the resultant mixed water temperature.

Circulating pump The circulating pump is sized to circulate a minimum of 3 gpm (0.2 L/s) per branch or the gpm (L/s) necessary to limit temperature rise of the circulatory water to 5°F (2.8°C), whichever is greater. Table 12-6 lists the circulating pump capacity needed to limit the temperature rise of the circulated water to 5°F (2.8°C). If a separate pump is used to circulate water between the evaporator and the storage tank, the energy input to this pump must be included in the heat gain.

Table 12-2 Drinking-Water Requirements

Location	Bubbler Service: Persons Served Per Gallon (Liter) of Standard Rating Capacity	Cup Service: Persons Served Per Gallon (Liter) of Base Rate Capacity
Offices	12 (3)	30 (8)
Hospitals	12 (3)	—
Schools	12 (3)	—
Light manufacturing	7 (2)	—
Heavy manufacturing	5 (2)	—
Hot heavy manufacturing	4 (1)	—
Restaurants		10 (3)
Cafeterias		12 (3)
Hotels (corridors)		—

		Required Rated Capacity per Bubbler, gph (L/h)	
		One Bubbler	Two or More Bubblers
Retail stores, hotel lobbies, office building lobbies	12 (3)	5 (20)	5 (20)
Public assembly halls, amusement parks, fairs, etc.	100 (26)	20–25 (80–100)	15 (60)
Theaters	19 (5)	10 (40)	7.5 (30)

Source: Reprinted from ARI Standard 1010, by permission.

Note: Based on standard rating conditions, with delivered water at 50°F (10°C).

Table 12-3 Refrigeration Load

	Btu/Gal (W/L) Cooled to 45°F (7.2°C)					
Water inlet temp., °F (° C)	65 (18.3)	70 (21.1)	75 (23.9)	80 (26.7)	85 (29.4)	90 (32.2)
Btu/gal	167 (13)	208 (17)	250 (20)	291 (23)	333 (27)	374 (30)

Multiply load for 1 gal (L) by total gph (L/h).

Table 12-4 Circulating System Line Loss

Pipe Size, in. (mm)	Btu/h per Ft Per °F (W/°C/m)	Btu/h per 100 Ft (W per 100 m) [45°F (7.2°C) Circulating Water]		
		Room Temperature, °F (°C)		
		70 (21.1)	80 (26.7)	90 (32.2)
½ (13)	0.110 (0.190)	280 (269)	390 (374)	500 (480)
¾ (19)	0.119 (0.206)	300 (288)	420 (403)	540 (518)
1 (25)	0.139 (0.240)	350 (336)	490 (470)	630 (605)
1¼ (32)	0.155 (0.268)	390 (374)	550 (528)	700 (672)
1½ (38)	0.174 (0.301)	440 (422)	610 (586)	790 (758)
2 (51)	0.200 (0.346)	500 (480)	700 (672)	900 (864)
2½ (64)	0.228 (0.394)	570 (547)	800 (768)	1030 (989)
3 (76)	0.269 (0.465)	680 (653)	940 (902)	1210 (1162)

Table 12-5 Circulating Pump Heat Input

Motor, Hp (kW)	¼ (0.19)	⅓ (0.25)	½ (0.37)	¾ (0.56)	1 (0.75)
Btu/h (W)	636 (186)	850 (249)	1272 (373)	1908 (559)	2545 (746)

Table 12-6 Circulating Pump Capacity

Pipe Size, in. (mm)	Room Temperature, °F (°C)		
	70 (21.1)	80 (26.7)	90 (32.2)
½ (13)	8.0 (99)	11.1 (138)	14.3 (177)
¾ (19)	8.4 (104)	11.8 (146)	15.2 (188)
1 (25)	9.1 (113)	12.8 (159)	16.5 (205)
1¼ (32)	10.4 (129)	14.6 (181)	18.7 (232)
1½ (38)	11.2 (139)	15.7 (195)	20.2 (250)

Notes: 1. Capacities are in gph per 100 ft (L/h per 100 m) of pipe including all branch lines necessary to circulate to limit temperature rise to 5°F (2.8°C) [water at 45°F (7.2°C)].

2. Add 20% for a safety factor. For pump head, figure longest branch only. Install pump on the return line to discharge into the cooling unit. Makeup connection should be between the pump and the cooling unit.

Storage tank The storage tank capacity should be at least 50% of the hourly usage. The hourly usage may be selected from Table 12-2.

Distribution piping

Sizing General criteria for sizing distribution piping for a central, chilled-drinking-water system are

1. Limit the maximum velocity of the water in the circulating piping to 3 fps (0.9 m/s) to avoid giving the water a milky appearance.

2. Avoid excessive friction head losses. Energy required to circulate water enters the water as heat and requires additional capacity in the water chiller. Accepted practice limits the maximum friction loss to 10 ft (3 m) of head per 100 ft (30 m) of pipe.

3. Dead-end piping, such as that from the main riser to the fountain, should be kept as short as possible, and in no event should it exceed 25 ft (7.6 m) in length. The maximum diameter of such dead-end piping should not exceed ⅜ in. (9.5 mm) iron pipe size (IPS) except on very short runs.

4. Size piping on the total number of gallons circulated. This includes gallons consumed plus gallons (litres) necessary for heat leakage.

Design layout General criteria for the design layout of piping for a central chilled-drinking-water system are

1. Keep pipe runs as straight as possible with a minimum of offsets.

2. Use long sweep fittings wherever possible to reduce friction loss.

3. In general, limit maximum pressure developed in any portion of the system to 80 psi (552 kPa). If the height of a building should cause pressures in excess of 80 psi (552 kPa), divide the building into two or more systems.

4. If more than one branch line is used, install balancing cocks on each branch.

5. Provide a pressure relief valve and air vents at high points in the chilled-water loop.

The following example illustrates the calculations required to design a central chilled-drinking-water system.

Example 12-1

Design a central drinking-water system for the ten-story building in Figure 12-15. The net floor area is 14,600 ft^2 (1356 m^2) per floor, and occupancy is assumed to be 100 ft^2 (9.3 m^2) per person. Domestic water is available at the top of the building, with 15 psig (103 kPa) pressure. Applicable codes are the *Uniform Plumbing Code* and the *Uniform Building Code*.

Solution

1. Number of drinking fountains required:

$$\text{Occupancy} = \frac{14,600}{100} = 146 \text{ people/floor}$$

$$\left(\text{Occupancy} = \frac{1356}{9.3} = 146 \text{ people/floor}\right)$$

The *Uniform Building Code* requires 1 fountain on each floor for every 75 people. So,

$$\frac{146}{74} = 1.94 \text{ fountains/floor}$$

Therefore, use 2 fountains per floor, or a total of 20 fountains.

2. Estimated fountain usage: From Table 12-2,

$$\frac{146 \times 0.083}{2} = 6 \text{ gph (22.7 L/h) per fountain}$$

3. Total anticipated makeup water:

6 gph × 10 fountains = 60 gph per riser, or 120 gph for 2 risers (Figure 12-15)

(22.7 L/h × 10 fountains = 227 L/h per riser, or 454 L/h for 2 risers)

4. Refrigeration load to cool makeup water: From Table 12-3, assuming 70°F (21.1°C) water inlet temperature,

120 gph × 208 Btu/h per gal = 25,000 Btu/h

(454 L/h × 16 W/L = 7,300 W)

5. Refrigeration load due to piping heat gain: Determination of heat gain in piping requires pipe sizes, but these sizes cannot be accurately known until the heat gains from the makeup water, piping, storage tank, and pumps are known. Therefore, assume 1-in. (25-mm) diameter chilled-water risers, circulation line, and distribution piping to the risers. Then, the heat gains in the piping system of Figure 12-15 are (from Table 12-4)

Risers: (120 ft) (490 Btu/100 ft)(2 risers) = 1189 Btu/h (349 W)
Distrib. mains: (90 ft) (490 Btu/100 ft) = 440 Btu/h (129 W)
Return riser: (330 ft) (490 Btu/100 ft) = 1620 Btu/h (475 W)
Total piping heat gain = 3249 Btu/h (953 W)

The water that must be cooled and circulated is at a minimum of 3 gpm (11.4 L/h) per riser, or a total of 6 gpm (22.7 L/h).

6. Refrigeration load due to circulating pump input: The pump head can be determined from data given in Table 12-7 and Figure 12-15. The results of the calculations are given in Table 12-8, with the indicated pumping requirements being 6 gpm (22.7 L/h) at a 25.77 ft (7.85 m) head. Data from one manufacturer indicate that a ¾-hp (0.56-kW) motor is needed. From Table 12-5, the heat input of the pump motor is 1908 Btu/h (559 W).

7. Refrigeration load due to storage tank heat gain: The tank is normally sized for 50% of the total hourly demand. Thus, for 100 gph (379 L/h), a 50-gal (190-L) tank would be used. This is approximately the capacity of a standard 16-in. (406-mm) diameter, 60-in. (1524-mm) long tank. Assume 1½-in. (38-mm) insulation, 45°F (7.2°C) water, with the tank in a 90°F (32.2°C) room. Assume an insulation conductivity of 0.13 Btu/h/ft² (0.4 W/m²). The surface area of the tank is about 24 ft² (2.2 m²). Thus, the heat gain is

(24)(0.13)(90 – 45) = 140 Btu/h (41 W)

8. Load summary:

Item		Heat Gain, Btu/h (W)	
Makeup water	=	25,000	(7,325)
Piping	=	3,240	(949)
Pump heat input	=	1,908	(559)
Storage tank	=	140	(41)
Subtotal	=	30,288	(8,874)
20% safety factor	=	6,050	(1,773)
Required chiller capacity	=	36,338	(10,647)

Table 12-7 Friction of Water in Pipes

GPM (L/h)	½-in. (13-mm) Pipe Velocity, ft/s (m/s)	Head, ft (m)	¾-in. (19-mm) Pipe Velocity, ft/s (m/s)	Head, ft (m)	1-in. (25-mm) Pipe Velocity, ft/s (m/s)	Head, ft (m)	1¼-in. (32-mm) Pipe Velocity, ft/s (m/s)	Head, ft (m)	1½-in. (38-mm) Pipe Velocity, ft/s (m/s)	Head, ft (m)
1 (227)	1.05 (0.32)	2.1 (0.64)	—	—	—	—	—	—	—	—
2 (454)	2.10 (0.64)	7.4 (2.26)	1.20 (0.37)	1.9 (0.58)	—	—	—	—	—	—
3 (681)	3.16 (0.96)	15.8 (4.82)	1.80 (0.55)	4.1 (1.25)	1.12 (0.34)	1.26 (0.38)	—	—	—	—
4 (912)	—	—	2.41 (0.73)	7.0 (2.13)	1.49 (0.65)	2.14 (0.65)	0.86 (0.26)	0.57 (0.17)	—	—
5 (1135)	—	—	3.01 (0.92)	10.5 (3.20)	1.86 (0.57)	3.25 (0.99)	1.07 (0.33)	0.84 (0.26)	0.79 (0.24)	0.40 (0.12)
10 (2270)	—	—	—	—	3.72 (1.13)	11.7 (3.57)	2.14 (0.65)	3.05 (0.93)	1.57 (0.48)	1.43 (0.44)
15 (3405)	—	—	—	—	—	—	3.20 (0.98)	6.50 (1.98)	2.36 (0.72)	3.0 (0.91)
20 (4540)	—	—	—	—	—	—	—	—	3.15 (0.96)	5.2 (1.58)

Note: Table gives loss of head in feet (meters) due to friction per 100 ft (30 m) of smooth straight pipe.

Table 12-8 Pressure Drop Calculations for Example 12-1

From[a]:	Pipe Length, ft (m) Actual	Equivalent[b]	Water Flow, gpm (L/h)	Selected Pipe Size (in.)	Pressure Drop, ft (m) 100 ft	Actual ft	Cumulative Pressure Drop, ft (m)
A to B	30 (9)	45 (14)	6 (23)	1	5.0 (1.5)	2.25 (0.7)	2.25 (0.7)
B to D	180 (55)	270 (82)	3 (11.5)	1	1.3 (0.4)	3.5 (1.1)	5.75 (1.8)
D to A	270 (82)	406 (124)	6 (23)	1	5.0 (I.5)	20.02 (6.1)	25.77 (7.9)

[a] Refer to Figure 12-15.

[b] Increase 50% to allow for fittings. If an unusually large number of fittings is used, each should be considered for its actual contribution to pressure drop.

Codes and Regulations

Most mechanical installations are subject to regulation by local codes, and chilled-drinking-water systems are no exception. They must comply with one or more plumbing, refrigeration, and electrical codes. The majority of such local codes are based on guide codes prepared by associations of nationally recognized experts.

One of these model codes has usually been selected by a particular municipality, or other governmental body, and modified to suit local conditions. For this reason, it is important to refer to the code used in the locality.

Local refrigeration codes vary considerably. The *Uniform Building Code* sets up guide regulations pertaining to the installation of refrigeration equipment. It is similar in most requirements to the ANSI B9.1 *Safety Code for Mechanical Refrigeration*, but there are some notable exceptions. It is, therefore, important that the local codes be carefully applied in the design of the refrigeration portion of chilled-drinking-water systems. Other local codes that merit a careful review are the electrical regulations as they apply to control and power wiring and ASME requirements for tanks and piping.

13 Bioremediation Pretreatment Systems

Pretreatment of effluent prior to discharge is a requirement established by federal legislation and implemented by federal regulations and state and local legislation. Pretreatment requirements apply both to direct discharges, i.e., to drain fields, streams, lakes, and oceans; and to indirect discharges, as in collection systems leading to treatment works. Pretreatment is required of all industrial discharges, which are all discharges other than those from a domestic residence. Pretreatment can involve the removal of metals, the adjustment of pH, and the removal of organic compounds. It is defined as "the reduction of the amount of pollutants, or the alteration of the nature of pollutant properties in wastewater prior to or in lieu of discharging or otherwise introducing such pollutants into a POTW [publicly owned treatment works] . . . . The reduction or alteration may be obtained by physical, chemical or biological processes, process changes or by other means, except as prohibited by 403.6 (d) [dilution]" (US Environmental Protection Agency. *Code of Federal Regulations*, Title 40, 403.3 [1]q).

Bioremediation is one method of simultaneously removing the pollutant from the waste stream and disposing of the pollutant by altering its chemical or physical structure such that it no longer causes depreciation of water quality, in the case of direct discharges, or interference or pass-through, in the case of indirect discharges. Generally speaking, bioremediation can be described as the action of living organisms on organic or inorganic compounds resulting in reduction in complexity or destruction of the compound. Typically, bioremediation processes are conducted at the source of the pollutant to avoid transporting large quantities of polluted waste water or concentrations of pollutants. The most common application of bioremediation to plumbing systems is for the disposal of fats, oils, and grease (FOG).

PRINCIPLE OF OPERATION

Bioremediation systems, as described here, do not include the practice of adding enzymes, bacteria, nutrients, or combinations thereof (additives) to grease waste drainage, grease traps, or grease interceptors. The use of additives in conventional apparatus is a cleaning method resulting in the removal of FOG from the apparatus and its redeposition downstream. Recombined FOG is usually a denser form, which is more difficult to remove from sewer mains and lift stations than the substance not altered by the application of additives.

Bioremediation systems are engineered systems containing the essential elements of a bioreactor that can be operated by the kinetic energy imparted from flowing water or mechanically agitated by various pumping and aeration methods. Bioremediation systems can be aerobic, i.e., requiring oxygen for the metabolic activity of the organisms; anaerobic, or not requiring oxygen; or a combination of both. The type of bioremediation system employed is determined mainly by the target compound and the organisms necessary to metabolize that compound. In the case of FOG, typically the application of bioremediation is aerobic. Figure

13-1 shows a kinetically operated aerobic bioremediation system.

Central to the operation of all on-site bioremediation systems applied to FOG are

1. *Separation*, removal of the FOG from the dynamic waste flow

2. *Retention*, allowing the cleaned waste water to escape save the static water content of the device

3. *Disposal*, metabolic disassembly of the FOG to its elements of hydrogen, oxygen, and carbon, usually in the form of water and carbon dioxide.

Incidental to the application of a bioremediation system to FOG are

1. *Sizing*, calculation of the potential maximum flow over a designated interval

2. *Food solids removal* from the liquid waste stream

3. *Placement*, to minimize the length of untreated grease waste piping.

Separation

Separation of the FOG with the greatest efficiency, as measured in percentage of FOG present in the waste stream and time necessary to effect separation, is essential to the accomplishment of retention and disposal. The standard for this measurement is Plumbing and Drainage Institute PDI-G101. Separation can be effected by simple gravity flotation, in which case the device has to be of sufficient volume to provide retention time and quiescence to allow ascension of suspended FOG (see Chapter 8, "Grease Interceptors"). Separation can also be effected by coalescence, coagulation, centrifugation, dissolved air flotation, and skimming. In these instances, for a given flow the device is typically smaller in dimension than in the gravity flotation design.

Because food particles generally have a specific gravity greater than one and are oleophilic, the presence of food particles will materially interfere with the efficient separation of FOG from the waste stream. Food grinders are typically not used upstream of bioremediation systems for this reason and because of the increased biological oxygen demand (BOD) the additional waste places on the system.

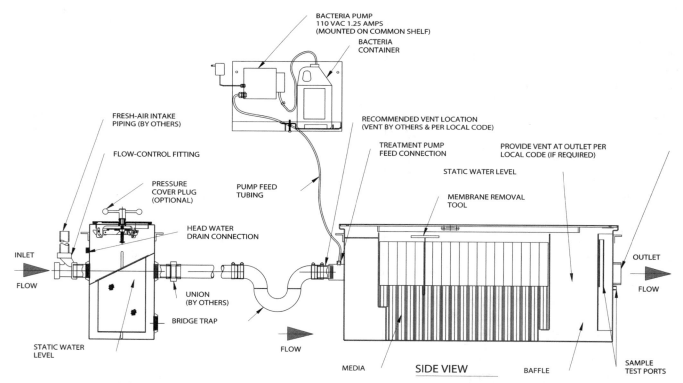

Figure 13-1 Kinetically Operated Aerobic Bioremediation System

Retention

The retention of FOG in a bioremediation system is essential to FOG's disposal by a reduction to its constituent elements. Retention is facilitated by baffles, compartmentalization, or sedimentation, depending upon the system design. Because only 15% of suspended FOG (at a specific gravity of 0.85) is above the water surface, bioremediation systems that retain FOG a greater distance from dynamic flows generally have greater retention efficiencies and capacities than those that rely on suspension alone.

Disposal

The disposal of FOG by biochemical processes within an on-site system is the single most distinguishing feature of bioremediation systems. The organisms responsible for metabolizing the FOG may be endemic to the waste stream or, more likely, seeded by means of a timed or flow sensitive metering device. Crucial to a disposal function equal to ongoing separation and retention rates is a sufficient population of organisms in contact with the FOG. While this is a function of sizing (see "Sizing Guidelines" later in this chapter), it is also a function of system design.

The mechanism typically utilized to provide a stable, structured population of organisms in a bioremediation system is a biofilm. Biofilms are controlled biological ecosystems that protect multiple species of organisms from washouts, biocides, and changing environmental conditions in the bioremediation system. Biofilm forms when bacteria adhere to surfaces in aqueous environments and begin to excrete a slimy, glue-like substance that can anchor them to all kinds of material—such as metals, plastics, soil particles, medical implant materials, and tissue (Center for Biofilm Engineering).

Biofilms are cultivated on structures of various configurations of the greatest possible surface area per given volume. The structure or structures are generally referred to as "media." The media may be fixed, i.e., stationary relative to the device and the waste flow; moving by mechanical movement, such as a series of rotating discs or small, ball-shaped elements; or moving randomly from the energy of the waste stream flow and/or pump or aerator agitation.

The organisms inhabiting biofilms reduce the FOG to carbon dioxide and water through a process called "beta oxidation," a catabolic process consisting of the shortening of fatty acid chains by the successive removal of two carbon fragments from the carboxyl end of the chain (*Dictionary of Bioscience*, p. 58). Bioremediation systems utilizing structured biofilms are much more resistant to the effects of biocides, detergents, and other chemicals frequently found in kitchen effluent than systems using planktonic application of organisms. The efficiency of bioremediation systems in terms of disposal is dependent upon the total surface area of the media relative to the quantity of FOG separated and retained, the viability and species diversity of the biofilm, system sizing, and installation.

FLOW CONTROL

Flow control devices are sometimes used with bioremediation systems depending upon system design. When flow control devices are prescribed by the manufacturer, generally they are best located nearest the discharge of the fixtures they serve. However, because bioremediation systems are engineered systems, the use and placement of elements of the system are prescribed by the manufacturer. In instances in which elements of a bioremediation system may be common to the plumbing industry, the manufacturer's prescription for the application of those elements to the system shall prevail over common practice or code requirements.

SIZING GUIDELINES

These guidelines are intended as a tool for the engineer to quantify the maximum hydraulic potential from a given facility. Typically fixture unit equivalency prediction sizing methods and other estimation tools based on utilization rate weighted factors are not acceptable sizing tools for bioremediation systems. Bioremediation systems must be capable of accommodating maximum hydraulic events without experiencing upset, blockage, or pass-through.

1. *Fixture inventory* Itemize each and every fixture capable of liquid discharge to the grease waste piping system including, but not limited to, sinks, hoods, ware washers, floor sinks/drains, and kettles. Grinder pulpers are generally not to be discharged to bioremediation systems. Review the manufacturer's requirements.

2. *Capacity calculation* Calculate the capacity of liquid retaining devices such as sinks (in gallons) as follows:

length × width × depth = cubic capacity, in.³ (cm³)

cubic capacity × number of compartments = total cubic capacity, in.³ (cm³)

total cubic capacity ÷ 231 = gal (L) capacity

gallons capacity x fill factor 0.75 = rated discharge, gpm (L/s)

(*Note*: If a 2-min drain duration is used, divide rated discharge by 2.)

3. *Rated discharges* Fixtures such as ware washers with a manufacturer's rated water consumption or single discharge rate are calculated at the greater rate.

4. *Floor sinks/drains* Floor sinks/drains are generally rated at 4.0 gpm. Count the number of floor drains/sinks not receiving indirect discharges from fixtures calculated above and multiply by 4.0 to determine gpm potential. Should this number exceed the total supply to the facility, select the smaller of the two numbers.

5. *Loading influences* Some manufacturers may prescribe multipliers for various facility characteristics such as cuisine to accommodate anticipated increased organic content per gallon of calculated discharge. Refer to manufacturer's requirements.

DESIGN CONSIDERATIONS

Each manufacturer of a bioremediation system will have specific design elements to establish fitness for the purpose of its particular design. Certain fundamental materials and methods utilized in the design and manufacture of bioremediation systems are indicated by the following standard designations:

- ASTM C 33, *Specification for Concrete Aggregates*
- ASTM C 94, *Specification for Ready Mix Concrete*
- ASTM C 150, *Portland Cement*
- ASTM C 260, *Specification for Air Entraining Admixtures for Concrete*

- ASTM C 618, *Specification for Fly Ash and Raw or Calcined Natural Pozzolan for Use as a Mineral Admixture in Portland Cement Concrete*
- Plumbing and Drainage Institute (PDI)-G101, *Testing and Rating Procedure for Grease Interceptors with Appendix of Sizing and Installation Data*
- American Concrete Institute (ACI) 318-89, *Specification for Steel Reinforcement*
- American Association of State Highway and Transportation Officials (AASHTO) H20-44
- IAPMO PS 1, *Prefabricated Septic Tanks*
- UL 1585, *Class 2 & Class 3 Transformers*
- US Environmental Protection Agency (USEPA) Methods 413.1
- USEPA 1664 & 1664-A, *FOG (Fats Oils & Grease) Measurement*

MATERIALS AND STRUCTURAL CONSIDERATIONS[1]

Materials

Concrete If concrete is used as a container for bioremediation systems, the concrete and reinforcement should be of sufficient strength to resist stresses caused during handling and installation without structural cracking and be of such corrosion-resistant quality to resist interior and exterior acids as may be present. Concrete should have a minimum compressive strength of 3,500 lb/in.² (24 132 kPa). Concrete should have a maximum water cementing materials ration of 6 gal/sack of cement. Concrete should be made with Type II or V, low alkali Portland cement conforming to ASTM C 150, *Specification for Portland Cement*, and should also include sulfate expansion option as specified in Table 4 of ASTM C 150 for Type II or V. Concrete should contain 4–7% entrained air utilizing admixtures conforming to ASTM C 260, *Specification for Air Entraining Admixtures for Concrete*. Concrete aggregates should conform to ASTM C 33, *Specification for Concrete Aggregates*. If ready mix concrete is used, it should conform to ASTM C 94, *Specification for Ready Mix Concrete*. Fly ash and raw or calcined natural pozzolan, if used as mineral admixture in Portland cement concrete, should conform to ASTM C 618, *Specification for Fly Ash and Raw or Calcined Natural Pozzolan*

[1] *Source*: IAPMO PS 118-2000.

for Use as a Mineral Admixture in Portland Cement Concrete.

Stainless steel Stainless steel used in bioremediation systems should be of type 316 or of some other type with equal or greater corrosion resistance.

Fiberglass reinforced polyester Bioremediation systems constructed principally of fiberglass reinforced polyester should comply with the minimum requirements expressed for septic tanks in Section 5 of IAPMO PS 1.

Polyethylene Bioremediation systems constructed principally of polyethylene should comply with the minimum standards expressed for septic tanks in Section 5 of IAPMO PS 1.

Structural Considerations

Bioremediation systems should be designed to handle all anticipated internal, external, and vertical loads.

Bioremediation systems containers, covers, and structural elements that are intended for burial and/or traffic loads should be designed for an earth load of not less than 500 lb/ft^2 (24 kPa) when the maximum coverage does not exceed 3 ft (0.9 m). Each system and cover should be structurally designed to withstand all anticipated earth or other loads and should be installed level and on a solid surface.

Bioremediation systems, containers, covers, and structural elements for installation in traffic areas should be designed to withstand an AASHTO H20-44 wheel load and an additional 3-ft (0.9-m) earth load with an assumed soil weight of 100 lb/ft^2 (4.8 kPa) and 30 lb/ft^2 (1.4 kPa) fluid equivalent sidewall pressure.

Internal construction of separations, coalescing surfaces, baffles, and structures that may compartmentalize fluids should be designed to withstand the maximum expected hydrostatic pressure. Maximum hydrostatic pressure should include the pressure exerted by one compartment at maximum capacity with adjacent compartments empty. The internal structures should be of suitable, sound, and durable materials consistent with industry standards.

In buried applications, bioremediation systems should have safe, reasonable access for prescribed maintenance and monitoring. Access could consist of horizontal manways or manholes. Each access opening should have a leak-resistant closure that cannot slide, rotate, or flip. Manholes should extend to grade, have a minimum size of 20 in. (0.5 m) diameter, or 20 in. × 20 in. (0.5 × 0.5 m) square, and should comply with IAPMO PS-1, Section 4.7.1.

Bioremediation systems should be provided with drawings as well as application and disposal function details. Descriptive materials should be complete, showing dimensions, capacities, flow rates, structural and process ratings, and all application and operation relevant facts.

DIMENSION AND PERFORMANCE CONSIDERATIONS

Bioremediation systems differ relative to type and operating method but should have a minimum volume-to-liquid ratio of 0.400 gal per 1.00 gpm flow rating and a minimum retention ratio of 3.75 lb FOG per 1.00 gpm flow. The inside dimension between the cover and the dynamic water level at full rated flow should be a minimum of 2 in. (51 mm). While the airspace should have a minimum volume equal to 10.5% of the liquid volume, air management and venting shall be prescribed by the manufacturer.

The bioremediation system separation and retention efficiency rating should be in accordance with PDI-G101. Bioremediation systems should show no leakage from seams, pinholes, or other imperfections.

Performance testing of bioremediation systems should demonstrate performance equal to or exceeding claims of the manufacturer and should have a minimum discharge FOG content not to exceed 100 mg/L. Performance testing should be conducted only by accredited, third party, independent laboratories in accordance with current scientific methods and EPA analyses procedures.

INSTALLATION AND WORKMANSHIP

Installation should be in accordance with the manufacturer's requirements. Bioremediation systems should be free of cracks, porosity, flashing, burrs, chips, and filings, or any defects that may affect performance, appearance, or serviceability.

REFERENCES

1. Center for Biofilm Engineering, Montana State University, Bozeman, Montana.

2. *Dictionary of bioscience*, 5th ed. New York: McGraw-Hill.

3. International Association of Plumbing and Mechanical Officials (IAPMO). 2000. *Uniform plumbing code.*

4. ———. PS 118-2000.

5. Plumbing and Drainage Institute. PDI G-101, *Testing and rating procedure for grease interceptors with appendix of sizing and installation data.* South Easton, MA.

6. US Environmental Protection Agency. *Code of federal regulations*, Title 40.

Index

dry-pipe sprinkler systems and, 2000 V3: 9, 11
fountains and, 2000 V3: 121–122
frost lines, 2000 V3: 226
gas piping and, 1999 V2: 196
ice and oxygen storage, 2000 V3: 61
ice as part of total load, 2001 V4: 130
ice inside water storage tanks, 1999 V2: 247
insulation and, 2001 V4: 126
irrigation system valves and, 2000 V3: 103
leaching trenches and, 1999 V2: 222
plastic pipe and, 2001 V4: 61
reduced-size venting and, 1999 V2: 50
swimming pool maintenance and, 2000 V3: 131
testing of cold-water systems, 1999 V2: 154
water meters and, 1999 V2: 115
well heads and, 1999 V2: 243
french drains, 1998 V1: 33. *See also* rubble drains
French, John L., 1999 V2: 38
frequencies (Hz, HZ)
 disturbing vibrations, 2001 V4: 160
 frequency ratios in vibration control, 2001 V4: 161
 measurements, 1998 V1: 41
 natural frequency of resilient mounted systems, 2001 V4: 160
 symbols for, 1998 V1: 19
frequency of ion regeneration cycles, 1999 V2: 305
fresh-air inlets, 1998 V1: 33
friction clamps, 2000 V3: 229
friction connectors, 1998 V1: 194
friction factors, 1998 V1: 19
friction head, calculating, 1998 V1: 7
 centralized drinking-water cooler systems, 2001 V4: 279
 pumps, 2001 V4: 108
friction loads, 2001 V4: 150
friction losses in flow
 bends in pipe and, 2001 V4: 70
 calculating friction head loss, 1998 V1: 2–3
 compressed air, 2000 V3: 78, 210, 211
 counterflow piping designs, 2000 V3: 178
 fountain display pumps, 2000 V3: 115
 fuel dispensers, 2000 V3: 170
 Hazen-Williams formula, 1998 V1: 2, 1999 V2: 116, 118, 119, 121
 liquid fuel piping, 2000 V3:170
 medical air, 2000 V3: 68, 74, 78
 medical gas piping, 2000 V3: 73
 medical vacuum systems, 2000 V3: 74, 79
 natural gas systems, 1999 V2: 183, 2000 V3: 253
 nitrogen systems, 2000 V3: 74, 77
 nitrous oxide, 2000 V3: 74, 76
 oxygen, 2000 V3: 74, 76
 pipe pressure and, 1999 V2: 122–132
 pressure and, 1999 V2: 125, 130
 sizing of branches, 1999 V2: 127
 standpipe systems, 2000 V3: 19
 steam pipes, 2000 V3: 187

submersible fuel pumps, 2000 V3: 170
swimming pool gutters and, 2000 V3: 142
vacuum cleaning systems, 1999 V2: 271, 272– 274, 274, 275
vacuum exhauster sizing, 1999 V2: 274
valves and threaded fittings, 1999 V2: 128
water in pipes, tables, 2001 V4: 280
water mains, 2000 V3: 8
water supply piping and, 1999 V2: 249
well pumps, 1999 V2: 245
front-end documents, 1998 V1: 64
front-loading skimmers, 2000 V3: 110
frost. *See* freezing temperatures
frost lines, 2000 V3: 226
frost proof flare nuts, 1999 V2: 196
frostproof closets, 1998 V1: 33
FRP (fiberglass-reinforced plastic). *See* fiberglass reinforced plastic
FRPP (flame-retardant pipe), 2001 V4: 64
FS. *See* US Federal Specifications
FS (flow switches), 1998 V1: 13
FSK (fiberglass cloth, skrim and kraft paper), 2001 V4: 118
ft, FT (feet). *See* feet
ft^2 EDR, 2000 V3: 178, 180
ft^3 (cubic feet), 1998 V1: 18
ft-lb, FT LB (foot-pounds), 1998 V1: 19
FTUs (formazin turbidity units), 1999 V2: 287
fu values. *See* fixture-unit values
fuel double containment systems, 2001 V4: 58
Fuel Gas Piping, 1999 V2: 214
fuel loads (fire hazards), 2000 V3: 2
fuel oil
 fuel oil return (FOR), 1998 V1: 10
 fuel oil supply (FOS), 1998 V1: 10
 fuel oil vents (FOV), 1998 V1: 10
 pipe bracing, 1998 V1: 168, 169
fuel/fuel oil pipes, 2001 V4: 35
fuel-gas piping systems. *See also* diesel-oil systems; gasoline systems
 conversion factors, 1999 V2: 212
 fuel gas, defined, 1999 V2: 213
 glossary, 1999 V2: 213–214
 liquefied petroleum gas, 1999 V2: 194, 196–197
 methane, 1998 V1: 132
 natural gas systems, 1999 V2: 173–194
 values of fuel gas, 1999 V2: 212
full port (100% area), 2001 V4: 91, 93
full-flow conditions (FF), 1998 V1: 1
full-port ball valves, 2000 V3: 72
fully recessed water coolers, 2001 V4: 271, 272, 274
fully-sprinklered spaces, 1998 V1: 15
fume hoods, 1999 V2: 334, 342
fumes, hazardous, 1999 V2: 284, 332, 333. *See also* gases
 acid-waste drainage systems, 2000 V3: 39
 filter cleaners, 2000 V3: 150
 in soil profiles, 2000 V3: 162

S

shock intensity of water hammer, 1999 V2: 132
shock treatments in pools and fountains, 2000 V3: 123
shopping centers, 1999 V2: 25, 2001 V4: 20
shops. *See* retail stores and shops
short circuiting in grease interceptors, 2001 V4: 171
short cycling in boilers, 2000 V3: 180
short-circuiting installations, 1998 V1:148
short-coupled pumps, 2001 V4: 107
Short-form specs, 1998 V1: 80
shot-in concrete anchors, 1998 V1: 165, 193
shower pans, 2001 V4: 15
shower valves
  flow rates, 2001 V4: 16
  installation, 2001 V4: 16
  types, 2001 V4: 15–16
showers
  acoustic ratings of, 1998 V1: 199
  body sprays, 2001 V4: 16
  emergency showers, 1999 V2: 332, 333, 344, 2001 V4: 17–18
  enclosures, 1998 V1: 118
  fixture-unit loads, 1999 V2: 3
  flow rates, 2001 V4: 15
  grab bars, 1998 V1: 118
  grates in school shower rooms, 1999 V2: 11
  gray-water supply and demand, 1999 V2: 25
  health-care facilities, 2000 V3: 32, 38
  hydrotherapy, 2000 V3: 35
  installation man-hour estimates, 1998 V1: 83
  labor rooms, 2000 V3: 36
  minimum numbers of, 2001 V4: 18–22
  patient rooms, 2000 V3: 34
  public areas in health-care facilities, 2000 V3: 33
  rates of sewage flows, 1999 V2: 237
  reduced water usage, 1998 V1: 125
  requirements, 2001 V4: 14–15
  resilient-mounting design, 1998 V1: 212
  seats, 1998 V1: 121
  shower compartment accessibility, 1998 V1: 115–119
  shower head acoustic ratings, 1998 V1: 199
  shower pans, 2001 V4: 15
  sodium hydroxide cross contamination, 2001 V4: 213–214
  spray units, 1998 V1: 114, 117
  standards, 2001 V4: 2
  swimming pool bathhouses, 2000 V3: 130
  temperatures, 2000 V3: 45
  thresholds, 1998 V1: 118
  water fixture unit values, 2000 V3: 217
SHP (shaft horsepower), 1998 V1: 22
SHR (sensible heat ratio), 1998 V1: 22
Shreir, L.L., 1998 V1: 152
shrinkage of ceramic fixtures, 2001 V4: 1
Shrive, Charles A., 1998 V1: 80
shrub sprinkler heads, 2000 V3: 103
Shumann, Eugene R., 1999 V2: 114

shutdown relays, 2000 V3: 24
shut-off devices
  defined, 1999 V2: 214
  fuel dispensers, 2000 V3: 165
shut-off valves
  earthquake-sensitive valves, 1998 V1: 164
  fountains, 2000 V3: 118
  gas hose connectors, 1999 V2: 196
  globe valves, 2001 V4: 92
  medical gases, 2000 V3: 71, 72
  natural gas, 1999 V2: 176
Shweitzer, 2000 V3: 97
SI units. *See* International System of Units
siamese fire department connections, 1998 V1: 15, 2000 V3: 11
  double-check detector valve assemblies, 2001 V4: 196
  surveying for cross connections, 2001 V4: 201
siamese fittings, 1998 V1: 36. *See also* fire protection systems
side reach for wheelchairs, 1998 V1: 106, 107
side vents, 1998 V1: 36
side-beam brackets, 2001 V4: 155
side-beam clamps, 2001 V4: 155
side-spray accessories, 2001 V4: 12, 14
side-suction pumps, 2001 V4: 105
sidesway prevention, 1998 V1: 194
sidewalk fire department connections, 1998 V1: 15
sidewall grab bars, 1998 V1: 110
sidewall heat loss in pools, 2000 V3: 144
sidewall sprinklers, 1998 V1: 16, 38
Siegrist, R., 1999 V2: 34
siemens, 1998 V1: 41
sight disabilities, 1998 V1: 101
signals for fire alarms, 2000 V3: 9
significant digits, 1998 V1: 40
significant movement, 2001 V4: 155
silencers
  on air compressors, 2000 V3: 202, 212
  on vacuum systems, 1999 V2: 268
silent check valves, 2001 V4: 93
silfos, 2001 V4: 87
silica, 1999 V2: 283, 2001 V4: 237
silica gel, 2000 V3: 204
silicates, 1999 V2: 282, 2000 V3: 147, 2001 V4: 251
silicon, 1999 V2: 281
silicon iron piping, 1999 V2: 15. *See also* duriron pipe
sill cocks
  backflow prevention, 2001 V4: 210
  hose bibb vacuum breakers, 2001 V4: 193
silt
  content of water, 2000 V3: 99
  loams, 2000 V3: 100
  removing, 1999 V2: 294
  silt density index, 1999 V2: 288–289
  in soil texture, 1999 V2: 218
  in water, 1999 V2: 282

U

Z